BEGINNINGS: psychology of early childhood

BEGINNINGS
psychology of early childhood

Barbara Sweany McClinton, Ph.D.
Blanche Garner Meier, Ph.D.

with 69 illustrations

The C. V. Mosby Company

Saint Louis   1978

The C. V. Mosby Company
11830 Westline Industrial Drive, St. Louis, Missouri 63141

Library of Congress Cataloging in Publication Data

McClinton, Barbara Sweany.
   Beginnings: psychology of early childhood.

   Bibliography: p.
   Includes index.
   1. Child psychology. I. Meier, Blanche Garner,
1944-   joint author. II. Title.
BF721.M13   155.4   77-17619
ISBN 0-8016-3217-X

GW/CB/B 9 8 7 6 5 4 3 2 1

To our favorite people

DAVID
JEREMY
ERNIE
NAOMA
SANDY

Preface

Beginnings: Psychology of Early Childhood is a text designed for use in introductory child development courses with an emphasis on early childhood. Basically, the book includes material on the infant, the preschooler, and the young child in the first years of school. Our own particular course in early childhood development deals with the child up to 8 years of age. Ending a discussion of development at a specific age level is impossible, however. Where necessary to complete a theoretical picture, such as Piaget's theory of mental development, we have touched briefly on slightly older children.

Our intention in writing this text is to provide students in applied training programs with a sound background of psychological principles. Too often there is a tendency to present these students with only techniques for dealing with children, without detailing the principles or experimental data on which these techniques are based. We have attempted to present solid psychological information in a simple, direct manner so that students may comprehend important concepts. We purposely tried to write in an informal style so that the student will not become bogged down in academic and psychological jargon and lose sight of the children about whom we are concerned.

In each chapter of this text we have described basic ideas and important research. Psychological theory is incorporated where it is relevant, but we have tried to maintain a balance between theory, research, and practical application of principles. We have tried to cover major topics and concepts in depth. This has resulted in limited coverage of some topics that you might feel are important. We hope that you will recognize the necessary limitations of coverage any book must have and use our text as a core around which other topics may be integrated in class time. We have attempted to point out relationships between concepts, theories, and data throughout this text in the hope that an image of the whole child will emerge.

With each chapter we have included a reading relevant to the topics discussed. We feel that students can better appreciate the science of psychology by reading firsthand the work of research psychologists. Perhaps in this way they will have a clearer understanding of what the psychology of child development is all about.

The production of this text has been a challenge that we could not have met without the support and encouragement of many people. We wish to express our gratitude to Dr. Brian MacWhinney of the University of Denver and Dr. Wanda Franz of West Virginia University, who critically and intelligently reviewed parts of our manuscript. They were both very helpful in pointing out ways to make our text clearer and more useful. In addition, we are indebted to Essex Community College for supporting us while this manuscript was written.

We are especially grateful to teachers who gave us the right start—Dr. Jay Eacker, Dr. Michael Rabinowitz, and Dr. Ellin K. Scholnick—and to colleagues who gave us help along the way—Dr. Elaine Bresnahan and Dr. Linda Davidoff.

We are also indebted to Mr. W. C. Baker of Doylestown, Pa., for providing us with many excellent photographs of children and to Maryann Yentzer for bringing Mr. Baker into our project and helping us so diligently herself.

Most of all we want to thank Sandy and David, our husbands, who sacrificed so much to allow us to accomplish our goals. To Jeremy, a special thanks for growing and developing so patiently on your own while "momma" spent her time describing development to others.

Barbara Sweany McClinton
Blanche Garner Meier

Contents

PART ONE
PSYCHOLOGY AND CHILDREN

1   Children and childhood: an introduction, 2

Early views of childhood, 3
Early scholars: their work with children, 6
  Charles Darwin: baby biography, 6
  G. Stanley Hall: questionnaires, 8
  Alfred Binet: intelligence testing, 10
  Arnold Gesell: developmental norms, 11
More recent contributors, 12
  John B. Watson: learning emotions, 13
  Sigmund Freud: personality development, 14
  Jean Jacques Piaget: mental development, 14
Summary, 16
A biographical sketch of an infant, 16
  Charles Darwin

2   Research with children, 22

Studies of individuals and groups, 24
Studies in natural settings and in laboratories, 25
Studies of correlations and causes, 26
  Correlational method, 26
  Experimental method, 28
Studies involving age, 31
Summary, 32
Peer influences on preschool children's willingness to try difficult tasks, 33
  E. Paul Torrance

3   Reading a research report, 36

Why bother with research reports? 37
Anatomy of a research report, 37
  Abstract, 37
  Introduction, 38
  Method, 39
  Results, 41
  Discussion, 46
  References, 48
Summary, 48

Contents

PART TWO
DEVELOPING BASIC SKILLS

4 **Developing perceptual skills,** 52

Studying children's perceptual abilities, 54
Seeing, 56
  What can infants see? 56
  Pattern discrimination and preferences, 59
  Perceiving depth and form, 62
  Looking at people, 64
  Stimulating visual development, 65
Hearing, 67
Touch, 69
Tasting, 71
Summary, 71
Stimulation of human neonates and visual attentiveness, 73
  Donald R. Ottinger
  Mary E. Blatchley
  Victor H. Denenberg

5 **Developing physical and motor skills,** 76

Pattern of physical development, 77
  Genetics, 77
  Prenatal development, 78
  Birth, 80
  Neonatal development, 81
  Course of physical development, 84
Role of experience in motor development, 88
  Skilled acts, 88
  Early experience and motor-skill training, 89
  Johnny and Jimmy, 90
Summary, 92
Action-schemes of 8-month-old infants, 93
  Claire B. Kopp

6 **Developing learned behavior,** 96

Classical conditioning, 97
Operant conditioning, 101
Learning by observation, 106
Learning social behavior: aggression, 107
Using learning principles to influence children's behavior, 111
  Reward, 112
  Punishment, 115
  Incentives, 117
  Modeling, 118
Limitations of learning theories, 118
Summary, 119

Televised aggression and the interpersonal aggression of preschool children, 121
    Faye B. Steuer
    James M. Applefield
    Rodney Smith

7   **Developing language,** 126

Stages of language acquisition, 128
   Crying and cooing, 128
   Babbling, 128
   First words, 129
   First sentences, 130
Language and maturation, 132
Theories of language acquisition, 133
   Learning theory, 134
   Psycholinguistic theory, 137
Processing speech, 140
   What the child hears and says, 140
   Mother's speech, 141
   How the child listens, 143
   Important speech cues, 144
Summary, 145
Verbal interaction in mother-child dyads, 146
    Joe Ernest Reichle
    Thomas M. Longhurst
    Lyanne Stepanich

PART THREE
DEVELOPING THOUGHT

8   **From 5 to 7 years: some changes in children's thought processes,** 154

Describing mental changes, 155
   Learning, 155
   Hypothesis testing, 158
   Perception, 158
   Spatial orientation, 160
   Intelligence test skills, 161
   Use of words, 161
   Memory, 162
   Effective reinforcement, 163
   Description of mental changes: a summary, 163
Explaining mental changes, 163
   Verbal mediation, 163
   Inhibition of associative thought, 166
   Attention, 167
   Piaget's theory, 170
Summary, 170
Persistent use of verbal rehearsal as a function of information about its value, 172
    Beth Ann Kennedy
    Dolores J. Miller

Contents

9 **A theory of intelligence: Piaget,** 176

Basic concepts of Piaget's theory, 180
Sensorimotor period, 182
  Stage 1: use of reflexes (birth to 1 month), 183
  Stage 2: first acquired adaptations and primary circular reaction (1 to 4 months), 184
  Stage 3: secondary circular reaction and procedures designed to make interesting sights
    last (4 to 8 months), 184
  Stage 4: coordination of secondary schemas and their application to new situations
    (8 to 12 months), 184
  Stage 5: tertiary circular reaction and discovery of new means through active
    experimentation (12 to 18 months), 185
  Stage 6: invention of new means through mental combinations (18 to 24 months), 185
Preoperational period, 188
  Egocentrism in language, 190
  Egocentrism in reasoning, 191
  Egocentrism in moral judgment, 192
  Immature thought processes, 192
Concrete operational period, 196
Formal operations, 197
Applications, 198
Evaluation of Piaget's work, 201
Summary, 202
Objective responsibility in children: a comparison with the Piaget data, 203
  Gene R. Medinnus

10 **Measuring intelligence,** 208

Intelligence tests then and now, 209
Correlates of IQ, 213
Poverty and intelligence, 215
Stimulating mental development, 216
  Harold Skeels: reversing retardation, 216
  Robert Rosenthal: self-fulfilling prophecies, 217
  Milwaukee Project: school at 4 months, 219
  Enrichment for normal children? 220
Heredity and intelligence, 220
Using and misusing IQ scores, 222
Summary, 223
The Milwaukee Project: early intervention as a technique to prevent mental retardation, 2
  Howard Garber
  Rick Heber

PART FOUR
DEVELOPING PERSONALITY

11 **Studying personality development,** 234

Biology, culture, and unique experiences, 235
Structural approach: Freud's theory of personality, 236
  Structure of personality, 237
  Stages of personality development, 238

Children's dreams, 242
Children's fears, 243
Evaluation of Freud's theory, 245
Behavioral approach: research studies of fear, 247
Development of fear, 247
Children's reactions to frightening situations, 248
Asking children about fear, 249
Inducing fear, 250
Reducing fear, 250
Summary, 252
What children fear, 254
Adah Maurer

12   **Social development,** 262

Attachment and infant sociability, 263
Theories of attachment, 264
Studying attachment, 267
Stranger anxiety, 269
Separation anxiety, 271
The child in the family, 272
The child beyond the family, 275
Summary, 278
Children's personal space as a function of age and sex, 280
Jacob Lomranz
Ariela Shapira
Netta Choresh
Yitzchak Gilat

13   **Sex-role development,** 285

Sex-role stereotypes, 286
What are little boys made of? What are little girls made of? 289
Infancy, 289
Aggression and dependency, 290
Theories of sex-role development, 295
Differential treatment of the sexes, 299
Summary, 300
Effects of sex typing in children's stories on preference and recall, 302
Sally A. Jennings

14   **Play,** 306

Theories of play, 307
Older formulations, 308
More recent formulations, 308
Psychoanalytic theory of play, 308
Piagetian theory of play, 309
Play patterns of early childhood, 312
Mastery play, 312
Fantasy play, 314
Social play, 316

Toys, 320
Summary, 322
The contents of boys' and girls' rooms as an index of parents' behavior, 323
   Harriet L. Rheingold
   Kaye V. Cook

PART FIVE
FOSTERING DEVELOPMENT

15   **Applying psychology to children,** 330

   "Expert" advice for rearing children, 331
      Benjamin Spock, 331
      Haim Ginott, 334
      Thomas Gordon, 335
      Lee Salk, 336
      Burton White, 337
   Educating young children, 339
      Preschools, 339
      Which type of preschool is best? 344
      Choosing a preschool, 345
      What about day care? 345
   Summary, 346
   Longitudinal development of very young children in a comprehensive day care program: the first two years, 347
      Halbert B. Robinson
      Nancy M. Robinson

PART ONE

PSYCHOLOGY AND CHILDREN

Chapter 1

Children and childhood: an introduction

Children are delightful and frustrating miniature inhabitants of our homes and world. They differ from adults in so many ways, yet ironically the most obvious difference of size is probably the least important or interesting difference. A few minutes of informal consideration of the probable activities of young children and adults in a park should make this point clear. While adults sit in the sun or shade reading, chatting, taking in the scenery, eating and drinking, or strolling casually along walks, children cannot be made to sit still. The list of possible child activities is endless and impossible to predict. The many differences among children and the special qualities of childhood make child study a challenge.

Developmental psychology is the field of study concerned with increasing our knowledge about children. Specifically, developmental psychology is concerned with describing and understanding the child's particular capabilities and qualities. It is important to understand the child's capabilities to see how they influence the way the child interacts with the world. When we understand the child better, we will be able to more intelligently provide positive experiences for children. Beyond understanding the child's particular qualities at any given age, developmental psychology is the study of how the child changes over time and becomes more like a maturely functioning adult.

In general, developmental psychology is concerned with all aspects of the developing child and as such is a very wide field of study. Psychologists who work in the area of developmental psychology frequently specialize in some particular aspect of development, such as the child's perceptual capabilities, social development, emerging personality, learning abilities, and cognitive (mental) capabilities. To better understand developmental psychology, it is helpful to consider who is interested in knowing about children.

Parents are interested in understanding children's behavior, but they are not alone. Many professionals whose work brings them into direct or even indirect contact with children benefit from solid information about children. Interested professionals include teachers, social workers, doctors and nurses, law-enforcement personnel, psychiatrists, and home economists, to name just a few. It is surprising that the interest in children has not been consistent historically. In the past, reformers of various kinds, churchmen, and philosophers were leaders in both concern for children and the study of childhood, while the interest of other groups, such as physicians, was less (Kessen, 1965). Even among psychologists, interest in child study has not always been strong and consistent. To understand these inconsistencies and to better appreciate developmental psychology today, consider some historical conceptions of childhood and some early techniques for studying children. Knowing the background of child study will not only help us understand the major areas of study in developmental psychology but will help us understand how information about children is gained.

EARLY VIEWS OF CHILDHOOD

The most surprising information that can be gained by exploring a historical perspective of child study is the realization that the concept of childhood has not been constant. Today, children are treated with care and concern and protected from exploitation by

3

R. Gates/Frederick Lewis, Inc.

Fig. 1-1. Children at one time were treated as miniature adults. No distinctions in dress or activity separated children from adults.

many laws. Our concern for children is further evident in the large numbers of students who enroll in developmental psychology courses. Because concern for children is so deep, today it is difficult to believe that it has not always been so.

In his history of the child, Kessen (1965) cites surprising statistics on the lives of children in seventeenth-century Europe. Not even physicians were much interested in children and childhood, as only a small percentage of children lived to be 5 years old.

Even into the eighteenth century, the lot of the infant did not improve much. One child out of three was placed in a foundling home. Kessen relates that abandonment was such a serious problem that at one time laws were passed that forbade women from transporting infants to large cities where foundling homes were located. With death or abandonment so likely for children, apparently there was little inclination to consider childhood as a special period of life. Fortunately, the medical profession became involved with children, and by the mid-1700s child mortality dropped from 300 to 400 deaths per 1,000 births to less than 25. It is interesting to note that mothers were admonished to feed newborns only milk, instead of butter and sugar, oil, boiled bread, gruel, or wine (Kessen, 1965).

Even with increasing chances for survival, there was still no real interest in children as special people. In the late 1700s and early 1800s, children's life spans had lengthened. They were put to work in factories and mines. Conditions for child workers were extremely bad. They worked 6 days a week, often starting before dawn and working late into the night. Kessen quotes a European law of 1833 that in essence protected children by restricting the work of those between the ages of 9 and 13 years to only 48 hours a week; however, children older than 13 were allowed to work 68 hours a week. This law applied only to children who worked in factories. Apparently, children as young as 4 years worked in mines in England and Scotland. At that time concern for children centered around their economic advantage as cheap labor. However, children became the object for concern of social reformers and churchmen. Reformers stressed the value of the child as a person, and churchmen saw the child as in need of salvation and religious education. The concern of the churchmen led to the belief that the child's innocence should be protected. This and the need to educate the child resulted in increasing segregation of the child from society in general.

In the late 1700s philosophers interested in the variety of people began to discuss children and childhood as they searched for the source of humanity's many differences. There was active interest in children and their characters. One of the most notable philosophic discussions of children is contained in Rousseau's *Emile*. Rousseau saw children as special and capable of directing their own development. Earlier, the philosopher John Locke had discussed children, but only to point out that they were essentially the same as adults and governed by the same laws of association in learning. Rousseau, however, emphasized the maturation of the child. He saw children as natural in the sense that he felt they would develop according to their own inner natures. Rousseau even felt the child's development if left alone would be better than if adults meddled in it. These philosophers, Locke and Rousseau, presented two very different concepts of the child, which for centuries have influenced workers with children. Locke felt the child was a product of his or her experiences; Rousseau thought that the child's own inherent qualities influenced development.

These two viewpoints are still viable (full of life) and essentially characterize two major theoretical orientations of child study. The Lockean point of view can be seen in theories of development that emphasize the importance of learning in development and the modifiability of the course of development. A specific example of this orientation

5

may be found in Watson's behavioristic approach to child study, discussed in the last section of this chapter.

Rousseau's concept of the child emphasizes the self-directing quality of the child's maturation. In other words, development is seen as an orderly progression through a series of predictable changes, which in turn leads to characteristic ways of dealing with experiences at various ages. This viewpoint is variously referred to as an organismic approach or simply a developmental approach and is illustrated more specifically in the discussion of Piaget, both at the end of this chapter and in Chapter 10.

It should be noted that, as philosophers, Locke and Rousseau did not study children in a precise or scientific manner; rather, they theorized (speculated) on the characteristics of childhood and of human nature in general. Although not exact descriptions of childhood, their philosophic statements mark an important beginning of new conceptualizations of children as more than incapable persons.

Once philosophers and scholars became interested in the nature of children and began studying them directly, rapid expansion of knowledge about children might be expected, but this was not the case. Any major new endeavor, especially a new field of study, requires time to define its questions and techniques for finding answers. Both the questions and the techniques used to answer the questions influence the type of information collected and its validity (correctness) and usefulness.

In the following section some early scholars are discussed, as well as the questions they asked and the methods they used to study children. Some ways of gathering information are more useful than others, but it is only through experience with various study techniques that the advantages and disadvantages of any technique are fully understood.

In considering the work of the following scholars, an attempt is made to highlight the advantages and disadvantages of their various techniques of study so that it might be better understood why today's psychologists study children as they do. Early methods were frequently speculative and imprecise, and early researchers were frequently hampered by lack of precise aids to observation, such as the camera and tape recorder. Nevertheless, the early scholars helped formulate the important questions about the nature of children and childhood that theorists and researchers are still concerned with.

EARLY SCHOLARS:
THEIR WORK WITH CHILDREN
Charles Darwin: baby biography

One of the early and notable scholars whose work gave great impetus to the study of children was Charles Darwin. After the publication of his theory on the evolution of species, the child became the object of direct study.

In a logical progression of ideas, Darwin moved from the contention that species develop to the idea that man develops. To understand the adaptations that fit humans for survival, childhood became a legitimate scholarly subject of concern. Not only did his theory give impetus to the study of children in general, but Darwin also published a discussion on the development of his own son. This was one of the earliest examples of a child-study technique known as the baby biography.

Baby biographies were more or less detailed accounts written by parents concerning the early growth of one or more of their children. The writers of early baby biographies often concentrated on describing the emergence (beginning) and changes of specific abilities of their children in an attempt to explain some phenomenon. Specifically, Darwin's account of his son makes frequent reference to animal behavior and capabilities, because he was interested in showing evolutionary trends.

In his article "A Biographical Sketch of an Infant," Darwin (1877) describes the development of reflexes and intentional movement in his son. He concludes that, since movement in reflex actions is so precise, poor coordination or lack of intentional movement must be due to lack of "will." Another of Darwin's observations concerns the development of the infant's vision. Darwin felt that his son could not fix his gaze any earlier than 9 days of age and from then to the 45th day the only object on which the child could focus was a lighted candle. In a later chapter the work of modern researchers who assert that infants are able to receive a wide variety of visual stimulation in the first days of life is discussed. This difference in observations is due to the fact that Darwin was relying only on his own informal observations, while researchers today make filmed records of eye fixations and are able to take precise measurements of eye focus. The informality of parental observations is one of the disadvantages of the baby biography as a technique of child study.

Darwin also describes the early appearance of anger in his son at 10 weeks of age. He describes him as frowning all the time he was drinking too cold milk. Darwin indicated that the infant looked like a cross adult forced into an unliked activity. This description illustrates another weak point of this type of child study. The writer often seeks to compare the child's behavior with that of adults. While this is not entirely detrimental, too much of this type of investigation is likely to cause the researcher to miss behavior that is essentially child behavior and not directly comparable with adult behavior.

In his discussion of fear Darwin describes, as more recent researchers do, how young infants show fear at unexpected loud noises and quick movements. Darwin's discussion also includes his preschool son's dislike of wild beasts in the zoo. Darwin makes an interesting speculation that this type of fear may be inherited from primitive times when beasts were real threats.

Affection and jealousy are also detailed in Darwin's account, and he discusses jealousy in dogs at the same time. Again this exemplifies the aims of early baby biographies. They were frequently written not as a pure description of child behavior, but as a means for the author to expand a theoretical point of view.

Frequently, a baby biographer speculated about the nature of some complex behavior, as Darwin did when he described early signs of shyness in his son. After Darwin's absence of 10 days, his 2-year-old son reacted by refusing to meet his father's eyes directly. Darwin classified this behavior as shyness; however, it should be noted that this is pure speculation. For example, later researchers have observed similar behavior and described it as a negative reaction to being "deserted." It takes the more precise techniques of child study described in Chapter 2 to really answer a question such as this. In any event, Darwin's article is interesting reading.

Baby biographies were quite common during the late 1800s and provided an important impetus to the study of children. However, baby biographies as a technique of child study have many drawbacks. As mentioned, they were often written not to describe the child but to support the writer's beliefs, and frequently they compared children with adults. Other problems include the suspect objectivity of the parent-writers; it is difficult to be completely objective when describing one's children. Another problem occurs if observations are not made regularly. The writer might miss small but important changes in the child or might fall into the habit of only recording very obvious or unusual behavior. Further dangers lie in the use to which these reports are put. Observations of one child do not necessarily apply to all or even most children. Darwin cautions his readers on this problem. Furthermore, the parents who in the 1800s kept detailed records of their children's development probably were not typical parents and probably had more than a passing interest in child rearing, which may have served to make their children different in many ways from other children. Adding to these disadvantages the lack of precise, rigorous observation discussed earlier, the disadvantages of the baby biography outweigh its advantages as a technique of child study. However, a main benefit of the early baby biographies is that they highlighted areas or problems of interest for later, more precise child studies.

Beyond providing an example of a child study, Darwin's work presented a rationale for studying children. It became increasingly obvious that in both children and animals it was possible to look at behavior and specific characteristics on a simpler level than it was possible to do with adults. However, psychologists avoided seriously studying children because the child was not suited to the methods of psychology. Early psychology of the structuralist school relied on the use of highly trained subjects who introspected (gave detailed accounts of their experiences). These subjects had to be able to communicate in a precise manner. Thus, neither children nor animals could function as psychological subjects during this period of psychological history.

G. Stanley Hall: questionnaires

In America in the late nineteenth century, child study was pursued by G. Stanley Hall, referred to by many writers as the founder of American child psychology. Hall, who was president of Clark University, made many contributions to psychology in America, including bringing Sigmund Freud to this country and helping to introduce Freudian psychoanalysis to American psychologists. Yet his most enduring contribution was his emphasis on child study. He felt that psychologists must study children to understand the behavior of adults. Hall also felt that institutions, such as the educational system, should be renovated and reorganized to better suit the growth and changes of children. Both of these beliefs, that studying children could clarify adult behavior and that child-centered institutions should better serve children, necessitated knowing more about children. To know more about children, child-study research needed to encompass more than a collection of parental records concerning a few children. Hall's solution for increasing knowledge about children was to study large numbers of children quickly through the use of questionnaires. By using questionnaires, much detailed information could be collected in a very short time. A single researcher or group of researchers could collect information from a large population of children without the time-consuming detailed observations that were required in writing baby biographies. While Hall was an active researcher at Clark, more than 100 questionnaire studies were conducted on a variety of topics (Kessen, 1965).

The results of a study conducted by Hall on the topic of dolls, originally published in 1896, are reprinted in Kessen (1965). This study was based on 648 questionnaires. The large number of children involved makes Hall's results more likely to be applicable to children in general than do the observations of one or two children.

In the "Study of Dolls," Hall tabulates and reports children's preferences for various types of dolls and the materials of doll construction that were most popular. These data (information) are of little real interest, but Hall's discussion of the findings is. Hall found that not only girls but boys were very interested in doll play. Hall felt that this tendency in boys should be encouraged because it would make them more sympathetic with their own future families. (Remember that Hall wrote this in 1896.) A second interesting discussion in Hall's paper concerns the use of dolls to develop children's awareness of right and wrong. Hall felt that as children become more aware of right and wrong, they work through their ideas by punishing "naughty dollies." This idea has been picked up by more recent researchers.

Through the use of questionnaires Hall hoped to find relationships between his subjects' early childhood experiences and their later personalities. He was also interested in the effect of various child-rearing practices. Typically, Hall directed his questionnaires to parents and teachers, who then supplied information on children. When the material was collected and summarized, Hall attempted to extract meaningful implications from it. For example, in one of his earliest studies, "The Content of Children's Minds" (1883; reprinted in Dennis, 1972), Hall asks questions about children's knowledge of natural phenomena. After tabulating the percentage of children who were ignorant or informed about such things as growing apples, Hall recommended that the best preparation for school that parents can give their children is to take them frequently to the country. Basically, Hall was encouraging parents to supply a variety of early experiences to their children, which most researchers today would heartily endorse. However, Hall's technique of study has been criticized for several reasons.

One major problem of Hall's study technique was that questions frequently were asked about past practices and behaviors; thus, the correctness of the responses is questionable. For example, try to remember when you stopped playing with dolls or building model airplanes. You may have a general idea, but are you sure? If possible, ask your parents and see if their recollections coincide with yours.

Another problem with relying on questionnaire data is the possibility that those who filled out the questionnaires did so in a manner they felt would please the researchers or even falsified their information to make themselves or their children look good. Furthermore, information obtained through a questionnaire is only as good as the questions asked. Suppose that, in studying doll play, Hall had directed his questions to parents of girls only. He would have missed the interest in dolls that little boys have. Although this example is purposefully obvious, it is not likely that any questionnaire maker will think of every relevant question.

Further problems arise in the use of these studies in that not everyone asked will fill out a questionnaire. The doll study discussed above was based on 648 replies; however, Hall sent out 800 questionnaires. There is no way of knowing how the other 152 subjects might have altered Hall's findings.

After considering these criticisms, recall that Hall and his method did give rise to the study of children in America. He emphasized the usefulness of child study and attempted to broaden knowledge about children by gathering information on large numbers of them. In doing so, Hall helped establish child psychology as an independent part of psychology.

Note that Hall's study of children did not require that he or his researchers ever have direct contact with them. Adults asked other adults about children. Although this procedure gave Hall much information, it is obvious that to really know children, researchers must interact with children.

Alfred Binet: intelligence testing

At about the same time (early 1900s) that Hall was sending out his questionnaires at Clark University, Binet was developing the intelligence test in France. Binet's purpose was to develop a reliable technique for identifying children who would not profit from schooling. The results of his work had important implications beyond the original purpose. In developing the intelligence test, Binet became involved with hundreds of children. To develop a test that would assess a child's abilities, Binet had to determine just what those abilities should be. He tested many children of different ages with a series of small tasks to determine the age at which most children can perform certain tasks. For example, when can most children tie a bow? You might have a general idea, and so did Binet. He asked several 3-year-olds to tie a bow and found that none of them could. Then he asked slightly older children and found that a few 4-year-olds could tie bows, many 5-year-olds could accomplish this task, and virtually all 6-year-olds could tie bows. In effect, Binet tested the task first, not the children. Once he established the proper age for accomplishment of a task, he used that task to determine whether a new group of children could perform tasks suited to their age. The importance of this procedure and intelligence testing are discussed in Chapter 10. The major point here is that Binet's work involved studying children in a precise way. Hundreds of children were tested, measured, and interviewed before Binet had developed a test that emphasized children's changing abilities related to their chronologic (physical) ages. Binet's task was a practical one and his work was practical. He did not draw implications or attempt to relate behavior and personality. He simply measured children and in doing so added real child observation to child study.

Lewis M. Terman developed Binet's test for use in the United States. His work and Binet's emphasized the changing abilities of children from later preschool years through mid-adolescence, since the test was developed in reference to the school system. Fortunately, a friend of Terman's, Arnold Gesell, became interested in studying the abilities of very young children and infants.

Arnold Gesell: developmental norms

Gesell's work centered on describing the developmental changes of infants and children up to the age of 10 years. While Binet had been interested in measuring children's capabilities to determine a child's level of mental functioning, Gesell was interested in describing the changes the child goes through during development. Working at Yale University for over 40 years, Gesell traced the development of motor behavior, language, visual capabilities, adaptive functions, and personal and social relations of children. By 1950, he had detailed 34 levels of maturity from birth to 10 years of age and had studied over 3,000 behavior items (Gesell, 1952).

Gesell started his detailed study of infant development in order to pinpoint developmental problems as early as possible. His original work was with older children who were handicapped in some way. He felt that these children could be better understood and helped if people knew more precisely what the development of a normal healthy child should be. Perhaps early diagnosis of a deviant developmental sequence could help the child whose development was not normal. With this goal in mind Gesell proceeded to describe infant development.

Gesell produced many volumes of detailed descriptions of children's behavior at various stages of maturation. He outlined what a normal child should be capable of doing at every age. For example, Gesell (1952) writes that at 18 months a child will scribble when given a paper and crayon. When this child is 2 years old, he or she is capable of making vertical marks, and 6 months later can add horizontal strokes to drawings. Between 3 and

Elaine M. Ward

Fig. 1-2. In developing norms for each level of development, Gesell and his associates even specified the types of strokes children make in drawing or painting. This little girl's painting contains primarily vertical strokes, typical of very young preschoolers.

4 years of age, the child is able to combine these lines to form a cross and should be able to draw a circle. By 5 years, the child should be able to draw a triangle.

With the publication of books full of such information, Gesell's work became very popular with mothers. Gesell established norms, or reference points, against which mothers could compare their children. Because of the sheer amount of descriptive detail of Gesell's books, it is easy to lose sight of what he was actually doing. He was attempting to establish norms so that children suspected of having developmental problems could be compared with a standard of normal development. Gesell probably never intended to provide mothers with a formal device for determining which neighborhood baby was the "best."

Beyond establishing much needed normative data on child development, Gesell attempted to present a theoretical picture of infancy. He felt that a child's development is basically the product of maturation, which is directed by inherited properties. This theoretical orientation is compatible with the philosophy of Rousseau discussed earlier. Gesell believed that environmental situations can modify the course of development to some extent but that the major component of development is genetic. Gesell also felt that infants are very capable creatures, again much as Rousseau did, and that the infant has a mind. He studied infants' behavior patterns in great detail because he felt that behavior is the best means of communication available to the infant. Gesell had a deep respect for the infant. He described the month-old infant as well organized, capable of registering pleasure and pain, responsive to environment, and adaptive. He even speculated on the more psychological aspect of development. He felt that part of the infant's developmental task involves learning how to distinguish between people and objects. This idea is interesting if you consider an infant's attraction to mechanical events, such as the opening and closing of venetian blinds, or the revolving of a mobile. Along these same lines, mirror images fascinate young children. Learning to separate people from objects is a lengthy and challenging task for an infant.

In a summary statement in 1952, Gesell specified his conclusions based on his extensive child study. He firmly believed that the infant has a mind, gained through the process of growth. Further, he believed that the child is a unitary action system of behavior that develops through a lawful sequence. Since the child's development is lawful, the child's maturity and the state of his or her nervous system can be inferred through behavioral tests.

Gesell's summary statement makes an important point. Researchers may be interested in many unobservable facets of children's lives, such as their minds, aspirations, or personalities, but all that can actually be researched and studied are their observable characteristics and behaviors. Gesell made an enormous contribution to our knowledge about children through his detailed normative data. He provided a sound descriptive base from which further work could be undertaken.

MORE RECENT CONTRIBUTORS

After the turn of this century, developmental psychology was influenced by increasing numbers of workers interested in understanding development. Many researchers and theorists have made major contributions to child study that have influenced the way present researchers study children. It is interesting that some of the most influential contributors to child study, John B. Watson, Sigmund Freud, and Jean Jacques Piaget, did not consider themselves specialists in developmental psychology.

John B. Watson: learning emotions

Watson's major contribution was to give developmental psychology a model for laboratory research and an interest in learning as a primary force in development. This view derives from John Locke's philosophy.

At the time Gesell was studying the development of infants and young children, Watson was also devoting time to child study. Although Watson's and Gesell's subjects of study were the same, their aims and beliefs were very different. While Gesell was interested in describing the process of the development of children through their behavior, Watson was interested in demonstrating how modifiable, or changeable, the developmental process is. While Gesell voiced a belief in the mind of the child and the importance of the child's inherited characteristics in determining the child's growth, Watson felt that only the observable behavior of the child is worth consideration and that the more important determinants of the child's growth are experiences.

Watson felt that the child's early reflexive behaviors are the base from which more complicated behaviors develop through learning. For example, Watson believed that fear, rage, and love are unlearned reflexes of infants and that from these three reflexes the child's emotional system develops. To substantiate his belief in the importance of learning in shaping or guiding the development of behavior (including behaviors typically considered emotions), Watson conducted a laboratory experiment designed to show how an infant can learn to fear an animal. This experiment is described in detail in Chapter 6. Without reading Watson's experiment, it is likely that you can imagine how a child might learn to fear an animal. Any child who has attempted to pet a neighbor's dog and has been nipped may learn to fear that dog and perhaps similar dogs. It is not the conclusion of Watson's experiment that was so important, but that he did not simply theorize about children's behavior; Watson experimented with behavior. Specifically, he stated what he thought caused children to behave in certain ways and then he manipulated events in such a way as to see whether he was right or wrong.

Watson's laboratory work focused on precisely controllable aspects of observable behavior and did much to move child study into psychological laboratories. Based on his experimental studies, however, Watson did make some generalizations about child development. In a discussion on childhood fear (reprinted in Kessen, 1965), Watson claimed that due to treatment from parents the child's emotional life style is formulated by the age of 3 years. Whether the child is happy and constructive or neurotic and complaining depends on what is learned from the parents early in life.

Watson's carefully controlled experiments were conducted to assess how experience and learning affect the development of children. His precise terminology and methods became models for child study and removed much ambiguity from child study.

With the use of controlled experiments researchers could do more than just describe children's behavior; they could attempt to look for the causes or reasons for children's behavior. However, as will be learned in Chapter 2, when researchers conduct carefully controlled experiments they in a sense create artificial situations and look at isolated bits of behavior. Laboratory experiments allow researchers to trace the causes of behavior, but at the same time the narrowness of life in the experimental laboratory may cause the researcher to lose sight of the total child. In spite of this limitation, experimental laboratory research of the type advocated by Watson dominated American child psychology during the first half of this century.

In conclusion, it should be repeated that Watson's experimentation with children was secondary to his interest in changing the methods and direction of psychology in general.

Sigmund Freud: personality development

Freud developed a theory of development dealing with the formation of the personality. His major aim was to clarify understanding of adult personality by tracing its development through early childhood. Because his major interest was the adult personality, Freud was not primarily a child psychologist, although he dealt with interest in early personality formation. Freud's work differs from the work of most other researchers whom we have considered in that he devised his theory from his treatment of disturbed patients.

At the time that Watson-type studies of learned behavior patterns dominated American child study, child study elsewhere progressed differently. Freud in his development of the psychoanalytic theory of personality emphasized the crucial importance of early childhood experiences in the formation of personality. While Freud's major aim was not to study children for the sake of understanding them, he saw that to understand the adult one must know the child that became the adult. Freud also was interested in the emotional development of the personality, but his understanding of development was very different from that of Watson. Freud saw the child developing through a series of conflicts stemming from within his or her own nature. Freud felt that emotional life is set very early in life, but that particular experiences are secondary to the child's own nature, which is full of conflicts and stress. This belief minimizes the modifiability of development and is considered by some to be rather pessimistic. Filtered into American culture through secondary sources, Freud's theory was seen as championing permissiveness in child rearing. It was thought that if some of the child's innate characteristics conflict with ideas of proper behavior, the stress of development can be reduced by removing some of the usual demands placed on children. It should be repeated that this reasoning was only inferred from Freud's work and should not be credited to him.

Jean Jacques Piaget: mental development

The final major figure discussed is the Swiss scholar Jean Piaget. Piaget, who has been a major force in child psychology through recent years, was interested in studying thought processes and the changes these processes go through with age. Like Freud, who wanted to understand personality, Piaget in trying to deal with cognitive (mental) phenomena found himself dealing with developing children. Although Piaget's interest was not originally in understanding child development, his work covers several areas of child development and has influenced many developmental psychologists and educators today.

Piaget's work differs in content and method from Watson's and Freud's. Piaget's work describes the development of the child's thought processes. Piaget felt that children actually think differently from adults. We all know that children have less experience and information than adults, which would affect their behavior; yet Piaget makes an even stronger statement by saying that children's thought processes change as they grow.

Piaget combined naturalistic observation with spontaneous experiments. A good part of his early work was based on observations of his three children. Typically, he spent hours watching them in their cribs, noting even the most ordinary occurrences and occasionally intervening to see what changes he could effect. For instance, if the infant was sucking on a rattle, he might take the rattle and lay it beside the baby's head just out of the line of vision to see if the child would look for the rattle. These interferences with the child's behavior were in effect unplanned attempts at verifying information gained simply through observation. These events and the fact that as his work progressed Piaget widened his field of observation and studied children in nursery groups and at play in parks make Piaget's work much more than the simple baby biographies of Darwin's day. Piaget also conducted interviews with children, during which he posed problems, which afforded him more opportunity to understand children and their thought processes. Piaget and his work and its importance are discussed in detail in Chapter 9.

W. C. Baker

Fig. 1-3. Childhood today is considered a special time of freedom from major responsibility. These boys enjoying tobogganing present a sharp contrast to eighteenth-century children, who labored all day alongside adults.

PART
ONE
＿＿＿

SUMMARY

Considering what you have just read, take another look at the children in your world. Their position in society has changed considerably over the past several centuries. As we watch children at play and at school, it is difficult to imagine them working in factories or mines, yet at one time the idea of children working was as acceptable as children playing is today. As our ideas about childhood have changed, so has our interest in the special qualities of children. With increased interest and need for information about children, the study of children has changed. No longer can casual observations offer valuable information. The business of child study has become increasingly precise and challenging.

REFERENCES

Darwin, C. A biographical sketch of an infant. *Mind,* July 1877, **7,** 285-294.
Dennis, M. (Ed.). *Historical readings in developmental psychology.* New York: Appleton-Century-Crofts, 1972, pp. 119-137.
Gesell, A. *Infant development: the embryology of early human behavior.* New York: Harper & Row, Publishers, 1952.
Kessen, W. *The child.* New York: John Wiley & Sons, Inc., 1965.

A biographical sketch of an infant

Charles Darwin

M. Taine's very interesting account of the mental development of an infant, translated in the last number of *Mind* (p. 252), has led me to look over a diary which I kept thirty-seven years ago with respect to one of my own infants. I had excellent opportunities for close observation, and wrote down at once whatever was observed. My chief object was expression, and my notes were used in my book on this subject; but as I attended to some other points, my observations may possibly possess some little interest in comparison with those by M. Taine, and with others which hereafter no doubt will be made. I feel sure, from what I have seen with my own infants, that the period of development of the several faculties will be found to differ considerably in different infants.

During the first seven days various reflex actions, namely sneezing, hickuping, yawning, stretching, and of course sucking and screaming, were well performed by my infant. On the seventh day, I touched the naked sole of his foot with a bit of paper, and he jerked it away, curling at the same time his toes, like a much older child when tickled. The perfection of these reflex movements shows that the extreme imperfection of the voluntary ones is not due to the state of the muscles or of the coordinating centres, but to that of the seat of the will. At this time, though so early, it seemed clear to me that a warm soft hand applied to his face excited a wish to suck. This must be considered as a reflex or an instinctive action, for it is impossible to believe that experience and association with the touch of his mother's breast could so soon have come into play. During the first fortnight he often started on hearing any sudden sound, and blinked his eyes. The same fact was observed with some of my other infants within the first fortnight. Once, when he was 66 days old, I happened to sneeze, and he started violently, frowned, looked frightened, and cried rather badly: for an hour afterwards he was in a state which would be called nervous in an older person, for every slight noise made him start. A few days before this same date, he first started at an object suddenly seen; but for a long

---

From *Mind: a quarterly review of psychology and philosophy,* 1877, No. 7.

time afterwards sounds made him start and wink his eyes much more frequently than did sight; thus when 114 days old, I shook a paste-board box with comfits in it near his face and he started, whilst the same box when empty or any other object shaken as near or much nearer to his face produced no effect. We may infer from these several facts that the winking of the eyes, which manifestly serves to protect them, had not been acquired through experience. Although so sensitive to sound in a general way, he was not able even when 124 days old easily to recognise whence a sound proceeded, so as to direct his eyes to the source.

With respect to vision—his eyes were fixed on a candle as early as the 9th day, and up to the 45th day nothing else seemed thus to fix them; but on the 49th day his attention was attracted by a bright-coloured tassel, as was shown by his eyes becoming fixed and the movements of his arms ceasing. It was surprising how slowly he acquired the power of following with his eyes an object if swinging at all rapidly; for he could not do this well when seven and a half months old. At the age of 32 days he perceived his mother's bosom when three or four inches from it, as was shown by the protrusion of his lips and his eyes becoming fixed; but I much doubt whether this had any connection with vision; he certainly had not touched the bosom. Whether he was guided through smell or the sensation of warmth or through association with the position in which he was held, I do not at all know.

The movements of his limbs and body were for a long time vague and purposeless, and usually performed in a jerking manner; but there was one exception to this rule, namely, that from a very early period, certainly long before he was 40 days old, he could move his hands to his own mouth. When 77 days old, he took the sucking bottle (with which he was partly fed) in his right hand, whether he was held on the left or right arm of his nurse, and he would not take it in his left hand until a week later although I tried to make him do so; so that the right hand was a week in advance of the left. Yet this infant afterwards proved to be left-handed, the tendency being no doubt inherited—his grandfather, mother, and a brother having been or being left-handed. When between 80 and 90 days old, he drew all sorts of objects into his mouth, and in two or three weeks' time could do this with some skill; but he often first touched his nose with the object and then dragged it down into his mouth. After grasping my finger and drawing it to his mouth, his own hand prevented him from sucking it; but on the 114th day, after acting in this manner, he slipped his own hand down so that he could get the end of my finger into his mouth. This action was repeated several times, and evidently was not a chance but a rational one. The intentional movements of the hands and arms were thus much in advance of those of the body and legs; though the purposeless movements of the latter were from a very early period usually alternate as in the act of walking. When four months old, he often looked intently at his own hands and other objects close to him, and in doing so the eyes were turned much inwards, so that he often squinted frightfully. In a fortnight after this time (*i.e.* 132 days old) I observed that if an object was brought as near to his face as his own hands were, he tried to seize it, but often failed; and he did not try to do so in regard to more distant objects. I think there can be little doubt that the convergence of his eyes gave him the clue and excited him to move his arms. Although this infant thus began to use his hands at an early period, he showed no special aptitude in this respect, for when he was 2 years and 4 months old, he held pencils, pens, and other objects far less neatly and efficiently than did his sister who was then only 14 months old, and who showed great inherent aptitude in handling anything.

Anger. It was difficult to decide at how early an age anger was felt; on his eighth day he frowned and wrinkled the skin round his eyes before a crying fit, but this may have been due to pain or distress, and not to anger. When about ten weeks old, he was given some rather cold milk and he kept a slight frown on his forehead all the time that he was sucking, so that he looked like a grown-up person made cross from being compelled to do something which he did not like. When nearly four months old, and perhaps much earlier, there could be no doubt, from the manner in which the blood gushed into his whole face and scalp, that he easily got into a violent passion. A small cause sufficed; thus, when a little over seven months old, he screamed with rage because a lemon slipped away and he could not seize it with his hands. When eleven months old, if a wrong plaything was given him, he would push it away and beat it; I presume that the beating was an instinctive sign of anger, like the snapping of the jaws by a young crocodile just out of the egg, and not that he imagined he could hurt the plaything. When two years and three months old, he became a great adept at throwing books or sticks, &c., at anyone who offended him; and so it was with some of my other sons. On the other hand, I could never see a trace of such aptitude in my infant daughters; and this makes me think that a tendency to throw objects is inherited by boys.

Fear. This feeling probably is one of the earliest which is experienced by infants, as shown by their starting at any sudden sound when only a few weeks old, followed by crying. Before the present one was 4½ months old I had been accustomed to make close to him many strange and loud noises, which were all taken as excellent jokes, but at this period I one day made a loud snoring noise which I had never done before; he instantly looked grave and then burst out crying. Two or three days afterwards, I made through forgetfulness the same noise with the same result. About the same time (*viz.* on the 137th day) I approached with my back towards him and then stood motionless: he looked very grave and much surprised, and would soon have cried, had I not turned round; then his face instantly relaxed into a smile. It is well known how intensely older children suffer from vague and undefined fears, as from the dark, or in passing an obscure corner in a large hall, &c. I may give as an instance that I took the child in question, when 2¼ years old, to the Zoological Gardens, and he enjoyed looking at all the animals which were like those that he knew, such as deer, antelopes, &c., and all the birds, even the ostriches, but was much alarmed at the various larger animals in cages. He often said afterwards that he wished to go again, but not to see "beasts in houses"; and we could in no manner account for this fear. May we not suspect that the vague but very real fears of children, which are quite independent of experience, are the inherited effects of real dangers and abject superstitions during ancient savage times? It is quite conformable with what we know of the transmission of formerly well-developed characters, that they should appear at an early period of life, and afterwards disappear.

Pleasurable sensations. It may be presumed that infants feel pleasure whilst sucking, and the expression of their swimming eyes seems to show that this is the case. This infant smiled when 45 days, a second infant when 46 days old; and these were true smiles, indicative of pleasure, for their eyes brightened and eyelids slightly closed. The smiles arose chiefly when looking at their mother, and were therefore probably of mental origin; but this infant often smiled then, and for some time afterwards, from some inward pleasurable feeling, for nothing was happening which could have in any way excited or amused him. When 116 days old he was exceedingly amused by a pinafore being thrown over his face and then suddenly withdrawn; and so he was when I suddenly uncovered my own face and approached his. He then uttered a little noise which was an incipient laugh. Here surprise was the chief cause of the amusement, as is the case to a large extent with the wit of grown-up persons. I believe that for three or four weeks before the time when he was amused by a face being suddenly uncovered, he received a little pinch on his nose and cheeks as a good joke. I was at first surprised at humour being appreciated by an infant only a little above three months old, but we should remember how very early puppies and kittens begin to play. When four months old, he showed in an unmistakable manner that he liked to hear the pianoforte played; so that here apparently was the earliest sign of an aesthetic feeling, unless the attraction of bright colours, which was exhibited much earlier, may be so considered.

Affection. This probably arose very early in life, if we may judge by his smiling at those who had charge of him when under two months old; though I had no distinct evidence of his distinguishing and recognising anyone, until he was nearly four months old. When nearly five months old, he plainly showed his wish to go to his nurse. But he did not spontaneously exhibit affection by overt acts until a little above a year old, namely, by kissing several times his nurse who had been absent for a short time. With respect to the allied feeling of sympathy, this was clearly shown at 6 months and 11 days by his melancholy face, with the corners of his mouth well depressed, when his nurse pretended to cry. Jealousy was plainly exhibited when I fondled a large doll, and when I weighed his infant sister, he being then 15½ months old. Seeing how strong a feeling jealousy is in dogs, it would probably be exhibited by infants at an earlier age than that just specified, if they were tried in a fitting manner.

Association of ideas, reason, &c. The first action which exhibited, as far as I observed, a kind of practical reasoning, has already been noticed, namely, the slipping his hand down my finger so as to get the end of it into his mouth; and this happened on the 114th day. When four and a half months old, he repeatedly smiled at my image and his own in a mirror, and no doubt mistook them for real objects; but he showed sense in being evidently surprised at my voice coming from behind him. Like all infants he much enjoyed thus looking at himself, and in less than two months perfectly understood that it was an image; for if I made quite silently any odd grimace, he would suddenly turn round to look at me. He was, however, puzzled at the age of seven months, when being out of doors he saw me on the inside of a large plate-glass window, and seemed in doubt whether or not it was an image. Another of my infants, a little girl, when exactly a year old, was not nearly so acute, and seemed quite perplexed at the image of a person in a mirror approaching her from behind. The higher apes which I tried with a small looking-glass behaved differently; they placed their hands behind the glass, and in doing so showed their sense, but far from taking pleasure in looking at themselves they got angry and would look no more.

When five months old, associated ideas arising independently of any instruction became fixed in his mind; thus as soon as his hat and cloak were put on, he was very cross if he was not immediately taken out of doors. When exactly seven months old, he made the great step of associating his nurse with her name, so that if I called it out he would look round for her. Another infant used to amuse himself by shaking his head laterally: we praised and imitated him, saying "Shake your head"; and when he was seven months old, he would sometimes do so on being told without any other guide. During the next four months the former infant associated many things and actions with words; thus when asked for a kiss he would protrude his lips and keep still,—would shake his head and say in a scolding voice "Ah" to the coal-box or a little spilt water, &c., which he had been taught to consider as dirty. I may add that when a few days under nine months old he associated his own name with his image in the looking-glass, and when called by name would turn towards the glass even when at some distance from it. When a few days over nine months, he learnt spontaneously that a hand or other object causing a shadow to fall on the wall in front of him was to be looked for behind. Whilst under a year old, it was sufficient to repeat two or three times at intervals any short sentence to fix firmly in his mind some associated idea. In the infant described by M. Taine (pp. 254-256) the age at which ideas readily became associated seems to have been considerably later, unless indeed the earlier cases were overlooked. The facility with which associated ideas due to instruction and others spontaneously arising were acquired, seemed to me by far the most strongly marked of all the distinctions between the mind of an infant and that of the cleverest full-grown dog that I have ever known. What a contrast does the mind of an infant present to that of the pike, described by Professor Möbius (*Die Bewegungen der Thiere, &c.,* 1873, p. 11), who during three whole months dashed and stunned himself against a glass partition which separated him from some minnows; and when, after at least learning that he could not attack them with impunity, he was placed in the aquarium with these same minnows, then in a persistent and senseless manner he would not attack them!

Curiosity, as M. Taine remarks, is displayed at an early age by infants, and is highly important in the development of their minds; but I made no special observation on this head. Imitation likewise comes into play. When our infant was only four months old I thought that he tried to imitate sounds; but I may have deceived myself, for I was not thoroughly convinced that he did so until he was ten months old. At the age of 11½ months he could readily imitate all sorts of actions, such as shaking his head and saying "Ah" to any dirty object, or by carefully and slowly putting his forefinger in the middle of the palm of his other hand, to the childish rhyme of "Pat it and pat it and

19

mark it with T.'' It was amusing to behold his pleased expression after successfully performing any such accomplishment.

I do not know whether it is worth mentioning, as showing something about the strength of memory in a young child, that this one when 3 years and 23 days old on being shown an engraving of his grandfather, whom he had not seen for exactly six months, instantly recognised him and mentioned a whole string of events which had occurred whilst visiting him, and which certainly had never been mentioned in the interval.

Moral sense. The first sign of moral sense was noticed at the age of nearly 13 months: I said ''Doddy (his nickname) won't give poor papa a kiss,—naughty Doddy.'' These words, without doubt, made him feel slightly uncomfortable; and at last when I had returned to my chair, he protruded his lips as a sign that he was ready to kiss me; and he then shook his hand in an angry manner until I came and received his kiss. Nearly the same little scene recurred in a few days, and the reconciliation seemed to give him so much satisfaction, that several times afterwards he pretended to be angry and slapped me, and then insisted on giving me a kiss. So that here we have a touch of the dramatic art, which is so strongly pronounced in most young children. About this time it became easy to work on his feelings and make him do whatever was wanted. When 2 years and 3 months old, he gave his last bit of gingerbread to his little sister, and then cried out with high self-approbation ''Oh kind Doddy, kind Doddy.'' Two months later, he became extremely sensitive to ridicule, and was so suspicious that he often thought people who were laughing and talking together were laughing at him. A little later (2 years and 7½ months old) I met him coming out of the dining room with his eyes unnaturally bright, and an odd unnatural or affected manner, so that I went into the room to see who was there, and found that he had been taking pounded sugar, which he had been told not to do. As he had never been in any way punished, his odd manner certainly was not due to fear, and I suppose it was pleasurable excitement struggling with conscience. A fortnight afterwards, I met him coming out of the same room, and he was eyeing his pinafore which he had carefully rolled up; and again his manner was so odd that I determined to see what was within his pinafore, notwithstanding that he said there was nothing and repeatedly commanded me to ''go away,'' and I found it stained with pickle-juice; so that here was carefully planned deceit. As this child was educated solely by working on his good feelings, he soon became as truthful, open, and tender, as anyone could desire.

Unconsciousness, shyness. No one can have attended to very young children without being struck at the unabashed manner in which they fixedly stare without blinking their eyes at a new face; an old person can look in this manner only at an animal or inanimate object. This, I believe, is the result of young children not thinking in the least about themselves, and therefore not being in the least shy, though they are sometimes afraid of strangers. I saw the first symptom of shyness in my child when nearly two years and three months old: this was shown towards myself, after an absence of ten days from home, chiefly by his eyes being kept slightly averted from mine; but he soon came and sat on my knee and kissed me, and all trace of shyness disappeared.

Means of communication. The noise of crying or rather of squalling, as no tears are shed for a long time, is of course uttered in an instinctive manner, but serves to show that there is suffering. After a time the sound differs according to the cause, such as hunger or pain. This was noticed when this infant was eleven weeks old, and I believe at an earlier age in another infant. Moreover, he appeared soon to learn to begin crying voluntarily, or to wrinkle his face in the manner proper to the occasion, so as to show that he wanted something. When 46 days old, he first made little noises without any meaning to please himself, and these soon became varied. An incipient laugh was observed on the 113th day, but much earlier in another infant. At this date I thought, as already remarked, that he began to try to imitate sounds, as he certainly did at a considerably later period. When five and a half months old, he uttered an articulate sound ''da'' but without any meaning attached to it. When a little over a year old, he used gestures to explain his wishes; to give a simple instance, he picked up a bit of paper and giving it to me pointed to the fire, as he had often seen and liked to see paper burnt. At exactly the age of a year, he made the great step of inventing a word for food, namely, *mum,* but what led him to it I did not discover. And now instead of beginning to cry when he was hungry, he used this word in a demonstrative manner or as a verb, implying "Give me food." This word therefore corresponds with *ham* as used by M. Taine's infant at the later age of 14 months. But he also used *mum* as a substantive of wide signification; thus he called sugar *shu-mum,* and a little later after he had learned the word "black," he called liquorice *black-shu-mum,* —black-sugar-food.

I was particularly struck with the fact that when asking for food by the word *mum* he gave to it (I will copy the words written down at the time) "a most strongly marked interrogatory sound at the end." He also gave to "Ah," which he chiefly used at first when recognising any person or his own image in a mirror, an exclamatory sound, such as we employ when surprised. I remark in my notes that the use of these intonations seemed to have arisen instinctively, and I regret that more observations were not made on this subject. I record, however, in my notes that at a rather later period, when between 18 and 21 months old, he modulated his voice in refusing peremptorily to do anything by a defiant whine, so as to express "That I won't"; and again his humph of assent expressed "Yes, to be sure." M. Taine also insists strongly on the highly expressive tones of the sounds made by his infant before she had learnt to speak. The interrogatory sound which my child gave to the word *mum* when asking for food is especially curious; for if anyone will use a single word or a short sentence in this manner, he will find that the musical pitch of his voice rises considerably at the close. I did not then see that this fact bears on the view which I have elsewhere maintained that before man used articulate language, he uttered notes in a true musical scale as does the anthropoid ape Hylobates.

Finally, the wants of an infant are at first made intelligible by instinctive cries, which after a time are modified in part unconsciously, and in part, as I believe, voluntarily as a means of communication,—by the unconscious expression of the features,—by gestures and in a marked manner by different intonations,—lastly by words of a general nature invented by himself, then of a more precise nature imitated from those which he hears; and these latter are acquired at a wonderfully quick rate. An infant understands to a certain extent, and as I believe at a very early period, the meaning or feelings of those who tend him, by the expression of their features. There can hardly be a doubt about this with respect to smiling; and it seemed to me that the infant whose biography I have here given understood a compassionate expression at a little over five months old. When 6 months and 11 days old he certainly showed sympathy with his nurse on her pretending to cry. When pleased after performing some new accomplishment, being then almost a year old, he evidently studied the expression of those around him. It was probably due to differences of expression and not merely of the form of the features that certain faces clearly pleased him much more than others, even at so early an age as a little over six months. Before he was a year old, he understood intonations and gestures, as well as several words and short sentences. He understood one word, namely, his nurse's name, exactly five months before he invented his first word *mum;* and this is what might have been expected, as we know that the lower animals easily learn to understand spoken words.

Chapter 2

Research with children

Do mothers who pick up and cuddle their babies have healthier and happier children? How would you go about finding an answer to this question?

One way to answer such a question is simply to give your opinion, based on whatever experience you have had with mothers and children. The main problem with opinions is that everyone has them. Without facts, proving that one opinion is more valid than another is impossible.

A second approach to answering such a question is to collect some ''expert'' opinions from the group of people who have the most experience with the problem, mothers. The drawback of this approach is that each mother is likely to favor whatever answer is comfortable for her. Mothers who like to pick up and cuddle babies will insist that the baby benefits from this treatment; mothers who do not enjoy this activity will reply that cuddling only spoils a baby.

A third possibility is to make casual observations of one or two children who receive a lot of cuddling and one or two children who receive only a little and to look for differences in the behavior of the children. The difficulty with this procedure is that casual observations are often inaccurate because the children observed may not be typical of all children and because the observer may overlook important details.

A fourth method for answering the question is to study the problem scientifically. The first step in a scientific study is to restate the general question in a specific form. The question about the effects of picking up babies might become, Does picking up a crying baby cause the baby to cry more? The second step is to make systematic observations of the behavior of interest. The observers must be careful not to allow any irrelevant factors (such as wet diapers) or outside interferences (such as a stinging insect) to mislead them into reaching a mistaken conclusion.

Of these four approaches to answering questions, psychologists prefer the scientific method because it provides answers that are most likely to be consistent and accurate.

Using the scientific method to study children is not as easy as it sounds. One problem is that some of the most intriguing questions about children do not lend themselves to scientific study. This problem is especially acute for questions related to the heredity-environment issue, such as, Is personality characteristic X primarily the result of genetic inheritance or is it primarily the result of learning and experience? The difficulty lies not in the design of the studies but in the ethics of the situation: it simply is unethical to systematically deprive a child of normal care for research purposes. A second problem is that comparing children of different ages often requires special methods. Suppose a study is designed to measure attention span at ages 3, 5, and 7 years. The psychologist must find an activity that is intensely interesting to children at each of these ages, a feat that requires some ingenuity. A third problem (which is not unique to psychology) is cost; scientific research is time consuming and often expensive. A fourth problem is that children are not always cooperative subjects. When a psychologist wants to test a child's memory, the child may prefer to inspect the automatic slide projector. When the psychologist asks the child to talk about a picture book, the child may suddenly become shy and silent. As any child psychologist can testify, Murphy's Law (In the most carefully controlled experiments, subjects behave as they _____ well please.) must have been written with children in mind.

In spite of its shortcomings, the scientific method is used by psychologists because it yields more valuable information than less systematic methods do. When designing a study of children's behavior, a psychologist must consider four questions: Should a few children be studied in detail or many children superficially? Should the research be conducted in a laboratory or in a real-life setting? Does the research question concern causes and effects? Which method will be most appropriate for comparing children of different ages?

STUDIES OF INDIVIDUALS AND GROUPS

A detailed description of the behavior (and often life history) of a child is called a *case study*. Darwin's baby biography (see Chapter 1) is an example of this approach to research with children. Case studies are most often used in clinical settings to trace the development of mental, emotional, or behavioral disturbances. In clinical case studies most of the information known about the child is likely to be included, but special emphasis is given to events the psychologist thinks may be related to the child's problems. By studying similar case histories a psychologist can develop ideas about possible causes of a disorder. Unfortunately, the case history approach cannot prove that a particular series of experiences caused a particular problem, because individual cases vary in too many details to allow exact, certain conclusions. Another problem with this approach is that part of the child's history is usually taken from family members, who may have forgotten or misperceived important events in the child's life. What case histories lack in precision, they usually make up in richness of detail and human interest. One especially engaging example of the case study method is Axline's (1964) account of Dibs, an intelligent young boy who was so withdrawn that his parents thought he was mentally retarded.

How might the case study approach be used to study the effects of cuddling on infants' psychological well-being? A detailed account of a child's early life would likely include references to cuddling and its aftereffects. If several case studies of infants were available, they might be compared, with close attention to details about physical contact between parents and children and notice of similarities among children who received unusually little (or unusually much) cuddling.

A case study is likely to provide information on many facets of a child's life that are irrelevant to a specific research project. A psychologist might prefer to study more children in less detail. The advantage of studying a large *group* of children is that more accurate conclusions can be drawn about children in general. Characteristics peculiar to one or a few children are less likely to cause confusion if many children are studied. The main drawback of group studies is the possibility that each child may be observed in so little detail that important insights are missed. Group studies can be done thoroughly, however, and generally they are more popular among psychologists than case studies are. The methods described in this chapter are used almost exclusively with groups rather than individuals.

STUDIES IN NATURAL SETTINGS AND IN LABORATORIES

Children (and adults) usually do not behave the same in strange surroundings as in comfortable, familiar settings. To determine how children behave in real life, the *naturalistic* approach is used. The naturalistic approach is to observe behavior in everyday situations, such as in homes, schools, playgrounds, or stores, rather than in a psychologist's office or laboratory. An observer who uses this approach tries to be as inconspicuous as possible to prevent interfering with the children's normal behavior. This method is often useful in the early stages of investigating a research problem because it provides ideas and hypotheses but seldom allows the observer to draw firm conclusions about causes of behavior. Sometimes, the researcher purposely interferes with the natural environment in some minor way to discover how the change in environment affects the behavior of the children.

The naturalistic approach is frequently used in *cross-cultural* research, in which children living in one society or culture are compared with children living in a very different setting. Many cross-cultural studies of children have been conducted by cultural anthropologists. Cross-cultural research often sheds light on questions involving heredity and environment. Within any particular culture, the environment of all children has many common elements, producing similarities in behavior that can masquerade as effects of heredity. If all children in the United States, for example, cry when angered, an American psychologist might conclude that crying is an inborn, hereditary reaction to anger. If, on the other hand, a cross-cultural study reveals that children in Guatemala do *not* cry when angered, the conclusion is that reactions to anger are learned, not inborn, since these reactions vary from one society to another. A cross-cultural study can, therefore, prevent conclusions that might mistakenly be drawn from observations in only one culture.

To use the naturalistic method to study babies' responses to cuddling (whether within or across cultures), a psychologist visits homes to observe how often mothers cuddle their infants and how the babies react. Based on these observations, the psychologist makes some guesses about the effects of cuddling, perhaps that physical contact quiets a child. After the initial observations, the psychologist might interfere slightly with a mother's cuddling behavior, perhaps by asking her *not* to hold the child for 10 or 15 minutes. The infant's behavior then allows the psychologist to confirm or to reject the guess made about the effects of cuddling. If such interferences are made, they are done on a small scale to prevent major disruptions of the natural home setting.

Research studies sometimes require special equipment and facilities not available in the average home or school. Elaborate play equipment, for example, or complicated recording machines (videotape and the like) are difficult to transport from one place to another. In such a case the research is conducted in a laboratory. Laboratories allow systematic control of the environment, so a child's behavior can be observed in a situation set up exactly as the researcher wants it. Psychologists often prefer laboratories to natural settings because of convenience. Laboratory observations may be distorted, though, if the behavior of the children is altered by the unfamiliar surroundings. If the behavior of a child is studied in a strange setting with a strange adult for the shortest possible period of time, extending the results to the normal behavior of children may prove difficult. **25**

STUDIES OF CORRELATIONS AND CAUSES
Correlational method

The correlational method is used to look for and then measure statistically the relationships that exist between variables. A variable is any event or characteristic of an individual that can vary, or be different for different people (or for the same person at different times). For example, age is a variable because different people are different ages and a person's age varies as time passes. Other examples of variables commonly studied in research with children are sex (some children are boys, some are girls), reading test scores (some children read at second-grade level, others at fourth-, sixth-, or eighth-grade level), educational level of the child's parents (perhaps eighth grade, high school, or college), and number of brothers and sisters (some children have none, others may have one, two, six, or more). One variable is often related to another in some predictable way. For example, children usually grow taller as they grow older. The variables height and age are therefore related to each other; as age increases, height increases also. To study this sort of relationship between variables, a psychologist uses the correlation method.

How can the correlational approach be applied to the research question about cuddling? The general research question must first be narrowed. One specific aspect of the cuddling issue is, Do children who receive more cuddling cry less than other children? The variables to be considered are (1) amount of cuddling a child receives, and (2) amount of crying by the child. Both of these variables can conveniently be expressed in numbers, such as the average number of minutes of cuddling (or crying) per hour. The psychologist then observes the number of minutes spent in each of these activities for, maybe, 1 hour a day for 10 days. Ordinarily, 20 or 30 children might be observed, because of individual differences among children. To provide a short example, suppose a psychologist observed only five children and recorded the following amounts of cuddling and crying.

Fig. 2-1. Children vary in height and weight, but generally, taller children are heavier.

Child	Average number of minutes per hour spent cuddling	Average number of minutes per hour spent crying
Kevin	3	36
Cathy	9	23
Matthew	10	18
Nina	13	6
Becky	15	4

Is there any relationship in these children between cuddling and crying? It seems that the babies who were cuddled less cried more and the babies who were cuddled more cried less. To confirm this conclusion (after observing more children), the psychologist would use *statistics*. Statistics are described in more detail in Chapter 3, but basically a statistic is a number that is calculated to summarize or describe a larger group of numbers. In the case of the correlational method, a correlation statistic is calculated to describe how closely related two variables are.

The correlational method may seem complicated, especially because of the statistics. This method is sometimes complex, but it is also very useful. A carefully conducted correlational study allows a psychologist to make *predictions* with precision and confidence. Suppose a researcher finds a strong correlation (close relationship) between mothers smoking during pregnancy and babies being smaller or less healthy at birth. On the basis of this study, it can be predicted that other mothers who smoke will have smaller or less healthy infants.

There is a danger, though, with correlational studies: readers often assume that a strong correlation between two variables means that one variable *causes* the other variable. Cause-and-effect relationships *cannot* be demonstrated in a correlational study. It would be a mistake to conclude that, because mothers' smoking and babies' poor health are simply "co-related," smoking causes the babies' problems. There may be a third variable, such as nervousness or chemical imbalance in the mother, that causes *both* smoking and babies' poor health.

The possibility of a third variable that causes both correlated variables is always present in a correlational study. Consider two examples:

1. The amount of liquor sold in the United States and the salaries of college professors are positively correlated; that is, the more college professors earn, the more liquor is purchased. Does this mean that paying professors more money causes them to splurge it all in bars? Though some people may suspect this is the case, a more likely explanation is that national prosperity causes both the increase in professors' salaries and the increase in liquor sales.

2. The higher the birth rate in New York City, the softer the asphalt of New York City streets. Though birth rate and softness of asphalt are correlated, neither causes the other. Birth rates typically are higher in the summer, when the heat softens the asphalt in the streets.

Because of the possibility of additional, undiscovered variables in correlational studies, conclusions regarding causes and effects are not justified in this type of study. If you like slogans, remember the psychologists' warning: *Correlation does not mean causation*.

Understanding that correlations do not imply causes is important, even if you never read a single research report or take another child development course, because this principle allows you to be more skeptical of everyday events, such as news stories or advertisements. Stories and ads on television and in magazines and newspapers often report correlational studies *as if* a cause-and-effect relationship were established. In an ad for a breakfast food, for example, a "teacher" claims that eating breakfast is "related to" (read "correlated with") doing well in school. The teacher advises feeding children nutritious breakfasts "so they will learn more efficiently." This last statement is based on the faulty assumption that breakfast *causes* the efficient learning, when all we know is that breakfast and learning are *correlated*. A likely third factor is social class. Studies have repeatedly shown that middle-class children perform better in school than poor children do; middle-class children are also more likely to eat breakfast. Though it seems sensible that hungry children will perform poorly in school, one *cannot* prove (on the basis of the correlational study) that feeding children will *cause* their grades to improve.

Experimental method

The experimental method is more powerful than the correlational method because it yields results that allow both predictions *and* conclusions about causes and effects. The basic strategy of this approach is to start with two or more groups of children that are *alike* in every way; one group is then given a special treatment or experience. If after the special treatment the original groups are *not alike,* it can be concluded that the special treatment *caused* the new difference between the groups.

With the experimental method, a new kind of question can be answered about our sample research topic, cuddling. This method is the only one that can be employed to answer questions such as, Does cuddling *cause* babies to sleep more? or Does cuddling *cause* babies to become overly dependent?

Consider the first question, Does cuddling cause babies to sleep more? The first step is to divide the children to be observed into two groups that are as similar as possible, with the same average age, same health, same temperament, same experience with cuddling, and (especially) same average time spent sleeping. Once the groups are sufficiently alike, the psychologist deliberately provides one group with cuddling experience that is different from that of the other group. For example, the parents of one group might be encouraged to cuddle their infants as much as possible, while the parents of the other group are prevented from cuddling their infants at all. The psychologist records how long the babies sleep each day. Note that the groups of babies are alike in every way *except* the one variable (amount of cuddling) being studied. If after 2 or 3 days one group of babies sleeps more than the other group, the psychologist can conclude that the difference in cuddling has *caused* the difference in sleeping. Because the groups started out alike and only the amount of cuddling was varied, only the cuddling could cause the difference between the groups in sleeping time found at the end of the experiment. Naturally, such an experiment would be quite brief, because long-term restrictions on physical contact are a hardship for both infants and parents.

The tricky step in the experimental method is to be certain the groups are alike before the experiment begins. Finding *exactly* identical groups is probably impossible, but psychologists frequently use three methods to make the groups as similar as is necessary for all practical purposes.

1. The individuals in the experiment can be *matched* according to important characteristics; then one member of each match is assigned to each group. In a two-group experiment on creativity, for example, a psychologist might match pairs of children in terms of age, sex, grades in school, and teacher's evaluation of creative ability. A 7-year-old boy with average grades and above-average creativity, for instance, would be matched with another boy with the same characteristics. One member of each pair would be assigned (by chance) to be in one group; the other member would then join the other group. Even though children *within* each group are different, each child in one group is quite similar to one child in the other group, making the two groups equivalent overall.

2. The same children can be members of both groups in a *before-and-after* experiment. Observing one group of children twice provides the same amount of information as observing two groups of children once. Observing the same children in each experimental condition makes it unnecessary to match children to find equivalent groups. In a study of the effects of frustration, for example, a child can be observed one day in a frustrating situation and another day in a normal situation. By repeating this procedure with 19 more children, the researcher has observed, in effect, a group of 20 children when frustrated and the same 20 children when not frustrated.

3. A large group of children can be *divided at random* (by chance) into two or more smaller groups. This technique, called random assignment of subjects to groups, is based on the assumption that differences among individuals are minimized or cancelled if the subjects (participants) are placed in groups entirely by chance. Suppose an experiment were designed to determine whether attending preschool increases intelligence test scores. Two groups are needed: children sent to preschool and children not sent. The groups must be alike, especially in intelligence, before the experiment begins. If 40 children are assigned completely by chance to be in one group or the other, each group will likely have some bright children, some average, and some below average in intelligence. For each child in the preschool group with an IQ (intelligence quotient) of, say, 106, there will probably be a child with a similar IQ in the other group. The result of random assignment will be groups with IQ scores (and other characteristics) that on the average are alike. After the groups are selected by random assignment, the researcher often measures important traits (IQ in this case) to be sure the groups are equivalent before the experiment begins.*

---

*The concept that random assignment cancels out individual differences is sometimes difficult to accept. To convince yourself, experiment with a group of at least 20 persons (perhaps your child development class). The people are likely to vary considerably in height. For each person in the group, put a small piece of paper in a hat, with an *A* written on half of the pieces of paper and a *B* on the other pieces. Mix all the pieces and have everyone draw out one. For those who drew a paper with an *A*, list their heights and average them. Then list the heights of the *B* group and average them. Because the people were assigned to the *A* or *B* group by "the luck of the draw," or random chance, some short people and some tall people are likely to be in each group. The individual differences should cancel out, and the average height of the *A* group should be quite similar to the average height of the *B* group; the groups are therefore equivalent.

The point to remember is that matching, testing children twice, and random assignment all result in similar groups, which can then be exposed to different conditions to
measure the effect of the experimental variable. Which of these three methods is best?
The answer depends on the purpose of the experiment and the resources of the researcher.
The *matching* technique is relatively costly and time consuming because a lot of information must be gathered about every child in the experiment, but this method provides
groups that are very similar. The *before-and-after* technique provides groups that are
even more similar. It is inappropriate for many studies, however, because the experience
of being in one group or condition may make the child ineligible for the other experimental condition. (If children are taught to read by method *A*, it is too late to teach them
to read by method *B*.) *Random assignment* is the most commonly used method because
it is quick, easy, and accurate enough for most purposes. The element of chance, though,
makes random assignment less reliable than the other methods. Psychologists deal with
this problem by assigning large numbers of children to each group, because having many
children in each group makes each child's idiosyncrasies less apparent.

Although the experimental method is more powerful than the correlational method
(because experiments allow conclusions about causes), experiments are not appropriate
for studying some kinds of questions. The method can only be used if the groups of subjects can be made alike at the start of the experiment.

Consider a study of social class and health. Are middle-class children healthier than
poor children? If they are, is the difference in health *caused* by the difference in income?
To answer the question about cause, two identical groups must be found, one of middle-
class children and one of poor children. But clearly, groups that are separated on the
basis of income can never be identical. The experimental method cannot be used to find
whether social class (or age, or race, or IQ, or sex, or any other intrinsic characteristic)
causes a behavior, because when we divide children into groups according to income (or
age, or whatever), the groups are no longer alike. The experimental method works only
with *alike* groups. In an experimental study, the *psychologist* must be able to decide
which group a child will be assigned to; if the group assignment is predetermined by some
characteristic of the child, the groups will not be alike.

Many studies of children combine the experimental and correlational approaches.
Consider a study of the influence of age and recent television viewing experience on reactions to a new program. The children can be assigned by chance to watch 6 hours of
TV a day or no TV at all for 1 month. Because the amount of recent TV viewing experience is varied experimentally, conclusions about recent TV viewing causing reactions to
the new show are acceptable. But the children cannot be randomly assigned to groups
based on age; they must be assigned on the basis of whatever age they are. Therefore, this
portion of the study is correlational.

Like the correlational method, the experimental method involves statistics. Statistics
are used in experiments to determine whether small differences between groups are due
to chance alone (see Chapter 3).

The experimental and correlational methods are employed to answer rather restricted
research questions. They are effective for gathering specific facts, but there is a danger

of losing an overall view of development if specific studies are considered alone. General conclusions must be based on many studies, which, like bits of stone in a mosaic, all contribute to an image of the pattern of development.

STUDIES INVOLVING AGE

In many studies of children, age is a variable; that is, children of one age are compared with children of other ages. Any of three different research designs can be adopted when age is a variable.

The same children can be observed year after year as they grow older. A study in which the same children are observed over a long period of time is called a *longitudinal* study. The Berkeley Growth Study of intellectual development is a good example of a longitudinal design (Bayley, 1968). Beginning with seventy-four 1-month-old infants in the early 1930s, Bayley and her associates tested the intelligence of the subjects many times as they grew older. The most recent tests were given to 54 of the original subjects at age 36. Bayley found that IQ scores of an individual can change considerably over time, but in general the subjects' IQs at age 36 were similar to their earlier IQ scores.

The main advantage of a longitudinal design is that it provides a good picture of individual development. This design is especially useful for observing development of intelligence and personality characteristics *within* individuals. This design has several disadvantages. It is expensive and requires a long time and a very patient researcher. The researcher often has trouble keeping track of all the subjects over the years. Perhaps the most significant problem in a rapidly changing world is that the longitudinal design is blind to the effects of cultural change. Children who are 5 years old this year, for example, may process visual information quite differently from children who were 5 in 1950, before the widespread availability of television. Because of cultural changes, a study started 25 years ago may no longer provide an accurate picture of children today.

The *cross-sectional* design is probably the most common method of making age comparisons. In a cross-sectional study, children of different ages are compared at one time. Since a child is only one age at one time, different children must be in different age groups. A psychologist interested in development of muscle coordination among preschoolers, for example, might test ten 2-year-olds, ten 3-year-olds, and ten 4-year-olds, all within 1 or 2 weeks.

The major advantage of the cross-sectional design is convenience; it can be completed very quickly, without waiting for children to grow older. One of the disadvantages of this design is that it does not provide information about continuous individual development. A second disadvantage, shared with the longitudinal design, is that it may be contaminated by cultural changes. Behavior differences between 2-year-olds and 5-year-olds, which *appear* to be explained by differences in age, might in fact result from an abrupt cultural change, such as the way infants are treated in hospitals. A third problem is that the researcher must be certain the groups are alike in every way except age. Comparing dissimilar groups, such as 4-year-olds who stay at home and 6-year-olds who attend school, yields confusing results; any differences in behavior can be related to either age or experience with school and playmates.

31

PART
ONE
=====

An ambitious researcher who is willing to invest the time and energy needed for the longitudinal approach but wants better control of problems associated with cultural changes can choose a third plan, the *time-lag* design. A time-lag design combines the longitudinal and cross-sectional designs by comparing children of different ages *and* following the development of children for several years. A time-lag design is useful, for example, in a study of age changes in sex roles. Children's ideas of behavior appropriate for each sex are likely to change as they grow older. What proportion of the change results from changes in age, and what proportion results from changes in society (attitudes of typical parents and teachers, for instance)? The study might be begun in 1978 with children of three ages: 3, 5, and 7 years. (So far, the study is cross sectional.) In 1980, another group of children, some 3, some 5, and some 7 years old, will be studied. (The 5- and 7-year-olds might be veterans of the first observations, 2 years before, but this is not a necessity.) In 1982, more children at each age will be studied. This design could be diagrammed as follows.

	Year		
	1978	**1980**	**1982**
Ages tested	7		
	5	7	
	3	5	7
		3	5
			3

Each year, comparisons across ages can be made to see whether ideas about sex roles change with age. Comparisons across years can also determine, for example, whether children who are 5 years old in 1978 have different ideas from children who are 5 in 1982. The time-lag design gives an indication of how much a child's ideas about sex roles are determined by age and how much by growing up in a particular time.

SUMMARY

Research with children is complicated. Information may be collected by studying an individual child in depth or by less detailed observations of many children. The observations may be conducted in children's natural surroundings or in unfamiliar places, such as specially equipped laboratories. Studies may be designed simply to find correlations between variables or to determine causes and effects. When age is a variable, the research plan may be cross sectional, longitudinal, or a complex time-lag design.

Which of these methods and designs is best for studying children? This question is a little like asking, What is the best way to spend a Saturday afternoon? No one approach and no one Saturday afternoon activity is intrinsically better than another. Some methods, like some activities, are more suitable than others for the time and situation and the intentions of the researcher. The researcher must consider the strengths and weaknesses of each approach and select the one that will be most effective for solving the problem at hand.

REFERENCES

Axline, V. M. *Dibs, in search of self.* New York: Ballantine Books, Inc., 1964.

Bayley, N. Behavioral correlates of mental growth: birth to thirty-six years. *American Psychologist,* 1968, **23,** 1-17.

Peer influences on preschool children's willingness to try difficult tasks

E. Paul Torrance

Some children apparently fail to learn because they are unwilling to try more and more difficult tasks. Others fail because they compulsively insist upon trying tasks too difficult for them to master. Thus, to guide a child's learning effectively a teacher must be able to influence his willingness to try tasks of appropriate difficulty.

In another source, the author has presented evidence to indicate that learners differing in tendencies to attempt the difficult need different kinds of feedback concerning their performance. Learners low in willingness to attempt the difficult appear to need evaluative feedback and external criteria. Those high in willingness to attempt the difficult seem to be hampered by this kind of feedback and need opportunities to test their own limits and push their limits forward. Thus, teachers should be aware of individual differences in willingness to attempt the difficult and to differentiate feedback experiences accordingly.

Almost all personality studies of productive, creative people show that such people enjoy a calculated risk in which success or failure depends upon their own ability. In fact, there seems to be a positive relationship between willingness to attempt difficult tasks and achievement. Studies of the lives of eminent people who have made important social contributions suggest that one of the essentials for high achievement is a strong tendency to attempt difficult tasks. Instead of just adapting or adjusting to their environment, they deliberately exposed themselves to possible failure and committed themselves to goals that required sustained expenditures of intellectual and physical energy and continued changes in behavior. Thus, it would appear that it is important to society that schools develop in children the ability to estimate their limits and a willingness to attempt difficult tasks.

The present study was conducted as a part of a sequence of activities to teach children to estimate more accurately their limits. It was designed specifically to determine the influence of three different peer conditions on willingness to attempt difficult tasks. The design of the study was suggested by the author's observations in working with United States Air Force personnel in advanced survival training that men were more likely to attempt difficult tasks and to test their limits in pairs than in individual or large group situations. The design of this study was also influenced by the finding of Miller, Bensen, Seidman, and Meeland that men have a greater tolerance of electric shock in the presence of a partner than when alone.

It was hypothesized that the five-year-old children in the present study would be more willing to attempt the difficult when placed in pairs than when alone or before a large group (a class of 22 peers).

PROCEDURE
Subjects

The subjects were 44 five-year-olds enrolled in an experimental preprimary educational program following [a] creative-aesthetic approach. The subjects were equally divided into two classes each taught by a master teacher assisted by a part-time teaching aide. The classes were integrated and roughly represented a stratified sample in a medium-sized Southern town. A deliberate attempt had been made to include some disadvantaged children in each class. While the

From *The Journal of Psychology*, 1969, **72**, 189-194.

majority of children in the two classes studied are white, almost all of the remaining children in the school are black.

The setting

Essentially the same behavioral settings were maintained in both classrooms. These behavioral settings were deliberately designed to encourage experimentation, manipulation, sociodramatic play, construction, and creative expression. The experimental materials (bean bags and waste baskets) used in this study had been available in both classrooms from the beginning of the school year but had been used almost entirely during free activity periods. The author was accustomed to working with each class for about one hour each week. Early in the school year during a free activity period, the author had encouraged some of the children to try to throw the bean bags into the basket from different distances. No systematic work had been done either to teach the children to estimate their limits or to encourage them to try the task at distances difficult for them to succeed. Any such learning prior to the present study was incidental.

Experimental material

The training and test task used in this study was adapted from Starkweather's test of willingness to try difficult tasks. Starkweather's test apparatus consists of a target game in which a ball is rolled from varying distances to a target enclosed in a box. A marker consisting of a strip of cloth calibrated for distance is used in determining what is difficult for each child and in setting the easy and difficult task. Prior to the development of this instrument, Starkweather had used a bean bag target game as a test of willingness to try difficult tasks but had abandoned it.

In the present study, the experimental equipment consisted of two sets of three 12-ounce bean bags each, a marker designating five levels of difficulty, and a waste basket. The equipment used in the study was quite similar to that which had been available in the classrooms from the beginning of the school year. However, no marker had been used prior to this time.

Orientation to the task

The target game was introduced as a part of the author's usual work with the children and was preceded by the reading and discussion of Mary McBurney Green's *Is It Hard? Is It Easy?* As the book was read, the author and the children talked about whether it was easy for each of them to skip, tie shoelaces, climb trees, catch and throw a ball, take a bath, hold tickly worms, whistle, somersault, and pound nails so they go in straight. They were told that they could make the bean bag target game easy or difficult by standing close or far away from the target. In all three conditions, children were given opportunities to practice the task to "warm up" and to find out what was hard and easy for them.

Peer conditions

Under all three conditions, each subject was given a practice session, an explanation of the scoring system (5 points for hitting the target from E, 4 points for hitting it from D, 3 points for hitting it from C, etc.), and three trials to hit the target.

For Conditions A and B, children were called from the classroom in random pairs to play the target game in the wide hallway just outside the classroom. Two sets of targets and markers were set up in such a way that the players were back to back and could not see what the other was doing. Under Condition A, the children practiced and played the game in pairs; under Condition B, they practiced and played alone. Under Condition C, they performed before the entire class and each class competed with the other for the ownership of a large ball unlike any available to them. After each child had performed, he was allowed to add whatever points he scored to the class score being kept on the blackboard. (The two classes achieved identical scores.) This procedure netted 22 subjects each in Conditions A and B and 44 subjects in Condition C. The 44 children in Condition C were the same ones who were in Conditions A and B. The study was conducted after the children had been in the preprimary program for about five months.

RESULTS

A rough test of the hypothesis already stated can be obtained by comparing the proportion of easiest tasks chosen under each condition. These percentages were as follows: Condition A (Pairs), 13.7 percent; Condition B (Alone), 36.5 percent; Condition C (Class), 86.5 percent. In all cases, the differences in proportions are statistically significant at the one percent level of confidence. When working in pairs, children least frequently tried the target from the easiest position. When performing before the class, they were most conservative and most frequently tried the target from the easiest position.

A somewhat more precise test can be made by obtaining a distance score for trial, adding the distance score for the three trials by each child, and comparing the differences in means for the three conditions. The means and standard deviations, respectively, for the three conditions are as follows: Condition A (Pairs) 12.1, 3.3; Condition B (Alone), 6.7, 3.9; Condition C (Class), 3.8, 1.6. An analysis of variance yielded an F ratio of 64.64, significant at better than the .01 level. A t ratio of 4.61 was obtained for the difference in means for Conditions A and B and one of 1.91 was obtained for the difference between Conditions B and C, the former being significant at better than the .01 level and the latter being significant at about the .05 level.

DISCUSSION

These results suggest that young children tend to be most willing to try difficult tasks when working in pairs and least willing to do so when performing before the entire class. In individual situations, they seem to be freer to adjust the difficulty of the task to their skill level than under the "pair" and "class" conditions.

One might question the extent to which one can generalize from the limited number of subjects included in this study. One might also wonder if the Creative-Aesthetic orientation of the program might not have influenced the results. Under the Creative-Aesthetic approach, there is constant emphasis on attempting difficult tasks and much effort is expended in developing a psychologically safe environment. Thus, it would be expected that children under the Creative-Aesthetic approach would feel freer than under other conditions to make errors or fail in the presence of the group. In both classes, however, the children were extremely reluctant to try the difficult before the class. Confidence in the results is strengthened by the fact that they were quite consistent within treatments and the differences between treatments were quite strong.

From these results, it would be expected that having children work on school tasks in pairs would influence them to try difficult tasks, while requiring them to perform before the entire class would discourage them from doing so. In the latter condition, none of the children in either class tried to hit the target from the five-point line and only two of them attempted to hit it from the four- or three-point line. When working in pairs, only three of the 22 children tried to hit the target from the easiest position; most of them held doggedly to the four- and five-point lines.

SUMMARY

In order to learn and to grow, children have to be willing to attempt difficult tasks. To facilitate learning and growth, teachers should be able to create the social or peer conditions conducive to attempting tasks of appropriate difficulty.

It was hypothesized that five-year-old children in an experimental preprimary school program would be more willing to attempt difficult tasks when placed in pairs than when alone or before their entire class.

The task used in this study was a target game in which the children attempted to throw bean bags into a basket from distances that made the task either easy or difficult, depending upon the choice of the child. In Condition A, the children played the game in pairs; in Condition B, alone; and in Condition C, before the entire class. There were 22 children each in Conditions A and B and 44 in Condition C.

The results clearly supported the hypothesis and further suggested that children are least willing to attempt the difficult when performing before the entire class.

Chapter 3

Reading a research report

Charles F. Few

Scientific knowledge about children advances, not by leaps and bounds, but by small steps. To be accepted by scientists, a fact or theory must be verified by careful research studies. When a research study produces interesting or useful information, a description of the study is published in a professional journal. More than 400 research articles are published each year in three major child psychology journals*; many more articles about children appear in journals devoted to general psychology, education, pediatrics, psychiatry, and clinical psychology. The research reports found in this book originally appeared in such journals. Each report represents one step in the slow accumulation of scientific knowledge about children.

WHY BOTHER WITH RESEARCH REPORTS?

People who are unaccustomed to reading research reports often find them dry, dull, confusing, full of minute details, and lacking in interesting insights about children. These characteristics are unfortunate side effects of psychologists' efforts to write in scientific style. This style was developed to communicate to experienced readers the most information with the fewest words. Because the readers are assumed to be interested in the research, the authors do not try to write in an entertaining manner.

Reading a research report is a skill, such as riding a bicycle, that can be perfected with some guidance and considerable practice. Some hints may help you learn this skill.

1. Start by carefully reading the summary or abstract. The details of the article will make more sense if the general theme of the research is understood.
2. Read the article once for meaning, temporarily overlooking the technical details. Beginners are often overwhelmed by the scientific terms and mathematical symbols. To prevent yourself from being overwhelmed, concentrate on grasping the basic ideas in the article and save the unfamiliar terms for later.
3. Reread the report, several times if necessary, picking up more details with each reading. Test your understanding of the article by trying to describe it in your own words.
4. Try to visualize what the psychologists and the children are doing in the study. Your imagination is what makes an article come to life.

Articles written in scientific style are usually divided into six sections, each with a different purpose: abstract (summary), introduction, method, results of the study, discussion of the results, and references. To help you understand the anatomy of an article, an example article has been "sacrificed for dissection." This article describes an investigation of sex differences in the typical play of 1-year-old infants.†

ANATOMY OF A RESEARCH REPORT
Abstract

The abstract is a short summary of the purpose of the research, the methods used, and the findings of the researchers. The abstract appears at the beginning of the article and is

---

*Child Development, Developmental Psychology, and Journal of Experimental Child Psychology.
†Goldberg, S., and Lewis, M. Play behavior in the year-old-infant: early sex differences. Child Development, 1969, 40, 21-31. © 1969 by the Society for Research in Child Development, Inc. All rights reserved.

rarely longer than one paragraph. Ordinarily it is set apart from the body of the article by italics, indentation, or smaller print.

---

32 boys and 32 girls, 13 months old, were observed with their mothers in a standardized free play situation. There were striking sex differences in the infants' behavior toward their mothers and in their play. Earlier observation of the mothers' behavior toward the infants at 6 months indicates that some of these sex differences were related to the mothers' behavior toward the infants. It was suggested that parents behave differently toward girls and boys, even as infants, reinforcing sex-appropriate behavior. This study emphasizes the importance of observing the freely emitted behavior of the very young child.

Introduction

The first section of the article proper is called the introduction, although it is not labeled as the other sections are. Most of the introduction is devoted to describing previous research studies on similar problems and explaining how these studies are related to the problem to be investigated. When previously published research is mentioned, the reference is usually given in the form Smith and Jones (1975), giving the last name(s) of the author(s) and the year of publication. More information about each reference cited appears at the end of the article. In addition to a review of other research, the introduction states the purpose of the research project, often in the form of the question to be answered or the hypothesis (expected result) to be tested. The following sample introduction is rather short, but more complicated research reports sometimes have lengthy introductions.

Until recently, the largest proportion of studies in child development gave attention to nursery and early grade school children. The literature on sex differences is no exception. A recent book on development of sex differences which includes an annotated bibliography (Maccoby, 1966) lists fewer than 10 studies using infants, in spite of the fact that theoretical discussions (e.g., Freud, 1938 [originally published in 1905]; Piaget, 1951) emphasize the importance of early experience. Theoretical work predicts and experimental work confirms the existence of sex differences in behavior by age 3. There has been little evidence to demonstrate earlier differentiation of sex-appropriate behavior, although it would not be unreasonable to assume this occurs.

Recently, there has been increased interest in infancy, including some work which has shown early sex differences in attentive behavior (Kagan & Lewis, 1965; Lewis, in press). The bulk of this work has been primarily experimental studying specific responses to specific stimuli or experimental conditions. Moreover, it has dealt with perceptual-cognitive differences rather than personality variables. There has been little observation of freely emitted behavior. Such observations are of importance in supplying researchers with the classes of naturally occurring behaviors, the conditions under which responses normally occur, and the natural preference ordering of behaviors. Knowledge of this repertoire of behaviors provides a background against which behavior under experimental conditions can be evaluated.

The present study utilized a free play situation to observe sex differences in children's behavior toward mother, toys, and a frustration situation at 13 months of age. Because the Ss were participants in a longitudinal study, information on the mother-child relationship at 6 months was also available. This made it possible to assess possible relations between behavior patterns at 6 months and at 13 months.

Method

The method section is a detailed description of how the research study was done. There are usually several subsections devoted to the subjects (participants), the procedure, and perhaps the apparatus or the test materials used. If the design of the study is quite complicated, with several groups of children treated in various ways, an additional subsection may be included to explain the design. A casual reader may find the many details tedious, but even the seemingly trivial facts must be reported for two reasons. First, other psychologists may want to replicate (repeat) the study, which requires exact knowledge of how the original study was conducted. Second, minor changes in method often produce major changes in results; if similar studies yield quite different results, a detailed method section can provide clues to account for the unexpected differences.

The subjects of a study are the children (or adults or animals) who are observed or tested by the experimenter. The description of the subjects is typically quite short but is especially important in studies of children. Small differences in the age, family background, personal characteristics, or method of selection of the subjects can results in large differences in the behavior of the children. For example, a task that is easy for 4-year-olds may be too difficult for 3-year-old children. Children selected from college nursery schools often behave quite differently from children selected from public day-care centers.

One feature of the method section of most articles is the use of operational definitions. Scientists attempt to state precise definitions for the words they use. In psychology, words are ideally defined in terms of numbers or in terms of specific observable behaviors. A very specific definition of this type, which tells the reader exactly how an event is measured or observed, is called an *operational definition*. Suppose a psychologist is studying children's sharing behavior. Everyone has an idea of what sharing is, but to determine exactly how much a child shares, the psychologist must decide which specific acts will be considered sharing (such as giving another child a toy or offering to give some pennies to a charity); the psychologist then counts the number of times these acts occur. This strategy of listing specific behaviors is used to define amount of physical contact in the sample article. A slightly different approach to operational definitions is to measure a trait, such as intelligence or verbal ability or anxiety, by administering a test; the trait is then defined by a score on the test.

One problem with an operational definition is that it may be limited to a certain situation. In a study of aggression in which children see an adult beating up a Bobo doll, a psychologist may define aggression as hitting, kicking, and pushing a Bobo doll. But this definition applies only to aggression studies with Bobo dolls; it certainly is not a general definition of aggression. A second problem is that different operational definitions of the same concept may produce contradictory results. Fear of dogs may be defined as a certain answer to the question, What are you afraid of?, or it may be defined as a child's refusal to pet a strange dog. A child may say, ''I'm afraid of dogs,'' but be willing to pet a friendly puppy. A third problem with operational definitions is that not all people agree that a particular behavior reflects a particular trait. Many people, for example, argue that scores on an IQ test are not an adequate measure of intelligence. The main advantage of operational definitions is precision: whether you agree with the author's definition or not, at least you know exactly how the author measured the behavior. Without this precision, psychologists cannot replicate and verify each other's research.

When reading the method section, imagine what the participants in the study are doing. The words have no meaning unless the reader can picture the events they represent.

METHOD
Subjects

Two samples of 16 girls and 16 boys each, or a total of 64 infants, were seen at 6 and 13 months of age (± 6 days). All Ss were born to families residing in southwestern Ohio at the time of the study. All were Caucasian. The mothers had an average of 13.5 years of schooling (range of 10-18 years) and the fathers had an average of 14.5 years of schooling (range of 8-20 years). The occupations of the fathers ranged from laborer to scientist. Of the 64 infants, 9 girls and 10 boys were first-born and the remaining infants had from 1 to 6 siblings.

The 6-month visit

The procedure of the 6-month visit, presented in detail in Kagan and Lewis (1965), included two visual episodes and an auditory episode where a variety of behavioral responses were recorded. The infant's mother was present during these procedures. At the end of the experimental procedure, the mother was interviewed by one of the experimenters, who had been able to observe both mother and infant for the duration of the session.

The interviewer also rated both mother and infant on a rating scale. The items rated for the infant included: amount of activity, irritability, response to mother's behavior, and amount of affect. For the mother, the observer rated such factors as nature of handling, amount of playing with the baby, type of comforting behavior, and amount of vocalization to the baby. Each item was rated on a 7-point scale, with 1 indicating the most activity and 7 the least. For the purpose of this study, it was necessary to obtain a measure of the amount of physical contact the mother initiated with the child. Since scores on the individual scales did not result in sufficient variance in the population, a composite score was obtained by taking the mean score for each mother over all three of the touching-the-infant scales. These included: amount of touching, amount of comforting, and the amount of play. The composite touch scores (now called the amount of physical contact) resulted in a sufficiently variable distribution to be used for comparison with the 13-month touch data.

The 13-month visit

Kagan and Lewis (1965), who employed the same 64 infants for their study, described the procedures used at 6 months, which were similar to those of the present (13-month) study. The only addition was a free play procedure, which will be discussed in detail below.

The playroom, 9 by 12 feet, contained nine simple toys: a set of blocks, a pail, a "lawnmower," a stuffed dog, an inflated plastic cat, a set of quoits (graduated plastic doughnuts stacked on a wooden rod), a wooden mallet, a pegboard, and a wooden bug (a pull toy). Also included as toys were any permanent objects in the room, such as the doorknob, latch on the wall, tape on the electrical outlets, and so forth. The mother's chair was located in one corner of the room.

Procedure

Each S, accompanied by his mother, was placed in the observation room. The mother was instructed to watch his play and respond in any way she desired. Most mothers simply watched and responded only when asked for something. The mother was also told that we would be observing from the next room. She held the child on her lap, the door to the playroom was closed, and observation began. At the beginning of the 15 minutes of play, the mother was instructed to place the child on the floor.

Measurement

Two observers recorded the *S*'s behavior. One dictated a continuous behavioral account into a tape recorder. The second operated an event recorder, which recorded the location of the child in the room and the duration of each contact with the mother.

Dictated recording. During the initial dictation, a buzzer sounded at regular time intervals, automatically placing a marker on the dictated tape. The dictated behavioral account was typed and each minute divided into 15-second units, each including about three typewritten lines. The typed material was further divided into three 5-second units, each unit being one typed line. Independent experimenters analyzed this typed material. For each minute, the number of toys played with and the amount of time spent with each toy was recorded.

Event recorder. To facilitate recording the activity and location of the child, the floor of the room was divided into 12 squares. For each square, the observer depressed a key on the event recorder for the duration of time the child occupied that square. From this record it was possible to obtain such measures as the amount of time spent in each square and the number of squares traversed. A thirteenth key was depressed each time the child touched the mother. From this record, measures of (a) initial latency in leaving the mother, (b) total amount of time touching the mother, (c) number of times touching the mother, and (d) the longest period touching the mother were obtained.

The data analysis presented in this report provides information only on sex differences (a) in response to the mother and (b) in choice and style of play with toys. Other data from this situation are presented elsewhere (Lewis, 1967).

Results

The outcome of a research study is reported in the results section. Psychologists use both words and numbers to describe the outcome of a study. The results section is often the most confusing because complicated ideas may be expressed in just a few words and the statistics are unfamiliar to most students.

Statistics are simply numbers used to summarize what the psychologist discovered in the study. There is nothing magical about statistics; any statistic can be translated into words, but it is more efficient to express an idea with a few numbers than with many words.

Two kinds of statistics are commonly used in psychological articles: descriptive and inferential. *Descriptive statistics* are used to describe or summarize a group of numbers. Percentages are perhaps the simplest example of descriptive statistics. Expressing a test score as a percentage is easier and more efficient than listing each question with an indicator of whether it was correct or incorrect.

Other popular descriptive statistics are the mean, the median, the range, and the standard deviation. The *mean* is the average score, obtained by adding all the individual scores and dividing by the number of scores. Consider the following hypothetical test scores.

2	Total of scores: 42
3	Number of scores: 7
3	Mean (average): $42 \div 7 = 6$
4	Median (middle score): 4
5	
6	
19	

The mean of this group is the total (42) divided by the number of scores (6), or 7. A mean familiar to most students is a grade point average, which is calculated by assigning each letter grade a number, adding the numbers representing a student's grades, and dividing by the number of grades earned.

The mean is often represented by the symbol $\overline{X}$. In the sample article, means are reported throughout the text and in the tables under the headings Girls and Boys.

The *median* is the middle score in any group of numbers that are arranged in order. Both the median and the mean are used to represent the typical score in a group, the score around which the other scores are centered. For the test scores listed above, the median is 4. Note that the median of these test scores is less than the mean. The mean is inflated by one extremely large score, 19. When one or two unusually large or unusually small scores are present, the median is a more representative or typical score than the mean. In most cases, though, the median and the mean are quite similar.

Sometimes it is useful to know how spread out the numbers are within a group. A simple way to indicate the spread is to give the *range,* or the difference between the highest and lowest numbers in the group. The range of the test scores above is the largest score (19) minus the smallest score (2), or 17. A problem with the range is that it is easily distorted by an extreme score. If the largest test score (19) is dropped, the range is only 6 minus 2, or 4. In the method section of the sample article, the education of the children's parents was described with both means and ranges: the mothers had an average of 13.5 years of schooling (range of 10 to 18 years), and the fathers had an average of 14.5 years of schooling (range of 8 to 20 years).

Another commonly used statistic for summarizing the spread of a group of numbers is the *standard deviation* (SD). To read research articles it is not necessary to be able to calculate a standard deviation*; it is only necessary to understand that the more spread out a group of numbers, the larger the standard deviation.

Descriptive statistics are used to summarize a group of numbers; *inferential statistics* are used to make comparisons between groups of numbers. The numbers represent the scores of the groups of subjects being compared. Whenever two or more groups of people are compared on some measure, such as height, the average scores or heights of the groups are likely to be somewhat different simply because of chance, because of naturally occurring differences among individuals. Small differences between groups often are due merely to chance, but large differences must be explained in some other way, usually by some real difference between the groups being compared. Inferential statistics provide an estimate of the likelihood that a difference between groups of numbers is due to chance alone.

---

*The formula for calculating a standard deviation is

$$SD = \sqrt{\frac{\Sigma(X_i - \overline{X})^2}{N - 1}}$$

where Σ is a summation sign (indicating that the values that follow are to be added), X_i represents each raw score, $\overline{X}$ represents the mean of the group, and N represents the number of scores in the group. The SD of the test scores listed above is 5.8. Without the extreme score (19), the SD would be about 1.5.

If an inferential statistic reveals that the probability of a chance result is very small, the difference between the groups is called *significant*. Note that statistical significance has nothing to do with the practical significance or importance of a result. Statistical significance means that the outcome of a study was probably *not* just chance or luck. Chance or luck is never completely ruled out; the probability level (significance level) tells what likelihood of a chance result remains.

The *probability level,* or *significance level,* which is reported along with the statistic, tells how confident the reader can be of the result. Statistics are usually reported in an article in the following form: $F = 10.59, p < .01$. $F = 10.59$ means that a particular inferential statistic (in this case one called an F ratio) was calculated and the answer was 10.59. The second notation, $p < .01$, gives the probability level. (Read $p < .01$ as probability less than $1/100$, or probability less than 1%). Loosely translated, $p < .01$ means that there is less than one chance in 100 that this value of the statistic $F(10.59)$ was obtained simply by luck. In other words, there are at least 99 chances in 100 that the differences between the groups compared can be explained, not just by luck but by real differences between the groups. In most research, $p < .05$ (probability of a chance result is less than five in 100) is considered acceptable, but $p < .01$ or $p < .001$ is preferred because they represent even lower probabilities of a chance result.

The F ratio is one of the most popular of many inferential statistics. In the sample article, Goldberg and Lewis rely on two less common inferential statistics: Mann-Whitney U and Fisher Exact Probability Test. A frequent shortcut in reporting statistics is also seen in this article; only the name of the statistic and the probability level are stated, with the numerical value of the statistic omitted.

An inferential statistic conveys a rather simple message: the result to which the statistic applies is significant, meaning it is unlikely that this result was due to chance alone. Understanding the differences among inferential statistics is not crucial for beginning readers of research reports if they recognize that these statistics are all used for the same purpose: to determine whether a particular finding is statistically significant.

One other statistic commonly used in psychological research is the *correlation coefficient*. A correlation coefficient expresses the extent to which two variables are related to each other, or correlated. For children younger than 12 years, height and age are two variables related to each other; as age increases, height increases. School attendance and grades in school are also correlated; students who often miss school usually earn poorer grades than students who attend regularly. Some events or variables are more closely related than others. Height and weight, for example, are more closely related to each other than are height and intelligence. A correlation coefficient is simply a number that expresses the relationship between any two variables.

A correlation coefficient can be a descriptive statistic (describing a correspondence between any two events) and it can also be an inferential statistic (testing a correspondence between two events for significance). The most commonly used correlation coefficient is Pearson's r.

Two elements of Pearson's r are important in interpreting the correlation between two variables: the size of the number and the sign (positive or negative) before the number. **43**

The size of r can vary numerically from 0 to 1.00. Larger r's express stronger correlations, or closer relationships. Two variables with a correlation of $r = .72$ are more closely related to each other than are two variables with a correlation of $r = .36$.

The size of the correlation indicates the *strength* of the relationship; the sign of the correlation indicates the *direction* of the relationship. A positive (+) correlation means that as one variable increases, the other variable also increases. Age and number of words understood are positively correlated, at least up to adolescence. As a child's age increases, the number of words understood also increases. A negative (−) correlation means that as one variable increases, the other variable decreases. A negative correlation does *not* mean

Table 1. Examples of correlations found in psychological research

r	Variables correlated	Interpretation of r	Source
+.75	Decision time in negative conflicts and decision time in positive conflicts	Strong, positive relationship between times to reach a decision in two conflict situations: children who took a long time with one decision also took a long time with the other. Time for one decision could be predicted from time for the other with considerable confidence.	Reppucci, 1970
+.68	IQ scores of siblings	Strong relationship: children with high IQ scores were likely to have brothers and sisters with high IQs, and children with low IQs were likely to have brothers and sisters with low IQs.	Laycock and Caylor, 1964
+.53	Height and speed in 25-yard dash	Moderately strong relationship: taller boys tended to run faster.	Govatos, 1959
+.26	IQ and popularity with peers	Rather weak relationship: the higher the child's IQ, the greater the popularity among friends, but many children did not fit this pattern, resulting in a low correlation.	Goldschmid, 1968
+.02	Dependence on adults and dependence on peers	Virtually no relationship between dependency with adults and dependency with same-age friends, indicating that one kind of dependency can *not* be predicted from the other.	Hetherington, 1966
−.22	Socioeconomic status and parents' difficulty supervising boys	Weak, negative relationship; as SES *increases*, difficulty supervising sons *decreases*, but the low correlation reveals that this relationship was not found in many families.	Weinstein and Geisel, 1960
−.48	Activity in free play and decision time in positive conflicts (boys)	Moderately strong, negative relationship; the *more* active the boy was in free play, the *less* time taken to reach a decision.	Reppucci, 1970
−.71	Duration of infants' crying and infants' ability to communicate by age 9 to 12 months	Strong negative relationship: the *more* the infant was allowed to cry, the *less* effective the infant was in using other means to communicate; high correlation means good prediction is possible.	Bell and Ainsworth, 1972

that the relationship between two variables is bad, or harmful, or undesirable, or weak. A correlation will be negative only because small values of one variable are associated with large values of the other variable. Zajonc (1975) reports that IQ and number of children in a family are negatively correlated. As the number of children in a family increases, the IQ scores of the children decrease. Note that the plus and minus signs affect *only* the direction of the relationship, *not* the strength of the relationship. Correlation coefficients of $+.83$ and $-.83$ represent equally close relationships. For some correlations taken from psychological research studies, see Table 1.

A significant correlation between two variables allows *prediction* of one variable from the other. For example, with Zajonc's findings, it can be predicted that children with one brother or sister will, in general, have higher IQ scores than will children with eight brothers and sisters. The most precise predictions are possible with the strongest correlations (largest values of r, disregarding the $+$ and $-$ signs). Correlations do *not* allow *conclusions about causes and effects*. A correlation cannot reveal whether variable A causes variable B, whether B causes A, or whether some third variable C causes both A and B. From Zajonc's research, it *cannot* be concluded that having large families *causes* IQ scores to decline. Other explanations are equally possible: perhaps a mother with a low IQ has children with low IQs because of heredity, and family size is a side effect of inability to comprehend or to use birth control. When interpreting correlations, remember that correlations yield no information about causes of events.

Only part of the results section of the sample article is included here because this section is quite long in the original research report. The omitted sections described the infants' toy preferences and amount of physical contact between mothers and infants.

RESULTS
Response to mother (13 months)

Open field. Boys and girls showed striking differences in their behavior toward their mothers (see Table 1). First, upon being removed from their mothers' laps, girls were reluctant to leave their mothers. When Ss were placed on the floor by their mothers, significantly more girls than boys returned immediately—in less than 5 seconds ($p < .05$ for both samples by Fisher Exact Probability Test). This reluctance to leave their mothers is further indicated by the time it took the children to first return to their mothers. Girls, in both samples, showed significantly shorter latencies than boys. Out of a possible 900 seconds (15 minutes), girls returned after an average of 273.5 seconds, while boys' average latency was nearly twice as long, 519.5 seconds. This difference was highly significant ($p < .002$, Mann-Whitney U test). All significance tests are two-tailed unless otherwise specified.

Once the children left their mothers, girls made significantly more returns, both physical and visual. Girls touched their mothers for an average of 84.6 seconds, while boys touched their mothers for only 58.8 seconds ($p < .03$, Mann-Whitney U test). Girls returned to touch their mothers on an average of 8.4 times, and boys 3.9 times ($p < .001$, Mann-Whitney U test). For the visual returns, the number of times the child looked at the mother and the total amount of time spent looking at the mother were obtained from the dictated material. The mean number of times girls looked at the mother was 10.8 (as compared with 9.2 for boys), a difference which was not significant. The total amount of time looking at the mother was 57.3 seconds for girls and 47.0 seconds for boys ($p < .09$, Mann-Whitney U test).

Finally, vocalization data were also available from the dictated material. The mean time vocaliz-   **45**

Table 1. Summary of infant behavior to mother in free play session

Behavior	Girls	Boys	p
Touching mother:			
$\bar{x}$ latency in seconds to return to mother	273.5	519.5	<.002
$\bar{x}$ number of returns	8.4	3.9	<.001
$\bar{x}$ number of seconds touching mother	84.6	58.8	<.03
Vocalization to mother:			
$\bar{x}$ number of seconds vocalizing to mother	169.8	106.9	<.04
Looking at mother:			
$\bar{x}$ number of seconds looking at mother	57.3	47.0	<.09
$\bar{x}$ number of times looking at mother	10.8	9.2	NS
Proximity to mother:			
$\bar{x}$ time in squares closest to mother	464.1	351.4	<.05
$\bar{x}$ times in squares farthest from mother	43.8	44.3	NS

Table 2. Summary of infant behavior during barrier frustration

Behavior	Girls	Boys	p
$\bar{x}$ number of seconds crying	123.5	76.7	<.05
$\bar{x}$ number of seconds at ends of barrier	106.1	171.0	<.001
$\bar{x}$ number of seconds at center	157.7	95.1	<.01

ing to the mother was 169.8 seconds for girls and 106.9 seconds for boys ($p < .04$, Mann-Whitney U test).

Another measure of the child's response to his mother was the amount of physical distance the child allowed between himself and his mother. Because the observers recorded which squares the child played in, it was possible to obtain the amount of time Ss spent in the four squares closest to the mother. The mean time in these squares for girls was 464.1 seconds; for boys, it was 351.4 seconds ($p < .05$, Mann-Whitney U test). Moreover, boys spent more time in the square farthest from the mother, although the differences were not significant.

Barrier frustration. At the end of the 15 minutes of free play, a barrier of mesh on a wood frame was placed in such a way as to divide the room in half. The mother placed the child on one side and remained on the opposite side along with the toys. Thus, the child's response to stress was observed.

Sex differences were again prominent, with girls crying and motioning for help consistently more than boys (see Table 2). For both samples, amount of time crying was available from the dictated record. Girls' mean time crying was 123.5 seconds, compared with 76.7 seconds for boys ($p < .05$, Mann-Whitney U test). Boys, on the other hand, appeared to make a more active attempt to get around the barrier. That is, they spent significantly more time at the ends of the barrier than girls, while girls spent significantly more time in the center of the barrier—near the position where they were placed ($p < .01$, Mann-Whitney U test).

Discussion

The author's comments about the study appear in the discussion section. The major findings, which were reported in the results section, are often repeated for emphasis in the discussion. If the author predicted specific results, the outcome of the study is analyzed in light of the predictions. Any unexpected or unusual findings are recounted and, if possible, explained. As the author reviews the results, relationships to studies by other authors may be noted. Ideas for follow-up studies to improve or extend the study are sometimes included at the end of the discussion. The discussion is often the most interesting section because it is the only part of the article in which the author can make speculations, state opinions, draw conclusions, and offer suggestions for using the research to understand children.

DISCUSSION

Observation of the children's behavior indicated that girls were more dependent, showed less exploratory behavior, and their play behavior reflected a more quiet style. Boys were independent, showed more exploratory behavior, played with toys requiring gross motor activity, were more vigorous, and tended to run and bang in their play. Obviously, these behavior differences approximate those usually found between the sexes at later ages. The data demonstrate that these behavior patterns are already present in the first year of life and that some of them suggest a relation to the mother's response to the infant in the first 6 months. It is possible that at 6 months, differential behavior on the part of the mother is already a response to differential behavior on the part of the infant. Moss (1967) has found behavioral sex differences as early as 3 weeks. In interpreting mother-infant interaction data, Moss suggests that maternal behavior is initially a response to the infant's behavior. As the infant becomes older, if the mother responds contingently to his signals, her behavior acquires reinforcement value which enables her to influence and regulate the infant's behavior. Thus, parents can be active promulgators of sex-role behavior through reinforcement of sex-role appropriate responses within the first year of life.

The following is offered as a hypothesis concerning sex-role learning. In the first year or two, the parents reinforce those behaviors they consider sex-role appropriate and the child learns these sex-role behaviors independent of any internal motive, that is, in the same way he learns any appropriate response rewarded by his parents. The young child has little idea as to the rules governing this reinforcement. It is suggested, however, that as the child becomes older (above age 3), the rules for this class of reinforced behavior become clearer and he develops internal guides to follow these earlier reinforced rules. In the past, these internalized rules, motivating without apparent reinforcement, have been called modeling behavior. Thus, modeling behavior might be considered an extension or internalization of the earlier reinforced sex-role behavior. However, it is clear that the young child, before seeking to model his behavior, is already knowledgeable in some appropriate sex-role behavior. In that the hypothesis utilizes both early reinforcement as well as subsequent cognitive elaboration, it would seem to bridge the reinforcement notion of Gewirtz (1967) and Kohlberg's cognitive theory (1966) of identification.

The fact that parents are concerned with early display of sex-role-appropriate behavior is reflected in an interesting clinical observation. On some occasions, staff members have incorrectly identified the sex of an infant. Mothers are often clearly irritated by this error. Since the sex of a fully clothed infant is difficult to determine, the mistake seems understandable and the mother's displeasure uncalled for. If, however, she views the infant and behaves toward him in a sex-appropriate way, our mistake is more serious. That is, the magnitude of her displeasure reveals to us the magnitude of her cognitive commitment to this infant as a child of given sex.

Regardless of the interpretation of the observed sex differences, the free play procedure provides a standardized situation in which young children can be observed without interference from experimental manipulation. While behavior under these conditions may be somewhat different from the young child's typical daily behavior, our data indicate that behavior in the play situation is related to other variables, that behavior can be predicted from earlier events, and that it is indicative of later sex-role behavior. The results of the present investigation as well as the work of Bell and Costello (1964), Kagan and Lewis (1965), and Lewis (in press) indicate sex differences within the first year over a wide variety of infant behaviors. The fact that sex differences do appear in the first year has important methodological implications for infant research. These findings emphasize the importance of checking sex differences before pooling data and, most important, of considering sex as a variable in any infant study.

References

Books and articles mentioned throughout the report are listed in the last section, the references. Only those references specifically cited or used in the article, not general references, are included in the list. Each entry in the references section gives all the information necessary for the reader to locate the book or article if desired.

The references are listed in alphabetical order by the last name of the first author listed for each article. If two or more articles of a single author are cited, they are listed in order of publication date. A line (_____) in place of the author's name indicates that the author is the same as for the previous article.

REFERENCES

Bell, R. Q., & Costello, N. S. Three tests for sex differences in tactile sensitivity in the newborn. *Biologia Neonatorum,* 1964, **1,** 335-347.

Freud, S. Three contributions to the theory of sex. Reprinted in *The basic writings of Sigmund Freud.* New York: Random House, 1938.

Gewirtz, J. The learning of generalized imitation and its implications for identification. Paper presented at the Society for Research in Child Development Meeting, New York, March, 1967.

Kagan, J., & Lewis, M. Studies of attention in the human infant. *Merrill-Palmer Quarterly,* 1965, **11,** 95-127.

Kohlberg, L. A cognitive-developmental analysis of children's sex role concepts and attitudes. In E. Maccoby (Ed.), *The development of sex differences.* Stanford, Calif.: Stanford University Press, 1966.

Lewis, M. Infant attention: response decrement as a measure of cognitive processes, or what's new, Baby Jane? Paper presented at the Society for Research in Child Development Meeting, symposium on "The Role of Attention in Cognitive Development," New York, March, 1967.

_____. Infants' responses to facial stimuli during the first year of life. *Developmental Psychology,* in press.

Maccoby, E. (Ed.) *The development of sex differences.* Stanford, Calif.: Stanford University Press, 1966.

Moss, H. Sex, age and state as determinants of mother-infant interaction. *Merrill-Palmer Quarterly,* 1967, **13** (1), 19-36.

Piaget, J. *Play, dreams and imitation in childhood.* New York: Norton, 1951.

Provence, S. Disturbed personality development in infancy: a comparison of two inadequately nurtured infants. *Merrill-Palmer Quarterly,* 1965, **2,** 149-170.

_____, & Lipton, R. C. *Infants in institutions.* New York: International Universities Press, 1962.

Seay, B., Alexander, B. K., & Harlow, H. F. Maternal behavior of socially deprived rhesus monkeys. *Journal of Abnormal and Social Psychology,* 1964, **69**(4), 345-354.

SUMMARY

Research reports are written in a standardized form, which includes an abstract, an introduction to previous research and the problem to be studied, a description of the research methods, a description of the outcome or results, and a list of references. Descriptive statistics (most often means and standard deviations) are used to summarize the numbers presented in the results. Inferential statistics are used to determine whether the results are significant, that is, unlikely to have occurred simply because of luck or chance. Research reports sometimes make rather dull reading because researchers tend to sacrifice style in order to gain accuracy and depth of detail.

REFERENCES

Bell, S. M., & Ainsworth, M. D. S. Infant crying and maternal responsiveness. *Child Development*, 1972, **43**, 1171-1190.

Goldberg, S., & Lewis, M. Play behavior in the year-old-infant: early sex differences. *Child Development*, 1969, **40**, 21-31.

Goldschmid, M. L. The relation of conservation to emotional and environmental aspects of development. *Child Development*, 1968, **39**, 579-589.

Govatos, L. A. Relationships and age differences in growth measures and motor skills. *Child Development*, 1959, **30**, 333-340.

Hetherington, E. M. Effects of paternal absence on sex-typed behaviors in negro and white preadolescent males. *Journal of Personality and Social Psychology*, 1966, **4**, 87-91.

Laycock, F., & Caylor, J. S. Physiques of gifted children and their less gifted siblings. *Child Development*, 1964, **35**, 63-74.

Reppucci, N. D. Individual differences in the consideration of information among two-year-old children. *Developmental Psychology*, 1970, **2**, 240-246.

Weinstein, E. A., & Geisel, P. N. An analysis of sex differences in adjustment. *Child Development*, 1960, **31**, 721-728.

Zajonc, R. B. Dumber by the dozen. *Psychology Today*, 1975, **8**, 37-43.

DEVELOPING BASIC SKILLS

Chapter 4

Developing perceptual skills

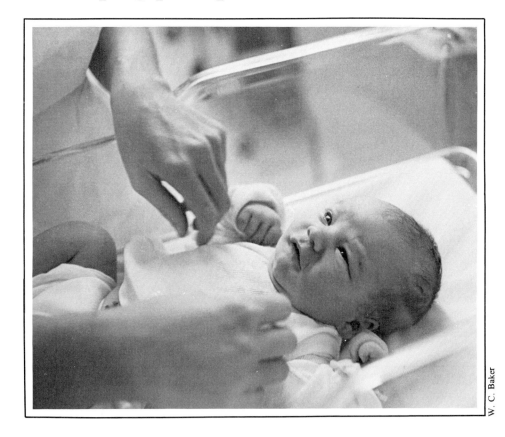

W. C. Baker

Eavesdropping is not a generally recommended way of doing research for a book; however, it occasionally provides usable material. When one of us (BGM) was viewing her newborn son in the hospital nursery, she observed the following interaction between two new fathers. The infant daughter of one father happened to have her eyes open and was lying with her head turned toward the observation window. Her obviously delighted father was bouncing up and down and waving both his arms at her. The second new father watched the behavior of the first for a short while and then sarcastically told the first father that he was wasting his time because babies cannot see. The first father stopped waving, looked very uncomfortable, and shortly thereafter walked away, while the second father continued to stare intently at his own sleeping infant. Can babies see?

The conflict illustrated by these two new fathers is not new. For years parents, physicians, philosophers, and many researchers have speculated over the infant's ability to receive sensory information from the environment. This question is important because the answer not only affects how people think of the infant but also the type of stimulation and environment that will be provided the newborn infant. For example, if parents believe that their newborn child cannot see or has extremely poor visual capabilities, they are not likely to provide the infant with anything special to look at; rather, they will wrap the infant warmly in a blanket and tuck him or her away in a dim, quiet corner of a room to sleep and grow. On the other hand, if the infant is capable of receiving information from the environment, treatment such as that described above will deprive the infant of the opportunity to begin learning about the world. Even more serious consequences develop if the infant has no opportunity to view the world. Without any stimulation the neural structures involved in vision will deteriorate (Hebb, 1972), damaging the ability to receive sensory information. These serious consequences are the result of extreme lack of stimulation brought about in experiments where animals were raised in total darkness for extended periods of time. In the normal course of child rearing, no infant is subjected to this type of visual deprivation; yet if the infant is capable of perceiving the world, it is important to provide the infant with all the sensory stimulation he or she is capable of responding to. It is through early sensory stimulation that infants begin to learn and interact with those around them. To facilitate this learning, we need to know what types of stimulation the infant can respond to and what conditions provide optimal stimulation.

Knowing what the infant should be capable of can also prevent needless worry about the normalcy of any particular infant. For instance, one worried mother was in a panic, fearing her daughter was almost blind. She was concerned because when she stood crossing her eyes and wrinkling her nose at her baby lying in the crib, the child seemed not to see these interesting contortions designed to amuse her. It was suggested to the mother that she bend over, bringing her face closer to the infant. When she did, the infant responded. Precise information about infant visual capabilities would have prevented this mother's concern. Unfortunately, this type of information has not been generally available until very recently because it is extremely difficult to assess the sensory capabilities in a nonverbal infant.

53

STUDYING CHILDREN'S PERCEPTUAL ABILITIES

To determine what an infant is capable of perceiving, a stimulus (object or event) must be presented and the infant must make some type of observable or recordable response. Observation is a difficult method for studying these responses, however, for several reasons. First, results of observations made by different spectators do not always agree, and second, responses the newborn infant is capable of making are limited.

Another difficulty for researchers in testing infants' sensory capacities is that infants are not very cooperative. They make poor subjects when they are sleeping, crying, or excited, and they spend a majority of their time in one of these ''uncooperative'' states. For sensory research, an infant ideally is in a quiet, alert state. Wolff (1959) reported that the longest period of quiet inactivity he observed in a newborn lasted a total of 7 minutes. Further, over a 24-hour period the total amount of time an infant spent in an ideal state for research was less than 30 minutes.

Another problem faced by researchers interested in the neonate's (newborn infant) sensory capacities is the effect of anesthetic administered to the mother during delivery. The neonate is affected for a period by the depressant quality of drugs given the mother during labor. When Stechler (1964) calculated the sheer amount of time neonates looked at an experimental stimulus, he found that neonates whose mothers had received drugs during labor had a mean looking time considerably less than the mean looking time of neonates whose mothers had not received drugs. In general, Stechler found that the more drugs the mother received late in labor, the less attentive the neonate was. These data imply that researchers interested in neonatal visual characteristics might have to limit their studies to infants of deliveries that were drug free. Stechler also mentions one further complication in doing visual research with neonates, that is, the practice of putting silver nitrate in the newborn's eyes, which for a couple of days may cause eyelid swelling.

Yet, as difficult as it is to assess what infants see, hear, smell, taste, or feel, there are several ways of asking these questions, and as a result the information being gathered has increased, both in amount and in refinement.

The most general technique of finding out what an infant attends to is careful, long-term observation. Observation of the child as a whole can be useful. A good observer will note not only what the infant appears to be looking at, but will also note changes in activity level and motor responses. When a visual stimulus attracts an infant's attention, a change in activity level is an indication that the child has noticed the object. If the child has been engaged in some type of motor behavior, such as leg flexing, the child is likely to freeze, or stop moving, while he or she orients to the new visual event. These same changes are also likely to occur as the child attends to other sensory inputs, such as a sudden or interesting sound. It is also likely that after the initial orientation the infant's activity level will increase. Another motor response accompaniment that occurs in older infants is reaching toward the object or making grasping movements with the fingers. A good observer will note these responses as well as the obvious indicators of attention, such as head turning or controlled eye movements.

An important factor in observing infants' visual capacities is to note their state of alertness. An infant in any state other than alert and quiet is not likely to respond in such a way that accurate answers to questions of visual capability can be determined. Another related factor that is easily overlooked is the position of the infant during the observation period. The most likely position of the infant during visual research is on his or her back. Indeed, many studies have been carried out with infants lying on their backs in a looking chamber where visual stimuli were presented directly over their heads.

Information has been reported (Fredrickson & Brown, 1975) that compares visual behavior of infants who were lying on their backs, propped up in a semireclining position, or held to the shoulder, where they viewed visual stimuli over the shoulder of an adult facing away from the stimuli. Fredrickson and Brown found that the visual behavior of infants held to the shoulder was much better than the visual behavior of infants in the other two positions. It may be that infants are more likely to be alert when they are picked up and moved to the shoulder than when they are left lying on their backs. Whatever the reason, careful attention to infant state of alertness, consideration of position, and inclusion of observation of motor behavior of the child all contribute to make observation a useful but difficult technique of determining what a baby sees.

Another important addition to the observation technique of asking questions was introduced by Robert L. Fantz, who developed a technique for assessing visual preferences. Rather than simply presenting a visual stimulus and noting whether an infant looked at it, Fantz began presenting two stimuli at a time under controlled conditions and noted which stimulus was looked at and the total fixation time (looking time) for each stimulus looked at by the infant. In order to judge which stimulus the infant was looking at, Fantz used the reflection of the stimulus on the cornea of the infant's eye. Using this technique, Fantz has explored the infant's visual acuity (ability to see clearly) and visual preferences. His addition to the observation technique, although very simple, has greatly expanded knowledge about infant vision.

A second major technique of finding out what infants can sense and respond to involves monitoring various physiological responses, such as heartbeat and respiration. These responses may be used as indicators that the infant is attending to some stimulus event. Typically, a baby's heartbeat is monitored for some period to determine its characteristic pattern, and then a stimulus is presented. The researcher notes whether there is any change in the baby's heartbeat rate. Generally, as the infant orients to the new stimulus, the heart rate slows down for a short period and then speeds up, or accelerates. This technique is frequently paired with the process of habituation to assess not only what the infant can perceive but also his or her ability to recognize an already perceived event. Habituation is the phenomenon of decreasing attention to a constantly repeated event. For example, you have probably noticed that sometimes when you enter a room it has a particular odor (perhaps the smell of bacon that had been fried for breakfast); yet after you have spent some time in the room, you no longer notice the smell. You might assume that the odor has dissipated or worn off; yet if you were to leave the room and then reenter, you would probably notice the odor again. What has happened is that your sense of smell has habituated to the constant odor to the point where you no longer notice it.

The way cardiac monitoring (recording heartbeat rate) and habituation are used together in sensory research is that an infant's heartbeat rate is established, a stimulus is presented, and heartbeat rate change is noted. Then the stimulus is repeated again and again until no heartbeat change occurs. When this happens, a second event may be introduced, and the researcher will watch to see if the heartbeat rate changes once more. If it does, it is an indication that the infant has noticed the difference between the two events.

A third major technique researchers use in studying infants' sensory abilities involves learning techniques. Learning is discussed in detail in Chapter 6, but basically in sensory research the infant is taught to make a response, such as head turning, to a stimulus; then that stimulus is changed in some way, and the researcher notes whether the learned response (head turning) occurs. If the response does occur, it is a possible indicator that the infant considers the two stimuli as essentially similar.

The refinement of these three general techniques of study—observation, physiological monitoring, and learning—allows researchers to ask increasingly sophisticated questions about infants and to receive useful answers. Our knowledge of the infant's abilities has increased in much rich detail.

In the past it was felt that the infant is a passive being, relatively insensitive to the stimulation of the environment. Today, the picture of the infant is much more interesting. Infants are surprisingly capable processors of sensory information. In general, infants' sensory systems are all present and operating at birth. Most researchers would agree that the newborn is capable of sensing light, dark, and movement at birth; is responsive to the location of sound and to sounds of different frequencies; is aware of changes in temperature and changes in body position; and is capable of responding to odors (Mussen et al., 1969). It is also felt that the newborn is somewhat responsive to the taste of various substances and reacts to some degree of pain.

In this chapter these perceptual capacities of infants are discussed in detail. The majority of discussion concerns the development of the infant's visual and auditory capabilities. This concentration is in part based on the obvious importance of the visual and auditory modes in the infant's learning about the world. Although all the sensory systems are important to the child's development, much, in fact most, of the sensory studies concerned with infants have concentrated on visual development. One of the reasons for this concentration on the part of researchers is that it is more difficult to tell when an infant is responding to auditory stimulation than it is when the infant attends to visual stimulation. In the past, unless the infant turned his or her head toward the locus of a sound or unless the researcher took the time to set up a learning-based discrimination task, it was difficult to assess an infant's response to auditory stimulation with any accuracy. However, with the aid of physiological monitoring, auditory research is much more profitable.

As each sensory system is discussed in turn, keep in mind that it is most important to discover what infants are capable of responding to, what attracts their attention, and what experiences contribute to their learning about the world.

SEEING
What can infants see?

Of all the questions about the sensory abilities of infants, perhaps the most frequently asked concerns the capacity for vision in the neonate. Does the new infant's wide-eyed stare provide him with any information? First, the infant's eyes and the control of them are slightly different from adults'. Infants will not necessarily always look at the same object with both eyes. There is poor muscle control and coordination, which may on occasion allow the eyes to drift off target. Second, the infant's eye is structurally different from the adult's. In his book on perceptual development of infants, Bower (1974) discusses work done by Mann in 1928, which indicated that the infant eye is shorter than the adult eye and that the fovea (area of clearest vision on the retina) is in a different position. When light strikes the infant's retina, it is likely to be 10° to 15° from the fovea, toward the inner side of the eye. As the infant grows, the fovea gradually rotates to the normal position. From this information it might seem that if the infant were looking with the right eye, for example, the eye might actually drift right of the target, so the image would fall on the fovea more directly.

Salapatek (1969) in discussing the visual behavior of infants less than 2 months old indicates that they do not fix their gaze centrally on a blank field but orient to the sides of the field. Further, when they gaze with their right eyes, they tend to look at the right half of a figure. Salapatek also comments that there is little tendency for the young infant to gaze at the central area of a figure. This information would seem to be complementary to the observations reported by Bower.

Another physical characteristic of the infant's visual system is important. The infant prior to 2 months has very little ability for visual accommodation. Accommodation is the process through which we adjust our eyes to focus on objects at varying distances. In accommodation the ciliary muscles change the shape of the eye's lens by either contracting or relaxing. The infant's control of these muscles is very poor, and apparently the newborn is unable to make focusing adjustments for distance. Haynes, White, and Held (1965) report that infants under 1 month of age have a focal distance of about 7½ inches. It is generally accepted by researchers that for the first few weeks of life the infant's field of clearest vision is between 7 and 8 inches. This being the case, if we return to the two new fathers in the beginning of the chapter, the second father was partially correct. The infant girl could not have seen her father clearly at the distance he was from her; however, it is possible that she received some information from his performance.

Several capacities for vision are developed and useful in the neonate. First, the neonate is sensitive to light, and the pupillary response (changes in the size of the pupil in relation to changes in brightness of light) is present even in premature infants. Not only is the infant responsive to definite changes in light intensity, but also appears to be sensitive to light through closed eyelids. Haith (1968) noticed that infant subjects who had their eyes closed during experimental testing would open their eyes widely when the experimental light was turned off and would then scan the dark experimental room. This observation would seem to indicate that the new infant tucked off in a dim corner of a room might not be too displeased with the situation.

The very young infant is also sensitive, or receptive, to color. Under very controlled conditions, equated for all possible cues for difference except color cues, Peeples and Teller (1975) concluded that 2-month-old infants have the ability to perceive color. It is generally believed not only that infants can see color, but that brightly colored objects are highly attractive to them. To verify this point, take a quick look at the toys in the infant section of a store; you are not likely to find a gray rattle! Fantz (1963) compared the attention of infants less than 5 days old to three black-and-white patterned stimuli and three brightly colored stimuli—white, yellow, and red circles. He found that the infants paid twice as much attention to the black and white patterns as they did to the brightly colored disks. In fact, none of the infants looked longer at the colored circles. This surprising finding apparently has not found its way to toy manufacturers or parents who purchase toys.

Besides being able to see light, the neonate is also visually responsive to movement. Greenman (1963) tested the ability of neonates between 15 minutes after birth and 4 days of age to visually follow a slowly moving object. He presented the neonates with a stimulus of bright red rings, which were slowly moved horizontally or vertically in front of the infants. He found that almost all the infants could visually follow the rings. Some neonates even turned their heads to follow the rings.

Not only do neonates detect movement, they are able within a short time to respond adaptively to movement. Ball and Tronick (1971) tested infants from 2 to 11 weeks of age in a situation where it appeared that a moving object would either hit them or move just past them. They found that the infants reacted to apparent hits by moving their heads back and bringing up their arms. In the miss sequences the infants tended to turn their heads as if to follow the object moving by. Obviously, by this age infants can process information about movement in a sophisticated manner.

So far we have considered some very basic aspects of neonatal and young infant visual capacity. The newborn is responsive to light and dark, can detect movement, and is able to track slowly moving objects with the eyes. Return once more to the two fathers in the beginning of the chapter. Is it possible that the infant girl could see her father? Obviously not in any detail, but if the illumination was optimal and his movements large enough and slow enough to attract her attention, it is just possible that she could detect some massive shape in a state of movement. This is probably far from the father's idea of the impression he was making, but he should have some consolation in that the second father was not correct either. If he had been closer, his daughter would have seen a lot more.

Recall that earlier it was stated that the neonate's vision was apparently clearest at about 7½ inches. At this distance the infant is apparently capable of seeing a great deal. Fantz, using the technique of presenting two stimuli at once, which was described earlier, has investigated the visual acuity of infants of various ages and found that they prefer to look at patterns rather than plain gray fields. Fantz was able to measure infant acuity by presenting infants with a plain gray square and a square of black and white stripes. Generally the infant will look longest at the stripes. In testing acuity Fantz narrowed the width of the black and white stripes. As long as the infant looks longer at the stripes, we know he or she can see them, because once the stripes become too narrow to see, both stimuli look the same. The infant sees two gray squares and there is no reason to look any longer at one stimulus than the other. In a summary of several studies, Fantz (1965) reports that at 2 weeks of age an infant can see stripes of ¹/₈ inch at a distance of 9 inches from the eyes; at 3 months of age and under optimal lighting conditions, an infant can see stripes of $1/64$ inch at a distance of 15 inches. By the time the infant is 6 months old, acuity is similar to that of an adult.

Once it has been established that the infant has the ability to perceive form and pattern, pattern discrimination can be explored further to determine what attracts attention and holds it. It is also possible to find out if the same visual events that are attractive to the very young infant are interesting to older infants. Knowing what is attractive not only helps to provide positive visual experiences for the infant but aids psychologists interested in knowing what kind of information the infant is getting about the world. If it is known what the infant is likely to look at, inferences can be made about what the infant is likely to know.

Pattern discrimination and preferences

It has been established that even newborn infants can discriminate patterns in their visual field and that they prefer to look at patterns rather than plain patches of color. Since these discoveries, numerous investigations have been made to determine what type of visual events infants of various ages prefer.

One of the earliest established preferences is that very young infants are attracted to visual stimuli that move. Once Fantz discovered that infants prefer patterned objects to

Barbara McClinton

Fig. 4-1. Even young infants exhibit a preference for patterned visual stimuli. This infant gazing at leaves on a plant clearly demonstrates this preference.

solid-colored stimuli, it was determined that infants prefer patterns that contain sharp contrast between dark and light elements of the pattern, such as black and white stripes or checks. After these initial discoveries researchers started defining these preferences in greater detail and have established a large body of information about the pattern preferences of infants.

That infants are attracted to pattern is highly significant because it means that, as they view the world, their gaze is attracted to objects that are patterned. Patterned objects are more likely to provide the infant with information than are unpatterned objects. An infant who gazes at a plant with speckled leaves is likely to be learning more than an infant gazing at a section of bright orange wall. If color were more attractive than pattern, a plain sheet of red construction paper would be more interesting than a white sheet of paper with a drawing on it. It should be easy to see how a preference for pattern is adaptive and a useful beginning for visual exploration.

Beyond simply studying pattern preferences, researchers have found it useful to compare preferences. Two types of comparisons that tell quite a bit about the infant are comparisons of stimulus patterns for complexity and novelty.

It is generally found that infants prefer more complex patterns to simple patterns. Most researchers agree on this point, but there is some disagreement as to what makes a pattern complex. Various studies have attempted to define complexity as number of pattern elements, size of pattern elements, angles contained in the pattern, and amount of contour. Regardless of precise definition, the more complex the pattern, the longer infants tend to look at it or the more frequently they choose to look at it. This tendency is also of adaptive importance. Generally, the more complex of two patterns contains more information. If the infant selectively attends to patterns that contain more information that infant is exposed to more information. It appears that the young infant is well equipped to begin actively responding to information present in the environment.

Novelty of pattern is perhaps even more important than complexity in what it can tell us about the infant. In studying novelty, researchers typically present one stimulus over and over again until the infant habituates to it (or stops attending to it) and then present a novel stimulus to see if the infant's interest picks up. This technique allows researchers to explore the degree of novelty that the infant notices.

A common variant of this technique is to present two stimuli at once over several presentations. One stimulus appears in all exposures, while the second stimulus is new on each trial. The researcher then can determine whether the infant prefers the old familiar event or the new one. Again, this technique allows the researcher to vary the amont of novelty in the second stimulus.

Fantz (1965), along with his many other investigations, explored infant preferences for novelty. He took eleven complex stimuli (magazine pictures) and presented the infant with ten trials. One picture was presented on each of the ten trials and became the constant stimulus. The other ten pictures were presented for one trial each. Fantz found that infants over 2 months of age showed decreasing interest in the constantly exposed picture and a high interest in novelty. Infants under 2 months showed no change in the amount of time they looked at the constant stimulus. Fantz felt that his data showed that infants over 2 months are able to discriminate between complex stimuli and are also able to recognize a familiar stimulus in which they lose interest in preference to a novel event. Several other researchers using similar techniques and more or less complex stimuli have reported the same findings.

That infants prefer novel stimuli is an apparently useful characteristic. If infants were attracted to patterns, even complex patterns, they would not engage in much visual exploration if an attractive pattern had the ability to capture attention and hold it. However, the fact that infants prefer novel visual events indicates that they are likely to move on to new objects for exploration once the old explored objects become familiar. Thus an infant gazing at a speckled plant is likely to turn attention to a mobile or some other interesting pattern once the speckled plant has been thoroughly investigated.

The preference infants show for novel stimuli not only indicates that they are likely to actively explore the world around them, but also provides researchers with a useful tool for testing an infant's ability to recognize previously presented material. Using the phenomenon of habituation, researchers have explored infant recognition abilities and found that by 3½ months of age infants can remember seeing a particular familiar visual event after only brief exposures (Martin, 1975). While this may not seem remarkable, consider the typical presentation used in these studies. These infants very likely were exposed very briefly to some abstract figure that they had never seen before; yet their responses indicate they were able to process this information and retain it. It is likely that their ability to process information about stimuli that constantly recur in their homes is even better.

Another consideration relevant to habituation research is that infants tend to vary greatly in how fast or slowly they habituate to a particular stimulus. Some psychologists think these different habituation rates may be related to important differences in the infants, such as birth condition, later IQ, and discrimination learning ability. DeLoache (1976) conducted a study in which she allowed all of her infant subjects to habituate, no matter how long it took them. She found no difference between fast and slow habituators in their abilities to respond to a new stimulus. These findings indicate that some infants process information more slowly than others, but once the information is processed, they are just as able to retrieve and use it as faster processors are.

So far we have considered only the pattern discrimination and perceptual development of infants under 1 year of age. There are some indications that the ability to perceive patterned stimuli and process visual information changes, or continues to develop, throughout early childhood as cognitive processes increase. In Chapter 8, changes in the perceptual abilities of older children that are important for letter recognition and discrimination are discussed.

Piaget (see Chapter 10) felt that the young child's ability to perceive a visual pattern in its entirety was hampered because the young child's perception was centered. What Piaget means by centered is that a dominant feature of the pattern catches and holds the child's attention and prevents him or her from seeing the pattern as a whole. Many researchers feel that this is likely to happen with infants, but few have considered that this might also happen with preschoolers. **61**

Piaget felt that preschool children are unable to reverse the figure and ground of an ambiguous or changeable stimulus, to simultaneously consider the parts and whole of a complex stimulus, to explore a visual array in an orderly fashion, or to make efficient visual comparisons of two objects separated in space (Elkind, 1975).

Elkind has conducted a series of investigations on these questions, using children who ranged in age from 4 to 11 years. When he tested children with figure-ground reversals, he found that the older the children were, the more likely they were to see both objects. Younger children could accomplish the reversal of the pattern in the more obvious or clear examples; however, they needed prodding and even masking of parts of the pattern in the more difficult figures.

In testing the ability of the child to see both the parts of a pattern and the whole, Elkind used drawings, such as a man made up of vegetables and a scooter made from pieces of candy. He found a regular increase with age of the children to perceive both the individual items and the patterns they produced. By age 9 years, children seem able to accomplish this regularly.

Elkind further tested Piaget's predictions and found regular increases with age in children's abilities to process information presented in visual patterns. Apparently, the ability to perceive patterned stimuli and process the information contained in the pattern increases throughout childhood.

So far we have considered the visual characteristics and capacities of the neonate and the abilities of infants and young children for pattern discrimination; now we will turn to consideration of the development of the perception of depth and form.

Perceiving depth and form

Perceiving patterns distinctly is not all there is to visual sensing of the world. We also need to locate objects in space in relation to each other and to ourselves. We need to appreciate depth and be able to recognize dangerous drop-offs and changes in level. We need to be able to perceive form and the solidity of objects as well as to recognize the same form from different orientations. Once we consider that these abilities are also involved in our visual perception, it should become clear that it is important to know when an infant is capable of perceiving depth and form.

Depth perception has obvious survival value. If we could not recognize drop-offs visually, the world would be a very dangerous environment for us. Parents are not likely to experiment to find out whether their infants perceive depth. Instead, parents are generally very careful to block off stairways and not leave infants unattended on the tops of furniture. Even if infants are able to recognize dangerous drop-offs, they lack the motor control necessary to respond appropriately when they reach the edge of a drop-off or the top of untended stairs. However, psychologists are interested in whether infants can perceive depth and how early this ability develops.

Gibson and Walk (1960) did an extensive study on the development of depth perception that dealt not only with human infants but with infants of several animal species. They devised a testing apparatus that they called the "visual cliff." The visual cliff is a large box that stands several feet high. The top surface is covered with sturdy glass.

Across the center of the box is a wide board used as a subject starting point. This board divides the top surface of the box into two halves. On one side of the board, checked material is affixed right below the glass surface, creating the appearance of a level and solid surface. On the other side of the board the checked material is several feet below the glass surface, on the floor. This side is in effect a visual drop-off. From the starting position on the board, this side looks like a "falling off" place.

Gibson and Walk tested 36 infants ranging in age from 6 to 14 months. The infants were placed, one at a time, on the starting board and then enticed by the mother or experimenter to crawl across the glass. Of the 36 infants tested, 27 crawled across the shallow side, while only three infants dared to crawl over the "deep" side. Some infants showed distress when asked to crawl over an apparent cliff. Evidently the need for optical support is strong, for several infants touched the glass and still would not venture across it. Gibson and Walk also report that some infants even backed onto the deep side while attempting to move away from it, but still would not cross the deep side.

These results are very strong indications that by 6 months of age infants are able to perceive depth. It is important to note that Gibson and Walk's subjects were all 6 months old or older, because it was necessary that they be able to crawl to participate in the study. The results indicate that by the time infants need to recognize depth, they are able to. However, these results do not give any information about how early a human infant can recognize depth.

Compos, Langer, and Krowitz (1970) used the same test situation as did Gibson and Walk, but by monitoring cardiac responses they were able to test younger infants. Compos and his associates reasoned that, since the infants expressed distress when they were placed on the deep side of the visual cliff, it might be possible that their heartbeat activity was different when they were placed on the deep side as opposed to the shallow side. Using this reasoning they tested two groups of young infants. One group was slightly under 2 months of age and the second group was about 3½ months old. They found differential cardiac response in infants on the two sides of the cliff, indicating that these babies were able to perceive that the two sides were different. These researchers felt, however, that the infants were only showing orientation, or attention to the difference, and not fear. They suggest that the infant first perceives the difference in depth and then through experience learns to fear the deep side.

These studies give indications that young children are able to perceive depth and spatial relations and that this ability adds dimension to their visual capabilities. Another result of being able to perceive depth is that it aids in perception of objects as being more than patterns or shapes. Objects are solid and possess characteristics that take up space. They have fronts, backs, and properties of depth. Furthermore, objects can be touched and picked up. At what point do infants begin to distinguish between flat patterns and solid objects?

Fantz (1965) has demonstrated that by 2 months of age infants spend more time looking at solid objects than they do at the same representations on a flat surface. Fantz sees a recognition of solidity and a preference for solidity as having important implications for development. This preference directs the child's attention to objects rather than to flat, patterned surfaces.

Looking at people

Of all the visual stimuli in the infant's world, perhaps the most meaningful for the infant's total development are faces. Knowing the characteristics and preferences of infant vision, it should not be difficult to predict infant responses to faces. Faces are powerfully attractive visual events.

First, faces are visual stimuli that have movement and sharp contrast. Consider an infant being held in a parent's arms and gazing into the parent's face. The face bending over to smile at the infant is probably close enough to be within the infant's area of clearest vision. Various parts of the parent's face are moving, and these moving features are presenting sharp contrasts. The lips part in a smile or in speech and present contrast with the white teeth. The eyes constantly dart back and forth, and the dark iris and pupil contrast with the white of the eye. Beyond presenting contrast and movement, the face is a three-dimensional solid object that has a relatively complex pattern of features. All of these characteristics should serve to make perception of faces an intriguing event for infants. Preferences for faces have been studied in detail, and theories about the perception of faces have been proposed.

Lewis (1969) conducted an investigation with infants ranging in age from 3 months to a year in which he speculated on the effect of meaningfulness in infants' responses to facelike stimuli. Lewis was interested in changes in responsiveness to facelike stimuli over the entire first year of life. He used as a response measure not only looking time but smiling and vocalization. Lewis found that facelike stimuli, as opposed to distorted faces, are more effective stimuli for younger infants than for older infants when amount of looking time was used as the response measure. However the more facelike stimuli elicited more smiling and vocalization throughout the experiment.

In doing this study Lewis speculated that younger infants would spend more time looking at the facelike stimuli, while older infants would be more interested in distorted stimuli. Lewis' speculation was based on the idea that young infants are interested in facelike stimuli because they are in the process of building a representation, or model, of what a face looks like. While they are building their model they pay close attention to events that give them usable information. However, once the model is built the infant spends less time looking at events that match the model, as that information has already been incorporated into the model. It is also just as likely that representations or events that do not match an established model, such as distorted stimuli, become increasingly interesting as the infant compares the discrepant visual stimuli with the established model.

It is interesting that, while distorted stimuli appear rather bizarre or even disturbing to adults, infants do not generally show signs of distress at these unusual faces. Lewis speculated that during the second half of the first year infants might fret or cry when they saw unusual stimuli, just as some do when they are approached by a stranger during this period. However, this relationship apparently was not established, as the infants showed interest and not fear at distorted faces.

In these studies even the youngest infants were attracted to facelike stimuli when the stimuli were nothing more than black-and-white line drawings. Imagine how much more attractive an actual face must be, with the characteristics of solidity, movement, and color. Infants' visual characteristics and preferences should cause them to fix their gaze on the faces around them very early in their development. The social implications of this behavior are many. Children will quickly become familiar with the people in the environment and also, because of the movement in the facial stimuli, will prefer looking at people over objects. Not only will infants become familiar with faces in the environment, but it is quite likely that an intense gaze trained on the face of a parent will evoke positive responses in that parent. It is very likely that parents whose infants gaze intently into their eyes will respond with delight, which will probably increase the stimulation of the infant in the form of cuddling, vocalization, and smiling on the part of the parents. As infants become older and start to respond to facial stimuli with vocalization and smiling themselves, the mutual smiling and vocalization on the parts of parent and infants should be quite rewarding to both. We will return to this idea in Chapter 12, where the social development of the child is discussed in detail.

Stimulating visual development

As was noted early in this chapter, infant visual development has stimulated much research and as a result quite a lot of information about visual development is known. The infant is a surprisingly capable processor of visual information from birth onward. Although initially the visual range of the infant is restricted due to poor accommodation, acuity (clarity) of vision is good if visual stimuli appear at the proper distance, and by 6 months of age the infant's acuity matches that of the adult. Knowing the range of infant vision and also how acute an infant's vision is should influence our thinking about and our behavior toward infants. Visual stimulation to newborn infants should be presented at close range. As the infant's acuity increases, visual stimulation need not be restricted to overly large patterns; rather, objects with finer detail can be presented for visual examination. It is possible that large-scale patterned objects may not be as stimulating to young infants as supposed. If the pattern is too large, the infant may find less contrast and contour than in a pattern of more detail.

Considering the preferences of infant vision is also important to provide the infant with appropriate stimulation as well as to understand the infant's behavior better. Initially, infants are attracted to stimuli that contain sharp contrast and movement. Appropriate stimuli might include patterned objects that move, for example, a white rattle with a black pattern on it, such as a geometric form. A second consideration might be a low-hanging mobile with sharply contrasted patterns. It also might make more sense for the stimulation of the infant if mobile parts were constructed so that the shapes and patterns were on the bottom of the hanging pieces to be directly visible to the infant lying on his or her back, rather than the present arrangement that presents a better view to adults standing alongside the crib.

As infants develop, they begin to show interest in complexity in pattern, which increases with age. By 2 months, infants seem to appreciate solidity in visual stimulation.

Barbara McClinton

Fig. 4-2. A visual event that combines detailed pattern and movement, such as this train mobile, is highly attractive for young infants.

At this point the infant would probably enjoy large graspable forms with detailed patterns, such as soft, patterned cloth balls.

Toward the end of the first half year of life infants are interested in objects or events that are meaningful, such as facelike patterns as opposed to complex patterns. Possibly, picture books with photographs of objects and animals would be stimulating.

After the early preference for meaningful stimuli, interest increases for more discrepant or unusual visual events. Discrepant stimuli might include fantasy objects, such as story books where animals wear clothes, people fly, and buildings have faces. Novelty of stimulation is apparently attractive to all ages. The ability to appreciate fantasy objects is related to the infant's understanding of reality. Until a child is aware that people cannot fly, this occurrence is not attractive as a discrepant event. The appreciation of discrepant events increases during the preschool period as the child develops more and more complex reality notions.

66   One final point that should be considered is that putting all of these characteristics together into one visual event provides a powerfully attractive experience for the child. You may have noticed the extreme fascination with which a small child watches television commercials. This is not surprising. Most commercials are highly contrasted, moving, visual events (even with the sound off). Further, they usually depict complex events that are meaningful to the child, for instance, a mother in the laundry room preparing to wash diapers. Yet almost always there is a discrepancy from the child's experience. No matter how many times the child has watched mommy put soap in the washer, he or she has never seen a huge arm holding a large box of detergent rise up out of the washer!

It is important to consider that all of these preferences serve to draw the infant into a close and active participation with the important and informative aspects of the environment. The more attentive the infant is to informative environmental aspects, the more the child will begin to learn. A demonstration of the effect of planned stimulation is presented in the reading at the end of this chapter.

While interest in the visual capabilities of the infant may be important, the visual channel is not the only system operating at birth and providing infants with environmental stimulation. We will now consider the infant's senses of hearing, touch, and taste.

HEARING

Infants show by various responses, such as change in motor activity level, changes in direction of gaze, and changes in cardiac responses, that they are sensitive to sound from birth onward. Bower (1973) reports a study done by Wertheimer (1962) that showed that infants of only 2 minutes of age moved their eyes in the direction of a series of sounds. This would seem to indicate that infants are not only sensitive to sound but are aware of the direction from which sound comes.

The neonate's ear structure is somewhat more elastic than that of an adult (Bench, 1973), which may affect the efficiency with which the infant processes sounds of differing frequencies. Changes in frequency result in the perception of changes in pitch (high or low sounds). Bench felt that infants probably are more efficient in processing low- to middle-range frequencies, which may account for differing responsiveness to high- and low-pitched sounds.

Several researchers have discussed infants' differential responses to sounds of high and low frequency (Eisenberg, 1970). It is generally found that low-pitched sounds tend to quiet a distressed infant, while high-pitched sounds tend to cause "freezing" behavior followed by agitation. It should be noted that parents almost universally coo to their fussy infants in low-pitched voices. Eisenberg felt that the different response to low-pitched sounds might be related to the development of the perception of speech, as most speech occurs at a relatively low pitch. It has been hypothesized in several sources that infants' constant exposure to speech attunes them to speech frequencies. Yet other research, such as Bench's discussion of ear structure, indicates that the difference may be physically rather than psychologically based. However, Eisenberg makes another interesting observation that throughout life we tend to consider high-pitched sounds as noisy and irritating. Again, this may be a physical characteristic. Whatever the reason for these differences, it should be obvious that if infants react differently to sounds that are high- and low-pitched, they are capable of detecting the difference.

Just how acute this difference detection is has been explored using various techniques, and there seems to be some agreement that the infant's ability to detect frequency differences may be sharp enough to detect a difference between a tone of 200 cycles per second (cps) and one of 250 cps. Eimas (1974) has conducted a research program designed to assess infants' ability to perceive sound distinctions that are important in speech. Using artificial speech and sophisticated equipment, Eimas has been able to present infants with speechlike sounds that vary in technical and small ways. He has been able to measure precisely how acute an infant's perception of sound distinction is. For example, infants of 2 and 3 months of age have shown differential responses to the sounds *p* and *b* when they occurred in the syllables *pa* and *ba*. If you say these sounds to yourself you should notice how much alike they are. Both sounds are produced in exactly the same place and in the same fashion, with only one difference. When we produce the *b* sound, our vocal cords are engaged; they are not engaged in the production of the *p* sound. Consider the confusion that frequently occurs in conversations over the telephone that results in explanations such as "*B* as in boat" or "*P* as in puppy." (The telephone is not a faithful transmitter of all the information needed to make important speech distinctions.)

Eimas concludes that infants are very capable processors of auditory information. Being able to attend to the fine differences in sounds is extremely important in order for the infant to be able to discriminate important distinctions in the speech signal and to be receptive to speech. The ability to process speech requires that very fine discriminations be made between meaningful sounds, which occur rapidly and indistinctly at best. It is interesting that when we speak there are no distinct breaks between the sounds that make up a word or even between most words. Say the word *pet* to yourself, pronouncing each letter separately. Then say the word as you normally would. See the difference! The infant's ability to respond to fine differences in sounds is crucial if he or she is going to respond to speech.

Another interesting aspect of audition is the child's ability to coordinate what is seen with what is heard. Recall that Wertheimer found that 2-minute-old infants searched visually for sound sources. Apparently this ability is part of the infant's initial set of responses. A rather controversial study that investigated this ability was conducted by Aronson and Rosenbloom (1971). Aronson and Rosenbloom placed infants from 1 to 2 months of age between two stereo speakers and ran the mothers' voices through the speaker system. The mothers were visible to the infants, but in an adjoining room behind a window. Aronson and Rosenbloom tuned the speakers initially so that the mother's voice appeared to be coming from her actual position. After the infant attended to the mother and her speech, the speakers were unbalanced so that her voice appeared to be coming from one side or the other and not from where she was. When this occurred, the infants responded with distress. Aronson and Rosenbloom took this as indication that infants have the ability to coordinate sound and sight and further that they expect them to coincide. Others have argued that the distress of the infants was due not to the discrepancy of this event with their expectations but to the fact that they were expected to attend to two stimulus events at once.

There is also evidence that infants even younger than 1 to 2 months are sensitive to the varied properties of sound. Mendelson and Haith (1976) indicate in a review of auditory research involving newborns that newborn infants are sensitive to intensity, frequency, duration, and possibly the location of sound. There is also an indication that the fetus is sensitive to sound during the last 3 months of the prenatal period. A growing body of research indicates that the infant is capable of processing important sound distinctions.

Mendelson and Haith (1976) have also attempted to demonstrate a relationship between the visual and auditory processing capabilities of the newborn. They conducted a series of studies with newborns, involving various relationships between auditory and visual stimuli. They demonstrated that sound occurring while the infant is scanning a lighted blank field tends to result in more controlled visual scanning, including wider eye opening. When the infants were scanning either a vertical or horizontal visual display, the occurrence of sound tended to produce more fixations toward the center of the visual field. The researchers speculated that this was the result of the centralized location of the sound stimuli. In a later study they varied both the location of the sound and the visual stimuli. In some cases the locations of the sound and the visual stimuli were similar; in some cases the sound came from the opposite side of the infant than the visual stimuli. In cases where the sound and visual stimuli matched, the infants' fixations were more constrained in the area of the stimuli. It is interesting that initially the infants responded to the sound by gazing in the direction of the sound but then began to fixate away from it.

Mendelson and Haith discussed the possibility that the infants fixated toward the sound, and when no change in the visual stimuli occurred, they looked away, perhaps in search of some change elsewhere. In a final study, Mendelson and Haith were unable to find a relationship between the effort needed to process in one sensory mode and the ability to process in another. They had speculated that the more complex one stimuli is, such as the visual one, the less attention there would be available for the second stimuli, the sound.

In a summary statement based on their series of studies, Mendelson and Haith conclude that the infant has the appropriate sensory capabilities and tendencies very early in life to begin forming concepts about spatially related events, such as sight and sound. They see the infant's tendency to respond to sound by visual scanning as an indication that the newborn infant is equipped to start gathering information from the environment.

TOUCH

The sensory channels that we have considered, vision and audition, are generally believed to be relatively advanced in the infant. Now we will turn to sensory systems that are not considered advanced in the infant. The first of these is sensitivity to pain. It is commonly believed that for the first few days of life the infant is relatively insensitive to pain stimuli. This may be due both to the characteristics of the infant and to the effect of pain-depressant drugs given to the mother during delivery. Whatever the basis for the belief, it is widespread and can be testified to by the fact that infant boys are routinely circumcised without any anesthetic. However, some researchers do not use infant boys in sensory studies because they feel that the effect of the circumcision makes them poor subjects. Obviously there is inconsistency in belief.

In the past, studies that have concluded that the infant is relatively insensitive to pain have relied on light pinpricks as the source of pain and have taken distress or withdrawal responses as indications that pain was felt. The general conclusions of these studies are that the head is more sensitive to pain than the extremities are. This is consistent with the pattern of neural and muscle development. The infant's nervous and muscular struc-

Barbara McClinton

Fig. 4-3. Although most researchers feel the sense of taste is not well established at birth, children of preschool age certainly develop definite taste preferences for sweet substances, such as ice cream.

ture develops from the head downward and from the center outward. Past studies have also indicated that there may be differential sex responsiveness to pain, with girls being more sensitive. Lipsitt and Levy (1959), using a technique of applying mild shock as a pain stimulus, have concluded that a degree of sensitivity to this stimulus is present from birth on and that infants gradually increase in responsiveness over the first 4 days of life. They also indicate that infants who suffered birth trauma or stress are less sensitive to pain.

TASTING

A second sensory system considered underdeveloped initially is gustation (sense of taste). Mussen, Conger, and Kagan (1969) report that neonates have little taste sensitivity. If one considers the bland substances newborns are fed, perhaps it is just as well. However, Engen, Lipsitt, and Peck (1974) indicate that the neonate 1 to 3 days of age has the ability to distinguish between two sweet substances differing in sugar concentration—sucrose and glucose. These findings indicate that the gustatory sense is operating initially. Engen and his associates were interested in the possibility that children avoid harmful substances, based on taste and smell. They discuss other studies on taste and report what all mothers and fathers know: by age 3 years, children have definite taste preferences.

SUMMARY

While we have not discussed all of the infant's sensory capabilities, it should be apparent that the infant has a highly capable sensory system operating at birth, providing the infant with basic information about the world. From the beginning, infants attend and grow in ability to attend to information presented to them. The infant is remarkably competent and should be treated as such.

REFERENCES

Aronson, E., & Rosenbloom, S. Space perception in early infancy: perception within a common auditory-visual space. *Science,* 1971, **172**, 1161-1163. Reprinted in L. J. Stone, H. T. Smith, & L. B. Murphy (Eds.), *The competent infant, research and commentary.* New York: Basic Books, Inc., Publishers, 1973, pp. 702-706.

Ball, W., & Tronick, E. Infant response to impending collision: optical and real. *Science,* 1971, **171**, 818-820. Reprinted in H. C. Lindgren, *Children's behavior.* Palo Alto, Calif.: Mayfield Publishing Company, 1975, pp. 818-820.

Bench, J. Square-wave stimuli and neonatal auditory behavior: some comments on Ashton (1971), Hall et al. (1968) and Leonard et al. (1969). *Journal of Experimental Child Psychology,* 1973, **16**, 521-527.

Bower, T. G. R. Stimulus variables determining space perception. *Science,* 1965, **149**, 88-89. Reprinted in L. J. Stone, H. T. Smith, & L. B. Murphy (Eds.), *The competent infant, research and commentary.* New York: Basic Books, Inc., Publishers, 1973, pp. 690-693.

Bower, T. G. R. *Development in infancy.* San Francisco: W. H. Freeman and Company, Publishers, 1974.

Bridger, W. Sensory habituation and discrimination in the human neonate. *American Journal of Psychiatry,* 1961, **117**, 991-996. Reprinted in L. J. Stone, H. T. Smith, & L. B. Murphy (Eds.), *The competent infant, research and commentary.* New York: Basic Books, Inc., Publishers, 1973, pp. 348-352.

PART TWO

Compos, J. H., Langer, A., & Krowitz, A. Cardiac responses on the visual cliff in pre-locomotor human infants. *Science,* 1970, **170,** 196-197.

DeLoache, J. S. Role of habituation and visual memory in infants. *Child Development,* 1976, **47,** 145-154.

Eimas, P. Auditory and linguistic processing of cues for place of articulation by infants. *Perception and Psychophysics,* 1974, **16,** 513-521.

Eisenberg, R. The organization of auditory behavior. *Journal of Speech and Hearing Research,* 1970, **73,** 461-464. Reprinted in L. J. Stone, H. T. Smith, & L. B. Murphy (Eds.), *The competent infant, research and commentary.* New York: Basic Books, Inc., Publishers, 1973, pp. 332-335.

Elkind, D. Perceptual development in children. *American Scientist,* 1975, **63,** 533-541.

Engen, T., Lipsitt, L. P., & Peck, M. B. Ability of newborn infants to discriminate sapid substances. *Developmental Psychology,* 1974, **10,** 741-744.

Fantz, R. L. Pattern vision in newborn infants. *Science,* 1963, **140,** 296-297. Reprinted in L. J. Stone, H. T. Smith, & L. B. Murphy (Eds.), *The competent infant, research and commentary.* New York: Basic Books, Inc., Publishers, 1973, pp. 314-316.

Fantz, R. L. Visual perception from birth as shown by pattern selectivity. *Annals of the New York Academy of Science,* 1965, **118,** 793-814. Reprinted in L. J. Stone, H. T. Smith, & L. B. Murphy (Eds.), *The competent infant, research and commentary.* New York: Basic Books, Inc., Publishers, 1973, pp. 622-630.

Fantz, R. L. Complexity and facial resemblance as determinants of response to facelike stimuli by 5 and 10 week old infants. *Journal of Experimental Child Psychology,* 1974, **18,** 480-487.

Fredrickson, W. T., & Brown, J. V. Posture as a determinant of visual behavior in newborns. *Child Development,* 1975, **46,** 579-582.

Gibson, E. J., & Walk, R. D. The "visual cliff." *Scientific American,* 1960, **202,** 64-71. Reprinted in *The nature and nurture of behavior: developmental psychobiology: readings from Scientific American with introductions by William T. Greenough.* San Francisco: W. H. Freeman and Company, Publishers, 1973, pp. 19-26.

Greenman, G. W. Visual behavior of newborn infants. In A. J. Solnit & S. A. Provence (Eds.), *Child Development.* Hallmark, 1963, pp. 71-79. Reprinted in L. J. Stone, H. T. Smith, & L. B. Murphy (Eds.), *The competent infant, research and commentary.* New York: Basic Books, Inc., Publishers, 1973, pp. 323-326.

Haith, M. Visual scanning in infants. Paper read at the Regional Meeting for the Society for Research in Child Development, Worcester, Mass., March 1968. Reprinted in L. J. Stone, H. T. Smith, & L. B. Murphy (Eds.), *The competent infant, research and commentary.* New York: Basic Books, Inc., Publishers, 1973, pp. 320-323.

Haynes, H., White, B. L., & Held, R. Visual accommodation in human infants. *Science,* 1965, **48,** 528-530. Reprinted in L. J. Stone, H. T. Smith, & L. B. Murphy (Eds.), *The competent infant, research and commentary.* New York: Basic Books, Inc., Publishers, 1973, pp. 618-622.

Hebb, D. C. *Textbook of psychology.* Philadelphia: W. B. Saunders Company, 1972, p. 121.

Lewis, M. Infants' responses to facial stimuli during the first year of life. *Developmental Psychology,* 1969, **1,** 75-86.

Lipsitt, L. P., & Levy, N. Electrotactual threshold in the neonate. *Child Development,* 1959, **30,** 547-554.

Martin, R. M. Effects of familiar and complex stimuli on infant attention. *Developmental Psychology,* 1975, **11,** 178-185.

Mendelson, M. J., & Haith, M. M. The relation between audition and vision in the human newborn. *Monographs of the Society for Research in Child Development,* 1976, **41**(4, Serial No. 167).

Mussen, H. P., Conger, J. J., & Kagon, J. Child development and personality. New York: Harper & Row, Publishers, 1969.

Peeples, D., & Teller, D. Color vision and brightness discrimination in two-month old infants. *Science,* 1975, **189,** 1102-1103.

Salapatek, P. The visual investigation of geometric pattern of one- and two-month-old infant. Paper read for the American Association for the Advancement of Science, Boston, December 1969. Reprinted in L. J. Stone, H. T. Smith, & L. B. Murphy (Eds.), *The competent infant, research and commentary.* New York: Basic Books, Inc., Publishers, 1973, pp. 631-637.

Stechler, G. Newborn attention as affected by medication during labor. *Science,* 1964, **144,** 315-317. Reprinted in L. J. Stone, H. T. Smith, & L. B. Murphy (Eds.), *The competent infant, research and commentary.* New York: Basic Books, Inc., Publishers, 1973, pp. 175-178.

Wertheimer, M. Psychomotor co-ordination of audio-visual space at birth. *Science,* 1961, **134,** 1962. Reprinted in T. G. R. Bower. *Development in infancy.* San Francisco: W. H. Freeman and Company Publishers, 1974, p. 118.

Wolff, P. H. Observation on new born infants. *Psychosomatic Medicine,* 1959, **21,** 110-118. Reprinted in L. J. Stone, H. T. Smith, & L. B. Murphy (Eds.), *The competent infant, research and commentary.* New York: Basic Books, Inc., Publishers, 1973, pp. 257-268.

Stimulation of human neonates and visual attentiveness

Donald R. Ottinger
Mary E. Blatchley
Victor H. Denenberg

During recent years there has been a rapid growth in theory and research regarding the role of experience preceding and affecting the beginning of cognitive development. The work of Piaget and Hebb are noteworthy; Hunt (1961) has emphasized that infantile experience plays a role in cognitive, as well as emotional, development; and Denenberg (1966) has argued that variation in stimulus input is necessary for optimal adjustment and performance.

Institutionalized infants were given increased stimulation in the form of rocking by White and Castle (1964) starting at 6 days of age for 30 days. Although the eyes of the experimental Ss were covered during rocking, at 6 weeks of age the experimental Ss exhibited more visual attention than a nonrocked control group.

Casler (1965), again using institutionalized babies, gave an experimental group extra tactile stimulation for 10 weeks and found the experimental group exceeded a control group on Gesell scores on adaptive language, and personal-social scales.

The purpose of the present study was to determine if supplementary stimulation experiences would alter visual attentiveness if applied during the neonatal period.

METHOD
Subjects

The Ss were 28 full-term neonates, equally divided into experimental and control groups. Both males and females were used. Permission to use S was obtained from both the mother and the responsible physician.

From *Proceedings of the 76th Annual Convention of the American Psychological Association,* 1968, **3,** 355-356. Copyright 1968 by the American Psychological Association. Reprinted by permission.

Test apparatus

A modification of the Fantz (1958) technique for measuring visual fixation was used. A display board constructed of plywood, painted blue, 32 inches above the floor and tipped forward at an angle of 75° to the floor, held the visual targets. Two targets were presented simultaneously on the board, and an observation hole was placed midway between the targets.

These targets, painted black on white posterboard, were used and were presented in all combinations in random order and balanced for side of presentation. The targets were 1, 3, or 5 black dots within the black outline of a circle. S was held by an assistant and placed midway between the targets, oriented to the center, and 19 cm. from the display board. E remained behind the display board and presented the stimuli without awareness as to identity of targets and observed the reflection of targets on the pupils of Ss eyes. E presented each set of targets for 30 seconds and operated electrical timers recording the time eyes were open and time eyes were open and on target. Lighting was provided by lamps on either side of S below his field of vision. Approximately 25 to 28 foot-candles were reflected from the targets and field.

Procedure

All Ss were pretested on the morning of the day following delivery, at least 12 hours after the event, and in a quiet room. Ss were again tested for visual attentiveness on the morning of the fourth postpartum day.

Supplementary experiences

As soon as the pretesting was completed, Ss in the experimental group were subjected to several types of stimulation:
1. Ss were held at the shoulder of E approximately 19 cm. from a rotating multicolored wheel for a period of 5 min.
2. Ss were held on E's lap and their backs gently rubbed for 10 min.
3. Again while being held to the shoulder of E, S was exposed for 5 min. to a flat circle on which a schematic face was painted. This rotated continually (30 rpm) around a brightly painted semisphere, thus passing in and out of S's field of vision.
4. Five min. of rocking and "mother talk" were given.
5. At the completion of the above routine, an electrical crib rocker was placed on the crib for 15 min. This provided a gentle shaking of the crib and baby.

This 25-min. procedure, exclusive of the crib rocker, was carried out twice a day, morning and late afternoon, for 3 days. The crib rocker was employed for 15 min., 6 times a day, at approximately 4-hr. intervals.

Totaling all forms of stimulation, there were 140 min. of supplementary experience for each of 3 days given to the experimental Ss. In addition, a plastic mobile was placed at the head of the crib, a pinwheel at the side, and abstract designs were used as crib liners.

Except for the pretesting, the hospital routine for the control Ss was not altered until posttesting. All babies were taken to their mothers 6 times a day for feeding. Each feeding period lasted approximately 1 hr. and if the baby finished before that time the mother had the option of holding the baby or replacing him in his crib. Flexibility of routine was provided by allowing any mother to hold her baby between feedings. Additional routine stimulation to the baby was provided by the hospital attendants who could pick up and comfort the babies if it seemed necessary. Each nursery was provided with continuous music if the attendant on duty desired to listen to it. Thus, hospital routine was left as undisturbed as possible and no baby was denied any attention or stimulation that existed in the usual routine.

RESULTS

The design thus consisted of experimental and control groups divided unequally into males and females, and pre- and post-test scores.

Table 1. Proportion of eyes-open time spent on target arc-sin transformation

Group	N	Pretest	Posttest
Experimental male	6	1.5704	1.7555
Experimental female	8	1.6957	2.0437
Control male	7	1.7159	1.5841
Control female	7	1.7502	1.7339

The data were analyzed by an unweighted means analysis of variance. Analyses were performed on the total time S's eyes were open and also on the proportion of this "eyes-open" total time that S's eyes were fixated on a target.

The analysis of variance on the total time the eyes were open during the testing periods produced a significant main effect for pre- and posttest at the .01 level. The eyes of both experimental and control groups were open more on the posttest on the fourth postpartum day than they had been during the pretest on day one. There were no other significant main effects of interactions on this variable.

Visual fixation time on target was expressed as a proportion of the total time that each S had his eyes on target for the time he had them open during a presentation. . . . The interaction of groups by pre- and post-test scores was significant at the .01 level. Experimental babies fixated on targets a higher proportion of time than did the control babies during the posttest. Thus, on the posttest all babies had their eyes open more than on the pretest, but the experimental babies spent a greater proportion of that time with their eyes fixated on the targets than did the controls. Group means are shown in Table 1, and the analysis of variance is shown in Table 2. (Omitted in the interests of brevity.)

DISCUSSION

The purpose of this experiment was to determine if supplementary stimulation experiences would increase visual attentiveness during the neonatal period. This phenomenon has been previously demonstrated in older infants and after longer periods of treatment than is employed in the present study, but this is the first time this has been demonstrated during the neonatal period.

The finding that both control and experimental groups had their eyes open significantly more during the testing on Day 4 than on Day 1 is interpreted as a maturational change or at least an interaction between maturation and the level of stimulation available from the hospital routine. The effects on fixation time are apparently related to experiences provided by the experimental treatment. The present study does not contain any information on the permanence of this produced behavioral change. The demonstrated plasticity of visual behavior in the human neonate would appear to be important if subsequent experiences were to follow that built upon this behavioral modification. The increase in amount and variability of stimulus input for the experimental group acted upon the neonate to increase visual attentiveness. Such an increase in visual attentiveness would appear to be beneficial for the organism in enabling him to attend to more complex aspects of the visual world at an earlier age. This capacity to respond to experiences while yet in the neonatal period and increase the development of an act as basic as attention suggests that a systematic program of stimulation and experience can be initiated during the neonatal period with the goal of increasing cognitive development. The determination of appropriate developmental experiences remains to be determined, but the goal of increasing the rate of cognitive development clearly calls for the necessary research to determine this program.

Chapter 5

Developing physical and motor skills

W. C. Baker

On our street there are two 5-year-old girls. Both are about the same height and weight. One has been riding a bicycle for almost a year and is the proud owner of a new 26-inch bike, which she rides with great skill. The other has had very little success in her attempts to master a smaller bike equipped with training wheels. Motor-skill development is not as routine as it might appear to be. Furthermore, although everyone knows that infants sit before they are able to stand and that they stand before they begin to walk, many aspects of physical development must be considered if our understanding of the developing child is to be complete. There is great variety and importance in the physical and motor development of children.

Knowledge of growth patterns is important in several ways. First, knowledge of growth patterns helps us understand and evaluate the response capabilities and resultant skills of the child at various ages. Further, knowledge of growth patterns is useful as an indication of when training in specific skills may be valuable and should also tell us where training will be ineffectual. Another reason for being aware of the normal growth pattern is to be able to recognize abnormal growth patterns and dangers to healthy, normal development.

PATTERN OF PHYSICAL DEVELOPMENT
Genetics

Life begins with conception, the union of an egg (ovum) and a sperm. The egg and sperm contain all the genetic material that will guide the individual's development throughout life. Because half of the child's genetic inheritance comes from each parent, the child is similar to both parents but has a unique combination of genes all its own.

The influence of genes is easiest to trace in the case of a trait determined by a single gene. Unfortunately for students of genetics, there are few single-gene traits. Most single-gene traits are rare diseases (such as phenylketonuria, PKU) or trivial characteristics (such as the ability to taste a bitter substance called phenylthiocarbamide).

Single-gene traits are either present or absent. Most genetically inherited characteristics, though, occur in degrees. At age 6 years, for example, children are usually about 43 inches tall, but many children are 40 or 42 or 44 or 46 inches tall, and a few may be as short as 38 inches or as tall as 48 inches. Traits that occur in degrees most often result from combined effects of many genes. Tracing the inheritance of these gene clusters becomes impossibly complex.

Humans do not ordinarily "inherit" characteristics as such, but merely as predispositions or tendencies to develop characteristics, given ideal conditions. Infants, for example, are born with a genetically preprogrammed timetable for developing physical skills, but this timetable can be altered if the growing child is poorly fed or has disease. Other traits that have a strong hereditary component are extroversion or introversion (degree of "outgoingness"), emotionality (usually displayed as degree of excitability or fearfulness), level of activity, certain mental disorders (such as schizophrenia and manic-depressive psychosis), certain physical disorders (such as diabetes, multiple sclerosis, and some forms of cancer), handedness (right or left), and intelligence. It is important to remember that whether each of these characteristics appears depends on whether it is "encouraged." A person with a genetic potential for diabetes is likely to develop the disease if given the typical high-sugar American diet, but if fed different foods, the same individual might never become diabetic. Similarly, a child who is inclined by heredity to prefer the left hand will ordinarily become left-handed. If the child is continually punished for using the left hand (as is common in some groups who consider left-handedness a sign of the devil), no one would be surprised if the child decided to "become" right-handed.

The influence of many genes is apparent from birth or even before. Genes determining blood groups, for example, act soon after conception, and one's blood type remains stable throughout life. Other genes have delayed effects. Genes controlling release of hormones, such as growth hormones and sex hormones, are active at some periods of development but relatively quiet at other periods. Genes regulating the timing of aging processes usually are inactive until decades after conception.

Prenatal development

The period of most rapid growth and development is the prenatal period. This is also a period when the child's development is susceptible to a great number of potential hazards. It is important, therefore, to consider at least briefly the child's development before birth.

The prenatal period begins at the moment of conception, when the egg of a woman is fertilized by the sperm of a man. This generally occurs in one of the fallopian tubes leading to the uterus.

After conception the fertilized egg (zygote) moves down the fallopian tube into the uterus and is implanted in the wall of the uterus. This process generally takes a week. During this time the zygote has already been undergoing cell division. After implantation and during the second week of development, the zygote becomes differentiated into the placenta and the embryo. This change marks the end of the germinal stage of prenatal development and begins the embryo stage of development. It should be noted here that many more eggs are fertilized than pregnancies are confirmed. It is estimated that about one third of embryos are spontaneously aborted without the woman's knowledge during the first 8 weeks of development (Tanner, 1970).

The embryonic period begins with the second week of development and lasts through the second month of development. During the embryonic period the embryo develops characteristics common to the mammalian class of organisms (Meredith, 1975). During this early period the nervous, circulatory and skeletomuscular systems begin to develop. The embryo also develops a rudimentary nose, mouth, and eyes, as well as some major organs and glands. Some ossification (hardening) of bony structures has begun, and for a time the embryo has gill arches, which become incorporated into the inner ear structure. Further, the rudimentary heart has been beating since the end of the first month of development (Watson and Lowrey, 1976). At the end of the embryonic period the embryo weighs about $1/14$ of an ounce and is about $1^1/2$ inches long.

The remainder of the prenatal period is the fetal period, and the developing child is now properly referred to as a fetus. The fetus undergoes various changes as it develops, with its most rapid growth occurring during the fourth prenatal month. It is obvious that the fetus changes remarkably in size; however, there are other changes as well. As indicated above, during the embryonic period the embryo possesses gill arches for a short time, and during the fetal period there are other transitory developments. In the early fetal period, the fetus develops and loses an external taillike structure, touch pads on the fingers, and a covering of body hair called lanugo. At one point in development, taste receptors are present not only on the tongue but on the tonsils, esophagus, and palate. These excess receptors are lost later during prenatal development (Meredith, 1975).

These are not the only dramatic prenatal changes. Various organs, glands, and bone structures shift position drastically as the fetus develops. For example, the heart originally is located in what develops as the lower face. It moves down and back to the correct position in the trunk and finally rotates counterclockwise and tilts from right to left (Meredith, 1975).

During the third to fifth prenatal months the fetus develops a number of structures and refinements. During the third month the male and female genital organs are differentiated, ossification of cartilage continues in such structures as fingers and toes, and the nails begin to form. By this time the fetus has begun to resemble a human.

By five prenatal months the fetus has hair on its head, is a foot in length, weighs a pound, and possesses all of its nerve cells. During the sixth month the nails that began growing during the third month reach the ends of the fingers. By the seventh month the fetus has developed eyelashes and eyebrows, and the eyelids are no longer fused together. The skin is red and wrinkly. During the eighth month fat develops under the skin, changing the "dried-up old man" appearance of the fetus to a more babylike one. The final month is generally one of growth and refinement.

So far we have discussed the developing fetus only in terms of its physical structure. As the fetus develops physically, it also becomes increasingly mobile. Gesell et al. (1940) discuss behavior patterning in the embryo and fetus. As indicated earlier, the embryonic heart beats as early as 4 weeks of development. Movement is also present in the arms and legs as early as 6 weeks. By 3 months and increasing through 5 months, the fingers flex and there is movement of the trunk and head as well as further arm and leg movement. By 5 months the fetus lashes its arms and legs around and makes rhythmic respiratorylike movements of the chest. By the end of the sixth month the fetus makes sucking motions. During the final months of prenatal development, movements of the fetus are well developed and strong enough to cause occasional discomfort to the mother. Unfortunately, the mother is not the only one likely to suffer discomfort or harm during pregnancy; the fetus is susceptible to various types of injury and illness long before birth.

The mother's nutrition and health have an effect on the developing child. Mothers who are severely undernourished are likely to have children of low birth weight. Further, research with animals such as rats has indicated that prenatal undernourishment results in lowered intellectual capacity. This topic is discussed in Chapter 9 under the general topic of intelligence.

It is also known that certain drugs taken by the mother affect the child's development. This was tragically illustrated in Europe several years ago when mothers who had taken the drug thalidomide had children who were severely deformed. The drug had particularly affected the development of the limbs, and many children were born with only stubs of arms or legs. It has become increasingly evident that the mother's use of drugs may result in the birth of an addicted infant. Even smoking appears to be related to prenatal development, as women who smoke tend to have smaller infants and more premature infants than do nonsmokers. Taking any kind of medication during pregnancy is highly unwise without a physician's supervision.

Another serious problem most people are aware of is disease during pregnancy. If the mother contracts an illness during pregnancy, the disease is likely to be passed on through the placenta to the fetus. Whether the disease is particularly damaging to the fetus depends on the stage of development of the fetus at the time of the disease. Structures and systems undergoing most rapid change and development are most adversely affected, as periods of rapid growth also appear to be periods of greatest vulnerability. The most dread disease of pregnancy is the type of measles known as rubella, which is likely to have a most serious effect on the fetus if the disease is contracted during the first trimester (first 3 months) of pregnancy. Rubella may cause multiple defects in the fetus, including damage to the heart, eyes, and ears as well as low birth weight and other possible damage if the disease has been severe.

Other diseases potentially hazardous to the developing fetus include smallpox and polio and the infection of syphilis. The effects of other diseases, such as mumps and chicken pox, are less well established, but it is believed that severe cases of influenza during the second trimester of pregnancy may increase the chances of spontaneous abortion (Dudgeon, 1968).

Although diseases in the mother are potentially harmful to the fetus, the fetus is not without protection. Generally, the mother's own immunities are effective in protecting her and the fetus.

Birth

Marking the end of prenatal development and the transition to further development as a neonate is the birth of the child. This is perhaps the most dramatic transition of development. The infant generally tolerates this transition remarkably well.

The length of the delivery period varies greatly along with the ease or difficulty of the process. Although some potential parents are apprehensive as the birth of their child approaches and worry about damage to the infant, the infant and the process are well suited to each other. For example, the pressure of passing through the birth canal helps drain fluid from the infant's lungs, and release from the canal generally causes a reflex expansion of the lungs, aiding the child's initial respiration (Eichorn, 1970). One of the most serious situations likely to occur is anoxia (lack of oxygen) during the birth, with resultant brain damage to the infant. However, the newborn seems able to undergo a longer period of anoxia at birth without apparent damage than at any later period. Some researchers are beginning to believe that there may be preexisting brain damage that leads to the failure of the child to breathe initially or to handle the period of anoxia associated with birth (Tanner, 1970).

Another concern about the birth of the infant is the effect of drugs given the mother during delivery. (Recall the discussion in Chapter 4 on the effect drugs may have on early sensation.) Other effects are also likely. It is believed that drugs given the mother are present in the infant for a longer time than they are in the mother, as the infant's system is not as efficient in ridding the body of the drug. Some researchers feel that the common delivery drugs affect the infant's responsiveness, respiration, sucking rate, and temperature regulation (Aleksandrowitz, 1974). However, there is still much to be learned about the effect of these drugs on the infant before a judgment can be made as to their safety.

Neonatal development

At birth there are several abrupt environmental changes for the neonate, but in most cases the infant is prepared for the changes or at least able to make compensatory adjustments for them. For example, the neonate's ability to regulate body temperature by sweating or shivering is not perfected, and the proportion of body fat is less in the neonate, providing poor insulation; therefore, the neonate's body temperature is unstable and drops quickly after birth. Nurseries are kept overly warm to help compensate for this; however, the infant also aids in its own temperature regulation by crying, which steps up metabolism (Watson & Lowrey, 1967).

The physical maturity of the newborn's several body systems is varied, with some systems being more advanced than others. There are also differences at birth between newborn boys and girls. In general, boys are heavier at birth, while girls have more body fat. Boys develop more rapidly at birth, while girls are more advanced in skeletal maturity. It has also been noted that premature girls are generally superior in developmental state than are premature boys.

At birth the infant's skull is relatively soft and, as the infant lies constantly with the head turned to one side, may become temporarily flattened. The bones of the skull are not only soft but are not completely fused. The newborn has six fontanelles (soft spots) where the bones are not fused. Frequently in a bald baby the fontanelle at the front and top of the skull can be observed moving in and out with the infant's respiration and circulation. This may be disturbing, but it is not at all abnormal.

The newborn's head is large in proportion to both the body and the face. The neonate's neck is short and the chest is rounded. At birth the skeletal musculature is approximately one fifth of the body weight and by maturity will increase to two fifths. The brain is already one fourth its eventual weight and will reach 90% of its total weight by the time the child is 5 years old.

At birth the spinal cord and the section of the brain known as the midbrain are developmentally the most advanced portions of the central nervous system. Most researchers agree that the cerebral cortex (the portion of the brain involved in our more complex behaviors) is not identifiable in the brain until 2 months of age, and even at this point all sections of the cortex are not evenly developed. The primary motor area is the most advanced section of the cortex, followed by the primary sensory area, primary visual area, and primary auditory area (Tanner, 1970).

The maturity of various areas of the infant's brain and nervous system is reflected in the neonate's sensory capacities and response capabilities. Although the human infant is relatively helpless and immobile compared with infants of some animal species, the maturity of the primary motor area of the brain suggests that the human infant has a response repertoire of several motor reflexes.

The infant's complement of reflexes is an important set of behaviors. Many of these reflexes are important for survival. The most obvious are the sucking reflex and the rooting reflex. An infant begins to suck if an object, such as a nipple or a finger, is placed in its mouth. The rooting reflex is closely related to the sucking reflex. If an infant is touched lightly on the cheek, he will turn his or her head in the direction of the stimulation and open his or her mouth in preparation for sucking. This reflex helps direct the infant to a nearby source of food. Other reflex actions that serve survival functions are coughing, sneezing, and blinking.

Reflexes are also important in that they are reflections of the maturity and state of the infant's nervous system. Examination of the infant's reflex repertoire is an important part of early physical examinations. Table 2 offers a listing of some major reflexes, along with a brief description of each reflex and its developmental relevance.

Table 2. Infant reflexes

Reflex	Description	Significance
Blink at bright light		Absent in infants with impaired light perception
Palmer grasp	Press rod into palm; fingers should curl around rod	Weaker on one side may be result of clavicle fracture; absent in some depressed infants or may be an indication of peripheral nervous system damage
Babinski's sign	Scratch sole from toe to heel; toes spread	Absence may indicate defect of lower spinal cord
Rooting response	Lightly touch side of cheek near mouth; head should turn to direction of stimulation	Absence may be due to barbituate depression; infant may turn away if satiated; high correlation with alertness
Placing response	Touch top of feet to table edge; infant puts feet on top of table	Absent with paresis of lower limbs

Adapted from Prechtl, Heinz, & Beintema. Neurological examination of the full term newborn infant. Little Club clinics in developmental medicine (No. 12). Spastics Society Medical Education and Information Unit in Association with William Heineman Medical Books Ltd., London, 1964.

Examination of reflexes is a useful diagnostic tool because reflexes are common to all infants and are not dependent on any experience or learning. When stimulated, the infant should respond automatically with the appropriate response. If the infant does not, it is an indication of an unusual situation or condition. Many reflexes also have predictable developmental courses in that they occur, peak in strength, and then disappear on a known schedule. Again, deviances from the normal cycle indicate potential problems. Reflexes may also be used to assess the state of the nervous system by stimulating them first on one side and then the other. For instance, an infant will grasp a rod pressed against its palm with such force that he or she can be pulled into the air by one hand. If this reflex is much weaker on one side than on the other, it is a sign of some problem.

While these early reflexes are useful indications of the state of an infant's nervous system and also of the rate of neurologic maturation, they are not early indications of the child's potential in either physical or mental skill areas beyond differentiating normal from abnormal development. Yet many parents and researchers are interested in identifying any behavioral characteristics that might be used as an early predictor of a child's later development. Many physical and motor characteristics have been used in these attempts to look for direct relationships between early and later behavior. Attempts have been made, all without much consistency or success, to relate infant's respiration rates, amount of crying, percentage of time spent in alert visual exploration, and other such behaviors to later temperament and general behavioral traits. Even specific predictors are difficult to develop. At one time it was felt that when a baby would begin to walk could be predicted by comparing the child's trunk length with leg length. It was believed that when the legs had reached 60% of the trunk legnth the child was ready to begin walking. However, the accuracy and usefulness of this indicator are questionable. Shirley (1931), who did an extensive study of children's motor development, did report that in general small and muscular children tended to walk earlier than short-legged heavy babies did. On brief consideration, this generalization would seem to be compatible with common sense and be a rather satisfying conclusion, but Shirley continues to caution that the condition of the child, thin versus heavy, may be related to the child's activity level, which would tend to favor earlier walking in the thin, more active child. She further indicated that it was quite possible that early versus late walking may be just as dependent on interest as on skill or physique. Unless the relationship between interest, skill, and physique is explored and understood, using just one component of the three (e.g., physique) as an indicator may be misleading more than just occasionally.

Another consideration related to predictions involves attempts to get early indications of a child's intelligence. It is frequently felt by pleased parents that if their child develops through the various motor milestones of sitting, standing, walking, and so on, with ease and ahead of "schedule," all should be well as the child enters school and begins to further exercise mental functions. Along the same lines, the parents of the late walker frequently are anxious about the child's capabilities in general. Although most knowledgeable persons recognize the groundlessness of these points of view, you will see in a later chapter that psychologists have relied very heavily on the measurement of motor skills in an attempt to assess the intelligence of preschool children. It should be noted that it is useful to be aware of the physical characteristics and the response capabilities of the neonatal period to understand the needs and behaviors of the neonate at this stage of development. Concern for early indications of later development should not obscure this purpose.

83

Barbara McClinton

Fig. 5-1. A considerable amount of nervous system development must occur before an infant is able to use fingers to pick up tiny objects, such as macaroni shells.

Course of physical development

The course of physical development and the acquisition and refinement of motor skills follow the pattern of neurologic development in the child. This pattern is said to proceed in a cephalocaudal and proximodistal direction. Cephalocaudal means that development proceeds from the head downward. Specifically, the child gains control of the head and eyes first, normally during the first 3 months of life. During the later months of the first half year of life, control extends to the arms and upper trunk. In the following 3 months, control of the lower trunk and legs increases (Watson & Lowrey, 1967). Proximodistal development refers to development from the center outward. For example, the child has control of the upper arm before the wrist and fingers.

The development of the child's brain continues for many years after birth. As researchers gain more knowledge about the development of the brain, our understanding of the child's capabilities increases as well. Fishbein (1976) summarizes the work of several researchers and presents an overview of brain development. Apparently the brain reaches a plateau of development at about 1 year. At this point most reflexes have disappeared, the child increases its motor capabilities and becomes more mobile, and the electroencephalographic (EEG) pattern of brain activity becomes more consistent. During the preschool and early elementary school years, the brain develops most of its connections between major areas and most myelinization (covering of nerve fibers) is completed. These events, especially the association of major brain areas, allow for greater complexity and integration of the child's behavior.

Along with neurologic growth, the child's development in other areas affects skills and capabilities. The relationship between the child's body and abilities is very strong. Tanner (1970) reports that in some primitive cultures, when a child's age is not known, a crude predictor that he or she is ready for work or schooling is whether the child can touch the left ear with the right hand, with the arm passing over the top of the head. According to Tanner this is a fairly accurate indication of maturity, because as the child grows, the head becomes smaller relative to the limbs and trunk.

The rate of growth is relatively predictable for children in general, yet individual differences make it difficult to make growth predictions for any one child. For what it is worth, Watson and Lowrey (1967) present an entire set of mnemonic devices referring to children's height and weight. By these standards, 3-year-old children should be 3 feet tall; 4-year-old children are generally 40 inches tall. A 3½-year-old child should weigh 35 pounds; a 7-year-old should weigh seven times birth weight.

Another commonly used growth predictor is that doubling a 2-year-old's height should give a good indication of the child's eventual height.

All of these should be regarded only as general indications of the pattern of growth. Individuals vary widely from any of these norms. For example, doubling a 2-year-old's height gives a better prediction for boys than for girls. Other conditions, such as the child's health and general nutrition, affect rate of growth.

Although weight gain varies widely, in general it is a fairly consistent process. At birth boys tend to weigh more than girls, but by age 8 years they are generally equal. Closely related to weight is the proportion of body fat. At birth girls have more body fat. Both boys and girls generally show a decline in body fat between 1 and 8 years of age. During this period boys lose more fat than girls do, so by age 8 girls still have a higher proportion of body fat.

Weight gain over the first year of life is generally fairly consistent. During the first 3 months, infants generally add 2 pounds a month, so by 5 months of age most infants have doubled their birth weight. After the first few months weight gain slows down to a pound per month. By the end of the first year most children weigh three times their birth weight, and by the end of the second year their weight is four times what it was at birth. During the second year of life, monthly weight increases are much smaller, usually about half a pound. Beyond the second year, weight gains are measured in years, with an average increase of 5 pounds a year being normal throughout childhood (Watson & Lowrey, 1967). There appears to be a tendency for weight gain in children to be more pronounced in the fall. Perhaps the return to indoor play and school account for this phenomenon.

Gains in height are also slightly different for the two sexes. Girls are generally smaller than boys at birth, and this difference continues until adolescence. Although girls are shorter than boys throughout childhood, during the preschool years girls grow faster than boys and are at all ages more physically advanced than boys.

Contrary to popular belief, the growth rate for height is relatively consistent in any one child. Children do not generally grow in spurts. Although the rate of growth between age 5 years and adolescence is very consistent for a child, large differences between children are not at all unusual. One interesting parallel is that while weight gain tends to be greater in the fall, height gain apparently is greater in the spring.

Just as growth is an orderly process, so is the development of motor skills. Shirley (1931) conducted an extensive study of the motor development of 25 children from birth to age 2 years. The children were visited daily while in the hospital after birth, once a week during their first year, and once every other week during their second year. During this time Shirley kept careful records of their health, growth, and nutrition and tested their skills in both gross and fine motor activities.

In summarizing her findings Shirley divided the motor-skill development of children into sets of skills she referred to as orders. In Shirley's framework there are five orders or levels of motor skills. The various skills within one order are closely related to each other. Specific skills in each order are organized according to the median time, in weeks, in which most children acquire that skill or develop that ability. Shirley indicates that development generally proceeds in the order listed, yet within an order level some children may reverse the positions of some skills. Although overlapping and changed order may occur within order levels, Shirley felt that there was a separation between order levels. This means that all children develop first-order skills before second-order, and second-order skills before third-order, and so on.

Shirley's first-order skills involve the acquisition of passive postural control. During the first order the infant gains control of the head and upper trunk. Most infants master the skills of the first order before 20 weeks of age. In progression, first-order skills include lying on the stomach and being able to lift the head, lying on the stomach and being able to lift the chest, stepping movements made when held erect, tensing in preparation for being lifted off the back, keeping knees straight when held erect, and being able to sit when supported at the ribs. This final skill includes complete control of the head.

Second-order skills involve postural control of the entire trunk and undirected activity. Second-order skills are generally acquired by 25 to 31 weeks of age. The 25-week-old infant generally is able to sit alone momentarily. Other second-order skills include lying on the stomach and making knee pushes or swimming movements, rolling over on the back, standing firmly when held erect, and being able to sit alone for 1 minute by the end of the second order.

Third-order skills involve active effort toward locomotion, with little success in the form of actual movement. For most children the third-order skills are gained by 37 to 39 weeks of age. The two third-order skills involve making some progress toward forward movement while lying on the stomach and scooting backward on the stomach. Many people are surprised to learn that infants quite frequently creep backward before they are able to move forward. Many a child has backed under a bed or into a corner while trying to head out into the world!

The fourth-order skill period runs from 42 to 47 weeks of age. Fourth-order skills involve actual locomotion by creeping. In this particular order the sequence of skills frequently is reordered. The child's postural control expands to include the lower limbs. This control is necessary for the child to be capable of the coordinated movements necessary for effective locomotion. Children in the fourth order tend to either master the coordination needed for creeping or the postural control necessary for standing, but rarely both.

The fourth-order skills are standing while holding onto furniture, creeping, walking when led, and pulling oneself up to stand while holding onto furniture.

Frequently there is a long time lag between the fourth- and fifth-order skills. The median age for the development of the most complex fourth-order skills is 47 weeks. Fifth-order skills generally do not develop until 62 weeks of age. The fifth-order skills, which are standing and walking alone, involve both postural control and the coordination needed for walking.

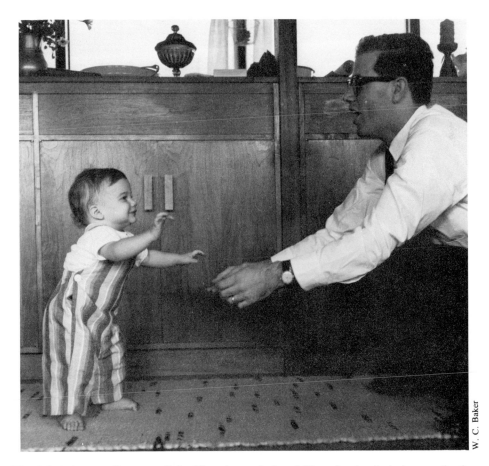

Fig. 5-2. It is generally not until the fifteenth month that children develop both the coordination and postural control necessary for walking.

Shirley also found a relationship between the infant's play tendencies and the five orders of motor-skill development. She saw the infant's play as exercise of newly acquired motor skills and emphasized that children tend to play at their exact level of motor skill and at their maximum strength.

Although most children progress through these periods at close to the median times indicated by Shirley, it is important to remember that there are vast individual differences in children and the rate at which they progress. Some children seem to enjoy motor activity more than others and devote more effort and time to these activities; other children seem much less interested. It is important to recognize these normal differences in children and not expect each child to follow a specified time table. The schedule included in this discussion is used only to give a rough estimate as to when to expect various motor milestones.

Just as Shirley's work details the development of locomotion skills in young children, it is possible to trace the development of sitting, standing, reaching, or grasping. One of the best sources for a detailed description of the development of all motor skills is the work of Gesell et al. (1940). (Recall that his work was discussed in detail in Chapter 1.) For example, Gesell's capsule description of 5-year-olds tells that their sense of balance is improved from what it was at 4 years; consequently, they can walk a 4-cm long balance board and skip and jump smoothly. It should take them 20 seconds to pick up 12 pellets and drop them in a bottle. Further, typical 5-year-olds should be able to wash their own faces and begin to speed up activities and stop dawdling as much as they did as preschoolers.

Gesell also characterizes the motor development of the first 5 years of life as the development from natural response activities to a wide range of specific motor skills. One of the most important features of motor development is the acquisition of postural control of the body. Before a child can master any complex physical activity, he or she must have the ability to automatically adjust and readjust body position to meet the demands of the new skilled act.

ROLE OF EXPERIENCE IN MOTOR DEVELOPMENT
Skilled acts

Once a child has gained postural control and some minimal locomotion skills, the possibility for mastery of skilled acts is increased greatly. Fishbein (1976) describes skilled actions as involving intentional sensorimotor actions accompanied by feedback as to how successful or appropriate the action has been. Each skilled act involves the child's postural control, movement capabilities, and abilities to manipulate objects.

Success in skilled action involves the mechanization of basic motor skills making up components of the skilled act as well as the child's abilities to recognize what skills are called for, what sequence they need to be in, and how to time the various components of the skill. All of these abilities take time to develop, especially for the more complex skilled actions. Fishbein states that children's abilities to handle skilled actions begin to increase from age 4 years onward, with the largest gain between the ages of 4 and

9 years. Therefore, it is unrealistic to expect young children to be proficient at motor acts that require quick decisions and quick movements. Fishbein illustrates this by explaining that a 6-year-old is not likely to have a good batting average because it takes the child a long time to decide whether to swing at a particular ball and a long time to actually make the swing. It is unwise to expect too much skill too early in such areas. The question arises, however, as to whether increased opportunity to practice facilitates motor skill development. Do children become better baseball players if they start early?

Early experience and motor-skill training

The question of early experience and motor-skill training is an interesting one that both parents and researchers have been concerned about, although for different reasons. Parents are generally concerned with helping their children acquire skills and develop as efficiently as possible. While researchers may also be interested in increasing the rate at which children develop skills, they are interested in training in motor skills to better understand both the skills and the developmental process. For example, if training in a skill is effective, that is, the child acquires the skill before an untrained child does, experience and learning must play a large role in the development of that skill. If the training given a child is ineffective, either the training was inappropriate and therefore we do not understand the components of the skill or maturation must play a more important role in the development of that skill than experience does.

Two general approaches have been taken in studying training in motor-skill development. One method is to compare the rate of development of children from cultures that differ in how much training is given children in motor skills or how early the training is given in a particular motor skill. For example, there are great differences among cultures as to when toilet training is begun. A concerned researcher might compare the time training is started and the success reached for various cultures and provide recommendations to the more "inefficient" cultures. An interesting example of this cross-cultural type of study was reported by Ainsworth (1967), who did extensive fieldwork in Uganda. There she found that children had traditionally been trained to sit alone. The training involved binding the child's trunk with a stiff material and placing the child in a hole. Ainsworth reported that untrained infants tended to sit alone before trained infants did. She speculated that perhaps only infants who were slow to develop were trained.

A second general method used to study the effect of motor-skill training has been to give extensive training or practice in a particular skill to half of a group of children who are at the same point of development and compare their performance with that of the untrained children at the end of a period of time. It is assumed that if maturation is crucial to the development of the skill, the untrained children when given the opportunity to exercise the skill will either be as proficient as the trained children or will catch up quickly, because both groups are at the same maturational level. However, if experience is the more important factor in the acquisition of the skill, the trained children's performance should be superior to the untrained children's.

The ideal subjects to use in this type of study are identical twins, because their innate characteristics are closely matched and individual differences are minimized.

Johnny and Jimmy

McGraw (1935) conducted one of the most intensive studies of motor-skill training using twin boys, referred to as Johnny and Jimmy. She worked with them from when they were 20 days old until shortly after their second birthday. During the period of the study the twins spent 8 hours a day in the laboratory, 5 days a week. The remainder of their time was spent with their family in their home. The major aim of the study was to give one twin extensive training in many areas of motor skills and to compare the performances of the two boys in each area. It was assumed that the family's behavior toward the twins would not seriously interfere with the experimental treatment and training, because there were seven children in the family and it was not likely that any special treatment or attention would be given the twins while they were at home.

There is one complicating factor to this study. McGraw selected her twin subjects with the belief that they were identical rather than fraternal twins; however, as they grew, there was some doubt that they were in actuality identical twins.

Johnny was chosen as the experimental twin because Jimmy appeared to be slightly stronger. Since Jimmy seemed to be developmentally advanced over Johnny at birth, if Johnny's training was effective, the gains over Jimmy would be more dramatic than if the stronger twin were trained.

When the study began, Johnny was given short training sessions every 2 hours during the day and Jimmy was left in a crib behind a screen. Periodically Jimmy would be tested on the skills in which Johnny had been trained, and relative performances of the twins were assessed.

During the first several months of the study Johnny's reflexes were stimulated as motor-skill training. When Jimmy's reflexes were stimulated during the test periods, there were no differences in performance. These results should not be unexpected, as reflexes are not dependent on experience.

As the twins developed, Johnny was given practice in all the motor milestones, such as rolling over, sitting, standing, and so on. Practice in rolling over did not particularly enhance Johnny's success, and although Johnny was given practice in sitting, Jimmy sat alone first. Both boys stood at about the same time, but McGraw reports that Johnny's standing was more mature than Jimmy's. At this point the training given Johnny had not noticeably increased his skills over those of his untrained twin brother.

As the study progressed, Johnny was given training in more and more complex and highly specific motor skills. He was trained to climb up and down steep inclines and to leap off high stools. He was trained to roller skate, to swim, and to dive. In all of these areas Johnny's performance differed from Jimmy's. When Jimmy was introduced to these tasks, both his initial and subsequent performances lagged behind Johnny's.

From these findings it would not be difficult to conclude that motor-skill training is ineffective in developing reflex behavior and apparently does not show much success in accelerating basic motor milestones, such as sitting and rolling over, but apparently training in specific complex motor skills, such as swimming or roller skating, does contribute to a child's mastery of these skills. However, it should be noted in reference to these more complex skills that Jimmy's performance also improved with practice.

McGraw emphasizes one major difference in the performances of Johnny and Jimmy. In all cases, Johnny showed more interest, less fear, and more confidence in performing these complex skills; Jimmy was not nearly as enthusiastic.

Following the 2 years of training and testing, McGraw and her co-workers introduced both boys to new complex tasks and novel situations to study the effect of Johnny's past training on his performance of novel tasks. The results were perhaps disappointing in that Johnny's past enrichment did not benefit him in highly novel situations.

Although the final results of this study are not quite what one might have anticipated, McGraw was able to make some interesting inferences about development and training. These include a reaffirmation of the belief that behaviors under infracortical control (not controlled by the cortex, such as reflexes, which are controlled by lower brain centers) are unaffected by specific training or practice. Other behaviors, however, may be influenced by practice to varying degrees.

McGraw feels that some behaviors appear early and are presumably controlled by lower brain centers, yet also appear later in development under cortical control. These behaviors disappear for a time while control is being developed in the higher brain center. For example, infants make reflex stepping movements at a very early age, yet do not show this behavior again until they are almost ready to walk. The point McGraw makes about these phenomena is that the greater the time lag in the appearance of a behavior and the reappearance of that behavior, the more likely that training will be effective in the acquisition of the more mature form of the behavior.

One final general conclusion that McGraw draws refers to the idea of critical periods of development. A critical period is assumed to be a point in the development of a behavior when experience or training influences the development of the behavior to a greater extent than at any other time. Some researchers qualify this definition by adding that training before or after this period not only has less effect but may be totally ineffective. McGraw feels that there is a critical period of development when motor-skill training is most effective, that is, the period when the skill is changing most rapidly. If training is introduced at the period of most rapid development of a skill, it will be most effective in the development of that skill. It should be obvious that it is not always easy to ascertain when this period of most rapid change occurs.

Based on studies of McGraw and others, it is apparent that early training in motor development does not exert much influence on the infant's acquisition of basic motor abilities, such as sitting or standing. Most children progress satisfactorily with the environmental stimulation found in almost all homes and institutions. However, there is benefit from specific training and practice of the more complex motor skills, such as swimming or skating. The more training and practice a child experiences, the more proficient that child should become. The question that is more difficult to answer involves the benefit of early training on the eventual level of proficiency in a skill. Does a child who begins swimming at 4 years of age have an edge over the child who begins at 8 years? Because many factors are likely to influence the eventual behaviors, identifying the effect of age of acquisition of the skill is almost impossible. For example, a relationship might be found between early training in swimming and eventual success in that skill, yet it is

W. C. Baker

Fig. 5-3. Some children seem to enjoy motor activity more than others and exercise newly found motor skills with great enthusiasm.

also highly likely that the child who begins to swim early is highly interested in swimming, lives in an environment that stimulates this interest, and is encouraged in this interest. Perhaps the only generalization that can be made is that while the skill is undergoing change or is developing, training in that skill is beneficial.

SUMMARY

Physical development does not take place in a vacuum. The environment provides the child with stimulation. If the environment offers appropriate and varied experiences, the child will likely develop motor skills of a satisfactory level. If the child experiences long periods of deprivation or illness, motor development is likely to be impaired or retarded, at least for the period of deprivation or illness and perhaps longer if it is serious. However, most children make compensatory gains, when conditions improve.

The development of motor skills and the development of the body also contribute to the child's social success and feelings of self-adequacy. If the child's skills are in line with the development of others, he or she develops a healthy concept of his or her own abilities. Generally the child feels competent and has normal acceptance by and success with peers. However, the child whose skills do not meet a certain level of acceptance or whose physical state differs greatly, such as in obesity, may have difficulty with peers and may also experience feelings of inadequacy. It is important to realize that young children as well as older children may suffer doubts about their abilities. It is equally important to realize that an understanding of physical development contributes to our understanding of the child as a whole.

REFERENCES

Ainsworth, M. D. *Infancy in Uganda: infant care and the growth of love.* Baltimore: The Johns Hopkins University Press, 1967 pp. 319-330.

Aleksandrowitz, M. K. The effect of pain relieving drugs administered during labor and delivery on the behavior of the newborn: a review. *Merrill-Palmer Quarterly,* 1974, pp. 122-141.

Dudgeon, J. A. Breakdown in maternal protection: infections. *Proceedings of the Royal Society of Medicine,* 1968, **61,** 1236-1243. Reprinted in L. J. Stone, H. T. Smith, & L. B. Murphy (Eds.), *The competent infant, research and commentary.* New York: Basic Books, Inc., Publishers, 1973, pp. 159-169.

Eichorn, D. H. Physiological development. In P. H. Mussen (Ed.), *Carmichael's manual of child psychology* (Vol. I) (3rd ed.). New York: John Wiley & Sons, Inc., 1970, pp. 157-283.

Fishbein, H. D. *Evolution, development and children's learning.* Pacific Palisades, Calif.: Goodyear Publishing Co. Inc., 1976.

Gesell, A., Halverson, H. M., Thompson, H., Ilg, L., Castner, B. M., Ames, L. B., & Amatrud, C. S. *The first five years of life: a guide to the study of the preschool child.* New York: Harper & Row, Publishers, 1940.

McGraw, M. B. *Growth: a study of Johnny and Jimmy.* New York: Appleton-Century-Crofts, 1935.

Meredith, H. V. Somatic changes during human prenatal life. *Child Development,* 1975, **46,** 603-610.

Shirley, M. M. *The first two years: a study of twenty-five babies. Vol. I. Postural and locomotor development,* Minneapolis: University of Minnesota Press, 1931.

Tanner, J. M. Physical growth. In P. H. Mussen (Ed.), *Carmichael's manual of child psychology* (Vol. I) (3rd ed.). New York: John Wiley & Sons, Inc., 1970, pp. 77-155.

Watson, E. H., & Lowrey, G. H. *Growth and development of children.* Chicago: Year Book Medical Publishers, Inc., 1967.

Action-schemes of 8-month-old infants

Claire B. Kopp

Departments of Pediatrics and Psychiatry
University of California, Los Angeles

Eight-month-old infants use a variety of structured actions, that is, "action-schemes" (Piaget & Inhelder, 1969) to interact with objects including mouthing, visual inspection, manipulating, banging, etc. These contribute to the organization of sensorimotor intelligence or goal-directed activities, or function as attentional aids. In view of their importance, the present study was designed to examine the influence of preterm birth and sex on action-schemes.

From Developmental Psychology, 1976, **12,** 361-362. Copyright 1976 by the American Psychological Association. Reprinted by permission.

Recent improvements in neonatal care have lessened the incidence of severe intellectual and neurologic deficits of preterm infants yet the proportion of children, particularly males, who have learning problems and normal intelligence has not declined (Davies & Stewart, 1975). At earlier age periods some preterm infants without evidence of developmental delay show similar signs of distractability and disorganized play. Since these signs are difficult to measure, utilization of a technique that allows microanalysis and quantification of action-schemes could be helpful in identifying subtle difficulties that emerge during infancy.

The sample consisted of 64 infants, equally divided by sex and term or preterm birth. The term infants were observed at a mean of 35.08 weeks (SD = .76) from their date of birth, the preterm infants at 34.9 weeks (SD = 1.29) from their expected date of birth. The infants met the criteria of no apparent neurologic deficit, no obvious developmental delay, and the ability to pick up cubes with thumb and fingers. Developmental data obtained at 4 months on all the preterm infants indicated no developmental deviance.

The infants, observed in a laboratory setting, were seated in a crib in front of a gray wooden table top (10.4 × 13.6 cm) adjusted to waist level. The mothers stood at the side of the crib and after a short adaptation period presented and removed objects at a signal from the examiner who was out of the infant's visual field. The entire procedure was videotaped. The objects used were chosen for ease of prehension, simplicity, and moderate interest—low wariness level. The first object presented, a single 2.5-cm red cube with a .8-cm white dot on each side, was placed 10 cm from the edge of the table top closest to the infant's chest. The second object consisted of three similar cubes tied together with white plastic cord. Each object was presented separately for 60 sec; the time was lengthened if the infant dropped the object on the floor.

One of the two examiners coded infant behaviors from videotapes, using slow motion, in order to give a detailed analysis of infant responses. Using previously written operational definitions, the examiners noted the type, duration, and frequency of each action-scheme. Results for the 1- and 3-cube situations were summed giving single duration and frequency scores. These scores formed the basis of statistical analyses. Periodic interobserver reliability checks (i.e., periodic coding of action-schemes by both examiners on the same babies) indicated coding agreement for duration averaged better than .90.

After grasping an object, 8-month-old infants commonly show the following types of object-related action-schemes: *mouthing, holding the object and looking at it, examining* (turning the object around in the hands), *waving and banging, sliding* the object across the table top, and *looking at the object without contacting it*. The data to be reported were measures of duration scores of these action-schemes.

The duration scores served as dependent variables in a 2 (Birth) × 2 (Sex) multivariate analysis of variance, which revealed a significant Birth × Sex interaction, F multivariate (7.54) = 2.99, $p < .01$; a significant birth effect, F multivariate (7.54) = 2.20, $p < .04$; and a significant sex effect, F multivariate (7.54) = 2.53, $p < .02$. The significant interaction indicated that overall durations of action-schemes were a function of preterm birth and sex. The significant main effects indicated that overall durations differed for term and preterm infants and for males and females.

As part of the overall multivariate analysis step-down F tests were performed to examine the contribution of each of the seven dependent variables. The variables initially were entered without an a priori order. Using the univariate Fs obtained in the Birth × Sex interaction analysis, the variables were reentered with the variable having the largest univariate F entered first and so forth. The step-down tests indicate the effect of each variable holding the preceding one(s) constant.

Birth × Sex step-down Fs indicated differences in duration of *examining* (F = 5.68, $p < .02$) and *looks at object—no contact* (F = 9.49, $p < .003$). *Examining* can be considered a type of active object exploration whereas *looks at object—no contact* can be labeled passive exploration, for the infant is not involved in holding the object as it is visually inspected. The full-term females contributed the longest duration of use for both action-schemes (*examining: M* = 22.90;

looks at object—no contact: $M = 9.74$), while the ful-term males ($M = 11.15, 3.15$), preterm females ($M = 13.44, 6.88$), and the preterm males ($M = 14.8, 7.35$) exhibited less.

Birth step-down Fs showed a significant difference between term and preterm infants on duration of *mouthing* ($F = 6.34, p < .01$), which was more pronounced for full term ($M = 27.92$) than for preterm ($M = 18.68$) infants. Mouthing was the most prominent action-scheme for the terms; the group difference, though, was mainly contributed to by the preterm males ($M = 13.91$), as their duration of mouthing was almost half that of the preterm females ($M = 23.45$). Another significant step-down F was obtained for the behavior *holds the object and looks at it* ($F = 3.99$, $p < .05$), with the preterm infants showing a greater amount ($M = 28.20$) than the full-term infants ($M = 19.85$).

Sex step-down Fs indicated one significant difference between males ($M = 5.25$) and females ($M = 8.31$) on *looks at object—no contact* ($F = 6.93, p < .01$).

Two other analyses were made to determine if clustering those action-schemes involved in direct object exploration, *(examining, mouthing, holding object and looking at it)* and those involved in large or ballistic-type movements *(waving and banging, sliding)* differed across the groups. Two 2 (Birth) × 2 (Sex) analyses of percentage of times indicated no significant differences for the first cluster and a significant main sex effect in the latter cluster with males showing a higher percentage of *waving and banging* and *sliding* ($M = 32.74$) than did females ($M = 15.44$).

Findings regarding the low-risk preterm infants are consistent with clinical descriptions. That is, in many ways they are similar to full-term infants, but group differences can be observed although they are subtle. In this study both groups demonstrated the same types of action-schemes and spent similar proportions of time involved in direct object explorations. Group differences were apparent in the duration of individual action-schemes. Of particular interest is the low duration of mouthing observed with the preterm males. Hand-to-mouth and object-to-mouth activities are major ways of learning and, for 8-month-olds, are prominent infant behaviors. Yet, the preterm male is atypical in this respect. It is possible that this low level of mouthing reflects a subtle aspect of behavioral disorganization; its developmental significance should be investigated.

Sex differences observed in manipulative action-schemes and in the cluster of ballistic-type movements are similar to previous findings. Males are more vigorous than females in manipulative activities. Additional research should be directed toward understanding these observed differences for later development.

REFERENCES

Davies, P. A., & Stewart, A. L. Low-birth-weight infants: Neurological sequelae and later intelligence. *British Medical Bulletin,* 1975, **31,** 85-91.

Piaget, J., & Inhelder, B. *The psychology of the child.* New York: Basic Books, 1969.

Chapter 6

Developing learned behavior

Elaine M. Ward

From earlier chapters and common sense, we know that learning has a tremendous influence on development. Recognizing the importance of learning, we are faced with the question of how children, even in infancy, are able to profit from their experiences. The answer to this question is not simple. Human beings have some basic capacities for learning from the moment of birth, perhaps even earlier. But there are some complex learning processes, which seem natural to an adult or even to a 12-year-old child, that are beyond the reach of a young child. In some ways, a young child must "learn to learn." Basic learning processes, the ones available even to infants, are the subject of this chapter. The more complicated learning processes will be set aside temporarily, to be described in a later chapter.

CLASSICAL CONDITIONING

Classical conditioning has been called the simplest type of learning because no particular effort is required of the learner. The learner merely makes an automatic reflex response to whatever stimulus the environment (or the psychologist) provides. You may recall that Pavlov's dogs, which could already salivate, were taught to salivate to a *particular stimulus* (a tone or bell); they learned this trick by classical conditioning. The essence of classical conditioning is not learning a new behavior but learning to produce an already established behavior in circumstances that previously did not provoke the behavior.

The most famous child-subject of a classical conditioning experiment is Little Albert (Watson & Rayner, 1920). In spite of some technical questions about the study,* Little Albert's experiences provide a good illustration of how classical conditioning can occur.

Watson and Rayner wanted to demonstrate that fears of everyday objects, which at that time were assumed to be symbolic of other unconscious fears, could be learned simply by conditioning. Little Albert, at 11 months of age, was not afraid of white rats, rabbits, or other furry objects. In fact, he had very few fears, except a fear of loud noises. Albert seemed an ideal subject for a study of conditioned fears.

Classical conditioning is accomplished in a straightforward manner (Fig. 6-1). Prior to conditioning, the subject reliably produces a certain reflexive reaction (the *unconditioned response,* UCR) whenever a particular event occurs (the *unconditioned stimulus,* UCS). In Little Albert's case, fear and withdrawal behavior (UCR) were displayed whenever he heard a loud noise (UCS). This stimulus and this response are called *un*conditioned because no conditioning is needed to make the stimulus elicit the response. It was not necessary to teach Albert to fear loud noises; this noise-fear relationship was already established, either as a reflex or by very strong previous learning.

Once the UCS-UCR relationship is known, another stimulus is introduced, which is a *neutral stimulus* (an event that does *not* elicit the unconditioned response or any similar

---

*Strictly speaking, Little Albert's fear was at least partly acquired by operant conditioning (see Reese & Lipsitt, 1970, p. 85, for an explanation). Even though elements of both types of conditioning are indicated in the Watson & Rayner report, the study is oversimplified in the following account to provide an example of classical conditioning with minimal confusion.

Fig. 6-1. Classical conditioning.

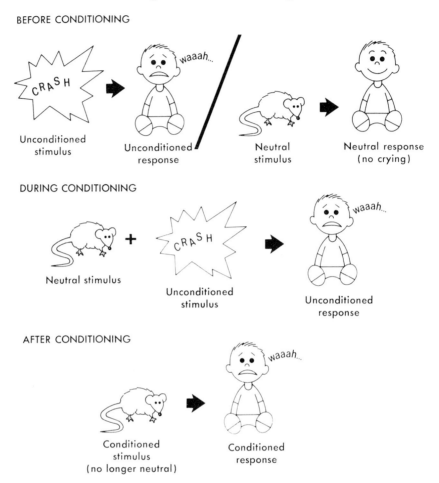

BEFORE CONDITIONING

Unconditioned
stimulus

Unconditioned
response

Neutral
stimulus

Neutral response
(no crying)

DURING CONDITIONING

Neutral stimulus

Unconditioned
stimulus

Unconditioned
response

AFTER CONDITIONING

Conditioned
stimulus
(no longer neutral)

Conditioned
response

behavior). For Albert, a white rat qualified as a neutral stimulus because Albert did not fear white rats; he liked them.

To produce classical conditioning, the neutral stimulus is paired with (presented just before) the unconditioned stimulus. To make the conditioning strong, this pairing of the stimuli is repeated many times.* The unconditioned response occurs with every paired presentation of the two stimuli, because the unconditioned stimulus "automatically" elicits the unconditioned response. Eventually, when the neutral stimulus is presented alone, it can elicit the unconditioned response. Since the neutral stimulus originally did not have this power but does now, it is given a new name: the *conditioned stimulus* (CS).

---

*"Real life" classical conditioning sometimes requires only one pairing of the neutral stimulus with the unconditioned stimulus, especially if the unconditioned stimulus is quite unpleasant (like a dog bite). In the laboratory, more pairings are usually necessary because for ethical reasons psychologists choose milder unconditioned stimuli.

The conditioned stimulus is any event that at first does not provoke the response being studied but by conditioning (CS-UCS pairings) develops the ability to provoke this response. To condition fear in Little Albert, every time Albert reached for a white rat (originally neutral stimulus), the psychologists made a loud noise (UCS). Naturally, Albert displayed fear (UCR). This procedure was repeated eight times. When the white rat was later presented alone (no noise), Albert cried and withdrew; the white rat had become a conditioned stimulus (CS) for fear.

The response to the conditioned stimulus often is not exactly the same as the response to the unconditioned stimulus, though it is very similar. Because the responses to the two stimuli may be slightly different, the response following the conditioned stimulus is given a new name, the *conditioned response* (CR). Some typical differences between UCRs and CRs (besides which stimuli provoke them) may be how quickly the responses are made after the stimuli appear, how long the responses last, how strong (or loud) the responses are, and so forth. Little Albert's CRs (crying and withdrawal in the presence of the white rat) were essentially the same as his UCRs (crying and withdrawal from the loud noise), but if Watson and Rayner had made very precise measurements of the CRs and UCRs, they might have detected some minor differences.

In spite of all the psychological jargon, the classical conditioning of Little Albert's fear was not complicated. At first Albert liked white rats but intensely disliked loud noises. After exposure to the rat in association with the loud noise on several occasions, Albert began to fear the rat. Albert's new fear was not restricted to the white rat but *generalized* (spread out) to similar stimuli. After conditioning he was also afraid of a white rabbit, a Santa Claus mask, and other furry objects that he did not fear earlier. Watson and Rayner originally planned to use conditioning to get rid of Albert's new fears, but publicity about the experiment produced such an uproar that Albert's mother withdrew permission for the psychologists to work with the child before they could recondition his positive responses to furry objects.

In the half century since Little Albert's unfortunate experiences, young children have been classically conditioned to produce many responses on cue, such as mouth opening, changes in heart rate and breathing, head turning, eye movements, changes in electrical conductivity of the skin, and movements of arms, hands, legs, and feet (see Reese & Lipsitt, 1970, for more details). Observant mothers often notice evidence of classical conditioning in their own infants: when placed in the usual feeding position (CS), infants as young as 3 weeks old may begin to suck (CR) before the bottle or breast (UCS) is available.

Modern studies of classical conditioning are much more refined than the early work of Watson and Rayner. A good example of how these experiments are carried out is provided by Kaye (1967). Kaye wanted to find out whether newborn infants are susceptible to classical conditioning. He was certainly not the first psychologist to ask this question, but earlier attempts to find an answer had not been designed in a way that would produce firm conclusions. Kaye chose sucking as the response to be conditioned. In some ways sucking is an ideal infant behavior for this purpose because (1) it is simple to observe and measure, (2) it can be easily elicited by placing a suitable object in a baby's mouth, and (3) it is one of the few well-developed skills that a newborn infant possesses. Unfortunately, sucking is also a favorite activity of infants, whether they are being conditioned or not. Because babies normally suck more at some times than others, the only way to determine whether sucking can be conditioned is to conduct an experiment that includes a conditioning group and several control groups.

In Kaye's experiment, a tone (neutral stimulus) was presented five times to 60 newborn infants (only 3 and 4 days old). Sucking occurred on about 40% of these "preconditioning" trials, which is not surprising considering how much time babies ordinarily spend sucking. Then ten of the infants were exposed to a standard classical conditioning procedure in which the tone was paired with a pacifier (UCS) placed in the baby's mouth for 19 seconds. Naturally, sucking (UCR) occurred when the pacifier was in the baby's mouth. This procedure was repeated 20 times. To measure conditioning, a test trial (CS-tone alone, without the UCS-pacifier) followed every fourth conditioning trial (CS-tone and UCS-pacifier paired). Sucking occurred on over 70% of the test trials, a marked increase from the 40% on the preconditioning trials. Five control groups of newborn infants were presented with various combinations of CS-tone or UCS-pacifier, but not in a way likely to produce conditioning. Kaye found a slight increase in sucking over trials in some control groups and a slight decrease in sucking in others, but no significant response changes were reported for any group except the "true" conditioning group.

Based on Kaye's study and many others, we can confidently conclude that newborn infants can learn by classical conditioning. Now another question arises: Does learning by classical conditioning become easier as a baby grows older? In many experiments, older

Charlie Westerman/Image, Inc.

Fig. 6-2. Specific fears may be learned by classical conditioning.

infants have developed conditioned responses more quickly than younger ones, but there are alternative explanations for these findings. For example, suppose head turning can be classically conditioned more quickly in a 6-month-old baby than in a 6-day-old baby. Is the improvement in conditioning due to age changes in learning capacity or to age changes in the ability to turn the head? Finding a suitable response to condition—one that is equally easy for babies of all ages tested—is quite difficult. Age changes in motivation, sensory abilities, and even time spent sleeping may produce results that masquerade as changes in ability to learn. Because of methodological problems in studies on this question, we cannot be certain whether there are age differences in the capacity for classical conditioning.

By now you may be wondering why, except for idle curiosity, psychologists are interested in the ability of an infant or even an older child to learn by classical conditioning. There are at least two practical reasons. Classical conditioning has been a very useful tool to find out what babies can and cannot do (see Chapter 4). The second reason is that many learning experiences, particularly learning of *emotional responses,* such as fear and love, are easily explained as cases of classical conditioning. If you ask why the sight of a fire engine brings shrieks of terror from Johnny but squeals of delight from Susie, the answer is likely to be found in principles of classical conditioning.

OPERANT CONDITIONING

Children, like other people (and other animals), learn to *increase* behaviors that produce pleasant consequences and to *decrease* behaviors that produce unpleasant ones. This type of learning is called *operant conditioning* (Fig. 6-3). In operant conditioning, the learner exhibits a behavior, either because of some other event or apparently spontaneously. The consequences of the behavior influence the learner's future behavior. If the behavior is rewarded, it becomes more likely to be repeated, but if the behavior is punished (or not rewarded), it becomes less likely to occur again. Psychologists call the behavior an *operant response* and the consequences a *reinforcement* (if the behavior becomes more likely) or a *punishment* (if the behavior becomes less likely). Some important differences between classical and operant conditioning are described in Table 3.

By applying reinforcement systematically, psychologists have been able to modify many behaviors of young children, such as smiling, talking, toilet behavior, cooperative play, aggressive play, scratching, biting, crying and whining, eating, temper tantrums, and going to sleep. For a demonstration of the technique, consider an attempt by Harris, Johnston, Kelley, and Wolf (1964) to eliminate the "regressive crawling" of a 3-year-old girl. After 3 weeks in nursery school, the girl was spending more than 80% of her time crawling or in a crouching position. Naturally, her social interactions with the other children were rather limited. The child's parents reported that this behavior had started some months before she entered school. The child's teachers had tried several methods to make the child feel more secure, but her regressive crawling continued. The psychologists observed that the teachers often gave special attention to the girl when she crawled but seldom responded to the less frequent "on feet" behavior (standing and walking). Suspecting the attention was reinforcing the crawling, the psychologists asked the **101**

Fig. 6-3. Operant conditioning.

BEFORE CONDITIONING

"Regressive crawling" is reinforced by
adult attention

DURING CONDITIONING

Crawling is ignored

Standing and walking are reinforced by attention

AFTER CONDITIONING

Walking continues   Crawling stops

Table 3. Differences between classical and operant conditioning

	Classical conditioning	Operant conditioning
What type of behavior is conditioned?	Reflexive	Voluntary
What is learned?	To produce an already established behavior when presented with a stimulus that previously did not elicit this behavior	To produce entirely new behavior or to exhibit established behavior more (or less) often than before
Does a specific stimulus elicit the behavior to be conditioned?	Yes, the UCS elicits the reflexive response	Not necessarily; voluntary behavior may occur "spontaneously," or a stimulus may "set the stage" for voluntary behavior to occur
What "causes" or strengthens learning?	Pairing of two events (the UCS and the CS) that *precede* the response	Reinforcement ("reward"), which *follows* the behavior
What role does the learner play?	Passive; the stimuli are presented to the learner	Active; the learner must produce a specific behavior to obtain reinforcement
Who learns by this method?	Humans, including newborn infants; all known animals, including single-cell animals; possibly even plants	Humans, including newborn infants; most animals

teachers to change their strategy. Rather than noticing crawling and ignoring on-feet behavior, the teachers were instructed to reinforce (with attention) standing and walking and to ignore the child when she crawled. Within a week, the girl's standing and walking were nearly normal. To be certain that the change in behavior was the result of the teachers' social reinforcements, the psychologists asked the teachers to resume the original procedure of ignoring on-feet behavior and attending to crawling. The girl reverted to her earlier behavior (80% crawling) within 2 days. Once the effectiveness of the teachers' social reinforcement was confirmed, they once again rewarded standing and walking and ignored crawling. The child soon began to stand and walk again, and "she quickly became a well-integrated member of the group."

Any behavior that a child can voluntarily produce can be modified by operant conditioning. The only problem is to choose an appropriate reinforcing (or punishing) event to follow the behavior. Even young infants can be influenced by a large number of reinforcers, such as a variety of foods, social reinforcers (smiling, talking, tickling, bouncing, cuddling, and the like), and interesting sights and sounds (pictures, moving dolls, moving wind chimes, and so on).

Older children are also easily influenced by these and other reinforcers. Adult attention may be the most powerful reinforcer for preschool children. Children who get little attention for good behavior sometimes resort to mischief, preferring unpleasant attention to none at all. Fun activities are also favorite reinforcers for preschool children; going to the circus or the zoo, "helping" mother or father, visiting friends or having guests, or simply going for a walk can act as reinforcement. Sometimes even work can reinforce desirable behavior: being forced to sweep the porch may be unpleasant, but being "allowed" to do it may be a privilege. The same objects or events will not necessarily be reinforcing for all children. Preschool children's preferences change quickly as they grow older, boys and girls prefer different rewards, and there are considerable individual differences in preferred objects (Witryol, 1971).

In spite of the seemingly straightforward relationship between reinforcement and behavior, reinforcement does not always have the effect that would be predicted by a devotee of operant conditioning. For example, based on operant conditioning principles, one might predict that picking up or attending to a crying baby would result in increased crying. This prediction was tested by Etzel and Gewirtz (1967). They observed excessive crying by two infants (6 weeks and 20 weeks old), who were healthy but living in a hospital. When the babies cried, their caretakers tried to quiet them. Reasoning that adult attention was reinforcing crying, Etzel and Gewirtz arranged for one caretaker to ignore the babies when crying but to reinforce them socially for smiling, vocalizing, and other behaviors incompatible with crying. This 15-minute procedure was followed once each day in a room that was new to the babies. After several days, a dramatic increase in smiling and decrease in crying had occurred with both infants in the experimental room. When the other caretakers discovered the results, they began to ignore crying and reinforce smiling, and the infants' behavior in the nursery soon became more agreeable.

Before jumping to the conclusion that an adult should never pick up a crying baby, consider a study by Bell and Ainsworth (1972). They observed infants' crying and mothers' reactions to crying in home settings during the first year of the infants' lives. The mothers were simply observed, not given suggestions or instructions regarding their babies. When mothers' responsiveness to crying early in the year was correlated with how much the babies cried later in the year, Bell and Ainsworth discovered that the babies who cried most often and for the longest time had mothers who were *least* responsive to crying. In other words, the mothers who picked up their babies and paid attention to them when they cried had babies who actually cried *less* as the year progressed. Another result of the study was that the babies who, by the end of the year, were most effective at communication (by facial expressions, body gestures, and noncrying vocalizations) were the babies whose mothers had been most responsive to crying throughout the year. It appears that mothers who attend to crying infants end up not with crybabies but with babies who express themselves in ways other than crying.

The results of one study, in which crying increases with attention, apparently contradict the results of the other, in which crying decreases with attention. A possible explanation is that the institutionalized babies in the study by Etzel and Gewirtz received attention *only* when they cried, but the home-reared babies in the Bell and Ainsworth report received attention when they were playing, smiling, cooing and babbling, and having a good time in addition to when they were crying. In that case, the moral of these studies is to give a baby attention when crying, but to also give plenty of attention at other times. The same principle could be applied to the problem of dealing with sick children. Mothers, intuitively understanding the power of attention, may ignore a sick child for fear

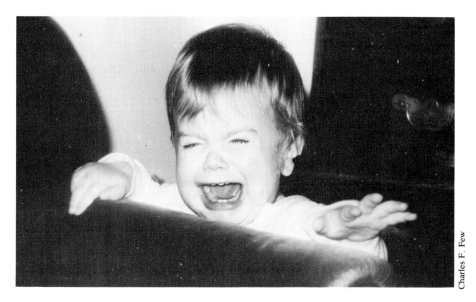

Charles F. Few

Fig. 6-4. Despite what our common sense tells us, paying attention to crying infants does not necessarily spoil them.

of producing a hypochondriac. If children get plenty of attention when well, comforting them when ill will probably only make them feel better.

Operant conditioning, like classical conditioning, has been attempted with children of all ages to determine whether learning capacities improve with age. As with classical conditioning, the studies do not provide conclusive results. The difficulty is finding a response to be reinforced that is equally easy for neonates and older children. But we have seen that young infants definitely are susceptible to operant conditioning. Psychologists have often used conditioning methods to determine what young infants are capable of doing. Operant techniques have been successfully used, for example, to find that 3-month-old infants recognize their mothers (Wahler, 1967) and that 4-month-old infants can tell the difference between familiar visual stimuli and new ones; they prefer to look at the new ones (Siqueland, 1966).

Some behaviors are more easily conditioned than others. Behaviors that have adaptive value (would help a child survive in dangerous surroundings) are especially resistant to conditioning. Crying when in distress, reacting negatively to pain, and fearing the dark are three examples of persistent behaviors that are not easily reduced by basic learning processes.

Many learning experiences are not "pure" cases of operant or classical conditioning but combine elements of both. Consider how a child might learn about bees. Before being stung, the bee itself is a neutral stimulus, probably an object of some interest to a young child. But if the sight of the bee (neutral stimulus) is paired with the sting of the bee (UCS), the result is likely to be tears and considerable motor activity (UCR). By classical conditioning, the sight of a bee (CS) on another occasion will provoke fear and perhaps **105** running away (CR). The same learning experience can also be analyzed as an instance of operant conditioning. The child sees a bee and reaches out to pet it (operant response). The sting of the bee (punisher) definitely decreases the chance that the child will try to play with the next bee he sees.

LEARNING BY OBSERVATION

Much learning occurs simply by observation of others, without any reinforcement or pairing of stimuli. Observational learning is an important source of social behaviors, such as cooperating or fighting, good manners or rudeness, sex-typed behavior, and temper tantrums. Specific skills, such as putting together a puzzle, spelling a word, or refusing to eat spinach, can also be learned by watching others. The power of observation as a learning technique is intuitively obvious to parents and teachers. Even young children use the technique to teach their peers, "Not that way, *this* way."

Defining the terms associated with learning-by-watching is difficult because these terms are not always used in the same way by all psychologists. *Imitation* most commonly refers to "copying" a specific behavior, such as sharing, biting, or tying a string, that has been observed in others. *Observational learning* usually means any learning that occurs while watching or listening to others, whether the learning involves a specific behavior, a class of behaviors (such as anxiety), or a concept. Observational learning is a general term; imitation is a special type of observational learning.

Another distinction between observational learning and imitation concerns the *performance* of the observed behavior. To qualify as imitation, the behavior must actually be repeated by the observer. Observational learning can occur with or without an actual repetition of the behavior in question. If a child sees a playmate drop a piggybank and pick up the pennies, he or she may learn (by observation) that pennies are in piggybanks, that a piggybank can be easily broken, and perhaps that the result of breaking a piggybank is an angry mother. This learning can occur and can be verified (by conversation or by watching how the child handles another piggybank) without any imitation of the "bank robbery."

The characters in an observational learning sequence have specific names. The person who demonstrates the to-be-learned behavior is called the *model,* while the person who is watching (and presumably learning) may be called the *learner* or the *observer.*

Observation is an important source of two general categories of behavior: much of our school learning (acquired by listening and watching) and many of our social behaviors. For an example of how children can learn by observation, consider a study by Bandura, Grusec, and Menlove (1967). These psychologists wanted to find out whether preschool boys and girls who were afraid of dogs could overcome their fear by watching another child playing comfortably with a dog. The children's initial fear of dogs was measured by their willingness to play with a cocker spaniel. Some of the children then observed a 4-year-old boy playing happily with the cocker spaniel in a party atmosphere or in a neutral setting. Other children attended the same number of parties with the dog present (in a cage) but without the fearless model; still others attended the parties with no dog present. After eight 10-minute sessions, each child was retested for fear of the cocker spaniel. A marked reduction in fear was found among the two groups of children who had seen the model playing with the dog, and their level of fear was still low in the presence of an unfamiliar dog. There was no significant change in the fear of the children who did not observe comfortable play with the dog. Children who had lost their fear of dogs were still free of the fear a month later.

What is learned by observation, apparently, is simply information (Bandura, 1971). This information can be how to do certain things, how *not* to do them, and what happens to other people when they do these things. What children learn by observation, therefore, is determined by their capacities for gathering information. The important factors are the child's attention, memory, and motivation. Other factors, such as reinforcement, are important only as they influence performance of what is already learned by observation.

Because imitation is not commonly displayed by infants but is well established by the time a child is a toddler, psychologists have tried to determine how the process develops, that is, how children learn observational learning. Children pass through a series of stages in which they become more and more skilled at imitation, according to Piaget (Ginsburg and Opper, 1969). By 4 months of age, an infant can be induced to repeat an already familiar action if the model demonstrates the action, but no new behavior can be learned by imitation at this age. The child's attempts to imitate gradually become more systematic, but unfamiliar actions of a model will not be imitated until about 10 months of age. *Deferred imitation* (observing an action, then imitating it at a later time) does not develop until about 18 months. Piaget reports that one of his daughters, when 16 months old, for the first time witnessed a temper tantrum by another child in a playpen. The next day, the normally placid girl imitated the tantrum behaviors when placed in her own playpen.

Under ideal conditions, an infant may be able to imitate at a younger age than reported by Piaget. As with other types of learning, the problem is to find a behavior that an infant can easily produce. Gardner and Gardner (1970) observed not-very-precise imitation of hand and mouth movements by their 6-week-old daughter. Infants may produce imitative mouth movements within the first week of life. The propensity to imitate appears to be present at birth, but the skills involved in observational learning become more refined throughout the first 2 years of life.

LEARNING SOCIAL BEHAVIOR: AGGRESSION

Except in a psychologist's laboratory, learning rarely occurs in one of the "pure" forms already described. Most real-life learning involves two or all three of the basic learning processes, and identifying reinforcements and other important elements is not always easy. To see how different learning processes can influence the same behavior, consider aggression.

Aggression is not a single behavior but a group of related, sometimes complex behaviors. Psychologists commonly define aggression as behavior intended to cause harm or pain (Aronson, 1972). Many other people have a different idea of what aggression is, such as being outgoing, putting one's best foot forward, and being a go-getter. This quality is likely to be called assertiveness by a psychologist. Whatever your own notion of   **107**

Fig. 6-5. Aggressive behavior can be influenced by all three basic learning processes.

aggression, we will restrict ourselves to the type of aggressive behavior in which a child attempts to inflict damage or discomfort, usually to another person or object, but occasionally to himself.*

For years a heated argument has centered around the origin of aggression: is it instinctive or learned? Proponents of the instinctive camp point out that many animals display aggression that apparently is not learned. Some of the most aggressive species of animals are found among the primates, a group that includes monkeys, apes, and humans. Furthermore, aggression among most animals can be easily modified by biologic means, such as injecting hormones, but cannot be as easily modified by learning. In addition, humans have engaged in violent and destructive behavior throughout recorded history. This widespread and persistent human characteristic has convinced many observers of human behavior that aggression must be part of our biologic heritage. On the other hand, proponents of the belief that human aggression is learned can muster considerable evidence to support their position. Though many animals are quite aggressive, chimpanzees and gorillas (our closest relatives in an evolutionary sense) are actually quite peaceable. Many people mistakenly think of these apes as violent, but studies of their behavior in natural settings reveal little aggression. When we look just at humans, we discover that in many societies people engage in little aggression. If aggression is an instinctive characteristic of our species, it would be prevalent in all human societies.

---

*Behaviors that appear to be aggressive in preschool children may actually be clumsy attempts to interact socially with other children. The child's intentions, whether malicious or sociable, are often difficult to determine.

Finally, aggression among humans definitely can be modified by experience, though whether it can be entirely eliminated is not known. The argument about the ultimate causes of human aggression is not likely to be resolved soon. Let us temporarily ignore the possibility of genetic predispositions and focus on how learning can influence aggression.

Much aggressive behavior, like other social behavior, is learned by observing others. Aggressive behavior can be induced in preschool children simply by showing a 5-minute film of an aggressive model (Bandura, 1965). Each child in Bandura's experiment viewed one of three films. In all three films, a man hit, kicked, and verbally abused an inflated Bobo doll in ways that young children are unlikely to do spontaneously. The films differed in what happened to the model after the aggressive sequence. In one film the model was lavishly rewarded with praise and foods that appeal to preschoolers, such as candy and caramel popcorn. In another film the model was punished in a dramatic way, including severe scolding and a spanking. The third film simply ended after the model's aggressive behavior, with no consequences following the aggression. After viewing one film, each child in the experiment was allowed to play in a room with a Bobo doll, all the toys used in the aggressive film, and a variety of other toys. The children displayed considerable imitative aggression when left to play alone. Less aggression was observed among children who had seen the model punished than among the other groups, indicating that consequences to the model definitely influence imitation. The girls in the experiment imitated much less aggression than did the boys. This sex difference is consistently found in similar studies, most likely because the behavior demonstrated by the model is not typical of the female sex role in our society.* Children as young as 3 years are acutely aware of sex-role-appropriate behavior, and in studies with an aggressive female model preschool children often comment, "She didn't act like a lady." When the children in Bandura's experiment were offered prizes to show what the model had done, they demonstrated nearly perfect memory of the contents of the film.

In a similar study, children's aggression was observed immediately after an aggressive film and again 6 months later (Hicks, 1965). The children were quite aggressive in the immediate test. After 6 months they showed little inclination to imitate the aggressive film (though they could recall more of the model's aggression than they imitated).

What is a reasonable explanation of children's imitation of violence immediately after they see it, but failure to imitate at a later time even though they remember the violence they saw? One possibility is that children will imitate violent behavior if they are "wound up" but not if they are in a calmer mood. Active, aggressive television shows are known to increase children's general level of arousal, as indicated by heart rate and blood pressure (Osbourne and Endsley, 1971). Perhaps by watching aggression a child learns how to aggress *and* is stimulated to perform what was learned, but after the stimulation wears off the child no longer is motivated to act aggressively.† Children who are

---

*This sex difference applies only to physical aggression. When verbal aggression is measured, girls and boys are equally abusive.

†Behaviors learned by operant conditioning are more likely to be performed when the individual is aroused. It is reasonable to expect that behaviors learned by observation operate on the same principle; once aggression is observed, whether it is imitated depends on how aroused the child is.

109

continually aroused, then, would be most likely to imitate aggressive models. This suggestion has been confirmed by Stein and Friederich (1972), who found that aggressive children are made more aggressive by watching violent television shows, but less aggressive children are not affected in the same way.

If observing violence makes a child more likely to attack a Bobo doll, will it also make a child more likely to attack another child? The answer appears to be yes. Several psychologists, using different methods, have demonstrated that after watching aggression children become more aggressive toward other children (Hanratty, O'Neal, & Sulzer, 1972; Liebert & Baron, 1972). For details about how watching television shows can affect children's play, read the article by Steuer, Applefield, and Smith (1971), at the end of this chapter.

What conclusions about allowing children to watch television can be drawn from these experiments? The most obvious conclusion is that watching violent programs will make children more violent, at least if they are already aggressive or stimulated in some way. On the other hand, children who watch a lot of television (and presumably violence) do not become as aroused physically by watching a gory show as children who seldom watch TV do (Cline, Croft, & Courrier, 1973). A possible implication of this study is that violent TV may inoculate a child against adverse effects of observing violence. (Another interpretation is that watching TV violence will make children less sensitive to real-life violence and therefore less likely to help a victim of violence.) An additional complication is the role played by parents. In experimental studies of imitating aggression, any nearby adults studiously avoid interfering with the children's behavior. But an adult who attempts to halt aggression among preschool children can easily do so (Smith & Green, 1975). Furthermore, many worthwhile social lessons may be learned by watching television. For example, first-graders who watched an episode of *Lassie* in which a boy helped a dog were more likely to help a puppy in distress, even though this interfered with a rewarding game, than were children who watched a nonhelping *Lassie* program (Sprofkin, Liebert, & Poulos, 1975). There is no easy solution to the problem of children and television. It probably is not possible (or even desirable) to shelter a child from viewing all violence, and any ill effects of watching limited amounts of televised aggression can be counteracted by adult direction of behavior and by exposing children to appealing shows that provide desirable models of behavior. The long-term effects of watching large doses of violent television are not known.

Though we have considered only observational learning of aggression, aggression can also be learned in other ways. No studies of classically conditioned aggressive responses have been conducted with children. In adults violence can sometimes be provoked by an aggressive stimulus, such as a gun or knife. A weapon probably acquires the power to spark aggression by classical conditioning in which the previously neutral weapon is paired with words or events that already elicit aggression. Words themselves can become "fighting words" by classical conditioning. It seems likely, therefore, that some aggressive responses can be classically conditioned in children.

Operant conditioning definitely plays a role in aggressive behavior. Davitz (1952) provides a straightforward demonstration of the effects of reward on aggression. Children at a summer camp were given "aggressive" training sessions over several days, in which they were encouraged and rewarded for playing active games in a highly aggressive manner. Other children were given an equal number of "constructive" training sessions, in which they were rewarded for creative and productive uses of art material and puzzles. After training, the experimenter deliberately frustrated the children by interrupting a movie they were watching at an exciting moment and taking away the candy they were eating during the movie. The children were then observed in a free-play situation. The children who had been trained to behave aggressively played in an aggressive manner, but the children who had been trained to behave constructively resumed their constructive play. Clearly, the rewards for earlier behavior influenced the children's reactions to frustration. This is especially striking because some psychologists have claimed that frustration automatically results in aggression.

As children grow older, the quality of their aggressive behavior changes. Hartup (1974) observed aggressive interactions of boys and girls, aged 4 to 7 years, in natural play settings. He found that the overall level of aggression decreased as the children grew older. Older children, however, were more likely than younger ones to direct their aggression toward people rather than toward objects. There were also age-related changes in children's reactions to specific provocations. Personal insults, for example, were likely to provoke physical aggression among the younger children, but most of the older children's reactions to insults were to return an insult. Hartup found interesting sex differences, too. Boys exhibited more aggression than girls, especially in the category of aggression toward people. But boys and girls reacted the same way to the same types of provocations. A possible interpretation of this finding is that sex differences in aggression are due to differences in the number or type of aggression-eliciting stimuli, *not* to differences in the way boys and girls react to a specific situation. Perhaps boys display more aggression because in our society boys are exposed to more aggressive circumstances.

Hartup's study emphasizes the significance of learning in the development of aggression, although the possibility of biologic contributions is certainly not eliminated. Hartup does not isolate a single way in which aggression is learned; he implies that aggression, like most complex behaviors, is influenced by many learning experiences involving all three basic learning processes. Psychologists separate these learning processes for purposes of explanation and research. In any given child the learning processes are like the three primary colors and all their combinations in a painting: examining one apart from the others prevents seeing and appreciating the overall effect.

USING LEARNING PRINCIPLES TO INFLUENCE CHILDREN'S BEHAVIOR

Learning plays an important role in many behaviors other than aggression. It is reasonable to expect that by understanding and using learning principles, one can have a tremendous influence on how a child thinks, feels, and acts. This expectation has been confirmed many times, both in scientific studies and in everyday experience. Simple as it sounds, even the most obnoxious behavior can often be controlled by systematically applying basic principles of learning.

Reward

Reward has a powerful effect on behavior: it strengthens or increases whatever be-havior was displayed immediately before the reward is given. To be most effective, the reward should be delivered as soon as possible after a desirable behavior. Providing an immediate reward is not always convenient or possible; if a reward must be delayed, it will be most effective if the child is reminded of the good behavior that earned the reward. Simply telling why a reward is being given will work well with school-age children, but for younger children (who often think nonverbally) words are not a sufficient reminder. A physical reminder, like showing the child what she did, will be more effective if the child is younger than 5 or 6 years old.

Just as delivering rewards strengthens a behavior, withholding rewards weakens a behavior. By *extinction* (failure or refusal to follow a behavior with reinforcement), undesirable behavior can be decreased or even eliminated. A common practical problem is to find the hidden reward for a behavior (like whining) that persists in spite of no appar-ent reward. If adults unknowingly reward whining (possibly by paying attention to a child who whines), discovering and discontinuing the unintentional reward will greatly reduce the offensive behavior.

Parents and other people who are concerned about the welfare of children often ex-press dismay at the idea of deliberately manipulating children with rewards and punish-ments. This can be a serious moral problem if the child is being manipulated for the exclusive benefit of an adult. But in most cases an adult who uses learning principles to modify a child's behavior has the welfare of the child in mind. The *intent* of an adult who applies these principles ordinarily is no different from the intent of one who employs more traditional child-rearing methods; the main difference is that learning principles, properly used, are more *effective* than less systematic approaches.

Parents are often disturbed by other potential problems with using rewards: a child may become dependent on them and demand more and more, or the child may see through the plan and refuse to be influenced by rewards. These problems arise only if rewards are used inappropriately. Many real-life rewards come not from other people but from the natural environment. A child who fiddles with the latch on the garden gate will be rewarded by unfastening it, and the next time he wants to get out of the yard he will try whatever method he was using just before the gate opened. If a child's environment can be arranged to encourage desirable behaviors and discourage unwanted ones, there is no need for an adult to hand out rewards every minue. It is true that even toddlers, who value their independence, resist blatant, mechanical attempts to control their behavior. Some subtlety is required to make reinforcements seem natural and acceptable to a child.

The word reinforcement often conjures up images of *material rewards,* like candy, money, or toys. Other kinds of reinforcements are likely to be more effective than ma-terial rewards, and people intuitively use them with children without being aware that they are reinforcements. *Social reinforcement,* such as attention, smiling, praise, cuddling, and talking with a child, is probably the most powerful reward for a young child. *Ac-tivities,* such as going to the park, having a friend visit, painting, playing on gym equip-ment, or any other out-of-the-ordinary pastime, are also effective rewards for children.

Social reinforcers and activities are inexpensive, readily available, and easy to provide many times a day. Another type of reinforcer is a *token,* a simple object that has no inherent value but can be traded for a desirable reward. For example, if a father places a check mark on a calendar every day his daughter makes her bed, and they agree in advance that 10 marks will entitle the girl to a movie, then each check mark is a token. Tokens work well in deliberate attempts to influence a specific behavior, but token systems may require more effort (and backup money) than other types of reinforcers and are therefore somewhat limited in usefulness.

There are two important rules to remember when using reinforcements:
1. A reward that is effective with one child will not necessarily appeal to another.
2. A variety of reinforcements is needed to prevent a child from growing tired of just a few. A mother who relied heavily on social reinforcements, especially praise, was caught by surprise when her 5-year-old son demanded, "Stop saying I'm a a good boy!'' The mother could have predicted that praise was not desirable to this boy, because praise was not producing a reinforcement effect; he was rowdy and difficult in spite of praise for occasional good behavior.

It is impossible to reinforce every desirable behavior every time it occurs. Fortunately, learning can proceed with *partial reinforcement* (reinforcement of some but not all instances of a behavior). Partial reinforcement results in slower learning of the behavior, but it also produces slower extinction. If Roger is given a desirable reward every time he puts away a toy, he will soon learn to put away his toys quickly and with little fuss. When an adult stops rewarding picking up, though, Roger will soon stop putting toys away. If, on the other hand, Michael is rewarded sometimes when he picks up his toys but not other times, his picking up will not improve as rapidly as Roger's. But when the rewards stop, Michael will continue to put away his toys much longer than Roger, even without rewards, because he learned with partial reinforcement.

In an ideal situation, a child learns quickly and maintains the behavior long after an adult has stopped dispensing rewards. One way to approach this ideal is to begin by reinforcing the behavior every time it occurs. After it is well learned, gradually decrease the rewards until very few of the desired behaviors are reinforced. Eventually, the behavior may be maintained with no external rewards at all. Reading is usually learned in this fashion. Beginning readers are praised for every correct sound or word, then for every correct sentence, then for a paragraph or story. Years later the learner still reads, often quite well, even though no one delivers praise.

The reader who no longer receives praise probably has developed *intrinsic* (internal) reinforcements for reading. There are many types of intrinsic reward, such as satisfaction of curiosity, feeling happy, or knowing that one is correct. Parents hope that many activities they find rewarding in and of themselves will also become intrinsically rewarding to their children. Sometimes providing *extrinsic* (external) rewards can stifle a child's internal motivation. For example, playing with puzzles is a desirable activity to most preschool children. Even after playing with puzzles once, children like to return to the same puzzles for more play. But children who expect and receive reward (chances to play with other fun toys) the first time they play with the puzzles are less interested in **113**

Elaine M. Ward

Fig. 6-6. Once a behavior is learned, it can be maintained by naturally occurring social reinforcement.

playing with puzzles a second time (Lepper & Greene, 1975). This decrease in interest in puzzles is found only among children who expect an extrinsic reward. The extrinsic reward apparently destroys the intrinsic reward for playing with the puzzles, or in other words, turns play into work. A word of caution, then, in delivering rewards: do not rely on them to the extent that a child's own motivation is stifled. The danger can probably be minimized by using partial reinforcement and nonmaterial rewards.

Sometimes basic learning principles do not seem to work very well. A parent or teacher may reward a certain behavior, only to discover that the behavior does not increase in strength. The rewarded behavior may even stop, and worse, some unpleasant behavior may take its place. This unhappy state of affairs usually results from a misapplication of learning principles. The example in which the mother's praise did not increase her son's good behavior demonstrates that what seems to an adult to be rewarding may not have the same effect on a child. Sometimes the wrong behavior is inadvertently rewarded. A mother who wanted her son to stop sucking his thumb rewarded the child for removing his thumb from his mouth, but thumb sucking actually increased. The mother was requiring the boy to put his thumb *in* his mouth in order to take it out and get a reward (Becker, Englemann, & Thomas, 1971). The mother would have been more successful if she had rewarded the child for *keeping* his thumb out of his mouth rather than for *taking* it out. A more common example of the same problem is a child who misbehaves in spite of considerable punishment. If a child gets little attention for good behavior, bad behavior may increase because of the attention it gains, even though the attention is unpleasant. A 6-year-old boy who received little attention at home or at school for good behavior began to spill paint, hit playmates, and vomit in class, and finally he ran naked during the parents' day program. When the school psychologist was consulted, the problem was quickly solved by instructing teachers to attend to the boy's good behavior.

Punishment

Whenever possible, psychologists recommend rewarding good behaviors rather than punishing bad ones. But sometimes punishment, like bug spray in a vegetable garden, is the most effective way to deal with a difficult situation. Punishment—the application of unpleasant stimuli to weaken a behavior—may be accompanied by at least two problems. Punishment may produce undesirable emotional responses, such as fear, apathy, or a feeling of helplessness. The second problem is that sometimes punishment does not effectively suppress the behavior in question. These problems are most likely to develop if punishment is misused. Often adults deal with misbehavior by "doing what comes naturally," which is whatever was done to them when they were young. This intuitive approach to punishment usually yields poor results because, even though it may make the punishing agent feel better, it does not effectively change the behavior of the misbehaving child.

The following guidelines make punishment more effective in stopping unwanted behavior. Some of these are familiar because they also apply to rewards.

1. Deliver the punishment immediately after the offending act. "Wait till your father comes home," a threat that is seldom followed up, is not nearly as effective in changing behavior as is a punishment given immediately.

2. If the punishment must be delayed, use a reminder (verbal with older children, visual with younger ones) to tell the child the reason for the punishment.

3. Make the relationship between misbehavior and punishment as clear as possible. Consistency helps, and "making the punishment fit the crime" is a good idea in some cases. For example, if a child paints designs on a wall, an appropriate punishment might be cleaning up the mess. This is *not* an eye-for-an-eye principle, however. If a child hurts someone, giving the child the same treatment in return is not advisable.

4. Deliver the punishment in a calm, matter-of-fact manner. Emotional punishments often are too harsh and tend to confuse the child about the reason for the punishment. **115**

The child may think the punishment is for making the parent angry and lose sight of the actual offense committed.

5. Choose a punishment that will be finished quickly. Young children have short memories, and a punishment is no longer useful when the child cannot remember the offending act. In many cases the purpose of a punishment is to convey information that a behavior is unacceptable. Short punishments convey just as much information as long ones. If the punishment is lengthy enough to stop the misbehavior, dragging it out over a longer period does not make it any more effective. One of the few advantages of an occasional spanking is that it lasts only a short time.

6. Use the *mildest* punishment that stops the misbehavior. This principle is often hard to accept because it contradicts common sense. Severe punishment increases the chances of unwanted emotional side effects, and there is evidence that mild punishment is more effective in the long run in helping children internalize society's rules. If a child is harshly punished, the punishment alone is enough to stop the misbehavior, at least while the punishing agent is present. But if a child receives a mild punishment, some mental effort on the child's part may be needed to justify stopping the misbehavior. This mental effort has lasting effects and controls the child's behavior long after the punishment is over. This idea was confirmed by a study in which preschool children were told not to play with an attractive toy, a robot. Children who were given a severe threat when told not to play with the toy were likely to play with it when the adult was later absent. But children who were given only a mild threat did not play with the toy later; in fact, they reported that the robot was no longer as attractive as it had been before (Freedman, 1965). Developing a dislike for the robot is an example of the type of mental effort that is likely to occur after a mild punishment but not after a severe one.

7. Once a punishment has been determined, do not allow the child to escape it by lying, hiding, running away, or any other behavior that merely compounds the crime, or the child may learn to be a con artist but will not learn to change the offensive behavior.

8. Avoid provoking the undesirable response that is to be punished. Pain, for example, often elicits aggression in a reflexive manner. Spanking a child for fighting simply makes the child more likely to fight, either right away or after the punishing agent is out of sight. A more effective way to deal with fighting is to isolate the offender(s) for a short time. Another common example of this problem is hitting a child for crying. Inflicting pain is probably the least effective method of stopping crying.

9. Avoid providing a model of the misbehavior. If the child is to be punished for using foul language, a scolding liberally sprinkled with offensive words will not be very effective. Similarly, it is difficult to justify biting a child for biting someone else.

10. Follow up punishment with rewards for good behavior. A misbehavior will not be effectively eliminated unless the child knows which good behavior is preferred. Telling or showing the child desirable behaviors and rewarding these when they occur helps the child learn new behavior patterns more quickly. Children do not learn by punishments alone.

Punishment, like reward, is in the eye of the beholder. If what seems like a punishment does not have the desired effect, try another approach. I (BGM) learned this the hard way while trying to teach my 3-year-old son to pick up his toys. I introduced a "naughty toy" bag, where toys left out at the end of the day would be imprisoned for a week. Rather than being upset about losing toys, my son thought this was a grand game and purposely left out toys to go in the bag. No longer was there a "naughty boy" in the house, just "naughty toys!" This ineffective punishment was soon eliminated. There is nothing wrong with the basic strategy of impounding toys, which is sometimes very useful. The only problem was that it was too appealing to the child.

Incentives

Curious children sometimes misbehave simply to find out what will happen. An infant who tries to put a finger in an electric socket will probably hear a resounding "No!" from a parent. The child is quite likely to crawl to the next socket and repeat the action, apparently to find out if this one is also forbidden. This sequence may be reenacted at five or six sockets before the child is convinced that he or she has discovered a general rule.

This type of misbehavior can often be avoided by explaining to the child in advance what the consequences of a particular act will be. Telling a child that punishment will follow the act is a *negative incentive*. Negative incentives can be quite effective in preventing a misdemeanor that is likely to occur otherwise. Promising a reward for an act is a *positive incentive*. Positive incentives are most useful for producing good behavior that is unlikely to occur spontaneously. All the rules for using rewards and punishments (variety, reminders, small magnitude, and so on) apply to positive and negative incentives.

People who disapprove of incentives frequently call them threats or bribes and claim they cause more harm than good. Incentives certainly can backfire if not used intelligently. A child actress is rumored to have refused to act in a certain scene unless given $5. The unsuspecting director, thinking $5 a small price for cooperation, willingly paid. The actress gradually increased the stakes until the prices for the last two scenes were $1,000 and a pony. The director had made a terrible mistake in allowing bargaining. To be effective, incentives must be offered with a take-it-or-leave-it attitude.

Critics of incentives also claim that any effects will be only temporary: as soon as the incentive is gone, the behavior returns. This may be true if incentives are misused, but the effects of well-thought-out incentives can be quite lasting. A mother who was about to resort to punishment to stop her preschool child's bedwetting decided, on the advice of her sister, to try bribery first. The mother offered the child a penny for each night the bed stayed dry, plus a three-penny bonus for a dry week. The bedwetting stopped immediately. The bribes continued for 2 weeks. The mother then announced that the child was old enough to keep the bed dry without pennies. The child had established a dry-bed habit during the 2 weeks and no longer needed the incentive.

Like rewards and punishments, incentives are most effective if the promised consequences seem natural and related to the behavior in question. Aware of the principle of incentives but not convinced it would work, I (BSM) tried it on a 4-year-old friend who had the unnerving habit of standing in the front seat of a moving car. On the way to visit the zoo, the child was told that she must sit down in the back seat or I would stop for safety reasons. As usually happens with incentives, the child tested me to see if I meant what I said. After one block the child stood up; I stopped abruptly. The child asked why the car was stopped, and I explained again about safety, sitting, and the incentive (progress toward the zoo). The child sat down for three more blocks, then stood up; I stopped again. The child immediately sat down without question and remained sitting all the way to the zoo. After this incident, the child sat calmly in the back seat whenever she rode in my car. The child's mother was amazed at this change in her daughter's behavior, but she refused to try the incentive technique herself (''Why, that's bribery''!). Needless to say, the child continued to stand in the front seat of her mother's car.

When using incentives, the adult must *always* be willing to carry out the promised consequences. The child is quite likely to test the adult's ability to follow through, and failure to keep the promise will make it impossible for the adult to use incentives with this particular child. Because carrying out the consequences is vital, think a moment before offering an incentive to a child. Avoid promising or threatening something you cannot in good conscience deliver.

Modeling

Because children learn so readily by observation, they will pick up behavior patterns of people around them. A woman who was entertaining overheard her 4-year-old daughter proclaim to her brother in a loud piercing voice, ''Don't do that! I've told you and told you! How many times must I tell you not to do that?''! The embarrassed mother politely apologized to her guests and said she had no idea how her daughter learned to scold like that. The mother then went into the daughter's room and said in a loud piercing voice, ''Don't talk like that! I've told you and told you! How many times must I tell you not to do that?''! There was no doubt in anyone's mind how the child had learned to scold.

Changing life-long habits is difficult for adults, and it is unreasonable to expect parents to set a good example in every realm of behavior. But parents can be aware that their behavior will be imitated. If they model behaviors they do not want to have imitated, parents can at least be forewarned and forearmed with other learning principles to counteract the effects of observational learning. Simply telling the child, ''Do what I say, not what I do'' is not enough; be ready with rewards, incentives, and if necessary punishments to modify the child's behavior.

LIMITATIONS OF LEARNING THEORIES

In spite of the marvels that can result from systematic applications of learning theories, it is a mistake to assume that all behaviors of children are learned in the simple ways described in this chapter. A child is not a blank slate on which experience draws the only marks. There are many examples throughout this book of the importance of genetic predispositions in developing certain types of behavior. Even the ability to learn can be viewed as a genetically inherited potential that allows children to develop behaviors suited for varied situations. Many behaviors can easily be modified by basic learning processes, but others are rather resistant to change resulting from experience. Powerful as learning theories are, they cannot by themselves provide explanations for all human behavior.

SUMMARY

Three basic types of learning—classical conditioning, operant conditioning, and observational learning—are available to a child from the moment of birth. These three learning processes can operate independently, but ordinarily they operate jointly to produce complex patterns of behavior, such as aggression. By using basic learning principles, a parent or teacher can easily and effectively modify a child's behavior. Even behavior problems that seem impossible can often be solved if learning principles are applied in an appropriate, carefully planned, systematic fashion.

REFERENCES

Aronson, E. *The social animal*. San Francisco: W. H. Freeman and Co., Publishers, 1972.

Bandura, A. Influence of model's reinforcement contingencies on the acquisition of imitative responses. *Journal of Personality and Social Psychology*, 1965, **1**, 589-595.

Bandura, A. *Social learning theory*. Morristown, N.J.: General Learning Press, Silver Burdett Co., 1971.

Bandura, A., Grusec, J. E., & Menlove, F. L. Vicarious extinction of avoidance behavior. *Journal of Personality and Social Psychology*, 1967, **5**, 16-23.

Becker, W. C., Engelmann, S., & Thomas, D. R. *Teaching: a course in applied psychology*. Chicago: Science Research Associates, 1971.

Bell, S. B., & Ainsworth, M. D. S. Infant crying and maternal responsiveness. *Child Development*, 1972, **43**, 1171-1190.

Cline, V. B., Croft, R. G., & Courrier, S. Desensitization of children to television violence. *Journal of Personality and Social Psychology*, 1973, **27**, 360-365.

Davitz, J. R. The effects of previous training on post frustration behavior. *Journal of Abnormal and Social Psychology*, 1952, **47**, 309-315.

Etzel, B. C., & Gewirtz, J. L. Experimental modification of caretaker-maintained high-rate operant crying in a 6- and a 20-week-old infant *(Infans tyrannotearus):* extinction of crying with reinforcement of eye contact and smiling. *Journal of Experimental Child Psychology*, 1967, **5**, 303-317.

Freedman, J. L. Long-term behavioral effects of cognitive dissonance. *Journal of Experimental Social Psychology*, 1965, **1**, 145-155.

Gardner, J., & Gardner, H. A note on selective imitation by a 6-week-old infant. *Child Development*, 1970, **41**, 1209-1213.

Ginsburg, H., & Opper, S. *Piaget's theory of intellectual development*. Englewood Cliffs, N.J.: Prentice-Hall, Inc., 1969.

Hanratty, M. A., O'Neal, E., & Sulzer, J. L. The effect of frustration upon imitation of aggression. *Journal of Personality and Social Psychology*, 1972, **21**, 30-34.

Harris, F. R., Johnston, M. K., Kelley, C. S., & Wolf, M. M. Effects of positive social reinforcement on regressed crawling of a nursery school child. *Journal of Educational Psychology*, 1964, **55**, 35-41.

Hartup, W. W. Aggression in childhood: developmental perspectives. *American Psychologist*, 1974, **29**, 336-341.

Hicks, D. J. Imitation and retention of film-mediated aggressive peer and adult models. *Journal of Personality and Social Psychology*, 1965, **2**, 97-100.

Kaye, H. Infant sucking behavior and its modification. (1967) Cited in H. W. Reese & L. P. Lipsitt, *Experimental child psychology*. New York: Academic Press, Inc., 1970.

Lepper, M. R., & Greene, D. Turning work into play: effects of adult surveillance and extrinsic rewards on children's intrinsic motivation. *Journal of Personality and Social Psychology*, 1975, **31**, 479-486.

PART
TWO
══════

Liebert, R. M., and Baron, R. A. Some immediate effects of televised violence on children's behavior. *Developmental Psychology,* 1972, **6,** 469-475.

Osbourne, D., and Endsley, R. Emotional reactions of young children to television violence. *Child Development,* 1971, **42,** 321-331.

Reese, H. W., and Lipsitt, L. P. *Experimental Child Psychology.* New York: Academic Press, Inc., 1970.

Siqueland, E. R. Two experimental procedures for the analyses of learning processes in human infants. (1966) Cited in H. W. Reese & L. P. Lipsitt, *Experimental child psychology.* New York: Academic Press, Inc., 1970.

Smith, P. K., & Green, M. Aggressive behavior in English nurseries and play groups: sex differences and response of adults. *Child Development,* 1975, **46,** 211-214.

Sprofkin, J. N., Liebert, R. M., & Poulos, R. W. Effects of a prosocial televised example on children's helping. *Journal of Experimental Child Psychology,* 1975, **20,** 119-126.

Stein, A. H., and Friedrich, L. K. Television content and young children's behavior. (1972) Cited in R. M. Liebert, J. M. Neale, & E. S. Davidson, *The early window.* Elmsford, N.Y.: Pergamon Press, Inc., 1973.

Steuer, F. B., Applefield, J. M., and Smith, R. Televised aggression and the interpersonal aggression of preschool children. *Journal of Experimental Child Psychology,* 1971, **11,** 442-447.

Wahler, R. G. Infant social attachments: a reinforcement theory interpretation and investigation. *Child Development,* 1967, **4,** 1079-1088.

Watson, J. B., and Rayner, R. Conditioned emotional reactions. *Journal of Experimental Psychology,* 1920, **3,** 1-14.

Witryol, S. L. Incentives and learning in children. In H. W. Reese (Ed.), *Advances in child development and behavior* (Vol. 6). New York: Academic Press, Inc., 1971, pp. 2-62.

Televised aggression and the interpersonal aggression of preschool children

Faye B. Steuer
James M. Applefield
Rodney Smith
University of North Carolina at Chapel Hill

Two matched groups of five preschool children each were exposed to either aggressive or nonaggressive television programs for a total of approximately 110 min over a period of 11 days. Interpersonal aggressive behavior immediately following viewing was recorded and compared with the same type of behavior during a prior 10-day baseline period. Ss who viewed aggressive television programs showed significantly greater increases in interpersonal aggression from baseline to treatment than did Ss who viewed nonaggressive programs. Results extended the generality of the previous finding that children's noninterpersonal aggressive behavior increased subsequent to viewing filmed aggression.

A number of investigations have demonstrated that children's aggressive behavior toward inanimate objects increases following exposure to filmed or televised aggression (e.g., Bandura, Ross, & Ross, 1963a,b; Hicks, 1965; Madsen, 1968; Walters & Willows, 1968). In these studies, the measurement of a child's aggressive behavior was made while the child played alone, offering the investigator no opportunity to assess the extent to which interpersonal aggressive behavior might have been influenced by the film. In very few instances has there been an attempt to determine the effect of filmed aggression on children's aggressive behavior toward other human beings.

Siegel (1956) observed children playing in pairs after exposure to an aggressive cartoon, but she did not distinguish between the interpersonal and noninterpersonal aggressive behavior of her subjects. More recently, Hanratty, Liebert, Morris, and Fernandez (1969), after exposing children to a model who aggressed against an adult human clown, observed the children playing with the toy clown or with an adult dressed as a clown. Children directed more aggression toward the doll than toward the human clown, although the human was assaulted by some of the children who had seen the film.

There is, then, very little evidence to indicate whether, if normal children are exposed to filmed or televised hostility, they will in fact be affected to the extent that they increase aggressive behavior against other persons. The present study was designed to determine whether the interpersonal aggressive behavior of preschool children would be increased by exposure to children's television programs which had been judged to be aggressive. To simulate natural play conditions, observation and measurement of aggression took place as subjects played together in small groups with minimum adult supervision.

METHOD
Subjects

*S*s were 10 preschool children at the Frank Porter Graham Child Development Center in Chapel Hill, North Carolina. The mean age of the sample was 51 months (range: 41-60 months). The

From *Journal of Experimental Child Psychology*, 1971, **11**, 442-447.

group was mixed racially and socioeconomically, and there were equal numbers of boys and girls, all of whom knew each other before the study began.

Experimental and control groups were composed of Ss matched for amount of time spent watching television in the home. Viewing time was determined by a questionnaire answered by parents several weeks in advance of the beginning of the experiment. The Ss were ranked on this measure, and for each successive pair of ranks (1 and 2, 3 and 4, etc.) one member was assigned to the experimental group and the other member to the control group.

Procedure

Experimental sessions of 10 min duration were held daily, 5 days a week. During a session, the two five-children groups played concurrently in separate experimental rooms, each of which was the mirror image of the other. The rooms, measuring 9 × 9 ft, were separated by an observa-

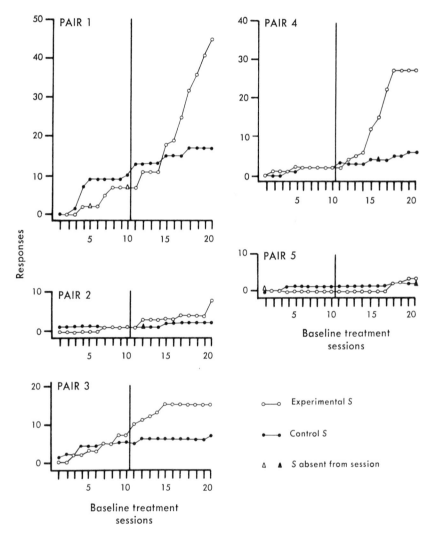

122 Cumulative frequency of physical interpersonal aggressive responses for five pairs of matched Ss.

tion booth with two one-way mirrors, one providing visual access to each room. Two observers (one at each one-way mirror) and a time keeper occupied the observation booth. Observers were systematically alternated from one group to the other. One adult male accompanied each group of children, but sat with his back to the room and did not participate in the play. Each adult remained with the experimental group one day and with the control group the next day throughout the experiment.

Experimental rooms contained the following toys: an inflated plastic punch-me doll, two wooden puzzles, six large cardboard blocks, two tow trucks, two plates, two cups and saucers, two spoons, a rubber knife, a plastic gun, a cowboy hat, a large cardboard carton, two plastic animals, a pail and shovel, and two bed pillows. At the start of each session, the toys were placed in predetermined standard positions about the room. The positioning in one room mirrored that in the other.

Each S was observed for a total of 2 min during a session—one of these minutes occurring during the first half of the session, one during the second half. Order of observation within each half session was randomly varied across sessions. A minute of observation was divided into twelve 5-sec intervals and, for each interval, an observer (O) noted the occurrence or nonoccurrence of physical interpersonal aggression displayed by the child he was observing.

Four basic patterns of behavior were designated as physical interpersonal aggression, namely: (a) Hitting or pushing another person with the hands or arms or with an object held in the hand; (b) Kicking another child; (c) Gross manipulative bodily contact with another person, which may include squeezing, choking, or holding down. (These behaviors were scored as aggressive only when resistance was evidenced by the recipient of the action.) (d) Throwing an object at another person from a distance of at least 1 ft. (This behavior was distinguished from throwing an object to another person.) The occurrence of one or more of these aggressive behaviors during an interval added one point to an S's aggression score. Thus an S's possible score for one session could range from 0 to 24.

The reliability of eight undergraduate volunteers who acted as Os was determined during fifty 1-min observations period prior to the experiment. Each observer was present for at least 10 of the periods. Os' aggression tallies were compared with the tallies recorded by a standard observer (one of the authors). The Pearson product-moment correlation between the two sets of scores was .84. Computations were based only on occurrences of aggressive responding.

The first 10 sessions of the experiment constituted a baseline measure of physical interpersonal aggression during unstructured play. For the next 11 sessions, each group viewed a videotaped television program of approximately 10 min duration immediately prior to free play. Viewing took place in the experimental room. The experimental group was always exposed to programs judged to be aggressive, while the control group always viewed nonaggressive programs. Os, who had been told that each group of children was viewing a random sequence of aggressive and non-aggressive films, entered the observation booth following the completion of the television programs.

Television materials were selected from Saturday morning children's program offerings. They featured various human and animated cartoon characters, with a preponderance of cartoons. Commercial messages were eliminated from the tapes. Programs were videotaped in black and white, with sound, using a Sony video tape recorder, Model CV2000 and were presented on a Sony monitor, Model CVM 2300U. The program segments ranged in length from 8 min 20 sec to 11 min 45 sec. All tapes were prescored according to the aggression measure used for the Ss' behaviors. Tape segments with more than 15 such responses were used as the aggressive television stimuli. The aggression scores on these tapes ranged from 15 to 32 with a mean of 22. Nonaggressive tapes were edited to contain no aggressive responses.

RESULTS

Examination of the cumulative aggression scores of individual pairs of matched Ss (Fig. 1) reveals that, while no pair's scores differed by more than three points at the end of the baseline **123** sessions, differences as great as 28 points were observed by the end of the 11 treatment sessions. All of the latter differences favored the S in the experimental group, although in one case the difference was only one point.

The shift in each S's mean daily aggression score from baseline to treatment condition is presented in Table 1. A positive score indicates an increase in physical interpersonal aggression; a negative score indicates a decrease. A t test for the difference between matched pairs (Hays, 1963) revealed that the experimental group showed significantly larger increases in aggression than the control group ($t = 2.34$, $df = 4$, $p < .05$, one tailed). The one-tailed test was used because an increase in aggression would be expected, based on results obtained with children playing alone.

Table 1. Difference in mean interpersonal aggression score between baseline and treatment sessions

Pair	Experimental S	Control S
1	2.57	−.36
2	.54	.00
3	.03	−.41
4	2.07	.20
5	.27	.00
Mean	1.10	−.11

DISCUSSION

A considerable degree of order can be noted in the data. During baseline observations, matched subjects showed a marked tendency to keep pace with one another in terms of the amounts of interpersonal aggression they displayed. Following the introduction of television episodes, the cumulative scores diverged, most dramatically in the cases of pairs 1, 3, and 4.

The regularity with which subjects in the aggressive treatment group emerged as more aggressive than their matched counterparts suggests that the television treatment influenced the change. It is possible, however, that one or two subjects were influenced directly by the television manipulation and that other subjects began to display more hostility in retaliation, independently of the television stimuli. The fact that some subjects began to increase their aggression scores above the baseline rate only late in the treatment portion of the experiment, suggests that this might have been the case. An alternative explanation is that these children took longer to respond to the influence of the television materials than the others.

The conditions of this study may be said to simulate the natural television-viewing and play situations of preschool children more closely than the conditions of other studies cited. Despite differences in the stimuli used and types of aggressive behaviors recorded, results of this study were substantially like those of previous investigations. Network children's programs were shown to affect the interpersonal aggressive behavior of preschool children in much the same way that films depicting aggressive behavior affected children's solitary play. The extent of the generality of these findings remains an important question, both within the preschool age group and across ages.

REFERENCES

Bandura, A., Ross, D., & Ross, S. Imitation of film-mediated aggressive models. *Journal of Abnormal and Social Psychology,* 1963, **66,** 3-11. (a)

Bandura, A., Ross, D., & Ross, S. Vicarious reinforcement and imitative learning. *Journal of Abnormal and Social Psychology,* 1963, **67,** 601-607. (b)

Hanratty, M. A., Liebert, R. M., Morris, L. W., & Fernandez, L. E. Imitation of film-mediated aggression against live and inanimate victims. *Proceedings of the 77th Annual Convention of the American Psychological Association,* 1969, **4**(Pt. 1), 457-458.

Hays, W. L. *Statistics for psychologists*. New York: Holt, Rinehart and Winston, 1963.

Hicks, D. J. Imitation and retention of film-mediated aggressive peer and adult models. *Journal of Personality and Social Psychology*, 1965, **2**, 97-100.

Madsen, C., Jr. Nurturance and modeling in pre-schoolers. *Child Development*, 1968, **39**, 221-236.

Siegel, A. E. Film-mediated fantasy aggression and strength of aggressive drive. *Child Development*, 1956, **27**, 365-378.

Walters, R. J., & Willows, D. C. Imitative behavior of disturbed and nondisturbed children following exposure to aggressive and nonaggressive models. *Child Development*, 1968, **39**, 79-89.

Chapter 7

Developing language

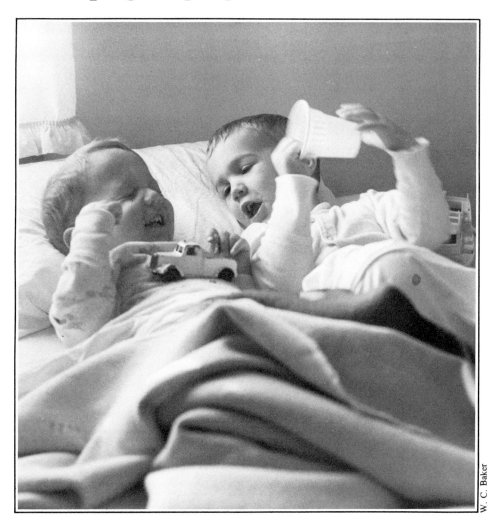

W. C. Baker

One of the most remarkable developments of early childhood is the acquisition of language. The child progresses rapidly from an infant whose major vocal activities include crying and cooing to a preschooler able to report in detail the many wonderful prizes contained in various boxes of cereal. Specifically, between the ages of 18 months and 3 years, most children master the basic structures of language, which allow them to communicate with others more or less efficiently. Before considering the details of this process, it is important to understand what is meant by the terms language and speech and to become aware of the complexity of language so that we can fully appreciate how remarkable the acquisition of language really is.

Language is a system of communication used by a group of people who share a large number of common responses. This system allows the members of the group to communicate with each other. Speech is the overt physical expression of language as an auditory signal. Having a system of communication (language) and a process through which the communication is exchanged (speech) allows individuals to efficiently convey information to other individuals. The relationship of language and speech is expressed in the basic task of language acquisition. The child must learn to relate sound and meaning.

This task is not as simple as learning vocabulary by rote because human language is highly complex. There are very few one-to-one relationships between particular sounds and a particular meaning, such as there is in some animal communication systems. For example, a sound described as a shrill bark is used by rhesus monkeys to express alarm and nothing else, while in human languages the same sound may express several meanings.

The complexities of language make language acquisition a difficult task. Even if a child has paired sound and meaning successfully or learned specific vocabulary items, meaning is also expressed in word order. The sentence "John hit Mary" does not express the same meaning as the same three words in the order "Mary hit John." A further complexity occurs with ambiguous sentences, where the same set of words may have several meanings. Consider the sentence "The shooting of the hunters was terrible." This might mean that the hunters came home without any game because all their shots went wild, or it could mean that the hunters themselves were victims of a hunting accident (possibly the result of wild shots from other terrible hunters). It is also possible to see this sentence as a negative opinion of hunting in general.

A third complexity of language is that the same meaning may be expressed by several different sound patterns. "John threw the ball" means the same as "The ball was thrown by John." Add to these problems the observations that an educated person may have a vocabulary of over 100,000 different words or that a typical student hears 100,000 words a day (Carroll, 1964) and it should become apparent that the task of acquiring language is a staggering prospect for an 18-month-old child.

Yet unless the child is severely retarded or suffers from a brain disorder or severe mental disturbance, all children acquire language, largely through their own efforts and without elaborate teaching programs such as those for reading. (An interesting observation is that not all children learn to read.) Furthermore, in the process of acquiring language most children go through similar steps or stages at about the same rate, so much so that these stages are generally accepted and well described.

STAGES OF LANGUAGE ACQUISITION
Crying and cooing

The earliest vocal behavior of infants is crying. Crying patterns in children change with age but persist as a distinct form of vocalization throughout development. It appears that during crying the child's vocal apparatus is relatively tense and rigid. These characteristics are very different from the flexibility of the vocal apparatus during speech. It is not generally believed that crying is part of the language development pattern, although through crying an infant can effectively communicate a need state to a parent.

A second form of vocalization develops around the sixth to eighth week of life. This type of vocalization is referred to as cooing. During cooing there is more flexibility in the vocal apparatus than there is in crying, and there appear to be relatively imprecise tongue movements not found in crying. Cooing frequently follows smiling and can be easily obtained from the infant during the third month of life. Toward the sixth month cooing sounds become more varied and it is at this point that the babbling stage of language begins.

Babbling

Babbling is characterized by short strings of relatively varied and distinct sounds accompanied by tonal variations (intonation patterns). Intonation patterns are tone variations of speech that add information and meaning to speech. For example, questions have a different intonation pattern than commands. In questions the voice rises at the end of the utterance. In addition to adding meaning to speech in this manner, intonation patterns help group meaningful sections of speech together by giving indications of the beginnings and ends of the groups. Intonation patterns are most easily detected if you listen to someone fluently speaking a foreign language. Since meaning is removed because you do not understand the words, it is easy to listen to just the sound pattern of the speech as the voice rises and falls. In a way, an infant's babbling sounds like a foreign language.

The babbling period generally begins when the infant is about 6 months old and lasts until approximately the end of the first year. During this period the child frequently vocalizes short strings of varied sounds accompanied by distinct intonation patterns. The babbling vocalizations are different from the cooing sounds in that the sounds are no longer continuous but are broken up into syllables. Syllables require not only the open vowel sounds that make up cooing but also the presence of consonants. The majority of speech sounds are consonants, which are different from vowels in that in the production of consonants the passage of air through the vocal apparatus is interrupted in some manner. This interruption requires coordination and more control of the tongue and lips than the production of vowel sounds does.

One of the child's earliest words is frequently papa or dada. This should not be surprising if one carefully examines the relationship of babbling and speech and the production of speech sounds. First of all, babbling is unstructured vocalization. The child utters many and varied sounds, without any apparent direct attempt to produce specific strings of sounds. It may be that the child produces more difficult or exotic speech sounds during babbling because the tongue, already in an unusual position, moves erratically to another difficult position. Speech requires structure. To produce a word, the child must utter specific sounds in a specific order. This requires organization and control. The consonant *p* is produced in the very front of the mouth, with the lips completely closed and the flow of air through the mouth completely stopped. The vowel sound *ah* is produced in a very different fashion. The sound is produced by a completely open, rounded throat and mouth. These two sounds are extremely different, and this maximum contrast should be easy for the child to intentionally produce (just as it should be easier for a child to learn the difference between a sharply contrasting pair of white and black blocks than between a yellow-orange and an orange block).

Incidentally, mothers frequently lament that their babies say papa before they say mama. To produce an *m,* the air flow must be channeled through the nose rather than the mouth. This requires movement of the velum in the back of the throat, which is not necessary in producing a *p.*

In summary, the babbling period starts when the infant is approximately 6 months of age and ends at about 1 year. During this period vocal activity is very frequent and the range of sounds produced is extensive. As the first words or intentional utterances begin to be produced, the overall frequency of vocalizations drops and the range of sounds produced is narrowed as the child concentrates on producing specific sound patterns or words.

First words

Somewhere around 1 year of age the child begins to produce isolated words. Parents readily identify these productions as communication and along with most psychologists reject the suggestion that the child is simply naming or labeling objects.

There are several indications that the child is expressing meaning with these early words. The same word may be uttered with different intonation patterns on different occasions. An excitedly squealed "Daddy" might be used to welcome the father back home and be taken as an indication that the child is pleased to see daddy. On another instance "Daddy" might be spoken defiantly or angrily as daddy attempts to carry the child off to bed. Along with these variations in sound patterns the situations in which the words occur make it obvious that the child is making a comment. Also, these single words often are accompanied by actions or gestures that help convey the child's message.

This period of language acquisition is often referred to as the period of holophrastic speech. The single word utterances are called holophrases and are believed to be an expression of a whole thought or message. In other words, a holophrase is an attempt by the child to express a *whole phrase* in a single word. It is believed that children's limited speech capacity restricts them to producing only one word at a time. This belief is strengthened by the fact that during this period the child may be able to utter quite a few words, yet it will be months before he or she attempts to combine them into two-word phrases. My (BGM) son provides a typical example. By around his first birthday he frequently produced a wide range of isolated words; however, it was not until just before he was 14 months that he first combined two of them and said "Plane bye-bye." When this combining begins to occur, generally during the first half of the second year, the child

enters the next stage of language acquisition, sometimes referred to as the period of telegraphic speech.

First sentences

The short two- or three-word utterances of children at this stage resemble telegrams.
Again it appears that the child's capabilities severely restrict the length of productions.
However, the child is very efficient at conveying meaning in this fashion. Almost no
one would misinterpret the message when a child says "Doughnut Mommy."

Children generally express the basic information-bearing words of the message and
omit the less informative words, such as articles, prepositions, and conjunctions. The
most frequent sentence relations expressed in these early speech strings are subjects,
verbs, and objects, with the verbs being the least frequent (McNeill, 1970).

Psychologists have studied these early speech strings in great detail. Their interest
in telegraphic speech centers on the way children structure these strings. Specifically,
researchers are interested in the types of sentence relations children are likely to express
and how frequently they use each type, such as the subject, object, and verb difference
just described.

Researchers are also interested in how children combine or order their speech strings.
They want to know whether a child combines words in a consistent fashion and whether
most children behave in a similar manner. To answer questions such as these and others,
researchers typically make periodic visits to the homes of young children and tape record
their speech over a short period of time. From these recordings a written data sheet, or
corpus, of the child's speech is developed. An example of a corpus is presented below.
Note that this research is an example of the naturalistic method described in Chapter 1.

CORPUS MATERIAL: JONATHAN; AGE, 28 MONTHS

Exchange between Jonathan and his mother while they are looking at a picture book:
Mother: It's a little man.
Jon: He's a big man.
M: He's a big man?
J: Yes.
M: Oh. He has a beard.
J: He's a monster.
M: He's not a monster, he's just a little man.
J: He's got a beard.
M: Uhum.
J: He's got a hat.
M: He's got a nice hat. Let's see what else we have here.
J: He's hiding.
M: He's hiding. Oh. He's hiding over there.
J: He a bear.
M: Does that look like a bear?
J: Yes.
M: Oh! Look at that; that's neat.
J: That's the bear?
M: That's the zoo. I'll take you to the zoo someday. OK?

J: I like that fox.

M: Yeah, That's the fox. He's going to the zoo. What's in the zoo there?

J: Some monkeys. Some bears.

M: Yeah, Some monkeys and some bears. What else?

J: Some elephants.

M: Is that an elephant?

J: Yes. It's in there.

M: What is he?

J: He's oh oh.

M: Is he an elephant?

J: Yes, he too old.

M: He's a too old, huh? What's that?

J: That an Indian.

M: What is? It's not an Indian. Look at that. That's a giraffe.

J: I like giraffes.

M: Where have you seen a giraffe? At the toy store?

J: Yes.

M: You remember seeing the giraffe at the toy store?

J: Yeah.

M: Uhum.

J: I want giraffe.

Fig. 7-1. By the time children are 3 years old, they have mastered the basic structures of language necessary for efficient communication.

131

By studying these records of children's speech, researchers hope to learn not only what young children say but, more important, how they arrive at such unique expressions as "Walking street," which is a child's comment on seeing a man walking up the street (Bloom, Lightbrown, & Hood, 1975). It is thought that understanding children's early speech production will tell us more about their cognitive (mental) capacities and give us a better understanding of the learning process. Recall that programs designed to teach reading are not nearly as efficient as children's independent language learning.

After children begin combining words they quickly expand their sentence strings. By the time most children are 3 years old they have mastered the basic structures of language and can express themselves in a satisfactory fashion. Much learning and refining occurs throughout early childhood, such as learning to use negation properly and how to rearrange sentences to express questions or passive relationships, but the basic language structure is generally mastered before children begin school.

LANGUAGE AND MATURATION

Almost every child learning to speak any language follows this general sequence of stages. This universality of sequencing indicates that maturation plays a large role in the child's early language behavior. Specifically, if a behavior is closely tied to maturation, that behavior develops in a regular sequence closely related to age, while environmental stimulation in regard to that behavior remains constant. In this case adults have been speaking to the child since birth. It is apparent that the onset of speech is related to changes within the child.

Language begins regularly when the child is around 18 months of age. A great many environmental factors, such as siblings, the social class of the family, whether the parents are deaf, or the language the child is exposed to, seem to have no effect on the time the child begins to speak. It also seems that the beginning of language occurs relatively independent of any particular need to speak. Most toddlers are able to make their needs known through actions or cries, yet they soon abandon these techniques in favor of speech. Because of these facts and others, there is an interest in the changing capabilities of the child that may be related to the beginning of speech. The most important source of these changes may be in the child's brain.

Lenneberg (1967) discusses in detail changes in the maturation of the brain and relates these to behavorial milestones. While it is believed that the number of cells in the brain does not increase after birth, the brain grows in a number of ways. For instance, the infant's brain cells are relatively isolated in the sense that there are very few connecting branches between them. During the growth of the brain the number of connecting branches (axons and dendrites) increases dramatically. Other changes in the brain include changes in brain weight, changes in the chemical composition of the brain tissues, and changes in the rhythm of brain waves. Using these changes in comparison with the state of the mature brain, Lenneberg calculates the percentage of the brain's maturity that has been reached when a behavioral milestone occurs. The approximate brain maturity is 50% when the child begins sitting regularly and is slightly above 60% when he or she begins walking. Telegraphic speech occurs when the brain reaches close to 70% maturity, and language is fully established by the time the brain's maturity reaches 85% (Lenneberg, 1967).

While these figures offer no explanation as to why these behaviors emerge at a particular time, they do indicate that the brain itself is well developed by the time the child is capable of using language.

Lenneberg argues very strongly that there is a critical period for the acquisition of language. Recall that a critical period is a time, before and after which the establishment of a behavior is impossible or at best extremely difficult. Lenneberg states that language learning apparently must take place between the ages of 2 and 13 years. This belief is the result of studying the effect of brain injuries at different stages of development as well as the effect of hearing losses at different ages.

Specifically, in most people the left hemisphere of the cerebral cortex is the dominant hemisphere and is most directly involved in language behavior. Lenneberg, in summarizing data on injuries to the left or right hemispheres of the cerebral cortex, concludes that early in development (the first 2 years) both hemispheres may be involved in the function of speech. If the left hemisphere is injured, the right hemisphere takes on the function of speech; however, once the left hemisphere has established control over the speech function, shift of the function to the right side is prevented even if the left hemisphere is injured and cannot control the function. By puberty, lateralization (establishment of specific functions in one or the other of the cerebral hemispheres) is complete. This means that the minor hemisphere no longer has the ability to acquire the function of the major hemisphere.

It is interesting to note here that during early childhood, one may readily acquire a second language (become bilingual) simply by being exposed to two languages. When the child grows older the acquisition of a second language can be accomplished only through conscious effort and directed study. Often when a second language is learned through conscious effort it is spoken with a foreign accent, while this is not the case of a second language acquired very early in life. From such information, Lenneberg has concluded that language acquisition is a process closely related to the maturation of the brain and, further, that language acquisition may not be possible once the brain has reached maturity.

Now that the process of language development has been described and we have briefly examined the maturational characteristics of language acquisition, it is possible to explore the question of how children acquire language.

THEORIES OF LANGUAGE ACQUISITION

Although many researchers are interested in how children acquire language, there are surprisingly few answers. The question is of great interest because of the remarkable facility shown by children acquiring this complex behavior. However, the question proves to be a difficult one to answer.

Although there are many approaches to this problem, two major theories of language acquisition are well defined, defended, and researched. One major theory expresses a belief that language acquisition can be explained on the basis of simple learning prin-   **133** ciples. The child acquires language through the formation of associations between words or between words and objects (or events) through the application of reinforcement. These associations are then strengthened by practice or repetition, and new responses (words or sentences) are acquired through imitation. This viewpoint relies heavily on environmental control for explanation of the development of language patterns. This viewpoint is referred to as the learning theory.

The second major point of view expresses a general belief that language is too complex and a child's use of language is too creative to be explained solely on the basis of learning principles, such as reinforcement, repetition, or imitation. It is believed that the child has an innate predisposition, or tendency, to learn language. In other words, something within the child directs or facilitates development of language. Briefly stated, this point of view holds that a child acquires language by listening to the speech around him or her and noting regularities. From these regularities the child forms hypotheses about speech, which are then tested or tried out. This theoretical viewpoint is referred to as a psycholinguistic theory.

In a very basic fashion, it is possible to say that essentially the learning theory viewpoint describes language acquisition as the acquiring of specific responses (words or sentence patterns), while the psycholinguistic viewpoint sees language acquisition as the acquisition of rules for the use of these responses. You might think of the two processes as complementary parts of a more general behavior. For example, when you learned to multiply, you first had to learn specific responses, such as $2 \times 6 = 12$. You probably never learned the specific response $341 \times 89 = 30,349$. Yet, since you have learned the rules of multiplication, you can easily find the answer. Language acquisition very likely involves both types of learning: specific responses and rules for use. Now look at both theories in detail.

Learning theory

Those theorists who study language development with an emphasis on learning rely heavily on the child's speech environment to help explain the language acquisition process. One major criticism that is often aimed at their work is that basic learning principles may be too simple to handle a behavior as complex as language. Further, the learning viewpoint emphasizes the importance of the establishment of an association between the verbal behavior and some reinforcement. With this requirement it is difficult to explain how the child acquires a new word or new combination of words.

One of the best known workers in the learning area of language is B. F. Skinner. In his book *Verbal Behavior* (1957), Skinner answers this criticism. He says that verbal behavior can be under the control of more than one aspect or variable of the environment. Since this is so, it is possible that variation in control may appear. When this happens, portions of verbal behavior may recombine, producing new combinations. This, in effect, gives the impression of a novel response.

There is also another way that learning theories account for the acquisition of new forms of speech. Skinner (1957) and Staats and Staats (1963) discuss the development of units. Staats and Staats talk about units on the speech sound level, while Skinner talks about units on the word level. At the word level a child may have already acquired a string of associated words in the form of a simple sentence. Examples might be "I saw a clown" or "I saw a pony." The phrase "I saw a . . . " begins to function as a unit because it has been associated in the same reinforcement situations. Therefore, in a similar situation a child may be observed to say "I saw a monkey." In this case there is a new combination.

Staats and Staats use the unit concept in much the same way, although they talk about speech sounds. A child who already has the various sound responses under control can combine them in new words much easier than if he or she had to start from the beginning.

Both the work of Skinner and that of Staats and Staats treat the acquisition of speech and language very similarly. Neither spends any time discussing the role of maturation in language development. Staats and Staats dispense with maturation as unnecessary for discussion because of the results of learning experiments that show that infant verbal behavior can be brought under environmental control. Rheingold, Gewirtz, and Ross (1963) studied the verbal behavior (crying or cooing) of a 3-month-old child. After 2 days of observation to establish the normal level of verbal behavior in the infant, the infant was reinforced for all verbal behavior by an experimenter who smiled, made soothing noises, and touched the infant when the child vocalized. This went on for two daily sessions, after which there was a day with no reinforcement. There was an increase of 86% more verbal behavior from the infant on the reinforcement days over the observation days. Staats and Staats see this type of experiment as indicating the strong effect of environment on the development of verbal behavior. The fact that learning can take place so early indicates to Staats and Staats the weakness of maturational variables in accounting for the development of verbal behavior.

To learning theorists, language development is seen as a continuous process making use of the same learning principles throughout the entire developmental period. The complex verbal behavior of the adult grows from the basic primitive speech sounds of the infant. This most primitive vocal behavior (crying) is seen by Skinner as an unlearned response of the infant. Crying is a function of deprivation and aversive stimulation. When crying brings parental attention, which is reinforcing, crying is no longer a reflexive response but is verbal behavior.

Staats and Staats also explain the development of verbal behavior from crying. They say that parents' voices acquire reinforcing power by association with positive reinforcement to the child. A simple and unfortunate example is that a child cries when stuck with a diaper pin (an aversive stimulus). The parent comes to see what is making the baby cry. While the pin is being removed, the parent talks to the baby. The parent's voice is then associated with the halting of aversive stimulation. When the baby makes a sound similar to the parent's sounds, the baby is reinforced in the same manner as when the aversive stimulation was removed.

Skinner adds that the vocal production of the child does not have to be exactly like that of the adult. The self-reinforcement may be the result of a part of the speech, such as similar intonation patterns. An important point to note here is that the child needs auditory stimulation for his own vocal behavior to become self-reinforcing.

According to these theories verbal behavior must occur before it can be reinforced. Once the verbal behavior occurs, the parents may help the child develop language. Early language develops primarily through shaping. The child utters sounds over a wide range. From this wide range of sounds a few get reinforcement because they are more similar to the sounds used in the parents' speech. The greater the amount of reinforcement, the more likely that speech sounds will be repeated and become more and more like the sounds of adults.

The change from similar sounds to first words is a result of the same type of differential reinforcement. Staats and Staats point out that once a child utters a word, the probability of doing so again is greatly enhanced because of the sheer amount of reinforcement those early words quickly receive.

This same idea explains how a child develops an incorrect form of a word, such as "wata," to the correct form "water." As long as "wata" brings reinforcement, it is not likely to change. However, if the child asks a neighbor for "wata" and the neighbor does not understand, the form is likely to change. When the child produces "water," reinforcement should be more general and faster.

Staats and Staats take the development of language from the use of single words to strings of words. If two or more words occur together under conditions of reinforcement, their association is strengthened to the point where one stimulus will call them all out. They then tend to function in chains, each one eliciting (calling out) the following word. Word chains can even develop vicariously from the child's listening to someone else.

Some people disagree with the points made by Staats and Staats. Denes (1966) is bothered by the idea that a child matches a model's speech and indirectly by the idea of vicarious learning from listening to someone else's speech. Denes states that the child's vocal mechanism is not enough like an adult's at this early age, so the child can never precisely match a model's sounds. Second, he finds it hard to believe that a child can learn from listening to the speech of others. In connected speech, there is little if any separation between sounds. He questions how the child learns to segment the speech signal before the concept of a word is acquired. To illustrate this problem, ask someone who speaks another language fluently to describe the location of his or her home in the other language. While the description is being given, try to count the words or sentences your friend uses. It should prove extremely difficult.

In addition to the methods of discrimination, where a general verbal form is differentially reinforced until it is a precise response ("wata" to "water"), and generalization, where a response is under the control of a wider range of similar situations (a child learns that home can refer to many different types of places where people live), Skinner lists more ways in which speech develops into a complex language system. New forms may develop where two or more forms have the same strength at the same time. For example, a child looking at a doll may say "pretty doll" and "new dress," since the doll looks pretty and has a new dress. The same situation evokes both responses and they are at the same strength. It is quite possible for the child to then say "pretty dress," which in effect is a new utterance formed from two others.

Forms may also deteriorate because precise reinforcement controls are relaxed, as

Elaine M. Ward

Fig. 7-2. Theorists who see the process of language acquisition as the result of simple learning principles would consider these children's play with telephones an example of strengthening language skills through practice and repetition.

when formal education ends and the child resumes saying ''Balmore'' instead of the ''Baltimore'' that the teacher insisted on. Forms may be elaborated when they deteriorate to the point where they are no longer distinguishable from other forms, thereby preventing proper reinforcement, such as the child who says ''yeah'' and ''naw'' in so much the same fashion that it is impossible to tell whether an answer is an agreement or disagreement. This child may soon be observed saying ''yes'' and ''no.'' Language becomes more abstract to the point where there is autoclitic behavior. Here words become reinforcing for other words. (Perhaps a good example is professors who love to hear themselves talk.)

This briefly is how the learning theorists look at language development. Change is determined from the environment by differential reinforcement. What the developing child brings to the learning situation is taken for granted. With a little thought, however, one can see how the maturation of the child could be related to this framework. As children mature and become more mobile, they are exposed to different situations (e.g., the child who modified ''wata'' because the neighbor did not reinforce that form). Also as children mature, they will probably be able to match more precisely the speech that models offer. They will be exposed to more situations, varying stimuli, and more reinforcing situations.

Psycholinguistic theory

The psycholinguistic theory of language development is best expressed by discussing the work of David McNeill (1970). McNeill discusses innate (unlearned) capabilities of the child that are necessary to acquire and develop language. Much of McNeill's general theoretical orientation stems from the work in linguistics by Noam Chomsky. McNeill bases much of his theory on the observation of small samples of children, which he

137

justifies by saying that the regularities in child samples from widely varying backgrounds indicate their universality and that therefore larger samples are not needed. Samples included English, Russian, and Japanese children.

By studying children from several language communities McNeill is able to broaden the statement of regularities in language development. Regardless of the language learned or the environment in which it is learned, all normal children speak a first word between 10 and 12 months of age and combine words between 18 and 20 months. McNeill's overall theory of language development rests on a principle of interaction between physical maturation and environmental learning. He spends much time relating what the child produces to what the child hears. His point, however, is that what the child produces is not learned entirely from what is heard. McNeill's theory attempts to explain what a child does with the language input (what is heard) to produce a particular output (what is said). The child's task is to draw some regularities from the language bombarding him or her. Further, what the child hears is in no way systematic or for that matter even grammatical.

McNeill believes that, whatever the internal capabilities of the child, they are such that any language can be acquired. In discussing how language is acquired McNeill uses Chomsky's idea that language exists on two levels, the deep structure level and the surface structure level. Briefly, the idea of deep structure is that it contains universal principles of language and is related to meaning. Supposedly, the deep structure of language is part of the "unaware" knowledge a fluent speaker has of language. The surface structure is related to the speech sounds of language. It is from the surface structure that the child must discover the regularities that underlie language. McNeill indicates that language is acquired when the child discovers the relationships that exist between the surface structure of sentences and the deep structure.

In addition to deep structure and surface structure, Chomsky discusses transformations. Transformations are the relations between the surface and the deep structure. While deep structure is universal (the same in any language), transformations are specific (different) for a given language. It is in the relation of the specific transformations to the universal deep structure that McNeill feels the interaction between the innate capabilities of the child and the environment take place. The deep structure is innate and unlearned, while the transformations must be learned. McNeill states that parental speech may be useful in learning the transformations.

Recall that learning theorists stress adult models for speech acquisition; from their theory it is easy to accept the idea that the more frequent speech events will occur more quickly in the child's speech. McNeill does not see this happening. He finds that the order of acquisition of inflections (meaningful word endings) in child speech is only weakly related to their occurrence in adult speech. He points out that the third-person inflection of verbs (the *s* endings, as in "Kim runs; I run") is the most frequent inflection in parental speech and the last to be acquired by the child.

McNeill also puts forth a case against the idea of practicing and reinforcement as strengthening a response. He points to an observation by Brown (1968). Brown examined the reinforcement children receive for their verbal expressions and found that a majority of the reinforcements are for the truth value of what is said rather than for the form in which the thought is expressed. For example, two children who have never been out of the city are taken to a farm, and one says in perfect form "I see a big doghouse." An adult hearing this comment made in reference to a barn is quite likely to say "No, no; that is a barn," while totally ignoring the perfectly formed sentence. Later, when the second child correctly identifies a cow by saying "Me seed biggie cowie," the adult is likely to express pleasure and praise the child for recognizing a cow. If a child is supposedly learning proper language through reinforcement, how is the child to know which reinforcements are for *what* is said and which are for *how* it is said.

McNeill also points to an observation by Ervin-Tripp (1964) that children early in speech use the correct forms of some irregular verbs, such as "went," not "goed." Later in development the correct form drops out. In other words, at one point a child may correctly say "I went for a ride on a train," then later will say "I goed for a ride on a train." This really is a step forward. The child has learned the general -*ed* rule and has overgeneralized its use. When the practiced associated form "I went" contradicts a transformation (the -*ed* rule), the practiced form loses.

This point gives a key to McNeill's theory. The important idea is that children seek regularities. Changes occur because the child discovers a regularity in the speech that is heard and applies the rule to all appropriate (and sometimes inappropriate) cases.

These regularity and rule-applying features of the child's language development are two reasons that McNeill does not feel that imitation is a technique of acquisition. He admits children will imitate, but stresses that they will only imitate forms or structures that they already possess; that is, if the child does not possess the appropriate deep structure for a form, he or she will not imitate that form. If direct instruction is repeated often enough, a child may add a new form in the imitation, but it will not be generalized to other situations or be incorporated into the system. Again Ervin-Tripp (1964) offers an observation that illustrates McNeill's point. She describes a case where a small child says "Nobody don't like me," and the mother replies "No, say nobody likes me." For eight repetitions the child persists with the original statement, then replies "Oh; nobody don't likes me." As McNeill (1970) puts it, "The contributions of parental speech are always most severely filtered through this system (the child's own rule system)."

One might ask why imitation could not help pair well-formed surface structures with a child's deep structure; McNeill has an answer. It appears that children change the adult versions into forms allowable in their own child systems. Cazden (1965) explored a closely related idea, that of expansion. In an expansion, an adult judges from the situation what a child meant to say and says it back in a well-formed sentence. This should help relate the meaning and the sound. For example, if the child says "Kitty runs," the parent may say "Yes, the kitty runs under the table." In the Cazden study the language complexity of a group of young nursery school children was assessed and the children were divided into two experimental groups. One group, the expansion group, spent half an hour a day for 5 days looking at pictures with the experimenter, who expanded every incomplete utterance the children made. The second group, the modeling group, spent the same amount of time with the experimenter, who never expanded their utterances but simply made relevant **139** comments when they spoke. At the end of the period the modeling group had gained more complexity in their speech than had the expansion group. This was not the expected finding. The results were explained in two ways: (1) the child may have not been paying attention (maybe because it became dull talking to someone who only repeated what you just said), or (2) the adult's expansions did not always fit the child's deep structure, even though the purpose was to pair the deep and surface structures so that the child could discover the proper transformations.

In summary, McNeill sees the learning of transformations as the critical problem in language acquisition. He sees in them the possibility that they describe the relationships to which children are predisposed. He gives them the role of hypotheses in children. These are the general ideas that children have about language and help explain the interrelations of the deep and surface structures. The child's goal is to find the hypothesis that applies most generally. McNeill further adds that generalizations are easily chosen because the child is predisposed to them; what is hard is to learn their modifications and exceptions. This possibly may be done by regular contact with the speech information provided by the speakers in the child's environment.

PROCESSING SPEECH

The two theoretical positions just described present very different ideas about how a child acquires language. People who believe in one or the other of these theories tend to study the acquisition of language in different ways. That each theory suggests very different types of research questions may help explain why there is so little real knowledge about language acquisition and even less agreement among psychologists who study this question. Many puzzling facts about children's language remain to be explained.

What the child hears and says

One of these puzzling phenomena is the unequal frequency of usage of the three major sentence elements (subject, verb, and object) by children who are producing two-word utterances. It has been noted that children tend to use the object noun with a higher frequency than the other two elements (Bloom, 1970). A second interesting phenomenon appears in a study by Shipley, Smith, and Glietmen (1969). They found that children had trouble following a command if it had an introductory nonsense word. They examined the possibility that this effect is related to the child's processing of a sentence. They felt that possibly the child processes sentences by listening to the very beginning and concentrating effort on the very first few words in order to understand what was said. In other words, the child processes or listens to sentences from the beginning to the end of the sentence. In regard to the high frequency of objects nouns in children's speech, Bloom theorizes that when a child constructs or speaks a sentence, he or she starts with the end, or the object, of the sentence. From this point the child builds longer utterances or sentences by adding more and more words from the end, working toward the beginning. For example, while buliding with blocks Jenny may first say "bridge." As she gains more ability a longer phrase may be made, such as "big bridge," and even later this phrase may be expanded to "build big bridge." The final step in this construction is "Jenny build big bridge." Keep in mind that this process of change and complexity takes place over a period of time and as the child gains the skill needed to string more and more words together.

These two points of view present interesting questions that need to be answered. Is it possible that a child listens to sentences from the beginning to the end and pulls the most information from the beginning, yet when starting to speak original sentences, builds from the end toward the beginning? This is a specific instance of the more basic question that language acquisition research needs to examine, that is, the relationship between the child's speech environment and the development of the child's own speech productions.

These problems have been treated in some form by some researchers, but they still remain. For example, in connection with the unequal frequency of usage for sentence elements, McNeill gives two plausible theoretical explanations for the frequent lack of verbs in early child sentences. One possibility is that, since most noun-noun child sentences include an animate noun (subject) followed by an inanimate noun (object), the verb must be an obvious action and therefore can be omitted. His second explanation is that verbs are words that are used to express a grammatical relationship (indicate a relationship between two other items, such as "She *owns* that car"). It appears that words that express relationships are added to a child's utterances only after words that are more concrete, such as nouns. Both of these explanations are speculative and imply that the child possesses a good deal of knowledge about verbs, even though they are used by the child infrequently.

Until recently, language acquisition research has virtually ignored the speech environment in which a child's language develops. For example, Friedlander et al. (1972), in a discussion of methods to study the language environment of children, explain that environment certainly must shape the development of a child's language, but there are no techniques for assessing the elements of language environments. This lack of investigation may initially seem to be an oversight, but from examination of past language acquisition studies, this lack of data on language environments does not seem so surprising. Early attempts to relate child speech productions to the speech children hear did not yield useful explanations.

An example of problems in assessing the effect of the language environment on a child's speech can be found in the confusing results of Cazden's (1965) study of the effect of expansion and modeling described earlier. Remember that Cazden found modeling to be more effective than expansion in developing children's language. A later study of these same two techniques by Feldman and Rodgen (1970) found more progress in the expansion group. Even exploration of such very specific questions about language environment has led to inconclusive results.

Mother's speech

While studies such as these lead to more confusion, researchers exploring the relationship between deep structures and surface structures argue that since there is no direct relationship between the surface structure and the deep structure, there is not much **141**

**PART
TWO**

Michael Hayman/Image, Inc.

Fig. 7-3. Many researchers believe the child's language complexity benefits from exposure to the speech of adult models.

use in trying to relate a child's speech to that of the parents, as any real relationship would only be at the deep-structure level. Following such arguments and the confusion of conflicting experimental results, attempts to relate a child's speech to that of the parents virtually stopped. Typical of those that can be found from this period of the late 1960s is Ervin-Tripp's (in Slobin, 1971) mention of the mother's speech in relation to the child's speech productions. She indicates that in general the mother tends to be repetitious and to use simple direct statements in speech to her child.

Moerk (1972) describes the parent's role as a teacher of language. The parent offers samples of language, a model to be imitated, and, of extreme importance, offers feedback to the child. The parent's role, incidently, involves both expansion and modeling. Moerk sees the child's repetitious daily routine and its accompanying repetitious speech as being ideally suited to teaching the child language.

In another study that attempts to analyze the speech environment of young children, Friedlander et al. (1972) also studied the verbalizations addressed to children. Similarly to Moerk, Friedlander and co-workers found both modeling and expansion being used in the child's environment. They quantified the amount of speech time taken up in various verbal activities. They found that the largest amount of speech directed to a child is noninteractive, such as the parent giving directions or commands to the child rather than questions and answers, modeling, or imitation. They also found, as would be expected, that the mother is the primary source of speech directed to the child and that she repeats herself frequently when speaking to the child.

A third study was conducted by Snow (1972), who investigated the speech of mothers to children of 2 years of age and to 10-year-old children to see if there was any difference in speech directed to younger children. She also investigated whether mothers and other adults addressed children in the same ways. Snow wanted to know if children hear typical adult speech. By giving mothers tasks to verbally describe to children, stories to make up, and physical phenomena to explain, Snow collected several samples of speech directed to children of both age groups. She found that mothers do modify the speech they direct to younger children. The speech directed to the 2-year-old group was more simple and redundant. Other adults were not as proficient in predicting the need for repetition with young children; however, they also used simple speech with the children. One interesting event that Snow reports is that mothers frequently omit verbs in speech to 2-year-olds, particularly when they are repeating utterances for the child. For instance, the mother might say ''Bring me the ball; the ball.'' This observation may help explain the unequal frequency of element usage that was mentioned previously.

How the child listens

Once a child's environment is described, it is also important to assess the child's interaction with it. One such investigation, mentioned earlier, was conducted by Shipley et al. (1969). They tested the ability of very young children, classified as using either holophrastic or telegraphic speech, to follow commands. The commands varied in that they contained nonsense elements as well as meaningful words. They found an increased interference with the child's compliance to a command if the command contained nonsense as the first word as opposed to other possible locations in the sentence. They speculated that the initial nonsense or unknown material at the beginning of an utterance turned the child off, or caused the child not to process the utterance. The results of this experiment indicate an important need to explore a child's speech processing capabilities and strategies.

It appears that studies dealing with a child's processing capabilities have been little more than initial explorations. Again this problem appears to be related to the trend of looking for deep structure guidance in the child's language development. The argument against studying processing and environment sounds convincing. If the child is using deep structure and learning transformations in language acquisition, there is little immediate use or need to study processing strategies because the deep structure will not be found in the surface structure of speech. It should be apparent, however, that to understand language acquisition we must know more than the structure of language. We should know what a child's language environment is like and how the child goes about getting information from the environment.

Important speech cues

Blasdale and Jensen (1970) feel that the child is sensitive to certain cues in speech and uses them in processing language. They explored this idea by presenting strings of four nonsense syllables to children aged 2½ to 3 years of age. They asked these children to repeat what they heard. The syllables varied in the level of stress (loudness) they received. Blasdale and Jensen found that the syllables receiving the strongest stress were recalled more often than words of lesser stress. They also found that the final syllable in a string was most frequently recalled. They concluded that children are sensitive to these cues of stress and placement, which often mark sentence information. They also believe that these cues may be used in speech processing by young children acquiring language. Other researchers frequently have found that young children often repeat the last word in a sentence.

Others have noticed that children center their attention on the stressed portions of language. Almost every parent knows that a small child attempting to repeat a multi-syllable word, such as tomato or pajama, often starts his own production with the stressed syllable, "mato" or "jama." In a study designed to explore this phenomenon Meier (1970) tested the effectiveness of stress cues in influencing a child's choice of word length when the word was unfamiliar. Specifically, 6-year-old children were presented with a sentence-length string of nonsense syllables and asked to repeat the last word. The last three syllables of the string were constructed so that the last word could appear to have one, two, or three syllables. Stress was varied in these strings so that it appeared on either the first, second, or third syllable from the end of the string. When the children were asked to repeat the last word of the nonsense string, they chose as the final word the last stressed syllable and all syllables following it to the end of the string.

Further information as to the effectiveness of stress cues in language processing is found in an unpublished paper by du Preez. He studied the effect of what he calls the tonic (referring to tone groups of information units of language) on a child's repetition of normal sentence strings. Each information unit is part of an intonation pattern that contains both old and new information. The new information is the tonic element and receives high stress. Du Preez found that children of 18 months are influenced by the stressed element in a sentence string. In working carefully with three children, du Preez was able to determine that they could imitate a sentence string beginning with the stressed element. Further, in normal sentence strings where there is expressed no question or doubt, the stress, or tonic, occurs at the end of the information unit. This observation brings together both stress and the position of most information at the end of the sentence, relating both these strong cues in what may be a highly efficient method for extracting information from sentence strings for a child. In pursuing his exploration, du Preez also moved the stress forward in the string and found that the children's imitation followed the movement of the stress. Du Preez says that stress, in effect, signals the child to pay attention. In much the same fashion as Moerk, du Preez sees that parent-child pair as optimal for teaching language. He feels that parents virtually "sing" language samples to their children, thus emphasizing the importance of intonation and stress to language understanding.

SUMMARY

The problems of language acquisition must be viewed from a new perspective and considered in relation to each other. How the child acquires language almost certainly is related to the perceptual capabilities and strategies of the child and the interaction of the child with the parents. One cannot simply examine a child's utterances in isolation and discover how the child came up with those particular productions. With all the contradictory positions and confusing information, the important point to keep in mind is that the child acquires language efficienctly and swiftly without direct teaching. This remarkable feat indicates that the learning capacity and capabilities of the preschool child are extremely well developed.

REFERENCES

Blasdale, R., & Jensen, P. Stress and word position as determinants of imitation in first language learners. *Journal of Speech and Hearing Research,* 1970, **13,** 193-202.

Bloom, L. *Language development: form and function of emerging grammars,* Research Monograph 59. Cambridge, Mass.: The M.I.T. Press, 1970.

Bloom, L., Lightbrown, P., & Hood, L. Structure and variation in child language. *Monographs of the Society for Research in Child Development,* 1975, **40**(2).

Brown, R. *Derivational complexity and order of acquisition in child speech.* Carnegie-Mellon Conference on Cognitive Processes, 1968.

Carroll, J. *Language and thought.* Englewood Cliffs, N.J.: Prentice-Hall Inc., 1964.

Cazden, C. *Environmental assistance to the child's acquisition of grammar.* Unpublished doctoral dissertation, Graduate School of Education, Harvard University, 1965.

Denes, P. B. Comments of preparations for discussion behaviorism with chimpanzees. In F. L. Smith and G. A. Miller (Eds.), *Genesis of language: a psycholinguistic approach.* Cambridge, Mass.: The M.I.T. Press, 1966.

Du Preez, P. *Units of information in the acquisition of language.* Unpublished dissertation, University of Cape Town.

Ervin-Tripp, S. An overview of theories of grammatical development (1964). In D. I. Slobin, *The ontogenesis of grammar.* New York: Academic Press, Inc., 1971.

Feldman, C., & Rodgen, M. *The effects of various types of adult responses in the syntactic acquisition of two- to three-year-olds.* Unpublished manuscript, University of Chicago, 1970.

Friedlander, B. Z., Jacobs, A. C., Davis, B. B., & Westone, H. S. Time sampling analysis of infant's natural language environment in the home. *Child Development,* 1972, **43,** 730-740.

Lenneberg, E. *Biological foundations of language.* New York: John Wiley & Sons, Inc., 1967.

McNeill, D. *The acquisition of language: the study of developmental psycholinguistics.* New York: Harper & Row, Publishers, 1970.

Meier, B. Unpublished pilot study, University of Maryland, 1970.

Moerk, E. Principles of interaction in language learning. *Merrill-Palmer Quarterly,* 1972, **18,** 229-257.

Rheingold, H., Gewirtz, J., & Ross, H. Social conditioning of vocalizations in the infant. In Staats, A., & Staats, C., *Complex human behavior: a systematic extension of learning principles.* New York: Holt, Rinehart and Winston, 1963.

Shipley, E. F., Smith, C. S., & Glietman, L. R. A study in the acquisition of language: free response to commands. *Language,* 1969, **45**(2), 322-337.

Skinner, B. F. *Verbal behavior.* New York: Appleton-Century-Crofts, 1957.

Snow, C. Mother's speech to children learning language. *Child Development,* 1972, **43,** 549-565.

Staats, A., & Staats, C. *Complex human behavior: a systematic extension of learning principles.* New York: Holt, Rinehart and Winston, 1963.

PART
TWO

Verbal interaction in mother-child dyads

Joe Ernest Reichle
Thomas M. Longhurst
Lyanne Stepanich

Department of Speech, Kansas State University

The verbal interaction of mothers and their children in mother-child dyads was examined in 24 children (12 2-year-olds and 12 3-year-olds) and their mothers. Each child was selected on the basis of age and pretest results indicating nondelayed receptive and expressive language function. The mother and her child were given an assortment of toys, and the mother was asked to play with her child. Tape recordings were made of each session. Analysis of the mother-child dyadic data revealed that the verbalizations of two groups of mothers differed significantly. Mothers of the older group of children used more complex expatiations and modeled interrogations. The occurrence of expansions and direct imitations was not a function of age of the child. The verbal interactions of 2- and 3-year-olds was significantly different in that 2-year-olds produced a greater percentage of imitations with reduction.

Recently many researchers have investigated the language mothers use when talking to their children (Broen, 1972; Brown, 1970; Brown & Bellugi, 1964; Friedlander, Jacobs, Davis, & Wetstone, 1972; Longhurst & Stepanich, 1975; Phillips, 1973; Snow, 1972).

Some of these researchers have specifically investigated the direct imitations and imitations with expansion or reduction in the interactions of mothers and children. Brown and Bellugi (1964) in a classic longitudinal investigation of three children and their mothers reported that mothers imitate their children's telegraphic utterances with expansion about 30% of the time. They also suggested that the children imitated the parents with reduction, although no specific frequency was reported. McNeill (1970) suggested that these children imitated with reduction about 10% of the parents' utterances. Friedlander et al. (1972) investigated the language interaction of two 1-year-old children with their parents. In the first family no expansions or reductions occurred. In the second family the mother expanded 3.7% of the child's utterances and the father expanded 8.2% of the child's utterances, while the child reduced .6% of the mother's utterances and none of the father's.

There are obvious problems with both of these studies. In both, the investigators have based their conclusions about expansions and reductions on a very small and select subject sample. Brown and Bellugi selected their three subjects because of their exceptionally high level of intelligibility and talkativeness. The two subjects used by Friedlander et al. were very young, and there may have been little opportunity for either expansion or reduction to occur naturally in their interactions, since the children were essentially nonverbal.

Another interaction called modeling or expatiation has been described by a number of authors (Bandura & Harris, 1966; Bandura & McDonald, 1963; Cazden, 1965; Muma, 1973; Feldman & Rodgen, Note 1). The incidence of expatiation in the language of mothers interacting with their children has not been reported however.

From *Developmental Psychology*, 1976, **12**, 273-277. Copyright 1976 by the American Psychological Association. Reprinted by permission.

Currently there are insufficient data available to describe adequately the natural occurrence of expansion and expatiation by mothers and imitation with reduction by children. The purpose of the current investigation was to describe some of the interactions used in mother-child verbal communication with larger and less select subject samples than those of previous investigations.

METHOD
Subjects

Twenty-four children, 12 males and 12 females, and their mothers served as subjects. These subjects represent two thirds of the subject population of a previous experiment (Longhurst & Stepanich, 1975), and the present report consists of a reanalysis of protocols collected in this previous study. Data from 1-year-olds in the previous study were not reanalyzed because almost none of the interactions of interest occurred. All subjects were from middle socioeconomic status families and were native English speakers. Twelve children were 23 to 35 months of age and 12 were 35 to 37 months of age. These age-groups were chosen for study because they represented chronological points at which two distinct levels of language development in children could be observed. Additionally, it is with these age-groups that previous authors have suggested that expansion, reductions, and expatiations should be most prevalent. No attempt was made in the current investigation to control for sex of the children, the educational backgrounds of the mothers, the ages of the mothers, or the ages and numbers of siblings. Developmental language level was determined by performance on the Receptive-Expressive Emergent Language Inventory (Bzoch & League, 1971). All children were judged to be nondelayed, and some were slightly advanced in their language development.

Experimental facility

All sessions were conducted in a small, quiet room containing a microphone, a table, two chairs, and a cabinet for the materials. The experimenter monitored the sessions through a one-way mirror in an adjoining room that contained a high-fidelity tape recorder.

Procedure

Prior to the session each mother was told that she and her child would be participating in a study of language development in children. The mother was also told that the experimenter was interested in observing and recording the verbal interaction between herself and her child. The experimenter assured the mothers that each tape would be coded to insure that neither her name nor the name of her child would be associated with the data. The specific details and purposes of the study were disclosed to the mothers only after the experiment in order that they might perform as naturally as possible during the sessions.

Each mother interacted with her own child in one session of approximately 20-25 minutes in length, and the middle 10-minute segment was selected for the analysis, since that was the segment previously analyzed (Longhurst & Stepanich, 1975).

Experimental condition

Immediately prior to the session, the mother was given a bag containing several farm animals and farm equipment made by Fischer-Price, Inc., and 10 colored blocks. The experimenter asked the mother to continue to play with her child until the experimenter indicated that it was time to stop. The purpose of this task was to replicate a situation that might naturally occur between a mother and her child in the home.

Protocol preparation and segmentation

Verbatim transcripts of the speech of both mothers and children were prepared, and the transcripts were segmented according to "thought unit utterances" rather than the traditional "per breath utterances." According to Miner (1969) utterances need not be complete and may occasionally extend across a pause (e.g., "See the big black dog [pause] run and hide"). Using thought unit segmentation, this example would be one utterance; if the traditional per breath utterance segmentation were used, this example would consist of two utterances. The thought unit utterance was chosen for analysis because the interactions under investigation often were not self-contained within per breath unit utterances.

Reliability for transcript preparation and segmentation was established by having a new transcript prepared and resegmented for two transcripts and then computing percentages of agreement. The words and segmentation points on the retyped version were compared with the original. Agreement for protocol preparation was 91% and 86%, and for segmentation 88% and 91%.

Performance measures

The experimenter categorized the mothers' utterances into five predetermined categories. The children's utterances were categorized into three categories. A percentage of occurrence for each category was calculated by dividing the number of utterances in a category by the partners' total number of utterances and multiplying by 100. For example, if a child produced 40 utterances and his mother expanded five times, the percentage for the expansion category would be 12.5. Examples of the categories are presented in the following display.

Mother's verbal interaction categories	Child's verbal interaction categories
Expansion	*Reduction*
Child: Horsey there.	Mother: A horsey is fat.
Mother: The horsey is there.	Child: Horsey fat.
Simple expatiation	*Direct imitation*
Child: Horsey there.	Mother: Horsey.
Mother: He's black.	Child: Horsey.
Complex expatiation	*Question*
Child: Horsey there.	Mother: —
Mother: He has a black nose and he's fat.	Child: How old horsey?
Modeled question	
Child: Horsey there?	
Mother: How does a horse run so fast?	
Direct imitation	
Child: Horsey there.	
Mother: Horsey there.	

A miscellaneous category was used for utterances that could not be categorized. This category was not subjected to any analysis. All of the categories have been previously described. Muma's (1973) descriptions of simple and complex expatiation as well as modeled questions formed the basis for the definitions used in the current investigation. Brown and Bellugi (1964) provided descriptions of imitation with expansion and imitation with reduction. An individual category for direct imitation by mother and by child was included, since many language intervention programs suggest the use of imitations to teach lower level communicative skills. Questions asked by the child were included because of speculation by Blank and Solomon (1968). They suggested that question asking is a requisite to the acquisition of higher level linguistic skill dealing with abstraction. Child questions was the only category that was not interactional in nature; that is, it did not have to precede or follow some other utterance to be categorized.

Mothers' verbalizations. An expansion was defined as a maternal utterance that (a) retained the same word order as the child's previous utterance and (b) contained the same content words but a greater number of function words, thus adding syntactic information. A simple expatiation was a maternal utterance that (a) was a simple utterance and (b) added referential information to the child's previous utterance. An expatiation did not have to retain the same word order or any of the words contained in the child's utterance. It may or may not have contained a greater number of words than the child's utterance. A complex expatiation was a maternal utterance that met Criterion b for simple expatiation and was either a compound, complex, or compound-complex utterance. A modeled question was either an expansion or expatiation but in question form. Direct imitations were maternal utterances that (a) retained the same word order and (b) contained the same words as the child's previous utterance and no additional ones.

Children's verbalizations. An imitation with reduction was a child utterance that (a) retained the same word order and (b) contained fewer function words than the mother's previous utterance. A question was defined as an utterance that (a) began with a *wh* word such as what, where, which, who, when, or how followed by an auxiliary or modal, (b) ended in a rising inflection, (c) contained an interrogative reversal, (d) ended with a tag and some minor miscellaneous categories. A direct imitation was a child utterance that (a) retained the same word order and (b) contained the same lexical items as the mother's previous utterance.

RESULTS

The data were analyzed in a series of one-way analysis of variance tests (Snedecor & Cochran, 1972) using the .05 level of significance. In each analysis of variance, the 2-year-old group mean percentage was compared with the 3-year-old group mean percentage within a given category.

There was no significant difference between the mean number of utterances by the mothers of 2-year-olds ($M = 82$) and the mean number of utterances by mothers of 3-year-old children ($M = 87$). There were fewer utterances by the 2-year-old children ($M = 40$) than by 3-year-old children ($M = 67$), and the difference was significant, $F(1.23) = 9.05, p < .006$.

There was a significant difference, $F(1, 23) = 4.85, p < .038$, in the mean number of complex expatiations used by mothers of 2-year-olds ($M = 7.1$) and by mothers of 3-year-olds ($M = 13.1$). Mothers of 3-year-olds ($M = 20.4$) used a significantly greater, $F(1, 23) = 6.58, p < .017$, percentage of modeled questions than mothers of 2-year-olds ($M = 10.4$). Differences between mothers of 2-year-olds and mothers of 3-year-olds, respectively, for expansion ($M = 4.3, M = 3.0$), simple expatiation ($M = 9.4, M = 5.9$), and direct imitation ($M = 5.3, M = 6.8$) were not statistically significant.

There were more imitations with reduction by 2-year-olds ($M = 21.4$) than by 3-year-olds ($M = 4.9$) and the difference was significant, $F(1, 23) = 10.19, p < .004$. Differences between 2-year-olds and 3-year-olds, respectively, for direct imitation ($M = 3.6, M = 3.2$) and questions ($M = 3.6, M = 13.2$) were not statistically significant.

DISCUSSION

Previous investigators (Brown, 1970; Brown & Bellugi, 1964) have reported that expansions account for about 30% of adult utterances addressed to children. A substantially lower frequency of occurrence was found in the present study. Expansions accounted for 3% to 4% of the mothers' utterances addressed to their children. Since the same definitions of expansion were used some other factor(s) must account for this difference. One possible explanation is that the present study used children of average ability while Brown and Bellugi's subjects were chosen for their exceptionally high ability in language. Additionally, Brown and Bellugi's data were collected in the home while the present study was conducted in a laboratory environment, although Friedlander et al. (1972), in an investigation in the home, reported results that were consistent with those of the present study.

Our results suggested that complex expatiation was far more prevalent than expansions in the speech of mothers of both 2- and 3-year-olds. Additionally, this behavior occurred more frequently in the speech of mothers of 3-year-olds than in the speech of mothers of 2-year-olds. This substantiated Broen's (1972) finding that mothers of older children use more complex ex-

149

pressive language constructions when interacting with their child. She suggested this tendency correlated with the child's increasing ability to decode complex grammatical constructions.

Broen (1972) also observed that the use of questions by mothers in mother-child dyads was related to the age of the child participating in the interaction. Leach (1973) suggested that expansions frequently co-occur with questions although no frequency of occurrence of this behavior has been previously reported. Results of the current investigation substantiate Leach's observation to the extent that it was found that modeling behaviors do frequently co-occur with questions. Broen's observation was substantiated as mothers of 3-year-old children produced nearly twice as many modeled questions as mothers of 2-year-olds. Future investigators in interaction behavior should consider a more thorough analysis of the role of questions in modeling behavior.

Brown and Bellugi (1964) reported that children frequently produced imitations with reduction. It is indicated from the results of the present study that reductions occur frequently in the speech of 2-year-olds only. Thus as the child's own language develops he/she imitates adults less frequently.

While imitation with reduction was the predominant interaction with 2-year-olds, questions were the most frequently occurring interaction of 3-year-old children. Although the difference is not statistically significant, 3-year-olds did produce over three times as many questions as 2-year-olds. So that, it can be argued that although 2-year-olds are dependent in the interaction, 3-year-olds begin to initiate interaction through questioning.

The application of interaction measures such as those presented here will hopefully provide a more comprehensive description of the influence that children and adults have on each other's language.

REFERENCE NOTE

1. Feldman, C., & Rodgen, M. *The effects of various types of adult responses in the syntactic acquisition of two- to three-year-olds.* Unpublished manuscript, University of Chicago, 1970.

REFERENCES

Bandura, A., & Harris, A. Modification of syntactic style. *Journal of Experimental Child Psychology,* 1966, **4,** 341-352.

Bandura, A., & McDonald, F. J. The influences of social reinforcement and the behavior of models in shaping children's moral judgments. *Journal of Abnormal Psychology,* 1963, **67,** 274-281.

Blank, M., & Solomon, F. A tutorial language program to develop abstract thinking in socially disadvantaged preschool children. *Child Development,* 1968, **39,** 379-390.

Broen, P. The verbal environment of the language-learning child. *American Speech and Hearing Association Monographs,* 1972, **17,** 1-65.

Brown, R. *Psycholinguistics.* New York: Free Press, 1970.

Brown, R., & Bellugi, U. Three processes in the child's acquisition of syntax. *Harvard Educational Review,* 1964, **34,** 133-151.

Bzoch, K. R., & League, R. *The Receptive-Expressive Emergent Language Scale for the measurement of language skills in infancy.* Gainesville, Fla.: Tree of Life Press, 1971.

Cazden, C. *Environmental assistance to the child's acquisition of grammar.* Unpublished doctoral dissertation, Harvard University, 1965.

Friedlander, B. Z., Jacobs, A., Davis, B. B., & Wetstone, H. S. Time sampling analysis of infants natural language environment in the home. *Child Development,* 1972, **43,** 730-740.

Leach, E. Interrogation: A model and some implications. *Journal of Speech and Hearing Disorders,* 1973, **37,** 33-46.

Longhurst, T. M., & Stepanich, L. Mothers' speech addressed to one-, two-, and three-year-old normal children. *Child Study Journal,* 1975, **5,** 3-11.

McNeill, D. *The acquisition of language: The study of developmental psycholinguistics.* New York: Harper & Row, 1970.

Miner, L. E. Scoring procedures for length-complexity index: A preliminary report. *Journal of Communication Disorders,* 1969, **2,** 224-240.

Muma, J. Language intervention: Ten techniques. *Language, Speech, and Hearing Services in the Schools,* 1973, **4,** 7-17.

Phillips, J. R. Syntax and vocabulary of mothers' speech to young children: Age and sex comparisons. *Child Development,* 1973, **44,** 182-185.

Snedecor, G., & Cochran, W. *Statistical methods.* Ames: Iowa State University Press, 1972.

Snow, C. Mothers' speech to children learning language. *Child Development,* 1972, **43,** 549-565.

DEVELOPING THOUGHT

Chapter 8

From 5 to 7 years: some changes in children's thought processes

Barbara McClinton

In a supermarket a 5-year-old boy "helping" his parents shop decided he must have a jar of peanut butter. Since his parents were two aisles away, he asked a friend of the family (who happened to be a child psychologist) where to find the peanut butter. The psychologist replied "It's at the end of this aisle, on the right-hand side, near the bottom of the shelf." (Stop reading for a moment and imagine what you would do if given these directions.) Instead of walking straight to the appropriate place, the boy wandered slowly down the aisle, looking up and down the shelves on both sides. Recognizing an opportunity to discover something about how a young child thinks, the psychologist stopped the boy (he had progressed only a few feet) and asked him some questions.

Psychologist: (to determine motivation) Are you still looking for the peanut butter?
Boy: Yes.
P: (to test memory) Can you remember the directions?
B: At the end of this aisle, on the right-hand side, near the bottom of the shelf.
P: (to test comprehension) Which is the right side of the aisle?
B: (growing a bit impatient) Over here (pointing to the right side).
P: (back to motivation) Fine. Let's see how fast you can find the peanut butter.
B: (obviously tired of all these silly questions) Well, that's what I'm doing!

Then the boy proceeded to wander slowly down the aisle, looking up and down, on both sides, in search of the peanut butter.

Why did the boy persist in using an inefficient method? He still wanted the peanut butter, he remembered the directions word for word, and he knew which was the right side of the aisle. He did not lack general intelligence (his IQ was well above average), and he was very adept with words (18 months later, at age 6½, he could read words such as fire extinguisher). Is it possible that children simply do not use information to solve a problem the same way adults do?

Psychologists who have studied children's mental processes have discovered that young children do not think and solve problems in the efficient manner they will when they grow older. It is not simply a matter of young children thinking slower or having less experience. Some thought processes, particularly the ones involved in solving relatively complex problems, appear not to be available to preschool children. According to White (1965), the period from 5 to 7 years is "a time of unusually significant change" in the way children think, perceive, and solve problems. In this chapter some of the changes are described and several possible explanations are presented.

DESCRIBING MENTAL CHANGES
Learning

Psychologists have devised many learning tasks to measure how quickly and efficiently animals and humans can solve problems. These tasks often have at least two common solutions: one solution that is likely if the learner uses only the basic learning processes (classical conditioning, operant conditioning, or observation) and a different solution that is likely if the learner uses complex reasoning and logic. A rat or monkey given such a problem is expected to choose the first solution; an adult human is expected to choose the second. For most of these learning tasks, a child younger that 5 years chooses the simple solution typical of animals; a child older than 7 years chooses the complex solution typical of adults. The years between 5 and 7 are a period of transition, when most children are developing the ability to find the adultlike solutions to these problems.

The *transposition* problem is an example of the type of learning task with a simple solution and a complex solution. One version of the transposition problem begins with two squares, one larger than the other. The subject guesses which square might be the correct one. If the guess is right, the learner is rewarded; if the guess is wrong, no reward is given. This procedure is repeated, with one size (large or small) always rewarded, until the subject repeatedly makes the right choice. (The position—left or right—of the correct size square is varied to be sure the learner responds on the basis of size.)

Once the subject has learned to choose one size consistently, a new problem (the transposition test) is introduced (Fig. 8-1). Suppose that the original problem consists of two squares, one that is 2 inches on a side and one that is 3 inches on a side. Suppose

Fig. 8-1. Stimuli for a transposition problem.

TRAINING TRIALS

TRANSPOSITION (TEST) TRIALS

If the larger square was correct during training

If the smaller square was correct during training

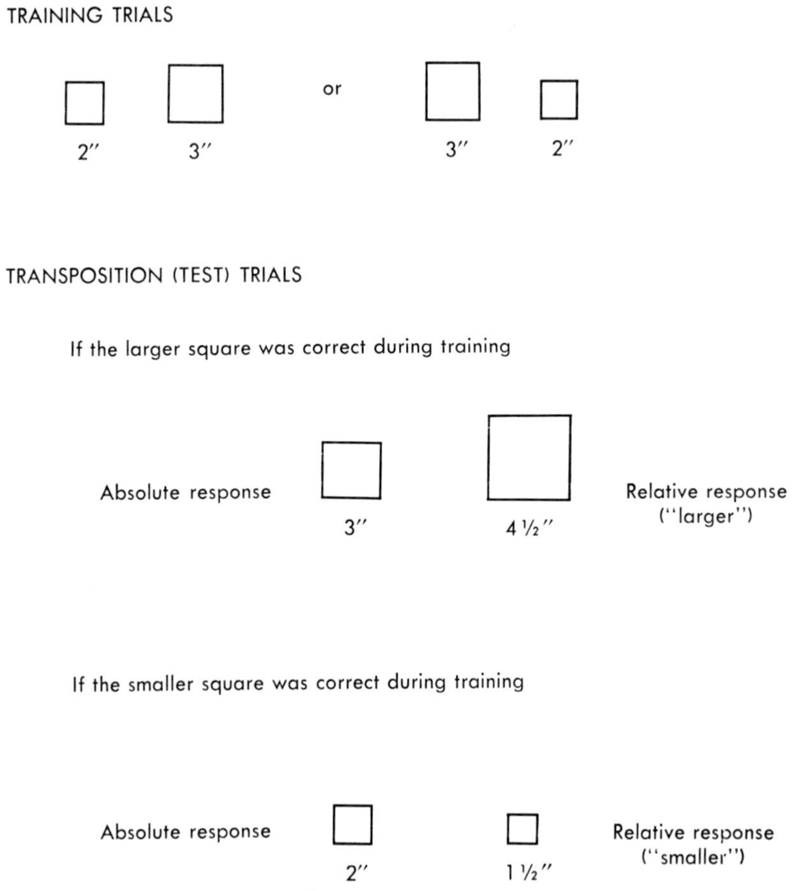

further that the large square (3 inches) is correct during training. For the transposition test, the stimuli might be one 3-inch square (the same absolute size as the orginally correct square) and one 4½-inch square (an even larger square). Subjects who respond only on the basis of physical characteristics of the originally correct square will choose the square most alike in absolute size, the 3-inch square. Such a solution is called an *absolute response*. Animals typically make an absolute response to the transposition problem. Subjects who respond on the basis of the relationship between the two squares ("The larger one is correct.") will choose the 4½-inch square because it is now the larger one. Such a solution is called a *relative response*. Adults typically make a relative response to the transposition problem.*

If an absolute response to the transposition problem is based on simple learning principles and if a relative response depends on more complex, logical thought, how will young children solve the transposition problem? In a classic study, Kuenne (1946) tried to answer this question with children aged 2½ to 5½ years. She found that performance both in the initial training and in the transposition test was related to age. Not surprising, the older children learned the original task more quickly. The older children were also more likely to choose the relative response on the transposition test. Kuenne also asked each child to tell her how the problem was solved. The children who could describe the solution in words ("The small one is right.") were most likely to choose the relative response. On the basis of her study, Kuenne suggested that children pass through two developmental stages of thought. In the *preverbal* stage, a child does not apply words to solving the problem, even though the words big and small may be known to the child; in this stage children, like animals, prefer the absolute response. In the *verbal* stage (usually beginning about 5 or 6 years of age) a child uses the words big and small to solve the problem; in this stage children, like adults, choose the relative response.

Kuenne's research marks the beginning of a long series of studies related to the theory that children need words to solve complex problems. This theory (verbal mediation theory) is discussed later in the chapter. When thinking about Kuenne's study, keep two ideas in mind:

1. The relationship between use of words and transposition was only a correlation. Correlations do not demonstrate causes. It is possible that some event, undiscovered by Kuenne, occurs in children at about the age of 5 years, which causes both an improvement in language and an increase in relational thinking in a transposition task.

2. Dozens of studies of transposition were inspired by Kuenne's work. From these studies psychologists concluded that transposition, which appears quite simple compared with other learning tasks devised by psychologists, is really a complicated matter. Children's solutions of the transposition problem can be influenced by many variables, such as the amount and type of pretraining, the sizes of the squares, the spatial arrangement of the squares, the timing of the trials,

---

*If the small square is originally correct, the new stimuli for the transposition test might be a 2-inch square —the same absolute size as the initially correct square—and a 1½-inch square—the same relative size (smaller) as the initially correct square.

the ability of the child to tell the difference between the squares, and the speed of the child's original learning, to name just a few. Many of these studies cannot be explained simply on the basis of using (or not using) words to solve problems.

Transposition is only one of many tasks designed to study children's learning. Some of the others are rather simple, but most are quite complex. Experiments with these tasks have strengthened the belief that children begin to develop an important new way of learning around the age of 5 years. The theoretical explanation of why this development occurs is still in dispute.

Hypothesis testing

A phone call wakes you out of a sound sleep. It is Monday morning. Sunlight is streaming in the window. Your first verbal thought is "What time is it? Did I miss my 9 o'clock class?" You glance at the clock; 10:23. Your second verbal thought is "What happened?" While jumping out of bed, you think of several possibilities: (1) you turned off the alarm and went back to sleep, (2) you forgot to set the alarm switch, and (3) you set the alarm but forgot to change the time back to 8:15. You look at the clock again. The alarm switch is still on; the first two possibilities are immediately discarded. The alarm timer says 11:00, not 8:15. The third possibility is confirmed. You have just engaged in a very adult thought process called hypothesis testing. *Hypothesis testing* is a strategy for solving problems, which involves (1) producing guesses or hypotheses about possible solutions and (2) systematically testing each guess against the real world, eliminating the ones that are not consistent with facts until only one hypothesis remains that seems to solve the problem.

Testing of simple hypotheses probably first develops around 5 years. This statement is tentative because much of the evidence for this strategy in children is indirect. Some very simple learning problems paradoxically become more difficult during and after the 5- to 7-year age range, possibly because the children expect complicated solutions and generate hypotheses about what these might be. The brighter children of this age have even more trouble with these simple problems than do the average children, probably because especially intelligent children develop the hypothesis-testing strategy at a younger age. (College students sometimes experience a similar problem when they choose the wrong answer to an easy multiple-choice question because the right one "is too obvious; it can't be right.") In most cases, though, hypothesis testing is a useful skill. Even in games such as hide and seek, children of 4 or 5 years typically run around looking at random, while older children systematically guess about likely hiding places.

Hypothesis testing is a thought process that is learned gradually throughout childhood and beyond. Though this mental strategy first appears in the 5- to 7-year age range, many years are required for it to develop fully. Even college students, who usually are rather efficient hypothesis testers, refine their techniques when necessary (Eimas, 1969).

Perception

Several changes in a child's perceptual preferences and abilities occur at about 5 years of age. One such change is a shift in the *dominant sensory mode* for exploring new

W. C. Baker

Fig. 8-2. At 2½ years of age, a child explores objects by touch. An older child is likely to look first and touch later.

objects. A dominant sensory mode is the sense (e.g., vision, hearing, touch, taste) that an unrestricted child uses to gather information. For example, an adult might investigate a new food by sniffing, but a young child might prefer touch to determine whether it is hard or squishy or suitable for finger painting. In studies of dominant sensory mode, Soviet researchers have observed that 3- and 4-year-old children explore new objects primarily by touch, but by 6 or 7 years children prefer visual exploration (White, 1965).

Within the visual mode, a shift occurs in the *dimension preferences* of children in the 5- to 7-year range. A *dimension* is a characteristic (such as size, shape, or color) that varies among the stimuli in a learning problem. For example, if a problem consists of two stimuli, a small red circle and a large red square, the dimensions of the problem are size (large or small) and shape (circle or square). Color is not a dimension of this problem because both stimuli are the same color, red. Children have predictable dimension preferences, which change with age. A dimension preference is the dimension of a problem that attracts the child's attention, the dimension the child will choose as the basis for solving the problem. The earliest dimension preference, appearing by age 2 years, is for position (left or right). Children of this age try to solve a problem by consistently choosing the stimulus on the left (or on the right); sometimes they never learn that color or shape or some other dimension is the relevant one. Three- and 4-year-old children prefer to solve problems on the basis of color or size. Shape (the dimension chosen by **159** most adults in such a task) becomes a preferred dimension at about age 6 years (White, 1965).

Cross-modal transfer also improves around age 5. *Cross-modal transfer* is using one sensory mode (such as touch) to demonstrate learning originally accomplished through another sensory mode (such as vision). Guessing what is inside a wrapped gift often requires cross-modal transfer: a child shakes and squeezes the package to guess what the present will look like. One way to test cross-modal transfer is to let a child look at a toy, then feel two toys that are out of sight; the task is to hold up the toy that was seen earlier. Children of 3 or 4 years find this task somewhat difficult, but by 5 or 6 a child is about as skilled as an adult at integrating information across sensory modes (McClinton, 1973).

Spatial orientation

Most children know the difference between up and down by 3 years of age, but correct use of the words right and left is not learned until about 5 or 6. (Apes and monkeys also learn up-down distinctions more easily than right-left ones.) Even at 6, the distinction is limited to the child's own right and left. Learning that right and left depend on one's point of view occurs still later.

A similar development occurs in overcoming confusions about reversed letters. Up-down discriminations (like telling the difference between *n* and *u* or *b* and *p*) typically are mastered at age 5 or 6. Left-right discriminations (like *b* and *d* or *p* and *q*) are learned a year or two later.

Elaine M. Ward

Fig. 8-3. Colors, shapes, sizes, and spatial arrangements are intriguing to young children.

These and other transitions in orientation indicate that during the ages of 5 to 7 years, children learn to process more information, and store it more efficiently, than they could when they were younger.

Intelligence test skills

Reliable predictions of adult intelligence test scores can first be made when a child is about 6 years old (Bayley, 1968) (for more details, see Chapter 10). There are at least two possible explanations for the high correlation between IQ at 5 to 7 years and adult IQ. One is that 5 to 7 is the youngest age at which questions on an IQ test are similar in form to questions on an adult IQ test. According to this explanation, the similarities in IQ scores can be accounted for entirely by the similarities in tests. The second explanation, which is consistent with other information about young children, is that children develop a new mode of thought at about age 6 years, which will continue through adulthood. This mode of thought is characterized by provisional action, planning, and abstract behavior. According to the second explanation, adult IQ can first be predicted accurately at age 5 to 7 years because this is the age when children first begin to think like adults.

Use of words

When children first learn language, words are used primarily to express feelings and to obtain desired results. Adults, though, use words for additional purposes: to direct their behavior and to solve problems. Repeating to oneself the steps in a process ("Turn it left, then wait for the light to come on, then pull. . . .") and using memory rhymes ("*I* before *e* except after *c*.") are simple examples of the directing and problem-solving functions of language. When speech can be used mentally to aid in thinking and problem solving, it is said to be internalized. The process of acquiring this verbal skill is therefore called *internalization of speech*.

Internalization of speech occurs during the preschool years, becoming complete by age 7. This gradual process can be seen in a series of studies described by Luria (1969). In these studies children's responses to verbal instructions were observed. Each child was seated in front of a light and given a rubber bulb to hold. If told "When the light comes on, press the bulb," a child of 1½ to 2½ years would press as soon as the instruction was given, even when the light did not come on. When told "Don't press," a child of this age would press even more energetically than before. By the age of 3½, a child could follow these directions but would be confused by more complicated ones. If told "Press when a red light comes on but not when a green one comes on," a child of 3½ would either press to both colored lights or not press at all. By 4 or 4½, a child could follow this sort of direction, but only if specifically trained to use phrases (such as "I must" or "I must not") to guide the pressing behavior. By 5 or 6 years of age the children could follow the verbal instructions appropriately.

Other adult uses of words also emerge during the years from 5 to 7. For example, the type of *word associations* given by children changes at about age 7 (Brown & Berko, 1960). Word associations are tested by asking the child to say the first word that comes **161**

to mind when the researcher says a word, such as cat. Very young children often produce associations that sound like the stimulus word but are not related in meaning. To
cat, a 2- or 3-year-old might say hat or sat. Associations of slightly older children are
typically related in meaning to the stimulus word, but a different part of speech; these
responses are often words that might logically follow the stimulus word in a sentence.
At 4 or 5, a child might respond to cat with meow or Scratched me. Children of 7, like
adults, usually give a word association in a part of speech that matches the stimulus
word and is meaningfully related to it. The response of a 7-year-old to cat might be dog
or whisker. This development represents a major change in mental style, from associations based on common word order to associations based on conceptual similarity.

Memory

Parents and other observers of children have often noticed that memory, like wine,
improves with age, at least for the first few years. But you can probably recall vividly
some of your early experiences, perhaps even from the age of 2 years. Do young children remember as well as older children and adults? There is no simple answer to this
question because memory is a more complex process than it might seem.

Remembering involves at least three events. *Acquisition* is the taking in of information to be remembered. *Retrieval* is locating the information where it is stored in the
brain and bringing it forth to demonstrate remembering. *Forgetting* is the loss of information over time. One of these three events that is *not* dependent on age is rate of
forgetting. In memory tests that separate rate of forgetting from other factors, preschool
children perform just as well as older children and adults (Belmont & Butterfield, 1969).
Acquisition and retrieval, on the other hand, improve with age, at least in certain circumstances. If the memory task is primarily verbal (such as repeating a story or a list
of numbers) or if it is made easier by advance planning or strategies (such as repeating
to oneself the items to be remembered) or if it requires reconstructing events (like describing a picture), preschool children will have more difficulty with the task than will
older children. Acquisition and retrieval of information also demand some interest
in the task and desire to do well. Preschool children may have trouble on some memory
tasks because of lack of attention or motivation. There are, however, some memory
tasks on which preschool children perform as well as adults; recognizing familiar pictures is an example (Levy et al., 1974). Recognizing pictures is easy for 3- and 4-year-
old children because (1) it depends primarily on images, not words; (2) trying to use
memory strategies does not help, and may hinder, performance on this task; (3) the child
merely points to the familiar items without reproducing them; and (4) pictures capture
the attention of young children.

One of the most important factors determining a child's performance on a memory
task is the task itself, because different tasks measure different abilities. In general, at
3 or 4 or 5 years, children will have some difficulties, which disappear by 8 or 10 or 12
(depending on the specific memory task).

Young children have one significant advantage over older children. Interference from
other information, which hinders memory performance from the age of 8 on, does not

affect children at 4 or 5 (Koppenaal et al., 1964). The period from 5 to 7, therefore, is a time of both gains and losses in children's memory.

What about your early childhood memories? Chances are you recall sights, feelings, and actions, especially those that were emotionally charged. Events that were primarily verbal or that could be remembered only with deliberate planning are not likely to have survived in your memory. Reconstructions (such as retelling the story or working in details you might have learned later) are a function of your adult mind, not of your memory as a young child.

Effective reinforcement

Most adults are not motivated to exert much effort for a raisin, a trinket, or a pat on the head from a psychologist. Young children, however, will work diligently for such rewards. Trivial material rewards, praise, and adult attention are effective reinforcers with preschool children, but they lose much of their appeal by about age 7. Older children and adults prefer "a more intellectual and abstract kind of reward," the knowledge that they were right (White, 1965). Considering that abstract thought first occurs in the years from 5 to 7, it is not surprising that an abstract reward (the joy of succeeding or the pride of accomplishment) should become a powerful reinforcer at about age 7. Some psychologists have suggested that differences in learning between middle-class and lower-class children can be explained in part because many lower class children make this shift in effective reinforcement at a later age or not at all.

Description of mental changes: a summary

Between the ages of 5 and 7, major changes take place in the ways children think. These changes are reflected in children's learning, use of strategies, perception, spatial orientation, capacity for abstract thought, use of words, memory, and motivation. The changes are more closely related to mental age than to chronological age (see Chapter 10). Bright children accomplish these feats somewhat earlier than do children of average intelligence, and retarded children lag behind the average. To borrow the words of Stevenson (1970), the preschool child "is viewed as a relatively rigid rote learner," whose learning, language, and thought are restricted, while the older child is "flexible and verbally facile" and able to solve problems deliberately and systematically.

EXPLAINING MENTAL CHANGES

Four theories have been developed that explain some or all of the mental changes that occur between the ages of 5 and 7 years: verbal mediation, inhibition of associative thought, attention, and Piaget's theory of cognitive development.

Verbal mediation

According to verbal mediation theory, thinking and solving problems in an adultlike fashion requires the use of words. An adult is often unaware of the significance of words in thought, because the words are produced covertly (silently), quickly, and with little effort. A child younger than 5 or 6, however, does not spontaneously use words to or-   **163** ganize thought, even though the necessary words may be simple and well known to the child. Kuenne suggested this theory to explain children's responses to the transposition problem. The concept was later tested, refined, and named verbal mediation by Kendler and Kendler (1962).

Verbal mediation theory is an elaboration of stimulus-response *(S-R)* learning theory, developed in the 1930s and 1940s to explain how animals (presumably including humans) learn. The basic idea of *S-R* theory is that a stimulus event *(S)* provokes a predictable response *(R)* by the experimental subject. Some extensions of the basic notion are:

1. New responses can be produced by manipulating stimuli in certain ways, for example, by delivering rewards.
2. Behavior (responses) can be controlled completely by controlling the environment (stimuli).
3. Complicated behaviors can be reduced to a series of simple responses, each provoked by specific stimuli.
4. Explanations based on thinking and other unobservable mental activities are unnecessary, because *S-R* theory can be expanded to explain even human learning in terms of concrete, observable stimuli and responses.

S-R theory enjoyed several decades of popularity among psychologists because it is simple and useful for explaining results of learning experiments. By about 1960, however, some psychologists suspected that some elements of complex human learning could not be explained by the simple *S-R* theory. The Kendlers, who were studying conceptual learning in children, developed an elaboration of *S-R* theory to explain complex human learning; this elaboration was verbal mediation theory.

In early *S-R* theory, only directly observable stimuli and responses were considered. A sequence of events could be described with a diagram of *S*s and *R*s; for example, the behavior of a child who ate a cookie could be represented by

$$S_{cookie} \rightarrow R_{eat}$$

A series or chain of *S*s and *R*s would be used to represent a more lengthy sequence of behaviors.

The Kendlers proposed that adult responses to learning problems, such as transposition, could be explained more completely if two new elements were added to the *S-R* scheme. They introduced the symbols for an internal response *(r)*, which is elicited (provoked) by the external stimulus *(S)*, and an internal stimulus *(s)*, which is elicited by the internal response and which in turn elicits an external response *(R)*. (Note: Capital letters represent observable events; lowercase letters symbolize internal, unobservable events.) With the introduction of the two new symbols, a simple *S-R* diagram becomes a more complicated *S-r-s-R* chain. The internal sequence *r-s* is called a *mediator* because it comes between and links together the external events *S* and *R*. If the *r-s* sequence involves words, it is a verbal mediator. *Verbal mediation,* then, is the intervention of an internal response *r* (words) and the internal stimulus *s* it elicits between an external stimulus *S* and an observable response *R*.

164   Think back to the transposition problem of Kuenne. According to the Kendlers' theory, the behavior of animals and preschool children can be diagrammed with a simple *S-R* model.*

$$S_{\text{transposition problem}} \rightarrow R_{\text{pointing to one square}}$$

Animals and young children presumably respond simply on the basis of stimulus characteristics. On the transposition problem they will therefore choose the square most similar in physical size to the originally correct square; that is, they choose the absolute response.

Older children and adults use words covertly to solve the problem; in other words, they use verbal mediation. Their behavior is represented as

$$S_{\text{transposition problem}} \rightarrow r_{\text{thinking "the big one"}} \rightarrow s_{\text{muscle stimulus}} \rightarrow R_{\text{pointing to one square}}$$

Since words such as "The larger one is correct" guide adults' responses to the initial problem, on the transposition test they will once again select the larger square, making a relative response.

Exactly why do young children have trouble with verbal mediation? One view is that children simply do not use words as mediators, even though the necessary words are familiar. Perhaps it never occurs to young children that thinking with words is a handy technique. This is the *mediation deficiency* explanation: children have mediators (words) available but for some reason do not use them. An alternative explanation is that young children may try to use words as mediators but are not skilled enough to produce the right words. Perhaps young children produce mediating words that are irrelevant to the problem and therefore lead them astray. This is the *production deficiency* explanation: children can use words as mediators, but they produce mediating words that are inappropriate.

If children fail to think like adults because they lack verbal skills, certain kinds of verbal experiences might help stimulate mental development. This suggestion is supported by the research of Hess and Shipman (1965), in which the problem-solving styles of 4-year-old children were related to the verbal stypes of their mothers. Each mother was observed teaching her child three simple tasks; in addition, both the mothers and the children were tested on several aspects of mental functioning. Middle-class mothers, as compared with lower-class mothers, gave verbal directions that were more reflective, more objective, more complex, more descriptive, and more likely to provoke abstract, organized thought. The children of the middle-class mothers, as compared with the lower-class children, were more likely to solve problems in a reflective way, to consider alternative solutions, to describe in words what they were doing, and to delay their responses long enough to analyze the problem. This study clearly demonstrates a relation-

---

*The Kendlers' theory was developed from research on different conceptual problems called reversal and nonreversal shifts. The *RV-NR* shift studies are not described here because the transposition problem is easier to understand and the application of verbal mediation theory is similar for both problems.

ship between mothers' language and children's thought. It does not prove that mothers' language style *causes* children to think in a certain way, however, because it is only a correlational study. There may be some factor not investigated by Hess and Shipman that is correlated with both social class and mothers' verbal style and that causes the differences in children's approach to problems.

The verbal mediation theory can possibly explain or be related to the changes in children's learning, the development of strategies, some changes in spatial orientation, the development of adult intelligence test skills, internalization of speech, and some memory changes that occur between the ages of 5 and 7. There are, however, several arguments against the verbal mediation explanation. One is that some children can solve problems in a verbally mediated way when they cannot describe the solution in words; conversely, some children can describe the solution, but solve problems as it they did not use verbal mediation. A second difficulty is that teaching a child labels for the stimuli does not reliably produce adultlike problem solving. A third argument is that deaf children (who are slow to develop verbal skills) learn to solve transposition-type problems at the same age as children who hear normally. From these and other research findings, it can be concluded that the development of verbal skills, specifically, verbal mediation, is *correlated* with but probably does not *cause* the changes in children's thought at 5 to 7 years.

Inhibition of associative thought

White (1965) proposed a theory to explain the changes between 5 and 7 years, based on (1) two levels of thought and (2) inhibition. *Inhibition* is holding back a response, or restraining behavior. According to White's theory, preschool children cannot or do not inhibit their responses. Adultlike thought is not available to children until they learn to inhibit, to take the time to consider a problem carefully. This proposal is not revolutionary; children are notorious for acting impulsively without reflection. Common admonitions to children (and impulsive adults) to "wait a minute" or "hold your horses" or "look before you leap" are evidence that we recognize the necessity of inhibition for complex thought. White's theory is noteworthy because he formalized this commonsense notion and conducted research to test it.

White suggested that adults can think at two levels. The *associative level* develops early in life and depends on conventional associative principles (simple forms of learning). Young children are limited to this level of thinking. Adults can think at this level, but ordinarily they prefer to think at the cognitive level. The *cognitive level* develops, or first becomes fully functional, between 5 and 7 years of age. The precise ways in which thought is processed at the cognitive level are not understood, but mental activity at the cognitive level is more complex, relational, organized, and abstract than at the associative level. In White's view, these two levels of thought are *temporally stacked;* that is, they require different periods to swing into operation. At the associative level, thought occurs very quickly; at the cognitive level, more time is required for a thought to develop. When a stimulus "initiates the hunt for a response," the fast-acting associative level of thought is tapped immediately. A young child will respond at this level, but an adult is more likely to *inhibit* the associative thought and wait for a response from the slower-acting cognitive level. Sometimes an adult responds at the associative level, particularly when stressed or pressured for a quick response, but ordinarily adults delay to allow a response from the cognitive level. For a child to develop adultlike thought, therefore, two events are necessary: the cognitive level of mental activity must be firmly established, and the child must learn to inhibit the speedy associative response for the slower cognitive response to occur.

White's theory can be used to explain the changes between 5 and 7 years of age, described earlier in the chapter. Inhibition theory might also be expanded to incorporate verbal mediation theory. One difference between White's two levels of thought might possible be that verbal mediation occurs only at the cognitive level. Producing words to direct thought certainly requires more time than impulsively responding without words, which is consistent with the suggestion that verbal mediation might be one of the slower cognitive-level functions.

White's theory can also be related to a series of studies of children's response style (Kagan and Kogan, 1970). Kagan has found that a child typically is either *impulsive* or *reflective* in thinking and problem solving. Impulsive children respond quickly on many tasks. Reflective children take more time to answer questions and solve problems. Reflective children also make fewer errors on memory tasks, make fewer reading errors, reason more effectively, process visual information more systematically, and in other ways demonstrate more advanced mental processes. Viewed in terms of White's theory, reflective children are more likely to inhibit the immediate, associative-level thought and act on the slower, cognitive-level thoughts.

Though White's theory fits the research data and is consistent with commonsense notions of children, it has one important weakness. The theory does not tell us exactly *what* happens in adult thought that takes more time than simple associations and is absent or only partially effective in the thoughts of a young child. One time-consuming mental process that develops during childhood and might account for the changes at 5 to 7 years is attention.

Attention

By the age of 7 years, two important changes occur in children's attention:

1. The length of time a child concentrates on a particular activity, commonly called *attention span,* increases. At 2 or 3 a child's interest darts from one thing to another very rapidly, but by 5 or 6 a single activity can attract a child's attention for a surprisingly long period.
2. The ability to discover the important features of a problem and to ignore the irrelevant or distracting ones improves markedly. In other words, a child learns to discover what is "worthy of attention."

Can improvements in attention account for the age-related changes in solving the transposition problem? Caron (1967) tried to answer this question with the three-choice transposition problem (large, middle-size, and small squares; the middle-size square is correct). Caron hypothesized that children of all ages use the same perceptual-explora- **167**

Fig. 8-4. A child of 5 or 6 can concentrate on a single activity for a surprisingly long time.

tory methods to solve problems; age differences result only because preschool children are less likely than older children to attend to the important features of the problem. The important feature of a transposition problem is size, but a young child may consider other irrelevant features (such as position) before thinking about size. When he presented the transposition problems, Caron obtained the results expected on the basis of previous research: more relational responding among 6-year-olds than among 4-year-olds and more relational responding among children who understood the concept of middle size than among those who did not. The interesting outcome of Caron's study was that when tasks were arranged in a way that drew attention to relative size, relational responses were made even by the youngest children and by the children who did not understand the words *middle size*. Since many of these children gave an adultlike response to the problem when they had *no* verbal concept of middle size, the verbal mediation theory cannot account for the results. Caron concludes that focusing a child's attention on the critical features of a problem results in adultlike solutions. This special focusing is probably unnecessary for children who describe the problem in terms of size, because their words reveal that these children have already decided that size is the relevant feature of the problem.

Considerable evidence points to the importance of attention in problem solving. Children can be easily distracted, and sometimes hopelessly confused, by adding more dimensions to a problem; adults simply take more time to sort out a problem with many dimensions. The difference between children and adults on this type of complex problem seems to be that children cannot easily discover which feature deserves attention.

Children also have biases that can misdirect their attention. One example is the "larger" bias that is common among young children. When size is a variable in a problem, most children choose the larger object first. The solution is therefore learned more quickly when the larger stimulus is correct than when the smaller one is. Color biases are common, too. When color is a variable, a wise psychologist will not make any stimulus red, because many children spontaneously choose red and stubbornly refuse to switch to another color. When the stimuli are letters of the alphabet, a child may respond to the initial of his or her name and show no interest in any other letter. An adult is less likely to fixate on a large stimulus or a red one or any other distinctive feature of the problem. Without the distracting biases of childhood, an adult can quickly eliminate an irrelevant feature of a problem and attend to something else.

Attention apparently is a significant factor in intelligence. Zeaman and House (1963) compared normal and retarded children's speed of learning simple discrimination problems. They found that retarded children learned the problems more slowly only because they took longer to direct their attention to the relevant feature of the problems. Once the relevant dimension was discovered, retardates arrived at the final solution just as quickly as did normal children.

The mental changes described earlier, which occur between 5 and 7 years, can be explained by increases in attention span and improvements in selective attention that occur in this period. Kagan and Kogan speculate that "central nervous system changes . . . may be responsible for the dramatic increase in performance between 6 and 7 in the child's capacity for sustained attention" (1970, p. 1301). If changes in attention at 5 to 7 years can be directly tied in with physical changes in the brain, attention theory will be strengthened considerably.

Verbal mediation theory can be incorporated in attention theory. Words, for example, can guide a child's attention to the important features of a problem. Attention can be directed to these features without words, too, but words are certainly helpful. Inhibition theory can also be viewed in terms of attention. Attending to the relevant features of a problem takes time, and time is available only if the child can inhibit an immediate response. Both verbal mediation and inhibition, then, can be encompassed by

169

attention theory. At present many child psychologists accept some version of attention theory as the best explanation of the transitions in mental functioning between early and middle childhood.

Piaget's theory

A fourth possible explanation of the mental changes at 5 to 7 years lies in Piaget's comprehensive theory of the development of intelligence. Piaget sees this age as a point of transition between two major periods in mental development. In the earlier stage (from 2 to about 6 or 7 years), a child's thought is determined primarily by perceptions. The preschool child is "locked in" to his or her own point of view and is unable to understand that there may be more than one way to look at a problem. In this period the child can consider only one aspect of a situation at a time; a problem that requires two features to be considered at once is beyond this child. When the child enters the next period, at about 6 or 7 years of age, thinking becomes more systematic, more factual, and more consistent with the concrete, physical world. The child's progress from one period to the next is, in Piaget's view, determined largely by maturation. The transition is relatively *in*dependent of specific learning experiences; it is dependent instead on a biologic timetable. Piaget has devised many imaginative ways to reveal the thoughts of children. His theory is an important alternative to attention theory and deserves more consideration than can be given here. Chapter 9 is devoted entirely to Piaget's theory.

Which theory is "true"? Probably none, in spite of the current popularity of certain theories among certain groups of psychologists. If the lack of a true theory bothers you, try to view theories as scientists view them. A good theory is not necessarily correct, but it explains the existing facts and stimulates future research. The future research inevitably reveals some weakness of the theory and results in the proposal of new theories. One characteristic of a good theory, therefore, is that it does not last forever.

SUMMARY

Important changes in children's thought processes occur between the ages of 5 and 7 years. Children develop more adultlike methods of learning, generating hypotheses and testing them, perceiving, responding to spatial orientation, answering questions on intelligence tests, using words (especially silently, "in the head"), and remembering. Four theories have been proposed to explain these impressive accomplishments. Verbal mediation theory is based on the ability to use words internally to guide thought. Inhibition theory emphasizes the ability to hold back or restrain responses, to allow sophisticated but time-consuming thought processes to occur. According to attention theory, these age changes result from learning to focus on or attend to important features of a problem. Piaget sees this time as a transition between two major periods in mental development; in his theory, the period from 5 to 7 years is only one of several "revolutions" in children's thought.

None of these theories is totally satisfactory, but one fact remains: between the ages of 5 and 7 years, a remarkable transition occurs in the way children think. The major implication of this is that a preschool child cannot be expected to think like an adult.

Young children are not "reasonable"—they often say one thing and do another, they have trouble following verbal directions (show works better than tell), they seem not to remember what they are told, they do not plan ahead, and sometimes they do not understand even a "simple" explanation from an adult. Much frustration can be avoided by keeping in mind the nature of a young child's thoughts.

REFERENCES

Bayley, N. Behavioral correlates of mental growth: birth to thirty-six years. *American Psychologist,* 1968, **23,** 1-17.

Belmont, J. M., & Butterfield, E. C. The relations of short-term memory to development and intelligence. In L. P. Lipsitt, & H. W. Reese (Eds.), *Advances in child development and behavior* (Vol. 4). New York: Academic Press, Inc., 1969.

Brown, R. W., & Berko, J. Word association and the acquisition of grammar. *Child Development,* 1960, **31,** 1-14.

Caron, A. J. Intermediate size transposition at an extreme distance. *Journal of Experimental Child Psychology,* 1967, **5,** 186-207.

Eimas, P. D. A developmental study of hypothesis behavior and focusing. *Journal of Experimental Child Psychology,* 1969, **8,** 160-172.

Hess, R. D., and Shipman, V. C. Early experience and the socialization of cognitive modes in children. *Child Development,* 1965, **36,** 869-886.

Kagan, J., and Kogan, N. Individual variation in cognitive processes. In P. H. Mussen (ed.), *Carmichael's manual of child psychology* (Vol. 1). New York: John Wiley & Sons, Inc., 1970.

Kendler, H. H., and Kendler, T. S. Vertical and horizontal processes in problem solving. *Psychological Review,* 1962, **69,** 1-16.

Koppenaal, R. J., Krull, A., and Katz, H. Age, interference, and forgetting. *Journal of Experimental Child Psychology,* 1964, **1,** 360-375.

Kuenne, M. R. Experimental investigation of the relation of language to transposition behavior in young children. *Journal of Experimental Psychology,* 1946, **36,** 471-490.

Levy, E. A., McClinton, B. S., Rabinowitz, F. M., and Wolkin, J. R. Two developmental studies of types of vicarious reinforcement on imitation and recall of a model's object preferences. *Journal of Experimental Child Psychology,* 1974, **17,** 115-132.

Luria, A. R. Speech development and the formation of mental processes. In M. Cole, & I. Maltzman (Eds.), *A handbook of contemporary Soviet psychology.* New York: Basic Books, Inc., Publishers, 1969.

McClinton, B. S. Cross-modal and intra-modal transfer of training in children. Unpublished doctoral dissertation, Tulane University, 1973.

Stevenson, H. W. Learning in children. In P. H. Mussen (Ed.), *Carmichael's manual of child psychology* (Vol. 1). New York: John Wiley & Sons, Inc., 1970.

White, S. H. Evidence for a hierarchical arrangement of learning processes. In L. P. Lipsitt, & C. C. Spiker (Eds.), *Advances in child development and behavior* (Vol. 2). New York: Academic Press, Inc., 1965.

Zeaman, D., & House, B. J. The role of attention in retardate discrimination learning. In N. R. Ellis (Ed.), *Handbook of mental deficiency.* New York: McGraw-Hill Book Co., 1963.

Persistent use of verbal rehearsal as a function of information about its value

Beth Ann Kennedy
Dolores J. Miller
University of Notre Dame

Sixty-two 6–7-year-old children participated in a serial recall task in which subgroups of "rehearsers" and "nonrehearsers" were identified by means of direct observation of semiovert verbalizations. The "nonrehearsers" were subdivided into equal groups both given training to verbally rehearse, but only one group received feedback relaying the strategy's value. When subsequently given the option of rehearsing, only those given feedback following rehearsal training persisted in using the strategy. The data suggest that one component of production deficiency, as it refers to rehearsal behavior in children, might be the absence of knowledge about the value of rehearsing.

Central to this project were the notions of the production deficiency hypothesis elaborated by Flavell and his colleagues. These investigators suggest the younger child tends not to produce relevant words at the appropriate point in the task situation, thus precluding any possible facilitative effect (e.g., Flavell, Beach, & Chinsky 1966).

Keeney, Cannizzo, and Flavell (1967) distinguished Producers and Nonproducers of rehearsal in a task that requires first graders to recall the serial order in which the experimenter had pointed to pictures of common objects. In a second session, the Nonproducers were trained to rehearse, and their recall scores then approximated that of the Producers. When given the option to rehearse or not during the remaining trials of this session, the Nonproducers generally abandoned the strategy. As noted by the authors, however, these children were not given feedback about the effect rehearsal had had on their recall performance. Such an omission may have accounted, in part, for the Nonproducers' lack of persistence.

In view of the procedures and results of Keeney et al. (1967), it could be suggested that one factor affecting voluntary production of a mediator like rehearsal, given it is in the child's repertoire, may be having a rationale for its use. To investigate this possibility, the present study was designed to replicate the method of Keeney et al. for detecting Producers and Nonproducers and for rehearsal training. The use of the newly trained strategy following presence or absence of information about its merit was then examined. It was hypothesized that, of the subjects given rehearsal training, only those receiving feedback would continue to use the strategy.

METHOD
Subjects

Sixty-two children, 6–7 years of age, were tested in a Jackson, Michigan, public school. The final sample consisted of 24 subjects who participated in both sessions of the experiment.

Apparatus

Pictures of six common objects (pig, moon, comb, apple, American flag, and flowers) were arranged in different random sequences on 15 display cards. In both sessions, the child wore a

From *Child Development*, 1976, **47**, 566-569. © 1976 by the Society for Research in Child Development, toy plastic helmet. The helmet's movable visor was covered with translucent tape and in its down position prevented the subject from seeing the surround.

Procedure

Each child was tested individually, with one experimenter administering the tasks and another scoring rehearsal and recall data.

Session 1. As in the Keeney et al. (1967) study, brief training was given on the concept of "same order" using colored blocks. Following this, the child was instructed on the use of the helmet during two three-item practice trials using picture materials. The child was instructed to look at each picture as the experimenter pointed to it, and then to lower the visor. In the 15-second interval while the visor was down, another arrangement of the stimuli was substituted. For recall, the child raised his visor and was told to point to the same sequence of pictures regardless of the new spatial locations of the items. Following Keeney et al., the number of items in the 10 subsequent trials was 5-4-3-4-5-3-2-3-4-5. Questioning about what the child had done to remember the pictures and naming of each of the objects followed.

Children were designated as Producers if they were seen to rehearse on nine of the 10 test trials. Those who rehearsed on one or none and in addition failed to report a rehearsal strategy were categorized as Nonproducers. Only subjects classified as Producers (6) and Nonproducers (18) were involved in session 2, held 3 weeks later. In addition to rehearsal data, each subject was scored for number of correct trials.

Session 2. The Nonproducers were paired on the basis of their recall scores of session 1 and then randomly assigned to either the Nonproducer-Feedback or Nonproducer–No Feedback group. All children were given an initial trial to assess stability of rehearsal behavior as classified from session 1.

Producers were given 10 trials as in session 1. Nonproducers in both experimental groups were shown arrays of new pictures, told to name each during experimenter pointing, then on signal to put the visor down and whisper the names over and over until time to raise the visor. Three practice trials were given using session 1 pictures. These stimuli and 10-trial sequence of session 1 were then used for subsequent test trials.

At the end of the 10 test trials, all children were given a brief stretch period. The experimenter told the Nonproducer-Feedback children, "My goodness, you did so much better when you whispered those names over and over. I guess whispering helped you remember the pictures better. Right?" Nothing of this nature was said to those comprising the Producer and Nonproducer–No Feedback groups, though the experimenter did exchange friendly words with them during this period. Prior to three more trials then given to all subjects, the children in the Nonproducer groups were told, "I'm not going to tell you to say the names over and over again anymore while we play the game. You can say them if you want to, but you do not have to. Okay?" The trials consisted of three, four, and five items.

Relevant rehearsal and recall data were scored as in session 1. An alternate scoring procedure, outlined by Keeney et al. (1967), was also used to focus on number of individual pictures correct. During both sessions, prizes were distributed as by Keeney et al.

RESULTS

Analyses were conducted to compare the serial recall performance of Producers and Non-producers for the 10 test trials of session 1; to determine the effects of rehearsal training for the 10 test trials of session 2; and to explore the effects of the feedback manipulation on both rehearsal and recall performance.

Session 1

Analysis of recall data for Nonproducers ($\overline{X}$ = 3.87) and Producers ($\overline{X}$ = 6.68) over test trials indicated superior performance for the Producers, $t(22)$ = 6.97, $p < .01$.

Session 2

Recall data of the Nonproducers ($\bar{X} = 8.16$) and Producers ($\bar{X} = 8.00$) for the 10 test trials were compared, $t(22) = -0.374$, $p > .05$. The lack of statistical significance between groups suggests the success of rehearsal training.

Comparison of rehearsal data for the final three trials of session 2 showed three of the nine No Feedback children abandoned rehearsal, two rehearsed on one trial, three on two trials, and only one on all three trials. In contrast, all nine Feedback children continued to rehearse on these trials as did all those in the Producer group. According to Fisher exact probability analyses, distributions of those children rehearsing versus those not rehearsing on all three trials of the final block were significantly different for the Nonproducer-Feedback and Nonproducer–No Feedback groups, $p < .01$. A significant difference was also found in the distributions of rehearsers and nonrehearsers for the Producer and Nonproducer–No Feedback group, $p < .03$. As evidenced in rehearsal data, those not given feedback rehearsed less frequently than children in the other two conditions.

Recall data, derived by the alternate scoring procedure, for block 3 (trials 8–10) and block 4 (trials 11–13) are shown in figure 1. A 3 (group) $\times$ 2 (block) analysis of variance for repeated measures yielded a significant main effect for blocks, $F(2,21) = 11.6$, $p < .01$, and a significant interaction for group $\times$ block, $F(2,21) = 9.37$, $p < .01$. The main effect for group only approached significance, $F(2,21) = 3.21$, $p < .06$. In view of the overall results of this analysis, blocks 3 and 4 were compared for each group to get at the nature of the recall most directly. The t tests showed that neither the performance of the Feedback group nor that of the Producers was significantly different from the third block of trials to the fourth block, $t(8) = 0.174$, $p > .05$, and $t(5) = 0.22$, $p > .05$, respectively. The only significant comparison was the difference in the blocks 3 and 4 recall performance of the Nonproducer–No Feedback group, $t(8) = 4.81$, $p < .001$, reflecting poorer performance of the final three trials.

In summary, the recall of the groups parallels their rehearsal performance. Producer and Nonproducer–Feedback groups continued rehearsing across blocks 3 and 4, and the recall perfor-

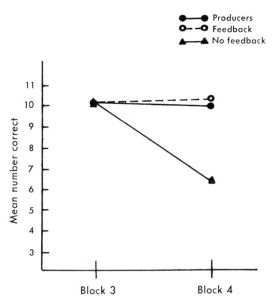

The mean number of pictures correctly recalled on blocks 3 and 4 in the groups.

mance for each was not different between the two blocks. The Nonproducer–No Feedback group rehearsed less in block 4 and concomitant recall dropped significantly from that of block 3.

DISCUSSION

The results of the present study suggest that persistent use and utility of a newly acquired rehearsal strategy may depend, at least in part, on having a rationale for engaging in such activity. Thus, one component of production deficiency, as it refers to rehearsal behavior in young children, may be the absence of knowledge about the value of rehearsing.

From a theoretical point of view, the rapid acquisition, use, or lack of use of rehearsal of the former nonproducing children would not be unexpected. The notions about intellectual development proposed by Piaget (Flavell 1963) anticipate these results in part. The distinction between underlying competence and performance as discussed by Flavell and Wolhwill (1969) also applies. Although age is not a critical index of developmental level, data from numerous studies suggest a child 6–7 years of age may possess the capacities of the late preoperational or early concrete operational phases of intellectual functioning. The basic potential to incorporate simple instructions, to conduct brief rehearsals, and to understand some simple cause-and-effect relationships should be part of the underlying cognitive repertoire brought to organism-environmental interactions. Such abilities, however, are not immediately reflected in reliable performance. Intellectual skills require experience to develop and organize. All children categorized as being in the same developmental level will not manifest equally skilled behavior, but the potential is there. The present experimental procedures simply provided the structure for and practice of a strategy within the child's range of competence. Thus, acquisiton of the strategy and its use during brief training was effected readily.

Use of rehearsal, or lack thereof, during the last block of trials may be explained similarly. While the child may have the ability to understand some cause-and-effect relationships, ability to detect them is a cognitive skill in itself requiring experience to develop. Present procedures provided an experience by making the relationship salient, through the experimenter's comment to one group. Knowledge of the effect of rehearsal evidently was sufficient reason for these children to persist for subsequent trials. Those not given a rationale abandoned the strategy, perhaps viewing rehearsal as extra work which they no longer were required to do.

Given that rehearsal has merit in a learning task, and the child proves capable of using it, the present data most directly suggest that relevant production deficiency may be overcome through training in the strategy which includes information about its benefits. The practical implications seem obvious. If the learning posture can be altered as readily with minimal feedback, consistent performance may evolve early on as a function of relatively few informative messages, saliently delivered, during early training. Further studies will be conducted to verify and extend the present findings. While spontaneous transfer of rehearsal strategy as a function of minimal feedback may obtain within task, transfer across tasks and time needs to be investigated systematically. Whether production of other types of mediators trained with such minimal feedback can be facilitated similarly will be examined also.

REFERENCES

Flavell, J. H. *The developmental psychology of Jean Piaget*. Princeton, N.J.: Van Nostrand, 1963.

Flavell, J. H.; Beach, D. H.; & Chinsky, J. M. Spontaneous verbal rehearsal in a memory task as a function of age. *Child Development*, 1966, **37**, 283-299.

Flavell, J. H. & Wohlwill, J. F. Formal and functional aspects of cognitive development. In D. Elkind & J. H. Flavell (Eds.), *Studies in cognitive development: essays in honor of Jean Piaget*. New York: Oxford University Press, 1969.

Keeney, T. J.; Cannizzo, S. R.; & Flavell, J. H. Spontaneous and induced verbal rehearsal in a recall task. *Child Development*, 1967, **38**, 953-966.

Chapter 9

A theory of intelligence: Piaget

Elaine M. Ward

The neighborhood play group has come in for cookies and milk, and the babysitter quickly provides each child with two cookies and begins to pour the milk. Aware that 4-year-olds are preoccupied with the ideas of being the "best," the "fastest," or getting "more" than someone else, the babysitter is very careful to pour the same amount of milk into each glass, as the 4-year-old judges make sharp-eyed comparisons. Unfortunately, there are six children and only five short, round tumblers. The sixth child gets milk in a slightly taller, narrower glass. As soon as this taller glass is set on the table, the recipient boasts "I got more milk; I got the most; I'm the best." Pandemonium reigns, and the babysitter's assertions that each glass is equally filled are ignored. The babysitter is unable to convince these children that they have all been treated fairly.

Incidents such as this are probably repeated daily in family groups, schools, and nurseries, while parents and teachers become frustrated in their attempts to explain to young children that although the milk level is higher in a narrower glass, there is just as much milk in a shorter and wider glass. Even demonstrations involving pouring the milk from glass to glass will not make much of an impression or end a heated argument. Why is it so difficult to reason with a child?

Several possibilities might come to mind in answer to this question. One is that it is unreasonable to expect a child to comprehend an abstract discussion that involves the relationship of height and width in containers of different shapes. Obviously! Yet it is important to note that even pouring the milk back and forth before the child's eyes will not end the debate. The reason is that young children apparently think differently from adults. Most people attribute the fact that children do not always behave in logical ways to the child's insufficient experience and resultant lack of knowledge, but this does not explain the fact that a demonstration will not end an argument. An interesting explanation of this phenomenon and a detailed theory concerning the development of thought processes in children can be found in the work of the Swiss theorist Jean Jacques Piaget.

Piaget was mentioned briefly in Chapter 1 as one of the important contributors to the field of child development. Piaget's theory is not strictly one of child development; rather, it is a theory of the development of intelligence. At one point in his career Piaget planned to spend just a few years studying children to further his study of intelligence and knowledge. Fortunately, Piaget's study of children has occupied more than just a few years. To understand and appreciate the basic concepts and aims of Piaget's theory, it is helpful to know a little about Piaget's personal history.

Piaget's initial interest was centered in the field of biology. Later he became interested in the more philosophic question of knowledge itself. This field of study is called *epistemology* and deals with the development and relationship of systems of knowledge. As Piaget moved from an interest in biology to an interest in knowledge, he also moved to an interest in studying children. The interest in studying children was actually a secondary interest, as Piaget began studying children to investigate the development of thought processes. In studying thought processes, Piaget has provided unique and important insights into the development of children.

Piaget's career is as unique and varied as his interests. He published his first scholarly paper when he was 10 years old and by the time he was 15 he had been offered the post of curator in a museum. Before he was 30 he had published five books, which present the original formulation of his ideas on the development of intelligence. Since that time he has defined and redirected his thinking and theory through the publication of more than 25 books and more than 50 lengthy articles (Flavell, 1963). This lengthy career began before Piaget was in his teens and has continued as he approaches his eighties. Piaget is a remarkable man.

The impact of Piaget's work on American child study has not been consistent over the years for a variety of reasons. First, Piaget's works are written in French and frequently there have been long time lags before his work has been translated into English. Second, Piaget's orientation and discussions are often incompatible with both the theoretical views of American psychologists and the methods of American psychology. For a long time American psychology was dominated by the concepts of learning theory (see Chapter 6). Piaget's discussion of abstract internal processes was not considered useful to people interested in investigating stimulus cues and reinforcement characteristics of children's environments. Finally, the types of questions that Piaget investigated and the way he investigated them were not entirely acceptable to American psychologists who were firmly entrenched in the experimental method (see Chapter 2). Piaget studied children by observing children.

As indicated above, the questions and topics that Piaget was concerned with were unique to his investigations and interests. Within the broader area of intellectual development, Piaget early in his career studied children's language, both for its content and structure, but also for an understanding of the child's ability to communicate. He also studied the child's ability to reason and understand the relationships expressed by such words as because and although. In the same manner Piaget investigated children's concepts of the world in regard to natural phenomena, much the way Hall did (see Chapter 1) when he asked children "Where does the sun go at night?" Piaget also studied events such as dreams. For example, he asked children where dreams were located. The children's answers indicated that they believed dreams were located in their rooms, their beds, their heads, or their eyes. An interesting sidelight here is that some children felt that others could not share or see your dreams unless they slept in your bed. A 5-year-old friend of mine (BGM) confirmed recently these ideas that Piaget collected early in the century by telling his father that the next time he had a bad dream he was going to kick it out of his eyes.

Another important topic that Piaget studied was moral judgment, including children's conceptions of naughtiness, lying, and punishment. Piaget presented children with hypothetical moral problems, such as which child is naughtier, a girl who tried to help her father by stirring his paint for him and spilled a whole gallon of paint on the driveway, or a girl who out of anger at being asked to help, drips a small amount of paint across a rosebush? This work is filled with examples of children busy being children. Piaget's interpretations of their responses and behaviors are insightful and offer the reader a perspective that can be useful in dealing with children in situations where logic fails, as in the milk glass problem described earlier.

Much of the material for these early investigations was gathered through careful observations of children (especially his own three children) and through rather informal questioning. Piaget would ask a child a question and then let the child's response guide him on to his next question to clarify the child's response or to expand it. The following conversations (Piaget, 1930) about causes of natural events are examples of this informal child-directed questioning.

> Grim (5 years old) was questioned near the banks of the Arve River, at a point where the current is strong and the slope is obvious.
> *Piaget:* Why does the water in the Arve move along?
> *Grim:* Because people make oars. They push.
> *P:* Where are the oars?
> *G:* In the boats there are men who hold them. They make it go.
> *P:* Do men make the water in the Arve go?
> *G:* With boats, great big boats.
> *P:* (There are a few skiffs downstream) Does the water run without boats?
> *G:* No, because that holds it back.
> *P:* Is the Arve running today?
> *G:* No . . . . It is moving along a little.
> *P:* Why?
> *G:* Because there are a few boats.

> Sala (8 years old)
> *P:* You have already seen the clouds moving along. What makes them move?
> *S:* When we move along, they move along too.
> *P:* Can *you* make them move?
> *S:* Everybody can, when they walk.
> *P:* When I walk and you are still, do they move?
> *S:* Yes.
> *P:* And at night, when everyone is asleep, do they move?
> *S:* Yes.
> *P:* But you tell me that they move when somebody walks.
> *S:* They always move. The cats, when they walk, and then the dogs, they make the clouds move along.

As Piaget continued his study of intellectual processes, his work shifted in both content and method. Piaget felt that his early directions were imprecise and that he could study intellectual processes more precisely by investigating questions about the child's understanding of number, classification, time, space, and velocity. In his investigation of these topics Piaget changed his technique of study and presented children with concrete problems that relied less heavily on language and hypothetical situations. For example, in studying number Piaget would place a row of pennies on the table and ask the child to make a second row that contained the same number of pennies. Once this was accomplished Piaget would rearrange his row of pennies and ask the child if there were still the same number of pennies in each row. Young children often said one row now had more pennies, even though no pennies had been added or taken away.

Along with the method of study, Piaget's interpretations of children's responses changed in his later work. In order to describe the underlying capabilities that direct the child's responses, Piaget began to use logical-mathematical structures in his descriptions   **179** and interpretations. He felt that descriptions in logical and mathematical terms made his points more precise and eliminated the vagueness he felt was inherent in the language of his early work. Further, he saw these structures as unifying his work and being more generally applicable to different content areas than the verbal explanations typical of his earlier work. It is true that the terminology and structure of his later work is more precise, more abstract, and hence less tied to specific situations, yet unless the reader is comfortable both with logic and mathematics, Piaget's later work is more difficult to interpret and it becomes more difficult to see the child behind the theory.

It should be noted here that in more recent years Piaget has also considered theoretically and experimentally the development of perception. You may recall from Chapter 4 a brief discussion of one aspect of his work in this area; however, due to the sheer amount of material even a brief consideration of Piaget's theory requires, we will not discuss Piaget's theory of perception in this chapter.

BASIC CONCEPTS OF PIAGET'S THEORY

The topics already mentioned are diverse and wide-ranging, and Piaget investigated many others that have been omitted. Piaget unites all these various topics in the general subject of intellectual development. He is interested in the structure, function, and content of intellectual processes and believes that these intellectual processes change in a qualitative fashion as they develop.

You may recall from Chapter 1 that Piaget at one point worked in Binet's laboratory and was involved in studying the intelligence test that Binet had developed. During this period Piaget noticed that children of different ages gave different types of wrong answers to the questions. In other words, there was a changing pattern of errors that children made with changes in age. This discovery has become a major cornerstone of Piaget's theory of intellectual development. Piaget sees intellectual processes as developing in a *qualitative* fashion. This means that children think in distinctively different ways at different ages. The changes in the child's thought are more than *quantitative* changes (changes in degree or amount). Older children think more logically and more efficiently than do younger children, not just because they have more information but because they are able to use that information in different ways from younger children. Older children have some mental abilities that simply are not available to younger children. Because Piaget believes that intelligence changes qualitatively as the child develops, his theory of cognitive development is a stage theory.

In discussing intellectual development Piaget begins with the behavior of the newborn infant and continues his discussion of intellectual functioning until the child's abilities are those of adult functioning. This point is reached in adolescence. In covering this span of 12 or 13 years of development, Piaget divides his discussion into four major divisions, which he calls periods, and several smaller divisions, which he calls stages. The following general discussion of periods should begin to help clarify the relationship between the structure, function, and content of intelligence.

The use of periods and stages in a theory of development implies a systematic sequence of changes during the course of development. If development involved continuous increments in ability (if one just got better and better as one grew) there would be no need for stages or periods of development. However, Piaget sees a definite need for periods of development. Each period is characterized by a particular way of behaving, or *functioning*, that is distinct from what went before it and what will come after. Yet each period is not isolated from the periods before and after. Each period incorporates the *function* and *structure* of the one before it and builds from that point. One important characteristic of the relationship between periods is that what the child has acquired in one period is reworked or reorganized as a newer way of functioning is developed in the next period. In this way each period is related to the others, incorporates the others, and builds on the others. In summary, each period is characterized by a specific mode of functioning that changes the structure or organization of the child's intellectual processes. It is possible to infer these structural differences by observing the child's interactions with various content areas.

Piaget's interest in biology significantly influenced his theorizing about the structure of intelligence, and he borrowed biologic concepts and terms to describe the intellectual processes.

Piaget sees intelligence as the result of two basic biologic characteristics that remain constant throughout development. These characteristics are a tendency to organize and a tendency to adapt. The tendency toward *organization* means that a person is a coherent unity in which events are interrelated and coordinated. The tendency toward *adaptation* means that a person is likely to make changes that ensure survival. These changes stem from interactions with the environment. The tendency to adapt is actually based on two specific processes called assimilation and accommodation. In *assimilation* the child (or adult) interprets or relates experiences to his or her present level or structure of understanding. In other words, the child interprets experiences in terms of how he or she understands the world, and this understanding may or may not match reality. If a child believes, for example, that eating watermelon seeds will cause a big belly, the child may conclude that a pregnant woman ate watermelon seeds (lots of them!). The child assimilates or interprets the new experience (seeing a pregnant woman) in terms of ideas already developed (that big bellies result from eating watermelon seeds). In *accommodation,* the structure of the child's understanding is changed by experiences. Suppose the same child is told that the pregnant woman has an unusual shape because she has a baby growing inside her. The child is likely to accommodate (change) his ideas about watermelon seeds (or his ideas about babies). He may conclude that babies come from watermelon seeds! Assimilation and accommodation are complementary processes that are constantly engaged as we experience our world.

In general, we tend to interpret each new experience in terms of what we have already experienced, what we already know. Sometimes this works, sometimes not. When it does not work, we distort our experience to fit what we know. However, after more interchanges with the world, we may encounter additional discrepant experiences that do not fit into the way we order the world. Then we must do some reordering of our understanding of the world. A very simple way of rephrasing what happens in assimilation and accommodation is that in assimilation the child "changes" the world and in accommodation the world "changes" the child. A small neighbor named Jonathan provides a nice example of assimilation. When Jonathan was about 2 years old, he fell and cut his forehead. He was rushed to the hospital in an ambulance. Afterward, when he talked about the event, he would say he had gone to the hospital in a fire truck. Jonathan was assimilating a new experience—ambulances—with something more familiar that he already understood—fire trucks. Because assimilation is a means of interpretation and understanding for the child, simply telling Jonathan that he meant ambulance did not help. In order for him to make the change in words from fire truck to ambulance, he had to develop a new understanding (an understanding that included ambulances, hospitals, doctors, and nurses) before he was ready to accommodate.

The structure of understanding that we have been referring to is made up of small units that Piaget calls *schemas*. The term schema is difficult to define or illustrate, but basically what Piaget means by schema is an organized cognitive unit. A schema originates as an action pattern that recurs frequently—so frequently that it becomes a unit, takes on independence from other actions or the original situation, and becomes useful to the child in organizing the world. Eventually these action patterns begin to function as cognitive units (symbols, memories, images). How this transformation occurs should become clear as the theory is detailed.

The concepts of organization and adaptation and of assimilation and accommodation make up Piaget's basic structure of the cognitive process. Recall that the child's cognitive abilities change qualitatively as the child develops. The basic mechanism of change in Piaget's theory is the process of *equilibrium*. It is the equilibrium process that produces growth and change through constant attempts to bring assimilation and accommodation into balance. When they are in balance, the child's behavior is relatively stable and his or her interactions with the world can be generally characterized and described as a specific period or stage. When they are unstable, there is transition, or change. Transition from period to period is the result of both maturation and experience. Further, experience involves more than contact with the world of objects; it involves the child's actions on the objects as well.

Before discussing Piaget's specific periods of cognitive development it should be emphasized that the age levels mentioned with each period are only approximate. What is important is the ordering of the periods, not the specific ages at which they are reached.

SENSORIMOTOR PERIOD

The sensorimotor period of development begins with birth and ends when the child has acquired the ability to use symbols. This generally occurs somewhere around the child's second birthday. This period is subdivided into six stages. Each stage is characterized by the development of a distinct functioning.

During the sensorimotor period the child's basic task is to coordinate the incoming *sensations* with *motor* capabilities. The child is confined to operating on the environment through actions only, and it is from overt action that intelligence and thought processes develop. In the beginning of this period the child is unable to differentiate self from the world of objects and see self as a separate entity. By the end of this period the child has made substantial progress and has developed a concept of objects. Being unable to differentiate oneself from the rest of the world in any sense is the most severe form of a general characteristic that Piaget calls *egocentrism,* or an inability to see the world from any point of view other than one's own. In sensorimotor egocentrism the infant is unaware of the existence of points of view at all.

Piaget has based the sensorimotor section of his theory on the careful observation of his three children. Much of his writing about this period involves the detailed description of a behavior example, which may be followed by a theoretical explanation of the event. Each observation is labeled with the child's name and age expressed in years, months, and (for infants) days. The following examples are quoted from *The Origins of Intelligence* (Piaget, 1952).

> At 0;1(1) Laurent is held by his nurse in an almost vertical position. He is very hungry. Twice, when his hand was laid on his right cheek, Laurent turned his head and tried to grasp his fingers with his mouth. The first time he failed, but succeeded the second time. But the movements of his arms are not coordinated with those of his head; the hand escapes while the mouth tries to maintain contact. . . .

> In the evening of 0;3(13) Laurent by chance strikes the chain while sucking his fingers. He grasps it and slowly displaces it while looking at the rattles. He then begins to swing it very gently, which first produces a slight movement of the hanging rattles and an as yet faint sound inside them. Laurent then definitely increases by degrees his own movements: he shakes the chain more and more vigorously and laughs uproariously at the result obtained. On seeing the child's expression, it is impossible not to deem this gradation intentional.

> At 0;9(16) Jacqueline likes the grape juice in a glass but not the soup in a bowl. She watches her mother's activity. When the spoon comes out of the glass she opens her mouth wide, whereas when it comes from the bowl, her mouth remains closed. . . . At 0;9(18) Jacqueline no longer needs to look at the spoon. She notes by the sound whether the spoonful comes from the glass or from the bowl and obstinately closes her mouth in the latter case. . . .

Stage 1: use of reflexes (birth to 1 month)

The reflexes the child is born with are the child's only means of operating on the world. These reflexes, however, are the important base from which the child's activity originates. Piaget uses the observation that infants tend to suck even when no stimulus is present, to introduce the concept of *functional assimilation* (if a person has a structure or schema available, there is a tendency to use it). This tendency to use existing structures is a basic force that stimulates activity *(generalizing assimilation)* to a variety of objects. Therefore, the infant begins to suck fingers, blankets, and so on, as well as nipples. This tendency apparently leads the infant to experiment with various objects, and as a result the infant begins to show a primitive type of recognition *(recognitory assimilation)*. For example, the infant begins to recognize that some objects are suckable and nourishing and that others are not. Thus, when hungry the infant is more likely to choose a nipple to suck than a blanket. Together these three tendencies are sufficient to begin to move the infant from a simple reflexive organism to one who is acting on the environment.

183

Stage 2: first acquired adaptations and primary circular reaction (1 to 4 months)

Piaget observed more definite signs of directed activity on the part of the infant during this stage. In particular, he noted that when a chance activity occurred involving the infant's own body and actions, the infant tended to repeat this chance activity. Piaget called this phenomenon the *primary circular reaction*. He saw its importance in that in repeating what was an accidental event, the infant showed some desire to set an action into motion, which usually involved some accommodation on the part of the infant. For example, an infant happens to bring his thumb and his mouth into contact while turning his head. To repeat this event, he must position both his hand and head properly, an act of accommodation. Also during this stage the infant shows a primitive *anticipation*, as he is quite likely to begin to suck as soon as he is placed in the usual feeding position.

Stage 3: secondary circular reaction and procedures designed to make interesting sights last (4 to 8 months)

The infant at this point makes significant progress in many areas of ability. One important ability that he has developed to the point of usefulness is visually guided reaching, which gives the infant more contact with objects. Partially related to this improved ability is what Piaget calls the *secondary circular reaction*. In this behavior sequence the infant begins to repeat a chance event that involves his actions and an object in the environment. For example, in moving about in the crib the infant's foot might kick the blanket up in the air, causing it to float down on his or her legs. In the secondary circular reaction the infant would then attempt to move the blanket again. Piaget saw this reaction as the early beginning of goal-directed activity.

Piaget also contends that during this stage the child may also show primitive *classification* of objects through recognitory assimilation. Piaget describes a behavior by Lucienne, his daughter (Piaget, 1952). Lucienne saw two toys hanging from the chandelier and shook her legs at them briefly. These toys had previously hung in her crib, where she had been able to kick them. Piaget saw her behavior as a recognition of the kickable toys and not a futile attempt to kick at toys at a great distance. This distinction and event are important. Piaget felt that she was indicating through a motor response (the only means available to her) that she recognized those toys as part of the group of kickable toys even though they were not available at that time for kicking. The fact that the infant uses motor responses as an indication of recognition is taken by Piaget as an illustration of his belief that thought processes stem from actions.

Stage 4: coordination of secondary schemas and their application to new situations (8 to 12 months)

During this stage the child shows more definite signs of goal-directed activity and the ability to use old schemas in new ways. The infant in the fourth stage will attempt to remove a barrier that separates him or her from a goal. For example, if a wad of blanket is in the child's way when reaching for a toy, the infant might hit the blanket out of the way. What is crucial here is that the hitting behavior has not been used previously to remove obstacles. This is an indication of the growing flexibility of the infant's behavior. Also during this stage the infant begins to show indication that he or she is able to anticipate events. For example, babies may begin to cry when they see adults put on their coats and are aware of the arrival of the babysitter.

Stage 5: tertiary circular reaction and discovery of new means through active experimentation (12 to 18 months)

Two major developments occur during this stage. The infant now actively pursues goals and through the process of trial and error may begin to use new means to reach goals. The infant also shows an interest in novelty for novelty's sake. This interest is the essence of the *tertiary circular reaction*. In the third circular reaction the child repeats previous behavior but now initiates changes in the repetitions. A child sitting in a highchair may begin to drop objects on the tray. After a few repetitions of this event, the child might vary the height of the drop over the tray or drop objects on the floor, first on one side of the chair and then on the other.

Stage 6: invention of new means through mental combinations (18 to 24 months)

This final stage of the sensorimotor period is really a transition to the next period. One major development in this stage is that the child is now able to invent new means to solve problems without the obvious trial-and-error process of stage 5. Piaget felt that by this point in development the child was capable of representing reality through symbols. The type of symbols Piaget was referring to are not words or thought, as we would normally consider thought, but are symbols involving motor responses, much as in stage 3, where Lucienne kicked at toys hanging from the chandelier. One of Piaget's most described observations best illustrates this point. While playing with Lucienne, at 1;4(0), he hid an attractive chain inside a small box.

> I put the chain back into the box and reduce the opening to 3 mm. It is understood that Lucienne is not aware of the functioning of the opening and closing of the match box and has not seen me prepare the experiment. She only possesses two preceding schemes: turning the box over in order to empty it of its contents, and sliding her fingers into the slit to make the chain come out. It is of course this last procedure that she tries first: she puts her finger inside and gropes to reach the chain, but fails completely. A pause follows during which Lucienne manifests a very curious reaction. . . . She looks at the slit with great attention; then, several times in succession, she opens and shuts her mouth, at first slightly, then wider and wider! . . . Lucienne unhesitatingly puts her finger in the slit, and instead of trying as before to reach the chain, she pulls so as to enlarge the opening. She succeeds and grasps the chain (Piaget, 1952).

The child was thinking through actions. As indicated earlier, Piaget felt actions were the forerunners of thought, and in this observation he felt he had seen an action-thought not quite internalized: not quite a mental symbol, yet an action functioning as a symbol. This idea of thought stemming from action may become more clear if you consider how new readers sometimes mouth or actually say aloud each word as they read. Another

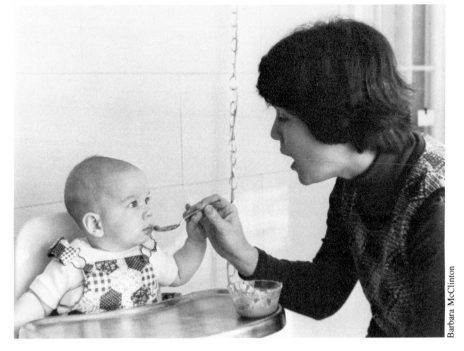

Fig. 9-1. Thought stems from action. Thinking about feeding the baby, the mother opens her own mouth.

example you may have observed occurs when a parent feeds an infant. As the spoon approaches the infant's mouth, the parent's mouth opens wide.

In the preceding section the sensorimotor stages have been described in general in terms of the major developments of each stage. Piaget, however, has traced the development of several special abilities through each of these stages.

One of the more important special developments that Piaget traced was the development of an *object concept*. Recall that to differentiate themselves from the world of objects in general, children must develop the idea that objects are stable events that have an independent existence of their own apart from the child's. You probably take this idea for granted. For example, if you drop your pencil on the floor and it rolls under your chair, you automatically reach down and feel for it with your hand. You assume it still exists, even though you can no longer see it. It takes an infant quite a time to reach this belief. During the first stage of development, objects are simply patterns of sights and sounds that appear and disappear in the infant's perceptions. By stage two, the infant will continue to stare at the spot from which an object disappeared. If an infant is shaking a rattle in his right fist, and the rattle falls out of his grasp, he will continue to stare at his hand and not look down to see the rattle lying on the blanket. The object really does not exist any longer for this infant until it reappears. In stage 3 the child anticipates the future position of a moving object and will look briefly in the direction where an object disappeared.

Fig. 9-2. Peekaboo is a favorite game of the child who has just developed object concept, because the child can make people "disappear" and "reappear."

This infant will look on the blanket for a dropped rattle but will give up the search if the rattle does not appear immediately. In stage 3 the child also will continue actions performed in relation to the object if he loses the object. In other words, in reaching for a moving object that moves out of sight, the child will continue to reach for it as the visual search takes place. A third development of this stage is the deferred circular reaction. The child performing an action in relation to an object stops the activity for something else but returns again to the original object and activity without any pauses or errors. A fourth development in object concept in this stage is that an infant can recognize a partially hidden object as the total object. All four of these events indicate that the infant is beginning to form a belief in the constancy of objects, but Piaget stresses that this belief is closely tied to the child's activity involving the objects.

By stage 4 the concept of object constancy is becoming stronger. The child now searches actively for a hidden object. The search involves new movements and activities, **187** indicating ideas of object constancy are being separated from the child's activity on the objects. However, although the child will search actively for an object, once it has been found in a certain hiding place the child tends to search there first, even when he or she sees it being hidden somewhere else. The object is still closely related to or part of its context in the child's world.

By stage 5 the child will search for a hidden object where it was last seen, regardless of where it was last found. However, if the object is moved while in hiding (such as shifting a penny from one closed hand to another), the child cannot cope with the invisible displacement even though the movement should be easily inferred. In the final stages the child is able to attribute permanence and independence to objects. The child can imagine several possible locations for an object and can handle the search for an object that has undergone invisible displacements (been moved while in hiding). When this point is reached the world becomes a much more stable place for the child. The child is able to use objects in play and in enriching skills. Objects are reliable, and the child's expectations concerning objects are frequently substantiated. As indicated earlier, Piaget outlines the development of several abilities in the same fashion as the idea of object permanence was outlined above.

At the close of the sensorimotor period (somewhere near 2 years of age) the child is able to act overtly on the world of objects and is no longer a passive part of a total undifferentiated whole. The child is able to pursue goals through activity and is beginning to be able to represent reality through action and rudimentary symbols. This acquisition of symbolic function begins to free the child from the concrete present, and eventually the use of symbols will enable the child to become part of the larger social system.

The development of symbolic function is the transition from the sensorimotor to the next period, which is that of preoperational thought. Piaget felt that the ability to refer to the world through the use of symbols developed from the child's imitation of objects and events. The first symbols are overt imitations of actions, such as Lucienne shaking her legs at her toys. These actions become less and less overt, such as Lucienne opening her mouth as she solves the matchbox problem, and eventually become internal images. For Piaget, early symbols probably take the form of images. These images are related to perceptual actions. For example, when viewing an object, your eyes move and trace the object for its outline and details. When you recall the object, your image of it may involve "internal" tracing of the object with imperceptible eye movements. The child's early symbols are felt to be highly personal and idiosyncratic. They are private, not social signs; yet they give rise to the child's ability to think representationally and to use language. These two abilities form the basis of the period of preoperational thought.

PREOPERATIONAL PERIOD

The period of preoperational thought begins when the child acquires the symbolic function (is able to make reference) at about age 2 years and continues until the child is approximately 7. During this period the child's thought processes are immature in several ways and frequently inconsistent as the result of the child being misled by perceptions. By the end of the period the child's thought will have matured to the point where he or she can operate on the world in both action and thought in a consistent, concrete fashion. The major task in the preoperational period is, in a sense, a reworking of all that was accomplished on the action level of the sensorimotor period into the representational thought level of the preoperational period.

A child in the preoperational period can be characterized as being highly egocentric (unable to see the world from any point of view except his own), dominated by perceptions, and having immature thought processes. This description sounds relatively pessimistic, yet the preoperational child is a fascinating study who generally meets the world with enthusiasm, wonder, and delight.

As Piaget developed this portion of his theory, he began to study children other than his own. The material on which the discussion of the preoperational period is based was gathered through observation and interaction with children in schools and at play. Piaget's early work on this period was based on observations and discussions he held with children. Much of his early work centered on the child's egocentrism and involved studying the child's use of language, ability to communicate, ability to reason, and concepts of

Elaine M. Ward

Fig. 9-3. Experimenting with mirrors is one way to learn about different points of view.

morality. Later Piaget changed his method of study and began presenting children with special problems to solve. He began to define the characteristics of the child's thought processes more precisely and to investigate more specific content areas, such as the child's ability to classify objects and understand numbers. In our discussion of the preoperational period we will first consider the child's egocentrism and then the more specific characteristic of preoperational immature thought, much in the same fashion as Piaget.

Egocentrism in language

Conversing with a 3-year-old can be a frustrating experience for an adult who wants information and is not aware of the egocentric nature of the preoperational child. An egocentric child is unable to take the point of view of another person and consequently does not tailor communications to meet the needs of the listener.

Piaget and his associates observed two 6-year-old boys at school for one month and kept a record of all they said. Piaget concluded that speech could be either egocentric or socialized. Socialized speech serves the purpose of communication. During socialized speech children convey information. In egocentric speech this is not usually the case. Piaget found that nearly half of the preoperational child's speech was egocentric, or did not convey information.

Egocentric speech has three major forms. The first of these is the monologue, frequently observed in young children. In the *monologue* a child is working (or playing) alone and talks as he works, often at great length. There are several speculative reasons for this. One possibility is that in the young child thought and language are not yet fully independent of action, and the child accompanies activity with the more newly acquired skills. As the child cuts a sheet of paper, he may say "cut, cut" all the while. Along slightly different lines, the child may not yet fully grasp the relationship of causality, actions, and thought-language. For example, the child stacking blocks may say "higher, higher" as a command or wish, perhaps expecting the words to effect the cause as well as proper stacking activity.

A second form of egocentric speech that might easily be mistaken for socialized speech is the collective monologue. In *collective monologues,* two or more children each carry on their own monologues in a group. It may appear on the surface that they are talking to each other, but closer examination indicates that they are not. First, the speaker, being egocentric, does not adapt speech to the needs of the listener; even if the second child wished to listen, he or she is not likely to be able to do so. Second, the children frequently talk simultaneously as they go about their activity, with no signs that they expect the others to listen. Further, the topics of conversation may bear no relation to each other. One child might discuss what he is eating for lunch (action and words undifferentiated), and the child next to him might respond with her own remarks about beating her brother at marbles as she rolls peas around on her plate. The reasons behind the collective monologues are the same as those for the simple monologues.

A third characteristic of egocentric speech is *repetition.* The preoperational child frequently repeats what has been said by another child and acts as if the repetition were a unique contribution to the conversation. My (BGM) son's nursery group provides a typical example. One evening when I picked up my son, I spoke to a little girl who was sitting with a group of seven other children. She responded by saying "Hi; here I am again." Each child in the group responded in turn with the same sentence, and each smiled and gave a "straight" rendition of the sentence without the giggling that follows a teasing remark by a preschooler. They each believed they were saying something important and unique.

Following these observations Piaget investigated egocentric speech and the preoperational child's ability to communicate by telling a simple story and asking the child to repeat the story. He determined that young children frequently use pronouns without indicating the referent. The reason for this and many other errors is that the child knows who is being referred to and assumes that the listener does as well. Along the same lines and for the same reasons, the child may leave out large portions of the story. Further, the child often repeats segments of the story out of order and frequently fails to connect causes and effects properly. All of these problems result from the child's inability to see the story as an integrated whole. These flaws in communication stem from the child-speaker, yet the failure to communicate is compounded if the listener is also a child. The child-listener generally assumes that he has understood the speaker! Another problem is that frequently the words of the speaker stimulate a sort of free association on the part of the listener, who then begins to think about and talk about an unrelated topic of his own. For example, one child may be recounting the story about Jack climbing a beanstalk, and the second child launches into a monologue about a puppy he saw at Grandma's. A likely connection is that grandma, who has a puppy, made him eat beans during his last visit. These egocentric speech patterns are also related to the content of thought and reasoning flaws of the preoperational child.

Egocentrism in reasoning

The preoperational child reasons from specific to specific: if mommy puts on her green dress, we must be having company because we had company the last time she wore it. This child also sees unrelated events as related if they happen to occur together. A child who was whistling as he played in the sandbox when it began to rain may not allow himself to whistle in the sandbox again for fear it may rain.

Preoperational thought is also characterized by animism, artificialism, and participation. In *animism* the child believes that inanimate objects are alive, and he or she might caution you to whisper in the garden at night so that you do not wake up the roses. In *artificialism* the child believes that natural objects were made by someone. A child hearing that the moon is very old and also knowing that his grandfather is very old might consider the possibility that his grandfather made the moon. Another flaw in the child's beliefs is the idea of *participation,* in which the child sees a connection between his activities and those of natural events. An example is the common belief that the sun follows the child around.

Many of these flaws combine and recombine along with the child's basic egocentrism to provide countless examples of inappropriate reasoning on the part of preoperational children. A typical example was provided by a neighbor who repeated to me (BGM) a re-   **191** mark made by her son about mine. Early in the summer, Richard saw my son at the community swimming pool. The two boys had not seen each other since the previous summer at the same pool. When Richard went home, he happily informed his mother that he had "found Jeremy right where I left him."

Egocentrism in moral judgment

Piaget also devoted much time to the study of children's concepts of morality. This work forms a separate theory with stages of development of its own, which overlap the periods of intellectual development. Due again to the sheer amount of material in Piaget's theory, we will only briefly consider a portion of Piaget's work on morality.

Piaget studied moral development by watching children play marble games and asking them questions about the nature of the rules of the game. (He equated being moral with following rules). Through this technique he developed his theory of moral development. He also studied moral judgment on the part of children, and this work illustrates the egocentric characteristic of the preoperational child. Piaget asked which child was naughtier, the one who accidentally spilled a large amount of paint or the one who purposefully splattered a small amount. The preoperational child, being essentially egocentric, is generally unable to take intentionality into account while judging another person's activity and so is likely to judge naughtiness on the basis of how much damage was done. Therefore, a preoperational level child is very likely to tell you that the helpful little girl who spilled a gallon of paint on the drive is naughtier than her sister who got mad and purposefully dribbled a little paint on the roses. Specifically, the egocentric child cannot take another's point of view, so is unable to consider the motivation of these two children and is forced to judge naughtiness by how much damage is done.

The child's conception of lying follows the same pattern. Unable to handle the idea of intention to deceive, a preoperational child is likely to judge the naughtiness of lying by the amount of exaggeration. The child who exaggerates by saying she saw a puddle as big as a lake is naughtier than the one who says he never left the backyard at all, when he did go next door against orders. The reason the second lie is less naughty is that he only went a *short* way out of bounds—a little lie; it would have been judged naughtier if the boy had gone a greater distance.

Before considering the next area of discussion, keep in mind that what was just presented was only a very minimal sample of Piaget's work on morality. However, being aware even minimally of the child's limitation of judgment should be useful and make for smoother interactions with children of this age. Now consider more precisely the specific characteristics of the thought processes of the preoperational child.

Immature thought processes

In addition to being basically egocentric, the preoperational child can be characterized as having immature thought processes. Piaget characterizes preoperational thought as being immature in at least six ways: it is centered, static, irreversible, unstable in equilibrium, based on action, and tied to how things appear in reality (Flavell, 1963). Of these, the first three are essentially the most important characteristics (Ginsburg and Opper, 1969).

Centered thought. In centered thought the child's attention is attracted by one facet of a situation and he or she is unable to take into account other features that are also important. Piaget's study of classification illustrates this point. If you give a child a group of red blocks and blue blocks that are all the same size and shape and ask the child to put together the blocks that are alike, the preoperational child will have no trouble because the blocks only differ in one way. However, if the group of blocks contained red cubes, red disks, blue cubes, and blue disks, the preoperational child will have difficulty sorting the blocks because thought is centered. The child at this level will center on one facet of the situation, either color *or* shape, and sort the blocks into two piles rather than four. This should happen even if the child is able to tell you that there are red disks, red cubes, blue disks, and blue cubes. Although this example sounds relatively straightforward, it is possible that other assortments may be made by the young child. The child may begin sorting on the basis of color, sort for awhile, and then be attracted by the shape of the most recent block sorted and begin sorting by shape, ignoring color altogether. The result will be two piles with no overall characteristic. Another possibility is that the child will not sort the blocks at all but will simply use the blocks to create a design. These last two possibilities are examples of the child's domination by immediate perceptions, or how things look, as well as centered thought.

Another example of centered thought that you might easily try with a preoperational child is to line up two pencils of the same length, one just below the other, so that they "start" and "stop" at the same place. Ask the child if they are the same size. The child should say yes. Then move the bottom pencil to the right a short distance and ask the child if the pencils are still the same size. If the child's thought is centered, he or she will judge equal size by the fact that both pencils start at the same spot or end at the same spot but not by both starting or ending points. A child judging by starting points will tell you the top pencil is longer; a child centered on the ending point will tell you the bottom pencil is longer. The child's thought centers on one aspect of the situation, and he or she cannot handle information about the beginning and the end at the same time.

Static thought. At the same time a preoperational child's thought is centered, it is also static. In static thought processes, the child is best able to handle information from situations undergoing change by making judgments based on the static beginning and end states, not the changes in between. Even when the child actually watches some transformation, he or she behaves as if unable to use the information about the transformation. For example, take three drawings of a glass, one upright, one tilted at a 45° angle, and one upside down, and ask a preoperational child to draw the water line in each glass. The child should have no trouble with the first and last pictures. In the first picture, the child should draw a wavy line across the glass parallel to the top and bottom; in the last picture the child may draw no line or a puddle under the glass. In the middle picture, he is most likely to draw a waterline parallel to the top and bottom of the glass, not parallel to the ground, as it should be. This should occur even if you fill a glass with water and pour it out several times in front of the child. The child's thought is centered on the static states and gains no useful information from the changing states between.

Irreversible thought. Perhaps the most important characteristic of immature thought and the most difficult to illustrate is the characteristic of irreversible thought. In irreversible thought the child is unable to undo mentally that which has been done in reality. For example, if you were to receive directions for driving to a friend's new apartment across town, you would simply follow the directions to get there with no problems. After you have spent some time there and are ready to return home, you will take advantage of *reversible* thought. Before you leave you will retrace backward the route you took to get there to make sure you can get back to where you came from. You will probably talk to your friend to make sure you have reversed the route properly. A preoperational child cannot do this.

A student in one of my (BGM) classes tested this example one semester by taking children (one at a time) of ages 4, 5, and 7 years, on a walk from an unfamiliar playground. After walking a short way, he stopped and asked the children to guide them back to where they had started. All the children thought it was a grand game, but only the 7-year-old could actually retrace the walk accurately. The preoperational child's thought is irreversible.

Each of the above immature thought characteristics can cause faulty reasoning and performance on the part of the preoperational child; however, in combination the effects of these characteristics can cause the child to behave in ways that seem inconsistent and puzzling. The combined effect of these characteristics can be found in what Piaget called the conservation problems.

Conservation problems. In studying the preoperational child's idea of number, volume, and other specific concepts, Piaget developed a series of problems called conservation problems. He wanted to find out if children were able to understand that matter undergoing transformations or obvious changes of state, could still be the same matter, or be conserved. There are several of these problems, but we will consider the conservation of a continuous quantity here, both to illustrate immature thought and to get back to the milk and cookies problem with which we started the chapter.

In presenting this conservation problem to a child, Piaget used two glasses or containers of the same shape and size. Call them glass A and glass B. Into each he poured colored water to the same level so that the child would agree that there was the same amount to drink in both glasses. Then Piaget poured the water from glass B into a new container that was taller and thinner (glass C) and asked the child if there was the same amount to drink in glass A as in glass C. A child whose thought is centered, static, and irreversible will answer no. Then Piaget poured the water from glass C back into glass B and asked the child to compare glasses A and B. The child then said there was once again the same amount to drink in glasses A and B. This same inconsistency will occur over and over each time water is poured into a different sized glass. Frequently Piaget would use a fourth container, a low wide one (glass D) and get the same results. Water in glasses A and B are the same, but when water from B is poured into C or D, the child says there is no longer the same amount. Generally when the water is in C (the tall thin glass), children believe there is more to drink in C than in A. When the water is in D (the short wide glass), they believe there is more to drink in A than in D.

Students who try this problem find that no amount of argument will convince a pre-

Fig. 9-4. Conservation develops through maturation and a variety of experiences with water and other liquids.

operational child differently. Even having the child do the pouring does not help. The reasons for the failure of the preoperational child in this situation are threefold.

First, the child's thought is centered. To understand that the water is the same in all containers, one must consider both changes in height and width when making the judgment of amounts. The preoperational child centers thought on either height or width to make comparisons, but not on both. Therefore, a child who centers on height will say glass C has more water than does A and that D has less water than A. A child who centers on width will say A has more water than B does and that D has more water than A.

A second reason for failure is that the preoperational child's thought is static. The preoperational child only gains information from the beginning and end points of the

195

process and gets no information from actually watching the transformation (the pouring water from glass to glass). This is why letting the child do the pouring does not help him correct his judgments. No matter how many times the water is poured back and forth, the child will still make his judgments solely on how the water level looks in the two glasses when the pouring is finished.

The third contributing factor to the child's failure is that the child's thought is irreversible. The child cannot mentally undo what has been done in reality. When the child is asked to compare the water in glass A and in glass C, he or she does just that: compares the way A *looks* with the way C *looks*. The child cannot mentally pour the water from C back into B and then compare A and B and get the correct answer. Even though the child sees the pouring back and forth several times, he or she cannot put the water mentally back into B to confirm that it is the same amount of water.

Until thought has matured, the child is not able to reason that there is the same amount of water in all the glasses. To do this the child's thought must move from centered to decentered. In *decentered* thought the child is able to consider more than one aspect of a situation. In this case the child would note changes in width and height.

The child's thought must also move from static to dynamic. In *dynamic* thought the child is able to attend to transformations between end states and gain usable information. The child would be able to benefit from seeing the water poured from glass to glass and note that no water was added or lost.

Finally the child's thought must move from irreversible to *reversible*. In this example the child could undo mentally what had been done, imagine the water from C back in B, and confirm that the water was the same in both glasses.

When the child's thought processes have matured to the point where the thought is decentered, dynamic, and reversible, the child makes the transition to the third major period, the concrete operational period.

CONCRETE OPERATIONAL PERIOD

The transformation into the concrete operational period generally occurs at around 7 years of age and usually continues until the child reaches adolescence. This period roughly covers the elementary school years. Because this period and the one following it extend beyond the early childhood years, they will only briefly be outlined to give an overview of Piaget's total theory.

The concrete-operational child's thought processes are mature in the three ways described above (decentered, dynamic, and reversible). Further, the concrete operational child has a coordinated cognitive, or mental, *system* with which to work. The sensorimotor child operates on the world entirely through actions, the preoperational child is able to add representation of the world to his operations, and the concrete-operational child organizes actions and representations into a coherent system or unity. Piaget saw this system as a complicated mental structure, which he described in mathematical terms. Because the concrete-operational child has a coordinated mental system, any change in one part of the system has implications for other parts. This means inconsistencies will show up and be detected. The concrete-operational child's system will not tolerate inconsistencies that the preoperational child did not even notice (for example, when water from glass B was poured into C it became more, and when poured into D it became less).

The concrete-operational child has advanced beyond the preoperational child in a number of ways. The concrete-operational child can classify objects along several dimensions. The concrete-operational child is also able to conserve where the preoperational child could not. He or she can grasp the relationship between various events and can create matching series of different kinds of objects without difficulty. This means the concrete-operational child can line up a series of paper dolls of varying heights correctly from largest to smallest and match a series of large to small boxes with the large to small dolls. The concrete-operational child is able to imagine an object or a scene from another perspective; the preoperational child cannot. For example, a concrete-operational child viewing an array of objects can rearrange the array to show how it would look if you were sitting on the other side of the table. In language and reasoning, the concrete-operational child is able to see the viewpoint of others and to communicate effectively with another person. The concrete-operational child is also able to share goals and cooperate with other people.

The name of this period, concrete operations, points out the major limitation of this period. The child's realm of operations is confined to concrete reality. The child learns from and best handles experiences that are real and concrete rather than abstract. For example, concrete-operational children can solve rather complex problems *if* they have the necessary materials to work with. Their technique of solving problems is unsystematic and inefficient at this period, but given the materials and the time, they can reach a solution. Because concrete-operational children work best in concrete reality, their instruction is more efficient if they learn by doing and from demonstrations rather than from abstract discussions or reading.

FORMAL OPERATIONS

The final period of Piaget's theory is the period of formal operations, generally reached in adolescence. The formal-operational child is no longer bound by reality, but is able to operate in the realm of possibility. The formal-operational child is able to think in terms of the hypothetical and in solving problems generates all possible solutions and then proceeds to select the best solution, without the trial-and-error process of the concrete-operational child. The formal-operational child can plan operations to a greater extent than can the concrete-operational child. Once again, Piaget describes the characteristics of the thought processes of this period in mathematical terms. This period is the culmination of the three that went before, and at this point the child can operate from a formal, reasonable base.

It can be noted here that formal-operational children are again in a sense egocentric in that their new preoperation with thought and their thought processes get them to believe in their own ideals to the point where the formal-operational adolescent begins to believe that he or she can change the world.

Flavell, who has written an excellent comprehensive book on Piaget's theory, sums up the general characteristics of the last three periods in this fashion:

> The preoperational child is the child of wonder; his cognition appears to us naive, impression-bound, and poorly organized. There is an essential lawlessness about his world without, of course, this fact in any way entering his awareness to inhibit the zest and flights of fancy with which he approaches new situations. Anything is possible because nothing is subject to lawful constraints. The child of concrete operations can be caricatured as a sober and bookkeeperish organizer of the real and a distruster of the subtle, the elusive, and the hypothetical. The adolescent has something of both: the 7–11-year-old's zeal for order and pattern coupled with a much more sophisticated version of the younger child's conceptual daring and uninhibitedness. Unlike the concrete operational child, he can soar; but also unlike the preoperational child, it is a controlled and planned soaring, solidly grounded in a bedrock of careful analysis and painstaking accommodation to detail (Flavell, 1963).

APPLICATIONS

Piaget developed his theory to explain how thought develops, not to provide practical knowledge regarding the rearing and education of children. Parents and educators, though, can hardly resist looking for ways to apply Piaget's ideas to children.

Elaine M. Ward

Fig. 9-5. Activity is more valuable than explanation to a young child.

One of the fundamentals of Piaget's theory is that children learn though *actions*. Incorporating new experiences (assimilation) and changing existing ideas or methods of thought (accommodation) are active processes. To foster a child's mental development, then, the child must be allowed to explore, to experiment, and to "reinvent" ideas, even though such activities are often accompanied by a certain amount of mess, noise, and apparent confusion. The role of a teacher or parent is not to provide explanations but to act as a "tour guide" who encourages curiosity, introduces children to new situations, and opens up interesting possibilities. (Before you conclude that Piaget advocates free schools and permissive childrearing, recall that he did not address himself to practical problems of teaching and parenting. The applications suggested here are merely extensions of Piaget's abstract theory to concrete situations.)

A second point derived from Piaget's work is that a *variety of experiences* is needed to stimulate mental development. The potential pattern of development is predetermined by biologic factors, but for this potential to be realized a child must have opportunities for many different experiences. Mental development does not depend on specific "educational" events but on chances to "play" with an interesting, varied environment.

A third concept derived from Piaget is that a child's learning is enhanced by *optimal cognitive conflict*. Cognitive conflict results from discrepancies between the child's knowledge and a new experience. The new experience must be somewhat familiar to the child, or assimilation will be hindered in one of three ways:

1. The new experience may be totally rejected. Try telling a "true believer" that there is no Santa Claus (or try telling a feminist that women should not attend college), and see how quickly your idea is rejected.
2. The new experience may seem to be accepted but without genuine understanding. The usual result of requiring students to learn material that is completely foreign to them is memorization and little evidence of comprehension.
3. The new experience may be assimilated to some unrelated structure and interpreted in an inaccurate way. Amusing examples of such misinterpretations are often found in student's papers; for example, "A spinster is a bachelor's wife"; "The equator is a menagerie lion running around the earth and through Africa"; "The student was expelled from school for using profound language."

A child will not learn from experiences too novel to be assimilated, but slight discrepancies between existing knowledge and a new experience (optimal cognitive conflict) will stimulate the child's curiosity and lead to self-motivated learning.

A fourth suggestion based on Piaget's theory is that *interaction with other children* will help a child outgrow egocentrism (seeing the world from one's own point of view). The child will discover that other children have different beliefs and opinions. Conflicts (both cognitive and emotional) inevitably develop between children, and by resolving these conflicts themselves, children can grow mentally. Adults should try not to interfere when conflicts arise (unless they become too serious), to give the children a chance to develop their own solutions.

A new approach to *intelligence testing* has been another outgrowth of Piaget's work. Traditional intelligence tests produce IQ scores that estimate how bright a child is com-

Elaine M. Ward

Fig. 9-6. Conflicts between children are unpleasant to watch, but they can promote mental growth.

pared with other children of the same age. (This topic is discussed in detail in Chapter 10.) Each question on such a test is designed to have a right answer, known by about half of the children at a particular age. The questions are chosen for their ability to distinguish bright children from dull ones. As an alternative to the traditional IQ test, Laurendeau and Pinard of the University of Montreal developed a test based on Piaget's theory. Questions for this new test were derived from Piaget's descriptions of thought at each period. The emphasis is not on comparing children with each other but on determining a child's level of mental development in terms of Piaget's theory. Questions are relatively unstructured, and the primary interest is not right answers but the child's explanation of whatever answer was given. Rather than an IQ score, the test results are presented in the form of a description of the quality of the child's thought. The Montreal method of testing requires about 10 hours per child, but a much shorter test (about 25 minutes) based on Piaget's theory has also been developed. The shorter test yields scores that compare favorably with scores on traditional IQ tests. Intelligence tests based on Piaget's theory are unlikely to replace the widely used IQ tests, but they appear to be a useful supplement to the traditional tests.

A final benefit derived from Piaget's theory is an *enriched understanding* of children's behavior. When a new mental ability is developed, a child likes to exercise, or "play with," the fascinating new skill (functional assimilation). By understanding how structures develop and at what periods, changes can be predicted in the typical activities of children as they grow older. For example, with the development of object concept in the sensorimotor period, the child becomes fascinated with objects that disappear and reappear. Peekaboo is a favorite game at 6 months or so, because it provides the child a chance to make people "disappear." Later in the sensorimotor period, the child purposely repeats actions to discover whether the results will always be the same (tertiary circular reactions). It should not be surprising that after 12 months or so a child will repeat "experiments" almost endlessly. When an infant purposely spills juice on the floor ten times to watch daddy's reaction, the weary parent can comfort himself with the thought that mental growth is indeed progressing.

Behaviors typical of the preoperational period can also be predicted from Piaget's theory. The preoperational child is dominated by perception. It is no wonder that this child will be easily fooled by illusions and simple magic tricks or easily frightened by "monsters." The child's reasoning never goes beyond the ways things appear. Similarly, the preoperational child has difficulty separating fantasy from reality. Dreams, for instance, are as real to a 3-year-old as events experienced while awake. The effects of egocentrism also can be seen in the preoperational child's behavior. If parents are divorced or a sibling dies, the child is likely to conclude that he caused the calamity. Children often wish a parent or sibling would "go away." From the child's viewpoint, mere wishing made the fantasy come true. Language skills become fully developed during the preoperational period. Children frequently engage in playing with words (imaginary conversations, storytelling, and the like) and experimenting with funny sounds.

Trying out new mental skills continues in the last two periods. A concrete-operational child has learned to categorize efficiently; some 8-year-olds endlessly sort baseball cards, by league, team, and position. The period of formal operations is marked by the ability to think ahead and anticipate possible outcomes. One "symptom" of this ability is intense interest at about 12 years in Nancy Drew and Hardy Boys mysteries. The capacity to think in the abstract also gives rise to concern about philosophic issues, such as religion and utopian societies.

The enriched understanding of children gained from Piaget allows an appreciation of the limitations as well as the accomplishments of children's thought. Some of the concepts we try to teach children in elementary school, for example, are probably inappropriate for concrete-operational children. A symbolic, abstract subject like math might better be saved for older children. Forcing children to learn concepts beyond their mental capacities leads to frustration, failure, dislike of the subject, and precious little comprehension. No wonder many young people hate math! Teaching and reasoning with children is easier if we recognize that children's thought is qualitatively different from our own.

EVALUATION OF PIAGET'S WORK

Any theorist who is as productive and original as Piaget is bound to be the target of criticism.

Piaget's methods of collecting data, especially the observations and interviews he conducted early in his career, are not as consistent and systematic as they might have been. Most of his observations were of the behavior of his own three children. The **201** similarities among his children (who, after all, were genetically related and reared in a single environment) led Piaget to conclude that the pattern of development he observed was universal. Later studies of other children and in other cultures have cast some doubt on the generality of Piaget's conclusions.

Piaget's published papers and books are unnecessarily difficult to read. The difficulty results partly from the complex, abstract nature of many of his ideas. But some of the difficulty is due to vague expressions, inconsistencies, and lack of operational (specific) definitions. Terms such as schema, for instance, are defined differently in different sources, and none of the definitions is crystal clear. Many of Piaget's interpretations are speculative and only loosely related to observed behavior.

Some implications of Piaget's theory, if carried to their logical conclusions, are difficult to accept. His emphasis on active rather than passive learning, for example, could be extended to the radical notion that teaching children is useless, and perhaps even harmful, for mental growth. (To be fair, remember that Piaget developed a theory of cognitive development, not a theory of education.)

Finally, even if one overlooks questionable methods, vague and inconsistent writing, and doubtful applications, there remains a problem of interpretation. What is the best explanation of facts Piaget collected? Some psychologists believe that Piaget's *maturation* (stages) theory is not supported by the data. Why accept a complex theory with many assumptions if a simpler, already accepted theory can explain the same facts? Possible alternative theories include *perception* (young children's strange answers to conservation problems and the like result from misperceptions of the situation, not from inability to think), *language* (children's difficulties in interviews result from misunderstanding Piaget's complicated questions), *learning* (children can be taught Piaget's concepts, but in our culture they ordinarily do not have the experiences necessary to learn them spontaneously for a number of years), and *motivation* (young children do not care enough about Piaget's problems to direct much effort or attention to solving them). Each of these theories has received some experimental support, but none explains all of Piaget's facts as well as Piaget's own theory. Piaget's theory has become more popular among psychologists in the last 15 years, partly because psychologists have come to recognize that biologic timetables are important in development, partly because of the elegance of the concepts of assimilation and accommodation, and largely because many of Piaget's descriptions of children's mental capabilities and limitations have been verified by experiments and by personal observations.

SUMMARY

Piaget began his studies of children as a means of discovering how adult thought develops. He made detailed observations of children, questioned them about numerous subjects, and (later in his career) studied their solutions to logical, symbolic, and mathematical problems. Piaget described two mental activities that continue throughout life: *organization* and *adaptation* (change resulting from interactions with the environment). Adaptation results from two complementary processes, which also continue throughout life: *assimilation* (taking in new information, interpreted in terms of existing structures) and *accommodation* (changing existing structures to fit new information). Children progress through four periods of mental development; in each period, thought is qualitatively different from the preceding period. During the *sensorimotor* period (birth to 2 years) an infant develops thought by coordinating sensations with motor activities. Symbolic thought is possible in the *preoperational* period (2 to 7 years), but the child's thought is egocentric and limited by appearances (perceptions). The child's thought becomes more systematic and realistic in the period of *concrete operations* (7 years to adolescence), but abstract thought is not possible till the period of *formal operations*. Piaget was not interested in practical applications of his theory, but parents and educators have tried to extend his work to everyday problems. In spite of criticism, Piaget's theory is gaining popularity among psychologists.

REFERENCES

Flavell, J. *The developmental psychology of Jean Piaget.* Princeton, N.J.: D. Van Nostrand Co., 1963.

Ginsburg, H., & Opper, S. *Piaget's theory of intellectual development: an introduction.* Englewood Cliffs, N.J.: Prentice-Hall, Inc., 1969.

Piaget, J. *The language and thought of the child.* London: Routledge and Kegan Paul Ltd., 1926.

Piaget, J. *The child's conception of physical causality.* London: Kegan Paul, 1930.

Piaget, J. *The origins of intelligence in children.* New York: International Universities Press, 1952.

Objective responsibility in children: a comparison with the Piaget data

Gene R. Medinnus

A. INTRODUCTION

In his discussion of the development of moral judgment in the child, Piaget (1948) described changes in moral judgment as a function of age insofar as the child's chronological age defines the nature and quality of his social relationships. Specifically, Piaget emphasized the importance of the progression from the constraint exercised by the unilateral authority of parental discipline in early childhood to a relationship of cooperation existing among peers in the later childhood years.

One aspect of moral judgment found in the young child under the age of 7 or 8 years is termed "moral realism" by Piaget. This he defined as "the tendency which the child has to regard duty and the value attaching to it as self-subsistent and independent of the mind, as imposing itself regardless of the circumstances in which the individual may find himself" (1940, p. 106). In other words, moral rules are regarded as right in themselves and they are applied in a relatively rigid manner. Moral realism possesses three principal features: *(a)* Duty is essentially heteronomous. Obedience to adult commands is good, and any act which does not conform to adult rules is bad.

From *The Journal of Genetic Psychology,* 1962, **101**, 127-133.

(b) Because of the externality of the adult-imposed rules, moral realism demands that the letter rather than the spirit of the law be observed. *(c)* Objective responsibility, in which an act is evaluated in accordance with its conformity to rules rather than in terms of its motive and in which consequences rather than intentions are stressed, arises from features *(a)* and *(b)*. According to Piaget, moral realism is due to the conjunction of two series of causes, the spontaneous realism and egocentricity of the thought of the child and the constraint exercised by adults.

The morality involving objective responsibility is gradually eliminated as the child passes from a status which requires obedience to one characterized by mutual respect and cooperation. Taking intention into account is made possible only when the child is able to go beyond his own immediate point of view; his thinking becomes less absolute and more relativistic in nature and he is able to ascribe motives to other persons' behavior.

Around the age of 7 or 8 years, the child's changing relationship with adults and with his peers is reflected in his moral judgment. Unilateral respect is gradually changing to mutual respect; cooperation is taking the place of constraint; autonomy is replacing heteronomy. Peer solidarity leads to the priority of equality over authority. Cooperation, suppressing both egocentrism and moral realism, promotes the interiorization of rules. Subjective responsibility, which stresses intentionality and the autonomy of conscience, supplants objective responsibility.

The present paper is concerned only with the shift from subjective to objective responsibility as it is reflected in children's attitudes toward lying. According to Piaget, a change occurs with age in the child's attitude toward lying; this shift is brought about as a result of the child's changing role in relation to others. The young child, impressed with adult authority, believes lying is wrong because it is forbidden by adults. Cooperation with peers convinces the older child of the necessity of not lying and of reasons for not so doing; rules become comprehensible and interiorized. Piaget distinguished three stages in this age progression (1948, p. 168): "In the first stage, a lie is wrong because it is an object of punishment; if the punishment were removed, it would be allowed." In the second stage, "a lie becomes something that is wrong in itself and would remain so even if the punishment were removed." In the third stage, "a lie is wrong because it is in conflict with mutual trust and affection."

B. PROCEDURE

1. Description of the subjects

Two hundred forty children, 30 boys and 30 girls at each of the following age levels, 6, 8, 10, and 12, served as Ss in the present study. The Ss were selected from the lower socioeconomic groups, specifically from Classes V, VI, and VII according to the Minnesota Scale for Paternal Occupations (1950). Children from these groups were used so that the sample would be as comparable as possible to that used by Piaget, who studied children from "the poorer parts of Geneva."

2. Method

Eighteen story-situations and questions drawn from Piaget were administered to each S individually. The Ss' responses to the questions were recorded verbatim by the examiner. Only the item involving the following two questions pertaining to lying will be discussed in this paper:

Question 1: Why is it naughty (wrong) to tell lies?

Question 2: Would it be all right to tell a lie if you didn't get caught and if no one punished you for it?

Four judges, graduate students in psychology, who were interested in this area and who were familiar with the work of Piaget, sorted the responses of the 240 Ss to this item. The directions for classifying the responses were based on Piaget's discussion of the three stages in the age progression from objective to subjective responsibility mentioned earlier. Examples of each stage, drawn from Piaget, were also furnished the judges.

The purpose of the judges' classification of the responses was twofold: first, it was desired to learn whether the responses were such that they could be classified according to the definitions and examples provided by Piaget; and second, the age relationship posited by Piaget was tested. This was done by using a 4 × 3 chi-square table (the four ages by the three stages). A response was placed in a given category when three of the four judges agreed in placing the response in that stage. The sex difference in response to this item was tested for significance by summing the number of responses falling into each category for the boys and girls separately over the four age levels.

C. RESULTS

High inter-judge agreement was shown in the judges' categorizations of the responses to the two questions. All four judges agreed in placing 181 of the responses in a given stage, while three out of four judges agreed on an additional 33 responses. Thus all four judges agreed on 75 percent of the responses and three out of the four judges agreed on a total of 89.2 percent of the responses. A response was placed in a given stage for the analysis of age changes only when three of the four or all four judges concurred in their categorization of that response. That the responses to this item by the Ss in the present study could be classified according to the scheme outlined by Piaget is indicated by the fact that all except 26 of the 240 responses were classified with 75 percent or greater inter-judge agreement.

Table 1 gives the number of Ss at each age level whose responses were classified into each of the three stages. Although there was a significant change with age in the Ss' responses, with a tendency toward a greater number of "mature" responses with increasing age, it can be seen from Table 1 that only 10, or 16.6 percent, of the responses of the 6-year-olds fell into Stage 1, and only 15, or 25 percent, of the 12-year-olds' responses were classified as belonging in Stage III. One hundred and sixty-two of the 214 classifiable responses were assigned to Stage II. The sex difference in response to this item was not statistically significant.

D. DISCUSSION

A brief review of Piaget's discussion concerning children's attitudes toward lying and an examination of the criteria which he employed to classify his Ss' responses would seem to provide some clues to the present results. Piaget regarded the constraint of adults upon the young child as the basis for the latter's "purely external and realistic conception of rules," which he defined in terms of the young child's tendency to "look upon lying as naughty because it is punished, and if it were not punished no guilt would attach to it." Proof of the fact that lies are forbidden by God or by parents rests upon the punishment which is received, and, if the punishment were removed, telling lies would be allowable. In the second stage, "a lie is wrong because it is wrong in itself and would remain so even if the punishment were removed." The single distinguishing feature between Stages I and II, then, is the child's response to the question, "Would it be all right to tell a lie if you didn't get caught and if no one punished you?" If the child answered "yes" to this question, his response was placed in Stage I; if his answer was "no," the response was placed in Stage II. In Stage III "a lie is wrong because it is in conflict with mutual trust and affection." An examination of the responses of the Ss in the present study to the question, "Why is

Table 1. Number of responses classified into each of three stages at the four age levels

Age	I	II	III
6	10	44	1
8	4	45	9
10	1	38	11
12	1	35	15
Totals	16	162	36

$\chi^2 = 22.33$.
$p < .01$

Table 2. Number of responses falling into each of two main categories at the four age levels

	Age			
Categories	**6**	**8**	**10**	**12**
1. A lie is wrong because it is forbidden and punished.	43	45	27	20
2. Answers denoting a concern with the consequences of a lie.	7	7	25	36

it naughty (wrong) to tell a lie?'' revealed a number of fairly specific, meaningful themes: *(a)* you get punished; *(b)* it is naughty; it isn't right; God, Jesus, or parents don't like it; *(c)* you get into trouble; *(d)* you hurt others; *(e)* you don't get any place; it just leads to more lies; *(f)* you always get found out anyway. By classifying the responses into these six categories, it was found that in general the number of responses falling into the first two categories decreased from age 6 through age 12 while the opposite was true for the remaining categories. Interpreting the six themes in terms of Piaget's discussion of moral realism and objective responsibility, it would seem appropriate to group together the first two themes on the basis of their explanation of lying as wrong because it is forbidden and because it results in punishment. The last four themes, on the other hand, seem to reflect the child's concern with the possible consequences which might arise from lying. Table 2 gives the number of responses at each age level when the themes are grouped on this basis. It can be seen that the answers of the 6- and 8-year-olds were essentially similar, with approximately 85 percent of the responses at both age levels falling into the first category. The 10-year-olds' responses were divided almost equally between the two types, while a greater number of the responses of the 12-year-olds indicated a concern with the consequences of a lie.

The point of the present discussion is that while the results obtained from classifying the responses of the Ss in this study to the question, ''Why is it naughty to tell a lie?'' according to the schema outlined by Piaget do not seem to be particularly meaningful, classifying the responses according to the major themes which they represent leads to results which are in essential agreement with the basic thesis detailed by Piaget. The young child considers lying as wrong only insofar as it is a transgression of the rules and precepts laid down by adults; this is a clear reflection of objective responsibility as defined by Piaget: an act is evaluated in accordance with its conformity to rules rather than in terms of its motive or its consequences. In evaluating lying, the older child, on the other hand, judges in terms of consequences, which indicates his ability to recognize reasons for the existence of certain rules and regulations; lying is wrong, not merely because it is proscribed by adults, but because of the undesirable consequences which may result from it.

The present finding concerning no statistically significant sex difference in response to the questions used agrees with the writer's results in the area of immanent justice (Medinnus, 1959), and is also in aggreement with Durkin's (1960) findings with regard to an examination of Piaget's notion of reciprocity between children.

Although in most current discussions of Piaget's contributions, writers (e.g., Ausubel, 1958, p. 567; Bloom, 1959) concur in emphasizing the stimulus to research which Piaget's writings have provided, a number of criticisms are inevitably voiced. While these criticisms center about his unstandardized methods of investigation and his overemphasis upon stages of development, it seems to the present writer that much of the controversy arises from the failure of follow-up studies by various researchers to reproduce or corroborate Piaget's original data. This may be due to a too-rigid adherence to the schemes Piaget outlined for the classification of responses, coupled with insufficient understanding of his basic theoretical position. In the present paper, for example, little agreement with Piaget's findings was apparent until the data were reexamined with regard to the actual themes present in the Ss responses. Further consideration of these themes in the light of Piaget's discussion of moral realism and objective responsibility revealed a meaningful relation of the present findings to his original propositions. Perhaps a situation exists in the area of moral judgment comparable to that described by McCarthy (1946) with regard to follow-up studies of Piaget's notion of egocentricity in children's language development. McCarthy pointed out that studies attempting to classify language samples based on a literal interpretation of Piaget's definitions emerged with much smaller percentages of egocentric responses, while researchers who devised their own definitions of egocentricity agreed much more closely with the percentages reported by Piaget.

E. SUMMARY

In the present study, 240 children, 30 boys and 30 girls at each of the following four age levels, 6, 8, 10, and 12, were administered a questionnaire consisting of stories drawn from Piaget's writings concerning moral judgment. The Ss were selected from the lower socioeconomic levels. The data obtained pertaining to objective responsibility as it is revealed in the children's responses to the question, ''Why is it naughty (wrong) to tell a lie?'' were presented and discussed.

High inter-judge agreement was found in the judges' categorizations of the Ss' responses to the two questions according to the scheme outlined by Piaget. Although there was a significant change with age in the Ss' responses, a majority of the responses at all age levels were assigned to Stage II. A reexamination of the data revealed a number of meaningful themes; when the responses were classified according to these themes, and the themes grouped in the light of Piaget's discussion of moral realism and objective responsibility, results in essential agreement with Piaget's basic thesis were obtained. No significant sex difference was obtained.

Several comments were made with regard to criticisms of Piaget's work and concerning follow-up studies designed to extend and evaluate his findings.

REFERENCES

1. Ausubel, D. P. *Theory and problems of child development.* New York: Grune & Stratton, 1958.
2. Bloom, L. A reappraisal of Piaget's theory of moral judgment. *J. Genet. Psychol.,* 1959, **95,** 3-12.
3. Durkin, D. Sex differences in children's concepts of justice. *Child Develpm.,* 1960, **31,** 361-368.
4. McCarthy, D. Language development in children. *In* Carmichael, L. *(Ed.), Manual of Child Psychology.* New York: Wiley, 1946. Pp. 476-581.
5. Medinnus, G. R. Immanent justice in children: A review of the literature and additional data. *J. Genet. Psychol.,* 1959, **94,** 253-262.
6. *Minnesota Scale for Paternal Occupations.* (Pub. of Inst. of Child Welfare) Minneapolis: Univer. of Minnesota Press, 1950.
7. Piaget, J. *The Moral Judgment of the Child.* Trans. M. Gabain. Glencoe, Ill.: The Free Press, 1948.

Chapter 10

Measuring intelligence

Elaine M. Ward

Imagine that you have never heard of an intelligence test. How would you go about determining a child's intelligence?

Might you observe the child, looking for intelligent behavior? Ask the child questions, listening for intelligent answers? Ask a teacher to rate the intelligence of the child compared with all the other children in the class? Time the child's attention to a mental task? Find out how many words the child understands? Test the child's memory? Measure the child's strength and physical coordination? Estimate the weight of the child's brain?

Any of these methods might be used to estimate a child's intelligence. Which is the best method? A best intelligence test cannot be chosen until we decide what intelligence is and why we want to measure it. If we define intelligence as common sense and measure it for the purpose of predicting whether a child can think of practical solutions to everyday problems, the test will not be the same as if we define intelligence as accumulated knowledge and measure it for the purpose of deciding whether to advance a child to the next grade in school. The best intelligence test is the one most suitable for the definition of intelligence and the purpose in measuring intelligence.

Unfortunately, psychologists, educators, and other potential intelligence testers do not agree on one single definition of intelligence. Teachers often define it as the ability to solve problems efficiently. Parents may define it as the ability to outshine other children, to earn better grades, or to make more clever remarks. Dozens of definitions have been suggested by psychologists, including—

Ability to think in abstract terms
Capacity for knowledge and amount of knowledge possessed
Ability to perform complex, abstract tasks efficiently and creatively
Capacity to think rationally and deal effectively with the environment
A collection of 120 distinct mental abilities
A quality of logic that emerges naturally as a child grows older
General ability to learn
Inborn, all-around, intellectual ability
Capacity to perform well in school
Whatever intelligence tests measure
No test can be suitable for all these definitions!

In contrast to the multitude of definitions, there are traditionally only two main purposes for measuring intelligence: (1) to observe how mental activity normally develops, with an eye toward similarities in development among normal children (Piaget); and (2) to identify differences among individuals to discover what causes some people to be brighter than others and to predict an individual's mental ability at an older age (Binet; Bayley; a host of other psychologists). Piaget's maturational approach to intelligence is described in Chapter 9; in this chapter the individual difference viewpoint is emphasized.

INTELLIGENCE TESTS THEN AND NOW

In 1882 Sir Francis Galton made the first systematic attempt to measure intelligence. Galton believed that keen senses produced keen intelligence, because an intelligent **209** person was one who efficiently gathered knowledge by observation. Galton set up an "anthropometric laboratory" and proceeded to test the sensory equipment of any person who would pay for the privilege. He found that sensory ability varied widely, but he was not able to relate this characteristic to other mental abilities. He persisted in his belief that intelligence was hereditary, because genius "clearly" ran in his family. (Galton's IQ is estimated at 200; the IQ of his renowned cousin Charles Darwin is estimated at a mere 135.)

The first intelligence test of the type used today was designed by two Frenchmen, Alfred Binet and Theodore Simon. In 1904 Binet and Simon were asked by the Minister of Education to find a way to identify at an early age children who were retarded and needed special schooling. Rejecting Galton's sensory capacity theory, Binet and Simon developed a series of intellectual tasks to measure skills like the ones required in school. The tasks varied in difficulty, and by testing young children the Frenchmen established an average score for each age, called a *mental age*. A child who achieved the same score as an average 6-year-old, for example, had a mental age of 6. Three important features of the Binet test have been retained in modern intelligence tests: (1) the purpose of the test was to predict success in school; (2) the test was heavily loaded with questions requiring use of words and reasoning; and (3) intelligence was measured on a relative basis, with comparisons among children and an emphasis on individual differences.

Binet's test was soon brought to America, where Lewis Terman of Stanford University thoroughly revised and standardized it. The new version, first published in 1916, was called the Stanford-Binet. Terman introduced the term *intelligence quotient (IQ)*, which expresses intelligence as the relationship between mental age and *chronological age* (the number of years since birth). To calculate an *IQ*, Terman divided mental age *(MA)* by chronological age *(CA)* and multiplied by 100 (to remove the decimal point). Expressed as a formula

$$IQ = \frac{MA \text{ (mental age)}}{CA \text{ (chronological age)}} \times 100$$

A 5-year-old *(CA)* who answers as many questions as the average 6-year-old *(MA)* would have an IQ of 6/5 × 100, or 1.20 × 100, or 120. If a 5-year-old answered only as many questions as the average 4-year-old, the IQ would be 4/5 × 100, or 0.80 × 100, or 80. Since most normal children achieve a mental age very close to their chronological age, most IQs are about 100. Today the tests are designed so that the average score is 100, and about two thirds of all children score between 85 and 115.

The modern Stanford-Binet presents a variety of challenges to a child. A 5-year-old, for example, is asked to fill in the details on a half-finished picture of a man; to fold a square of paper as shown by the tester; to define ball, hat, and stove; to copy a square; to identify similarities and differences between pictures; and to arrange two triangles into a rectangle. At age 6 the tasks include defining simple words; explaining differences between objects, such as wood and glass; telling what part of a picture is missing; counting; and tracing simple mazes with a pencil. These problems are essentially similar to tasks at school, especially because they require watching an adult and following directions.

Elaine M. Ward

Fig. 10-1. IQ tests for school-aged children emphasize following directions and other skills essential for success in school.

How well does the Stanford-Binet fulfill its originally intended goal, to predict success in school? The correlation between IQ and school performance is moderately high, about 0.60. This means that some children with high IQ scores may do poorly in school and some with low scores may do well, but ordinarily children with high scores earn high grades and children with low scores earn low grades. This relationship between IQ and grades is not surprising, because IQ tests measure mental activities that schoolwork requires. The failure of IQ scores to predict school performance in some cases may result from nonintellectual factors, such as a child's lack of interest in schoolwork.

The Stanford-Binet is an individual intelligence test administered to one child at a time. Individual testing is still the preferred method for preschool children, but group tests have been developed for school-age youngsters. The typical group test measures many of the same skills as the Stanford-Binet. One adult can test many children at once, but the test must be administered and timed precisely according to the instructions, and children who have trouble following directions may receive artificially low scores. The best group IQ tests predict school performance nearly as well as the Stanford-Binet.

Originally the Stanford-Binet was designed for children of any age from 3 to 18 years. In 1937 a test for 2-year-olds was added. A number of other intelligence tests appeared in the 1930s or later, including the well-known Bayley Scales of Infant Development. The Bayley Scales measure mental and motor skills from 2 to 30 months of age. The Motor Scale tests abilities, such as holding the head up, sitting, standing, going up and down stairs, grasping small objects, and throwing a ball. The Mental Scale includes behaviors, such as looking at objects, shaking a rattle, smiling, babbling, imitation, looking for hidden objects, and following simple directions. Like the Stanford-Binet, the Bayley Scales are scored by comparing number of items passed to the infant's age. Unfortunately, scores obtained on the Bayley Scales during the first 2 years of life are only slightly correlated with scores obtained on other tests after 4 years. These low correlations mean that scores at age 4 cannot be predicted with any certainty before age 2. (Adult IQ cannot be accurately predicted until about 6 years by any test. This may be because intelligence does not stabilize until age 6, but it is more likely because the abilities measured before 6 years are very different from the abilities measured by an adult IQ test.)

W. C. Baker

Fig. 10-2. Infant development scales measure attention and motor skills as well as social skills.

Many other measures of mental development are commonly used with young children, especially in situations where the Stanford-Binet is impractical. The Peabody Picture Vocabulary Test is especially appropriate for children with speech impairments, cerebral palsy, short attention span, or other problems that make testing difficult. The child is shown a series of pages, each with four pictures, and is asked to point to the picture that represents a particular word. The Peabody test can be used with children as young as 2½ years. Administration, scoring, and figuring IQs are simpler than for the Stanford-Binet. Scores on the Peabody and the Stanford-Binet are quite similar ($r = 0.71$), but the Peabody does not predict success in school quite as well as the Stanford-Binet.

A test that is especially appealing to children is Goodenough's Draw-a-Man test. The child simply draws a picture of a man or woman. This test is easy to administer but tricky to score. Scoring depends on the basic structure of the drawing (for example, are two arms and two legs present?) and details, such as eyes, fingers, and elaborate clothing. Inexperienced scorers may have problems with the Draw-a-Man test, because judgments are often necessary. This test is less useful as a predictor of school success than either the Stanford-Binet or the Peabody.

CORRELATES OF IQ

Literally hundreds of studies have been devoted to finding traits that are correlated with intelligence (see Reese & Lipsitt, 1970, for a thorough review). Remember that when two characteristics are highly correlated, one can be confidently predicted from the other. Correlations do *not* indicate that one of the characteristics causes the other. Factors that "cause" intelligence are complex almost beyond imagination. Be careful not to assume that intelligence is shaped by one or only a few factors.

The moderately high correlation between IQ and school performance has already been described. Another reliable correlation, which has been confirmed time and again, is between IQ and socioeconomic status. Children from middle- and upper-class homes consistently score 10 to 20 points higher on IQ tests than do children from poor homes. Social class differences do not appear until 3 years of age. It is not clear whether younger children are immune to social class effects or infant tests are not sensitive to social class differences (Golden et al., 1971). Of all the factors included in socioeconomic status (income, occupation, education, attitudes), parents' education is most highly correlated with children's IQ scores. This means that parents' level of education is a better predictor of children's IQ than any other element of social status.

Another factor clearly related to IQ is ethnic or racial background. Black children, Indian children, and Spanish-American children typically score 15 or more points lower, on the average, than do white or Oriental-American children. In many cases, ethnic background is also correlated with social class; separating these variables is difficult. In the few studies in which social class was carefully controlled, racial and ethnic differences tend to disappear.

City-reared children typically score higher on IQ tests than do children from rural areas. This difference is most striking when the rural areas are most isloated. As the children grow older, the detrimental effects of living in an isolated place are exaggerated. It is possible that the decrease in intelligence over time occurs because the more intelligent children move out of the rural area, but a more likely explanation is that the harmful effects of living in a boring, unstimulating environment add up, year after year, as the children grow older.

Several characteristics of parents (besides education) are correlated with IQ scores. Parents' and children's IQs are only slightly correlated before the children reach the age of 2 years, but they grow more and more similar as the children grow older. By age 6, parent-child correlations approach 0.50. The increase in similarity between intelligence scores of parents and children over time suggests that family setting plays a major role in development of mental skills.

Children of demanding, "pushy" parents have higher IQ scores than do children of unconcerned parents who make few demands and show little interest in their activities (Kent & Davis, 1957). Parents who provide an all-around stimulating home environment have children with higher IQ scores. In one study, parents who had high expectations for the child, who encouraged vocabulary development, who created learning situations in the home, who assisted with homework and school activities, and who were aware of their children's mental abilities had children with higher IQ scores. The correlation between IQ and this type of home atmosphere was remarkably high (0.69) (Wolf, 1964).

IQ and family size are significantly related, although the correlations are fairly low (about 0.30). Children's IQ scores are higher in smaller families. (Small families are likely to have higher socioeconomic status; again, there are problems in separating the variables.) In addition, within a family the firstborn child is likely to have a slightly higher IQ than later children. One possible explanation is that children from large families, especially later born children, receive less adult attention than do children from small families (Zajonc, 1975).

IQ can also be predicted by certain personal characteristics of a child. Children with high IQs are more likely to be independent, competitive, and willing to wait for rewards (Sontag & Baker, 1958). Bright children as young as 5 years are significantly more assertive and more willing to knock down a barrier to get a toy (Dorman, 1973). Creativity and intelligence are also related, but in a complex way. A certain level of intelligence is a prerequisite for creativity; above this level, intelligence and creativity are unrelated (Torrance, 1967). Healthy children score higher on IQ tests than do children with short- or long-term illnesses, but perhaps sick children are simply less interested in playing games with a psychologist. Many other personality traits have been correlated with intelligence, but most of these studies deal with older children and adolescents.

IQ is often assumed to be related to a child's sex, age, and general learning ability, but contrary to some of our most cherished beliefs, these relationships are weak or nonexistent.

Boys and girls score equally well on IQ tests because the tests are designed that way. Questions that one sex answers more easily than the other are dropped from the test. Children certainly accumulate more knowledge as they grow older, but their intelligence *relative to their agemates* does not change much. Because IQ is a relative measure and because the formula adjusts for age, IQ does not change much as children grow older. The one exception is that children in restricted environments, such as isolated farms or orphanages, lose IQ points as they grow older.

IQ is related to school-type learning situations, but many other learning tasks (like memory tests or concept-formation tasks) are not necessarily easier for children with higher IQs. Stevenson (1970) states that IQ cannot be defined as a general ability to learn, because on tasks that are different from the usual IQ test problems, children with high IQs are not always the most speedy learners.

POVERTY AND INTELLIGENCE

Lower than normal measured intelligence is associated with both physical impoverishment (disease and malnutrition) and environmental impoverishment (lack of suitable stimulation), especially if these conditions occur early in life.

Distinguishing the various effects of physical impoverishment is difficult because in many cases several negative factors occur together. IQ can be depressed by numerous diseases. Genetic diseases usually produce the most severe effects. Genetic disorders known to affect IQ are Down's syndrome (mongolism, a disorder related to the presence of an extra chromosome), phenylketonuria, or PKU (lack of an enzyme needed to digest proteins, which results in slow poisoning as the proteins accumulate), Tay-Sachs disease and Spielmeyer-Vogt disease (disorders related to accumulation of certain fats in the nervous system), and cretinism (abnormally low levels of hormones usually produced by the thyroid gland). The effects of contagious diseases are usually less devastating, but brain damage and loss of IQ can occur from complications of simple diseases such as measles, especially if high fever is present. Diseases contracted by a pregnant woman, such as German measles and hepatitis, can depress the IQ scores of her child.

Of all negative influences on intelligence, malnutrition may be the most widespread throughout the world. Lack of adequate food, and especially lack of protein, is clearly associated with a dazed, dull look in children and abnormally low intellectual functioning. Underfed children certainly lack the energy and curiosity needed for close attention and complex, logical problem solving. There is also evidence that physical damage to the nervous system results from malnutrition. Most of the experiments on malnutrition involve animals, for obvious ethical reasons. Compared with female rats fed high-protein diets, female rats systematically deprived of protein, starting a month before and continuing through pregnancy, have smaller offspring with fewer and less developed brain cells. Similar results are found in comparisons of malnourished and normal children, especially if nutrition is poor during pregnancy or at a young age. A group of well-fed African children was compared with a group from the same area that experienced severe malnutrition in the first year of life. By the age of 7 years, the malnourished group was markedly inferior in body size, head size, and IQ. For these children malnutrition occurred during a crucial period for brain development, when the brain is still growing rapidly. Malnutrition at an older age is not likely to have such serious effects **215**

(Bayley, 1970). Although these studies deal with effects of severe malnutrition, moderate malnutrition also depresses IQ but to a lesser extent.

Children who are well nourished and free of disease must also live in surroundings that stimulate intellectual growth if they are to develop normal mental skills. Physically normal children who are reared in unfavorable settings, such as orphanages, score much lower than average on IQ tests and other mental measures. Dennis (1960), for example, found that gross retardation was typical of children reared in orphanages in Iran, where the infants and toddlers had very little contact with adults (they were not even held during feedings) and few interesting objects to look at or explore. Although the children received enough food and had no significant diseases, they were smaller than normal, lagged way behind normal children in motor development, scored very low on IQ tests, showed little interest in people, and had a dull, vacant look. One indication of the overwhelming consequences of this unstimulating environment was that by age 4 only 15% of the children could walk alone. Children who were adopted from the orphanage before 2 years of age recovered almost entirely from their earlier retardation, but the negative effects of the orphanage persisted in children adopted after they reached 2 years.

Children who remain with their parents can experience similar retardation if their chances for mental exercise are limited. Children reared in canalboats in England seldom attended school or engaged in any activity except traveling up and down the canals, with occasional chances to play along the banks of the waterways. At age 4, the average IQ of these children was about 90; by age 14, it had dropped to about 65. These children apparently had normal mental potential, but their drab, uneventful life style was not suitable for developing this potential (Gordon, 1923). Similar cultural retardation can be seen in children who live in isolated Appalachian communities, where few adults can read or write, children have little contact with the outside world, and daily life is routine and unstimulating. It is quite likely that lack of appropriate stimulation is at least partly responsible for the low IQs typically found in other deprived environments, such as inner-city slums.

STIMULATING MENTAL DEVELOPMENT
Harold Skeels: reversing retardation

One of the earliest experimental attempts to increase IQ started by accident. Harold Skeels was the staff psychologist at an overcrowded and understaffed orphanage that provided very little to stimulate a child's mental development. Two 18-month-old girls who were "clearly retarded" were sent to a home for retarded children. Six months later, Skeels visited the home for the retarded and, to his surprise, the girls appeared completely normal. He discovered that the toddlers had been "adopted" by older retarded girls, who played "aunts" and "mothers" and lavished attention on them.

Was it possible that generous attention from retarded teenagers could improve the mental development of normal but unstimulated infants? To test this radical idea, Skeels arranged for 13 more orphans to be transferred to the home for the retarded. At 18 months of age, all 13 children were considered unsuitable for adoption because of "ob-

216

vious mental retardation'' (their average IQ was 64). Twelve other children who stayed at the orphanage were chosen for a comparison group (their average IQ was 87). Two years later, all 25 children were retested. The "retarded" group had an average IQ of 92, a remarkable gain of 28 points. The outcome of the study was not entirely happy, though, for the IQ scores of the "normal" group that stayed at the orphanage had dropped an average of 26 points, to 61.

Eleven of the 13 children who had been sent to the home for the retarded were eventually adopted. Years later, Skeels (1966) located them again and found that all 13 were self-supporting; most of them had finished high school; 11 were married. The children who had remained at the orphanage had not fared as well. Four were still in state institutions; one had died in an institution; the others were unskilled laborers or were unemployed. Difficult as it may be to believe, variety of stimulation and affectionate attention from older people (even if retarded) are more beneficial for growing children than is scant attention from normal adults in an orphanage.

Robert Rosenthal: self-fulfilling prophecies

In another well-known experiment, Robert Rosenthal tried to encourage mental growth simply by telling teachers to expect certain children to "bloom" intellectually.

Rosenthal and Jacobson (1968) selected a school with 650 children, mostly lower class, about 20% Mexican. They described the children as attractive and sociable. The teachers were well educated, experienced, and "dedicated." In the spring of 1964, Rosenthal and Jacobson administered the Harvard Test of Inflected Acquisiton to all children who might return to the school in the fall. This test was described to the teachers as a predictor of academic blooming. It was actually a standardized, relatively nonverbal IQ test. The following fall, each teacher was given a list of the names of several children who were supposedly identified by the test as potential bloomers. The teachers were told to expect special improvements from these children. In actuality, the names of the bloomers were chosen entirely by chance; their scores on the IQ test were no different from the scores of the other children.

In the spring of 1965 all children who had been tested a year before were tested once again. Both the bloomer group and the control group had higher IQ scores than in 1964, but the gains in IQ were much greater for the bloomers. The biggest differences were found in first and second grade. In first grade, the control group gained an average of 12 points; the scores of the bloomers increased by an amazing 27 points. In second grade, the control group improved by 7 points, the bloomers by 17 points. The IQ scores of some bloomers jumped by more than 40 points!

Rosenthal and Jacobson concluded from their study that children's IQs are shaped at least in part by adults' expectations. They labeled this effect the *self-fulfilling prophecy* because the expectation seems to come true by its own accord. If these results could be obtained simply by giving teachers one bit of information, imagine the consequences of parents' expectations. Why were the effects of expectations greatest for the youngest children? IQs of younger children may be more malleable; younger children may be more sensitive to subtle cues from teachers; or older children may have established repu-

217

tations at school that were stronger determinants of expectations than was the advice of a psychologist.

A dramatic study like this is a likely target for criticism. Other psychologists have faulted the study for possible bias in the IQ test chosen, for misuse of statistics, and for not identifying in detail exactly how expectations operate. Some studies designed to replicate the experiment have not obtained the same results (perhaps the teachers had already heard about the trick). Other studies have confirmed the conclusion that mental growth can be encouraged simply by expecting it.

The powerful effect of expectations is also demonstrated in a rather frightening observational study in an urban ghetto kindergarten (Rist, 1970). The kindergarten teacher was considered a star of the school by both the principal and the other teachers. Thirty normal eager children entered the class in the fall. Within 2 weeks, the teacher had assigned them to sit at one of three tables. One difference among the tables was physical appearance of the children. Children at table 1 wore clean, relatively new clothing; they were light skinned; their hair was neatly cut; and none of them smelled of urine. At table 3, the children wore old, dirty clothes; most of them were dark skinned; most of them had uncombed, matted hair; and they often smelled of urine. A second distinguishing characteristic was social behavior. Children at table 1 were assertive, confident, and eager to be near the teacher and to gain her attention. Children at table 3 were more shy and often lingered around the edges of groups surrounding the teacher. A third distinction was use of language. The children at table 1 spoke freely to the teacher, usually in standard American English. The children at table 3 spoke to each other but rarely to the teacher, and they spoke in black dialect almost exclusively. A fourth difference was relative socioeconomic status. Parents of children at table 1 earned more money, had more education, and had fewer children than parents of the other children. None of the children at table 1 but half of the children at table 3 were from families receiving welfare. Asked how she decided where to seat a child, the teacher replied that the "fast learners" were at table 1, while the children at tables 2 and 3 "had no idea of what was going on in the classroom." (No formal test scores were available for the children when they were assigned to tables. On an IQ test given later in the year, children at table 1 scored slightly but not significantly higher than those at tables 2 or 3.)

These children were observed periodically for 3 years. The kindergarten teacher spoke to the children at table 1 politely and frequently; children at the other tables were often ignored and sometimes belittled. By the end of kindergarten, children at table 1 were progressing well, but children at tables 2 and 3 were characterized as withdrawn, inattentive, and lagging behind in their work.

The first- and second-grade teachers also assigned students to tables on the basis of "learning ability." All but two of the children who started kindergarten at table 1 were still in the favored group (the Tigers) at the end of second grade. Two children were demoted to the middle group (the Cardinals) because "neither could keep a clean desk." Children who initially were assigned to table 3 were without exception still in the lowest group (the Clowns). In the first weeks of kindergarten, the children's schoolwork was similar at all three tables, but after 3 years of being labeled as bright, average, or dull, the children were living up (or down) to their reputations. The kindergarten teacher's expectations had come true. These children were victims of a self-fulfilling prophecy.

Milwaukee Project: school at 4 months

Recognizing the importance of early experience in mental development, educators and the federal government joined forces in the 1960s to provide stimulating preschools for deprived youngsters. The program was optimistically called Head Start. Four- and 5-year-old children from poor families were enrolled in classes specially designed to encourage growth of intellectual skills and to prepare the children for elementary school. The youngsters' IQ scores increased. But in spite of high expectations, by the end of first grade, children from Head Start programs performed no better in school than did children from similar backgrounds who had no preschool experience.

Head Start apparently was too little, too late. Rather than trying to build up already low IQs of 4-year-old children, Richard Heber proposed that IQ deterioration might be *prevented* at an earlier age. Heber was concerned with cultural-familial retardation: low IQ with no known physical cause, frequently found in deprived families. He reasoned that Head Start programs had two inherent weaknesses: they did not reach children until 4 years of age and they did not involve the child's family. Heber hoped to encourage normal mental development by stimulating infants and educating their mothers about child care (Garber & Heber, 1973).

Heber launched his project in 1966 in an area of Milwaukee that had the highest population density, the lowest income, and the worst living conditions in the city. He purposely chose retarded women to participate in the study because children of retarded women living in slum conditions are highly likely to be retarded themselves.

To qualify to join the project, a woman needed a young baby and an IQ of 75 or less. Heber recruited 40 qualified women and assigned them at random to one of two groups. The 20 women in the control group cared for their infants on their own, but the children were tested periodically. The 20 women in the experimental group were visited daily by members of Heber's staff until their babies were about 4 months old. From 4 months to 2 years, the children were taken to the Infant Education Center every day, where trained teachers worked with them individually. The mothers were encouraged to visit the center, too, for social activities and discussions about rearing children. After 2 years, the children were placed in groups of six (with three teachers), and the size of the groups increased as the children grew older.

On the basis of previous studies in Milwaukee, Heber predicted that by 5½ years of age the children's IQ scores would have been, on the average, about 75. The average IQ of the control group at 5½ was 91. (This is higher than expected, perhaps because these children had been tested 15 times in 5½ years.) For the experimental group, the average IQ was 125. Heber's program clearly was successful, not only in preventing retardation but in stimulating intellectual growth beyond the normal range. (An interesting sidelight of the project is that the mothers became more sociable and more confident. Younger children of mothers in the experimental group also scored higher than expected on IQ

219

tests, though not as high as children in the program. Training the mothers seems to have lasting beneficial effects.)

As the children grow older, will these remarkable IQ scores be maintained? It is too early to tell. After entering school, the IQ scores of the experimental group dropped slightly, but at age 9 they remained 20 points higher than the scores of the control group (Heber, 1976).

Heber's research program has been criticized for possible bias in IQ testing, for not separating all the variables that distinguish the two groups, and for the high cost (about $30,000 per child). Heber tried to avoid bias by having children tested by strangers who were not told which group the children were in. He agrees that it would be desirable to have several groups to separate, for example, effects of training the child from effects of training the mother. This study was planned to demonstrate that IQ deterioration can be prevented. It was not designed to tease out individual variables influencing IQ. As for the cost, Heber argues that $30,000 is far less than the cost of special schools, vocational rehabilitation, and (probably) unemployment or welfare payments over an entire lifetime.

Enrichment for normal children?

Reports of the marvelous effects of stimulating environments often inspire parents to rush home and hang a mobile over baby's crib or start teaching their 2-year-old the ABCs. Children reared in middle-class homes ordinarily receive plenty of intellectual stimulation. David Elkind (1970) argues that special stimulation programs and academically oriented preschools are beneficial for underprivileged children, but for middle-class children they are redundant. If a normal child is exposed to an appropriate variety of experiences, which is usually the case in middle-class families, additional enrichment does not make the child brighter.

HEREDITY AND INTELLIGENCE

The question of the role of heredity in determining intelligence has been hotly debated for decades, at least since Sir Francis Galton's announcement that genius ran in his family. The influential British psychologist Sir Cyril Burt devoted his career to studies of heredity and intelligence. He concluded that 85% of the individual differences in IQ scores can be attributed to genetic factors. His many research studies, particularly those comparing IQs of identical twins raised together and separately, have provided the cornerstone for modern theories tracing inherited aspects of intelligence. There is only one flaw in Burt's studies: late in 1976 they were revealed as a fraud; the charming and witty Sir Cyril invented them. You can imaging the furor this discovery caused in psychological circles. Not only did Burt deliberately fake his data, but he also wrote articles praising his work and published them under fictitious names! Psychologists who have proposed hereditary theories of intelligence were quite embarrassed by the whole affair.

In spite of the black eye Burt has given to hereditary theories, there is considerable evidence that much of variation in IQ scores is due to genetic inheritance. The strongest

Table 4. Correlations between IQs of related and unrelated individuals

	Obtained median *r*	Number of studies
Identical twins reared together	+.87	14
Identical twins reared apart	+.75	4
Fraternal twins, same sex	+.56	11
Fraternal twins, different sexes	+.49	9
Siblings reared together	+.55	36
Siblings reared apart	+.47	33
First cousins	+.26	3
Second cousins	+.16	1
Parent (as adult) and child	+.50	13
Parent (as child) and child	+.56	1
Grandparent and grandchild	+.27	3
Unrelated persons		
Foster parent and child	+.20	3
Children reared together	+.24	5
Children reared apart	−.01	4

Adapted from Wilson, J. A., Robeck, M. C., & Michael, W. B., *Psychological foundations of learning and teaching* (2nd ed.).

evidence comes from studies comparing IQs for close and distant relatives (Table 4). Even when Sir Cyril Burt's research is omitted, dozens of studies remain. The general conclusion of these studies is that the closer the genetic relationship between two individuals, the more similar their IQ scores are likely to be.

Much of the controversy over the role of heredity stems from Jensen's article about racial differences in IQ. Jensen (1969) argued that attempts to raise IQs of deprived children in programs such as Head Start have failed. From studies comparing IQs of twins, he concluded that 80% of the individual differences in IQ can be attributed to genes. He suggested that genetic factors be considered in designing future educational programs. The hotly disputed item in the article is Jensen's proposal that the clear-cut differences in IQ between whites and blacks are genetic.

Challengers of Jensen's proposal point out that the racial differences in IQ (about 15 points, on the average, between whites and blacks) can be explained by social class differences in IQ, since a high proportion of blacks are poor. When income, education, occupation, and other socioeconomic factors are controlled, racial differences in IQ tend to disappear. (A question remains: why are so many blacks poor, if not because of genetic predispositions that make success in our society difficult?) Black children adopted by white families have higher than normal IQs (average IQ is 110 for children adopted in the first year of life). Natural children of the same parents score at about the same level (average IQ is 114)(Scarr and Weinberg, 1976). If racial differences in IQ are wiped out in studies controlled for social class and in studies of adopted children, can these differences still be attributed to heredity? Probably not.

Whatever one's opinion on the race and intelligence issue, the fact remains that heredity plays a major role in determining IQ. What a child inherits is not a specific

221

IQ score but probably a number of skills, such as speed of reflexes, speed of habituation, and predispositions to learn certain kinds of behaviors easily. Jensen and his followers state that 80% of the variation in intelligence results from heredity; environmentalists claim the figure is closer to 30% or 40%. Skeels' orphanage study and Heber's Milwaukee project are strong arguments in favor of the importance of environment. (All of Heber's subjects, by the way, were black.) At present we know that both heredity and environment are crucial, but we cannot pinpoint the relative contribution of each factor. Whatever the role of heredity, the more important problem now is to find out how environments can be designed to encourage development of intelligence.

USING AND MISUSING IQ SCORES

Anthony spent the first 9 years of his life with an alcoholic schizophrenic mother, who kept him locked in the apartment and forbade him to go to school. When Anthony's mother went out drinking, she left a padlock on the refrigerator so Anthony and his sister would not eat all the food. Anthony was rarely spoken to and he rarely spoke. When Anthony was sent to a foster home, his IQ was 68. Seven months later his IQ was 91. It could have been higher, but his verbal skills were still weak. Did Anthony's *intelligence* change, or just his ability to take a test?

People who know little about IQ tests often believe that intelligence and IQ are the same thing. They are not. Though we never settled on a single definition of intelligence, all but one of the definitions listed at the beginning of the chapter represent intelligence as an ability or capacity. This intellectual competence cannot be measured directly, but it is assumed to be a lasting characteristic of an individual. IQ, on the other hand, is only a test score, a number indicating performance in a particular setting on a particular day when in a particular mood. A person's IQ can change from day to day or year to year. Even trivial factors like the friendliness of the tester and the pace of the test can influence an IQ by 10 or more points. (Patty Hearst "lost" almost 30 IQ points as a result of her kidnapping. A few months after her return, her IQ was about the same as it had been before her ordeal.) Longitudinal studies show that changes of 15 or more IQ points over a period of years are common. A number that changes as easily as IQ clearly is not a precise measure of a stable, lasting characteristic.

Unfortunately, parents and educators often forget that IQ is merely a measure of performance. When parents find out their child's IQ score, they often make comparisons and worry about differences of a few points. In schools, IQ scores alone are commonly used to assign children to various educational programs, as if IQs were an absolute yardstick of mental ability. An IQ can set a teacher's expectations for a child, which as we have seen can influence the child's behavior. For these and other reasons, many school systems have stopped wholesale IQ testing. A few cities have even prohibited routine testing by law.

If IQ tests cause so much trouble, why use them at all? One reason is to identify seriously retarded children, especially at a young age. (With older children, one rarely needs a test to spot serious retardation.) A second reason is to simplify psychological research. Psychologists often need an estimate of mental ability in learning studies, for example, to discover whether learning speed is related to level of mental development. Another use in research is to describe the subjects in a study so the reader can tell whether they are bright, average, or perhaps retarded. A third reason for testing IQ is to help pinpoint specific learning problems. An IQ test included in a series of other tests can be useful to determine, for example, whether a child's poor schoolwork is due to low general intelligence or weakness in a certain area, such as vocabulary, or some other cause, such as hearing loss or emotional disturbance. An IQ score alone is not a complete measure of mental ability any more than height alone is a complete measure of physical ability.

SUMMARY

IQ tests have been widely used in the United States for more than 50 years. Most IQ tests are "descendents" of Binet's test, which was designed to predict how well a young child would perform in school when older. By age 6 years, adult IQ can be predicted with considerable accuracy. IQ is correlated with a number of variables, including socioeconomic status, racial and ethnic background, place of residence (city or country), family size, parents' behavior toward their children, and certain personality traits. Children who suffer from malnutrition or certain diseases and children who live in deprived environments do not fully develop their mental abilities. Certain kinds of mental retardation can be prevented or reversed if action is taken when the children are still very young. Some psychologists believe that intelligence is mostly inherited genetically; others believe that environment is much more important than heredity in shaping intelligence. Evidence is available to support both sides of the heredity-environment controversy. The most serious problem with IQ tests today is misinterpretation and misuse of scores by people who do not understand the tests' purposes and limitations.

REFERENCES

Bayley, N. Development of mental abilities. In P. H. Mussen (Ed.), *Carmichael's manual of child psychology* (Vol. 1), 1970, pp. 1163-1209.

Dennis, W. Causes of retardation among institutional children: Iran. *Journal of Genetic Psychology,* 1960, **96,** 47-59.

Dorman, L. Assertive behavior and cognitive performance in preschool children. *Journal of Genetic Psychology,* 1973, **123,** 155-162.

Elkind, D. The case for the academic preschool: fact or fiction? *Young Children,* 1970, **25,** 27-34.

Garber, H., and Heber, R. The Milwaukee project: early intervention as a technique to prevent mental retardation. University of Connecticut Technical Paper, March 1973.

Golden, M., Birns, B., Bridges, W., & Moss, A. Social-class differentiation in cognitive development among preschool children. *Child Development,* 1971, **42,** 37-46.

Gordon, H. Mental and scholastic tests among retarded children: an inquiry of the effects of schooling on various tests. London: Board of Education, Educational Pamphlet, 1923. Cited in J. Wilson, M. Robeck, & W. Michael, *Psychological foundations of learning and teaching.* New York: McGraw-Hill Book Co., 1974.

Heber, R. Intensive intervention program prevents retardation. *APA Monitor,* 1976, **7**(9/10), 4-5.

Jensen, A. R. How much can we boost IQ and scholastic achievement? *Harvard Educational Review,* 1969, **39,** 1-123.

PART THREE

Kent, N., & Davis, D. R. Discipline in the home and intellectual development. *British Journal of Medical Psychology,* 1957, **30,** 27-34.

———— Reese, H. W., & Lipsitt, L. P. *Experimental child psychology.* New York: Academic Press, Inc., 1970.

Rist, R. C. Student social class and teacher expectations . . . the self-fulfilling prophecy in ghetto education. *Harvard Educational Review,* 1970, **40,** 411-451.

Rosenthal, R., & Jacobson, L. *Pygmalion in the classroom.* New York: Holt, Rinehart, and Winston, Inc., 1968.

Scarr, S., & Weinberg, R. A. IQ test performance of black children adopted by white families. *American Psychologist,* 1976, **31,** 726-739.

Skeels, H. M. Adult status of children with contrasting early life experiences: a follow-up study. *Monographs of the Society for Research in Child Development,* 1966, **31**(Whole No. 3).

Sontag, L. W., & Baker, C. T. Personality, familial, and physical correlates of change in mental ability. In L. W. Sontag, C. T. Baker, & V. L. Nelson (Eds.), Mental growth and personality development: a longitudinal study. *Monographs of the Society for Research in Child Development,* 1958, **23,** 87-143.

Stevenson, H. W. Learning in children. In P. H. Mussen (Ed.), *Carmichael's manual of child psychology* (Vol. 1), 1970, pp. 849-937.

Torrance, E. P. The Minnesota studies of creative behavior: national and international extensions. *Journal of Creative Behavior,* 1967, **1,** 137-154.

Wolf, R. M. The identification and measurement of environmental process variables related to intelligence. Unpublished doctoral dissertation, University of Chicago, 1964. Cited in H. W. Reese & L. P. Lipsitt, *Experimental child psychology.* New York: Academic Press, Inc., 1970.

Zajonc, R. B. Dumber by the dozen. *Psychology Today,* 1975, **8,** 37-43.

The Milwaukee Project: early intervention as a technique to prevent mental retardation

Howard Garber
Rick Heber

. . . The Milwaukee Project, as it has come to be known, represents an attempt to prevent intellectual deficits in "high-risk" children by early intervention. The intervention technique employs an intensive educational program for the very young high-risk child, beginning before six months of age. The label "high-risk" is a statistically based term which reflects that certain children have a critically high probability of being mentally retarded by the time they have reached maturity. This probability level is determined by a number of factors which include low maternal IQ, low socio-economic status (SES), low IQ of siblings, large-sized families, etc. Evidence from extensive survey work showed that the offspring of mentally retarded, low SES mothers, although testing at regarded levels on IQ instruments at maturity, test at normal levels very early in life.

From *National Leadership Institute—Teacher Education/Early Childhood.* University of Connecticut Technical Paper, March, 1973.

The Milwaukee Project undertook to prevent this decline from occurring by having a group of children participate in an intensive early education program, beginning before six months of age.

It is just this point that may not be well understood. The Milwaukee Project was designed as a study to prevent mental retardation—cultural-familial mental retardation—by intervening very early in life. The study was not designed to raise IQ levels, but to permit continued normal intellectual development by mitigating environmentally depressing events. . . .

Approximately ten years ago, faced with problems associated with early detection of mental retardation, the University of Wisconsin Research and Training Center established the High-Risk Population Laboratory. The main purpose of this effort was to provide opportunity for prospective longitudinal investigation into the problems of mental retardation, in contradistinction to the almost exclusive reliance upon retrospective techniques. Further, the intent of the laboratory was to bring into accessibility for research purposes the sub-population of the mentally retarded labeled the cultural-familial retarded, which previously has been essentially unavailable to investigators. This group of retarded reside in the community and remain undetected for two reasons: (1) they have relatively mild intellectual deficits which are most difficult to detect in the very young; and (2) they are without major related physical problems. Ordinarily, neither of these characteristics alone would be sufficient to precipitate the attention of responsible agencies to these individuals.

The approach used by the High-Risk Population Laboratory in its search for a technique for early detection was to develop sufficient information to permit the diagnosis of cultural-familial retardation. In order to compile this information, a door-to-door survey was conducted in an area of the metropolitan community of Milwaukee which had previously been identified as having an extremely high prevalence of retardation. This area of the city has the lowest median educational level, the lowest median family income, the greatest population density per living unit, and the highest rate of dilapidated housing in the city. *Though the area comprises about 2 percent of the population of the city, it yielded approximately 33 percent of the total number of children identified in school as educable mentally retarded.* In our first survey, all families residing in this area who had a newborn infant and at least one other child of the age of six were selected for study. All members of the family, both children and adults, received an individual intellectual appraisal. In addition, extensive data were obtained on family history, including the social, educational and occupational history and status. This approach provided us with some key variables that appear to be sufficiently sensitive to the existence of cultural-familial retardation to be used as a signal for such.

The population survey data produced some striking data on the prevalence of retardation in depressed urban areas, on the distribution of retardation among families living in the high-risk area, and on trends in intelligence as a function of age of children and adults residing in the area. *For example, it was found that the high prevalence of mental retardation identified with Milwaukee's inner core population was strikingly concentrated among families where maternal intelligence was depressed, particularly where the family was large.* From our survey sample it was found that the prevalence of IQs of 75 and below was 22 percent, i.e. in these families where there was a newborn and at least one child of age six or greater. This selection procedure resulted in a sample of much larger than average families, and an increased prevalence of sub-75 IQs. However, it was found that 45.4 percent of the mothers who had IQs below 80 accounted for 78.2 percent of all children with IQs below 80. Moreover, it was found that depressed maternal intelligence was even a better predictor of depressed child intelligence for the older (above age six) than for the younger children. The most startling aspect of this data is that on infant intelligence tests, children of mothers above 80 IQ and below 80 IQ did about equally well. *After the infancy period, though, the children whose mothers had IQs greater than 80 appeared to maintain a fairly steady intellectual level, while the children whose mothers had IQs less than 80 exhibited a marked progressive decline in their intellectual level.* (See Figure 1) This trend toward a decline in measured intelligence for children in disadvantaged environments has wide acceptance as a general characteristic of a "slum" environment population, although this set of data indicates that this trend in declining intelligence as age increases is restricted to offspring of the "less bright" mothers.

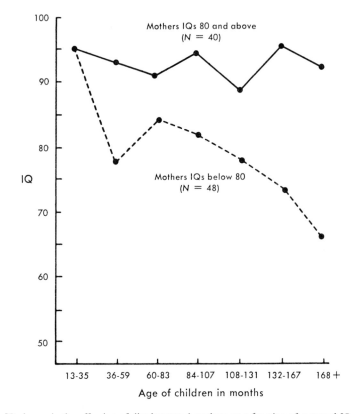

Mothers IQs 80 and above
(N = 40)

Mothers IQs below 80
(N = 48)

IQ

Age of children in months

13-35   36-59   60-83   84-107   108-131   132-167   168+

IQ change in the offspring of disadvantaged mothers as a function of maternal IQ.

SELECTION OF RESEARCH FAMILIES

As a consequence of the survey data, we have utilized maternal IQ as a basis for selection of a group of newborns, with confidence that a substantial percentage would be identified as mentally retarded. In other words, to identify the "high-risk" families within the "high-risk" residential area, the variable of maternal intelligence was utilized as a selection criterion since it proved to be the most efficient predictor of low school-age offspring intelligence.

The High-Risk Population Laboratory maintained a survey of births in the high-risk area. By first screening and then administering individual tests of intelligence, we identified those mothers of newborns who were mentally retarded, i.e. who had full-scale WAIS IQs less than 75. From this pool of candidates, accumulated over an eighteen-month period, we drew 40 mentally retarded mothers and randomly assigned them to either the Experimental or Control condition, after they had been invited to participate in a study of child development being conducted by the University of Wisconsin. All of the families selected were of Negro extraction.

The Experimental group, beginning within the first few months of life, was to undergo a comprehensive intervention in their social environment, the objective of which was to displace all of the presumed negative factors in the social environment of the infant being reared in the slum by a mother who is herself retarded. We are, thereby, testing the "social deprivation" hypothesis of etiology by seeing whether it is possible to prevent retardation from occurring in the offspring of these retarded mothers.

Should the Experimental children enter school and exhibit normal intellectual functioning we will know that it is possible, through our experimental program, to prevent mental retardation from occurring at the present high frequency of children raised in these circumstances. If the children are assigned to classes for the retarded at the rate of those without training, our program has not been successful.

The experimental intervention is comprised of two components: (1) the maternal rehabilitation program and (2) the infant stimulation program which are described below.

THE MATERNAL REHABILITATION PROGRAM

A two-phase program was initiated to better prepare the experimental mothers for employment opportunities and to improve their homemaking and child-rearing skills. Through improved employment potential, increased earnings, and self-confidence, it was hoped that positive changes in the home environment would occur. The rehabilitation program consisted of adult education classes to teach the mothers basic academic tools necessary for vocational adaptability, and finally, an occupational training program to teach specific vocational skills. . . .

THE INFANT STIMULATION PROGRAM

The program is, in its most basic sense, designed to facilitate intellectual development of very young children. The plan is concerned with (1) a physical location which promotes learning, (2) a staff to manage and arrange instruction for children, and (3) the educational program.

Physical plant

Over the years, the project has been located in several facilities. When all of the children were around six months of age, a large fourteen-room duplex served our needs very well because of the many "nooks and crannies" where teachers could work with children on a more intimate one-to-one basis. . . . The entire program is now housed in a leased school facility located adjacent to one of the inner-city's churches. This building, complete with six classrooms, a gymnasium, office space, and a lunch room is well suited to the needs of the program.

The staff

At the onset of the stimulation program we chose to employ a paraprofessional staff. The persons chosen were, in our judgment, language facile, affectionate people who had had some experience with infants or young children. The majority of these "teachers" resided in the same general neighborhood as the children, thus sharing a similar cultural milieu. The teachers ranged in age from approximately eighteen to forty-five with most of the teachers in their mid-twenties. Their educational experience ranged from eighth grade to one year of college. The teachers were both black and white.

The teacher of an infant had the major responsibility of establishing initial rapport with the infant's mother. This was done during a brief period, ranging from two to eight weeks, when the teacher worked with her child in the home until the mother expressed enough confidence in the teacher to allow the child to go to the center. . . .

Educational program

When the children first entered the project (by six months of age), they were each assigned a teacher. If the match proved satisfactory, the child remained with her as his primary teacher until he reached twelve months of age. At that time the child was gradually paired with other teachers and children. By the time he was fifteen to twenty months old, depending on the child, he was grouped with two other children and came into contact with three different teachers. This situation held for just his academic-learning environment. Actually each child was in contact with most of the other children and teachers.

The teacher who was assigned to an infant was responsible for his total care, including: feeding and bathing, cuddling and soothing, reporting and recording general health as well as organizing his learning environment and implementing the educational program. Within the context of the educational program, the teacher was expected to follow and expand upon a prescribed set of activities. Her job was to make these activities interesting, exciting and varied. She was also required to "objectively" evaluate and report the child's progress, pointing out areas of apparent difficulty. . . .

The intent of the education program was to provide an environment and a set of experiences which would allow children to develop to their potential intellectually as well as socially, emotionally, and physically. The specific focus of the educational program was to prevent from occurring those language, problem-solving, and achievement motivation deficits which are associated with mild mental retardation and severe disadvantagement.

The general educational program is best characterized as having a cognitive-language orientation implemented through a structured environment by prescriptive teaching techniques on a daily basis (seven hours per day, five days per week). This program and schedule was coupled with a high teacher-child ratio, affording an opportunity to present a variety of cognitive tasks to evaluate their effectiveness, and to provide both direct and non-direct teaching within both small and large groups. . . .

Thus the Milwaukee Project attempted to change the expected course of children who were at high-risk for mental retardation. The plan was to implement a comprehensive family intervention, beginning in the home.

The program for the retarded mothers was designed to modify those aspects of the environment which the mother herself creates or controls. Each day, her child was picked up at home and brought to the Infant Education Center for the entire day. These children are the Experimental group. The Control group is essentially the same kind of children whose mothers were in the original pool of high-risk families from which were drawn both the Experimental and Control group families. The children in the Control group are seen only for testing, which is done on a prescribed schedule for both groups of children.

ASSESSMENT OF DEVELOPMENT

In order to assess the effects of the kind of comprehensive intervention we have made with the natural environment of the infant reared by a retarded mother, we have undertaken an intensive schedule of measurements.* Our schedule of measurement includes measures of physical maturation, standardized and experimental measures of developmental schedules of infant adaptive behavior, standardized tests of general intelligence, an array of experimental learning tasks, measures of motivation and social development, and a variety of measures of language development.

Both the Experimental and Control infants are on an identical measurement schedule. Infants are scheduled for assessment sessions every three weeks. The particular measures administered at a given session depend upon the predetermined schedule of measures for that age level. A particular test or task is administered to both Experimental and Control infants by the same person; the testers are not involved in any component of the infant stimulation or maternal program.

In the first 24 months of life, the measurement schedule was largely restricted to general developmental scales and emerging vocalization and language.

Gesell data

The Gesell Developmental Schedules were administered to Experimental and Control infants at the ages of six, ten, fourteen, eighteen, and 22 months. [Ed. note: These schedules measures motor, adaptive, language, and personal-social development.]. . . .

The Gesell data is roughly comparable for both groups to fourteen months with performance on all scales slightly in advance of test norms. At 22 months, performance of the Experimental

---

*Because of the obvious limitations of this report, only a portion of the measurements are reported here.

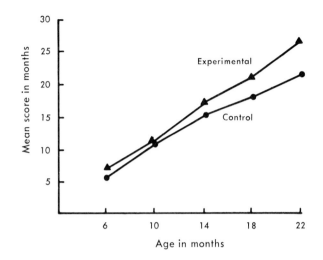

Composite of four Gesell scores.

group is clearly accelerated while the Control group performs at or slightly below norms for the four scales.

Learning

Beginning at 24 months, increased emphasis was given to experimental, direct measures of learning and performance, as well as to the standardized tests of general intelligence.

The learning tasks chosen were those that, on the one hand, would characterize the developmental learning process and on the other hand were tasks that could be repeated yearly. By repeating tasks we could keep pace with the increasing CA's of our Ss and yet maintain a continuity of task which would permit evaluation of developmental changes in performance. *Obviously, the exceedingly complex nature of cognitive growth required more than a single measure of intellectual development, such as is obtained from IQ tests. Thus, a more comprehensive picture of the growth of cognitive abilities was attempted by an array of experimental learning tasks (see, e.g., Stevenson, 1972).*

Most importantly, we were concerned with delineating some of the characteristics of early learning behavior that are either facilitating or interfering with learning. We wanted information on the response patterns or behavior style, and we wanted information about the role of attention in early learning. These tasks, therefore, not only provided a measure of the differential development of the learning process in the children, but increased our understanding of how certain performance variables relate to cognitive growth.

One experimental task has been concerned with development of the child's attention to color and form and the response strategy employed. It is a color-form matching task in which the child may respond consistently according to one of the dimensions: color or form. He cannot respond consistently if he does not attend to one dimension or the other, especially if he uses a response strategy such as position responding or alternation responding. In this case, responding to the dimension of either color or form is more developmentally advanced than ignoring the color-form dimension and responding, e.g., to position. This test has been administered four times. During the third year of life, none of the Controls demonstrated a dimensional response (i.e., in terms of color or form). By contrast, over half of the Experimental group (55 percent) showed unidimensional responding. In the fourth year of life and during the fifth and sixth years as well, this differential performance was maintained. There are two notable points: (1) three-fourths or more of the Ex-   **229** perimental group showed unidimensional responding at each successive testing, while even at the fifth and sixth year testings the percentage of the Control group showing unidimensional respond-ing was comparable only to the Experimental group's first test performance, nearly two years before; and (2) the Experimental group showed a significant shift to form, which is quite consistent with other research indicating advanced developmental performance. . . .

Language development

A child's acquisition of language occurs in a surprisingly short period of time. Although grammatical speech rarely begins before eighteen months of age, the basic process appears com-plete by the age of three and one-half. Furthermore, at this age level, it is probably language facility which most clearly differentiates the cultural-familial retardate from his non-retarded peers. It is for this reason that we have given so much emphasis to both the development of the children's language abilities and the measurement of this aspect of behavior. Our concern is both with the quantitative and qualitative differences in the developing language structures of these two groups. . . .

The first statistically significant difference in language development appeared at eighteen months on the Language scale of the Gesell Developmental Schedule. At this testing age the Ex-perimental children were two months above the norm and three months ahead of the Controls. By 22 months the Experimental children were over four months ahead of the norm and six months ahead of the Controls. This trend of differential language development has continued, and perhaps in even a more dramatic way. In fact, some of the most striking differences in the performance of the Experimental and Control children are reflected in the research measures of language per-formance. . . .

MOTHER-CHILD RELATIONSHIP

Each mother . . . creates an environment for her child which is quite different from that cre-ated by other mothers, even though all live in the same environment. Indeed, it is the very nature of the environment created by the mother which influences social, emotional, and cognitive de-velopment. The investigation of this relationship has been studied in detail by Hess and Shipman (e.g. 1968). They found that the mother's linguistic and regulatory behavior induces and shapes the information-processing strategies and style in her child and can act to either facilitate or limit intellectual growth.

Mildly retarded mothers tend to regulate behavior by using imperatives and restricted com-munication—a behavior control system which can [limit] intellectual growth in her child. Fur-thermore, the nature of this interaction is such that it induces a passive-compliant attitude by weak-ening the child's self-confidence and dampening motivation. We are quite concerned, therefore, in determining the nature of the mother-child relationship, especially after having intervened in this critical process.

In the mother-child interaction most sophisticated behavior—such as the initiation of problem-solving behavior by verbal clues and verbal prods, or the organization of tasks with respect to goals in problem-solving situations, etc.—is done by the mother. However, where the mother is of low IQ, the interaction is more physical, less organized, and less direction is given to the child. Indeed, while this was the case in the Control group mother-child dyads, it was quite different in the Ex-perimental dyads.

We used a specially prepared mobile laboratory for all experimental sessions. The testing room was equipped with videotape and sound recording equipment, so that the entire session with each family was recorded for later analysis. The mother and child are brought to the laboratory and seated at a table. Part of this research involved explaining to the mother the tasks she and the child were to perform. First, she was to tell the child a story based on a picture, which afforded us the opportunity to measure the mother's language facility. Second, the mother was told to teach the child a block sorting task and how to copy three designs on a toy Etch-A-Sketch. The behavior between the mother and child was rated on a scale with rating categories divided into various kinds of physical and verbal behaviors, with additional categories to indicate whether the behavior was active or passive.

We found that the Experimental dyads transmitted more information than the Control dyads, and this was a function of the quality of the Experimental child's verbal behavior. The Experimental children supplied more information verbally and initiated more verbal communication than found in the Control dyads. The children in the Experimental dyad took responsibility for guiding the flow of information—providing most of the verbal information and direction. The mothers of both dyads showed little differences in their teaching ability during the testing session. However, in the Experimental dyads, the children structured the interaction session either by their questioning or by teaching the mother. As a result, a developmentally more sophisticated interaction pattern has developed between the Experimental children and their mothers, which contributed to faster and more successful problem completion.

It is apparent from this description of a portion of the data of the mother-child interaction, that the intervention effort has effectively changed the expected pattern of development for the Experimental dyads. Moreover, the result of what might be termed a reciprocal feedback system, initiated by the child, has been to create a more sophisticated and satisfying interaction pattern in the Experimental dyad. In fact, there is some evidence that the Experimental mothers may be undergoing some changes in attitude and self-confidence. The Experimental mothers appear to be adopting more of an "internal locus of control"—an attitude that 'things happen' because of their decisions and actions and not purely by chance or fate. Thus, the intensive stimulation program, undergone by the Experimental children, has benefited both the Experimental child and the Experimental mother by broadening their verbal and expressive behavioral repertoire.

MEASURED INTELLIGENCE TO 66 MONTHS

The standardized tests of intelligence included the Cattell, Stanford-Binet, and Wechsler Preschool-Primary Scale of Intelligence (WPPSI). The Cattell test, extending into the Binet, was scheduled at three month intervals beginning at CA 24 months and at six month intervals from CA 48 months on. The graph illustrates the course of intellectual development for the two groups from twelve months until 66 months of age. The data presented use scores derived from the Gesell schedules from 12 to 21 months, and Cattell and Binet scores from 24 to 66 months. The mean IQ at the upper age level of 66 months is based on approximately half of the group, because at this time not all of the subjects have reached this age.

The mean IQ for the Experimental group based on the means at each age interval from 24 to 66 months is 123.4. For the Control group, mean IQ for all testings is 94.8. At the latest age point the Experimentals are just above their mean, at 125 (s.d. = 8.5) while the Controls have slipped below their overall mean to 91 (s.d. = 9.1). The discrepancy between Experimental and Control group performance at each three month test interval varies from a minimum of 23 IQ points at 24 months to over 30 IQ points at 66 months.

These data summarize the present differential development between the Experimental and Control groups. The dotted line on the graph [Figure 3] represents the mean IQ's of offspring of mothers with IQ's below 75, taken from our original population survey. This is referred to in our study as the Contrast group. It depicts the pattern of development expected for our actual Control group. You will recall that our hypothesis was in terms of preventing the relative decline in development of the Experimental group which we see in the Contrast group and which we can begin to see in the Control group. In sharp contrast is the Experimental group's performance, to date, on the standardized tests of measured intelligence, indicating a remarkable acceleration of intellectual development on the part of these children exposed to the infant stimulation program. Further, their performance is quite homogeneous as contrasted with that of the Control group where less than one-fourth of the Ss test at or above the norms with the remainder trending toward sub-average performance.

It is important to point out that there is reason for caution in the interpretation of such data, par-

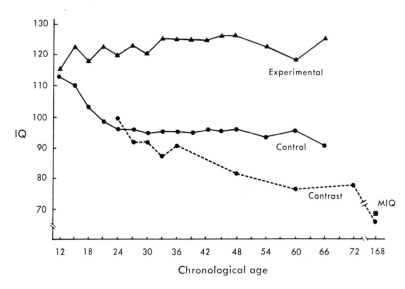

Mean IQ performance with increasing age for the experimental and control groups in comparison to the high-risk survey contrast group.

ticularly when one considers the numerous pitfalls and hazards of infant measurement. The Experimental children have had training, albeit fortuitously, on items included in the curriculum which are sampled by the tests, while the repeated measurements have made both groups test-wise. It is well to point out, however, that curriculum materials and tests used are standard fare for early education programs everywhere. All in all, it does seem that the Experimental group has benefited from the intensive training program, a program to which no comparable group of infants has ever been exposed, to the best of our knowledge. We have tried very hard to answer whether it has been simply a matter of training and practicing specific skills. In fact, extraordinary precaution has been taken to separate the development of the curriculum and the assessment program. Two separate staffs have been employed. It is obvious to most researchers that, to some extent, infant intelligence tests must contain material which approximates material used in preschool curricula, primarily because of the limited variety of material for this age. To circumvent this problem somewhat, we have employed other measures of performance, which minimized the stock item, and thereby afforded additional insight into the differential development of these children. As could be seen in the measures of learning and language development, the differential performance discrepancy is consistent with the IQ measures, indicating advanced intellectual development of the Experimental group. What is more, there is considerable difference in the pattern or style of behavior between the groups—particularly the tendency to stereotypy of response exhibited by the Control group, which certainly is antagonistic to successful learning performance.

Thus, infant testing difficulties notwithstanding, the present standardized test data, when considered along with performance on learning tasks and language tests, indicate an unquestionably superior present level of cognitive development on the part of the Experimental group. Also, the first "wave" of our children are now in public schools. *None* have been assigned to classes for the retarded and we are collecting data on school performance generally.

PART FOUR

DEVELOPING PERSONALITY

Chapter 11

Studying personality development

W. C. Baker

Jenny is a "little lady." She always wears a dress, and every afternoon she has tea with her dolls.

Christy wears jeans, T-shirts, and lots of dirt. She ignores the dolls her grandmother gives her. She prefers electric trains and erector sets.

Jenny volunteers to help her mother carry chemistry books home from the library. She "reads" the books along with her mother. After 7 months in first grade, she can sound out words such as semiconductor.

Christy's parents seldom see her with a book. They do not know that Christy hides under the covers at night, looking at books with a flashlight (which is kept under the bed for just this purpose).

BIOLOGY, CULTURE, AND UNIQUE EXPERIENCES

How do children develop the set of characteristics we call personality? This question is one of the most persistent in psychology.

One important determinant of personality is *biologic predispositions,* genetically based tendencies to acquire certain characteristics. Biologic predispositions do not absolutely determine a trait; they simply increase the chance that the trait will develop if circumstances are favorable. Genetic codes determine species characteristics, such as (for humans) language capacities, large brains, physical structures resulting in walking on two feet, refined hand structure, and timetables for maturation. Genetic codes also influence a multitude of individual characteristics, such as basic tempermental traits (e.g., nervousness), physical build, resistance to some diseases, handedness, intelligence, and certain abilities (e.g., musical talent). There is even some evidence for genetic bases of interests and tastes, such as preference for English rather than history, or Bach rather than rock (Nichols, 1976).

A second major influence on personality is *culture.* By culture is meant experiences common to members of a particular group. American children are, on the average, more aggressive and less obedient than are Chinese children living in Taiwan; this difference has been attributed to cultural differences in disciplinary techniques (Niem & Collard, 1972).

The third important factor in personality development is *unique experiences,* events that occur to some children but not to others. Experiences such as being an only child or losing a parent through death or separation obviously have major effects on personality. But even apparently trivial experiences, such as the name given to a child, can be significant. Children with socially desirable names, such as Karen or Michael, are more popular with other children than are children named Elmer or Adele (McDavid & Harari, 1966). Children's names influence adults, too. Teachers are likely to give a higher grade to David than to Hubert, even when the papers written by the two boys are identical, apparently because of a negative impression of boys with strange names like Hubert. It is surprising that for papers written by girls, the teachers gave higher grades to Bertha than to Lisa. Perhaps the teachers felt sorry for girls saddled with disagreeable names (Harari & McDavid, 1973).

Although we know that biologic predispositions, culture, and unique experiences   **235** all contribute to personality development, we are faced with a major problem: personality is an elusive concept that is difficult to define.

Personality can be viewed as a structure (somewhat like the floor plan of a house) that is determined very early and endures with only minor changes (like occasional re-modeling) throughout the life of the individual. The structure is hidden from view, but feelings, thoughts, and actions give hints about the structure. Psychologists who adopt this point of view typically generate theories to describe the structure of personality and to suggest how it might have developed. These theories are often speculative, that is, rich in thought and intuition but lacking in research evidence to support them.

Personality can also be viewed as simply a collection of behaviors that are often repeated, with no underlying structure. Most of these behaviors are learned and, like habits, tend to persist for a long time. Major changes are possible, though, because of new learning experiences. Psychologists who adopt this point of view typically conduct research to find out how specific behaviors or characteristics develop. They might study, for example, aggression, altruism, anger, cooperation, curiosity, dependency, happi-ness, intelligence, jealousy, leadership, morality, popularity, responsibility, self-con-cept, sex roles, sociability, zealousness, or any other behavior that is a component of personality. Research studies yield a wealth of facts, but facts alone do not provide an organized, comprehensive picture of personality.

No chapter can cover every facet of personality. For this chapter, Freud's theory was chosen to represent the structural approach. Freud's work is often criticized, but his ideas continue to influence our reactions to children. The behavioral approach is rep-resented by studies of fear. Fear has been the topic of surprisingly few research studies, considering how common a feeling it is for children. Other elements of personality, such as attachment to others, sex typing, and play, are discussed in following chapters.

STRUCTURAL APPROACH: FREUD'S THEORY OF PERSONALITY

Sigmund Freud (1856-1939) did not consider himself a psychologist. Psychologists in Freud's day studied the workings of the conscious mind; Freud devoted his career to studying the unconscious. Freud likened the mind to an iceberg: the visible portion of the iceberg was analogous to consciousness, and the vast mass of ice hidden under water represented the unconscious. Since early psychologists studied only what was visible, it is no wonder that Freud thought psychology would never amount to much.

Freud was a physician. He graduated from the University of Vienna Medical School in 1881 and specialized in the treatment of nervous system disorders. He had hoped to become a research scientist, but, because he was a Jew, the few academic posts avail-able in Vienna in the 1880s were not open to him.

Freud suspected that many of the patients he treated had no physical cause for their maladies. He tried treating these patients with the new talking-out technique developed by Joseph Breuer, a personal friend. After several successes with the "talking cure," Freud applied it to all of his patients. He developed the technique of free association, by which the patient was to say whatever came to mind, with no censoring or embel-lishing. He also became interested in interpreting dreams, which he considered the "royal road to the unconscious." From the mental wanderings and dreams of adult patients, he constructed a theory of the development and structure of the personality. Although much of the theory deals with early childhood, he had only one child "patient" (Little Hans), who was analyzed on the basis of the boy's father's reports to Freud; Freud met the child only once.

According to Freud's theory, personality development is primarily a biologic event, based on instincts and guided by maturational processes. Instincts in this context are motivating forces, the propelling factors of the personality. Instincts supply both the energy and the direction for fulfilling one's needs. Freud believed that experiences play a small role in shaping the details of a personality, but basic personality structure is a species characteristic that unfolds in the same sequence in all persons. (Since Freud's death, his followers have placed much more emphasis on personal experiences and less emphasis on instincts.)

Structure of personality

Freud proposed that the personality contains three systems, or parts: the id, the ego, and the superego. These parts interact in complex ways, so that one rarely if ever acts alone in an adult. (Since only the id is present at birth, the interactions of the parts must be somewhat different in infants and young children than in adults.)

The *id* contains all the instincts and psychic energy present at birth. The id is essentially a collections of urges, needs, and wishes. Tension builds up within the individual when the demands of the id are not satisfied. The tension becomes unpleasant as it continues to increase, and relief of the tension is pleasurable. The id tries to discharge the tension and bring physical pleasure, but it cannot accomplish this directly. The id is handicapped because it has no way to communicate its needs to the external world; therefore it cannot act by itself to release tension and bring pleasure.

To serve the id, the *ego* emerges. The ego deals directly with the external world to find means to satisfy the demands of the id. The ego is a realistic thinker and engages in reality testing (forming plans to satisfy an urge and trying the plans until one is found that works efficiently). The ego is never completely separate from the id. The id and ego work together to bring pleasure to an individual: where there is a will (id), there is a way (ego).

As the id and ego become skilled at satisfying needs, some restrictions become necessary; a child must learn which methods of finding pleasure are socially acceptable. The third part of the personality, the *superego,* develops to control the child's impulsive behavior. The superego is sometimes called the moral arm of the personality. It represents the internalized standards of society and is established by reward and punishment. Unlike the ego, which deals with the real world and strives for pleasure, the superego deals with the ideal world and tries to reach perfection. The superego has two subsystems: the *ego-ideal,* which rewards a person for good behavior with feelings of pride, and the *conscience,* which punishes a person for bad behavior by producing guilt. (Before Freud's day, the conscience was considered a gift from God to mankind that enabled people to be more god-like.) The superego functions to provide self-control **237** when parental or societal control would otherwise be necessary. In a way, the superego is like carrying a scolding parent around inside one's head. Unpleasant as this prospect sounds, the superego is essential for social behavior. Without it, the ego might decide that the most efficient way to gratify the id's demand for lunch is to steal it from an acquaintance.

In normal people, these three systems of the personality work together harmoniously. Conflict among them is an indication of neurosis.

Stages of personality development

The id, ego, and superego emerge in response to problems that face a growing child. All personality development, in Freud's view, is essentially a process of developing new methods of dealing with difficulties, such as frustrations, conflicts, and threats. Two important methods are used to resolve these problems: identification and displacement.

In the most general sense, *identification* is matching a mental image (idea or memory) to an object or event in the real world. Because a mental image cannot satisfy a need of the id, the ego finds some physical object that matches the image; the object then satisfies the need. In the process of trying out methods of satisfying physical urges, children are likely to observe that their parents have developed some clever techniques for satisfying urges. The children often adopt these techniques as their own. One form identification can take, therefore, is the adoption of characteristics of another person (especially a parent) and making these characteristics part of one's own personality. A small boy who walks with the same peculiar gait as his father is demonstrating identification. Children often use identification to try to gain a parent's love or to defend against a parent's anger. Battered children, for example, tend to be exceptionally dependent on and imitative of the parents who abuse them. Identification is not just imitation, though; it is an unconscious process by which people broaden their personalities. Children may identify with parents, other children, animals, fictional characters, and even their own fantasies. As they grow older, children are likely to identify with teachers and other powerful adults and to incorporate traits of these people into their own personalities.

Displacement occurs when an impulse cannot be satisfied by the original object choice; because the original object is unacceptable or unavailable, the impulse is displaced or transferred to a substitute object. For example, if a boy grows up wishing he could marry his mother, he may choose a wife very similar to his mother. Freud suggested that Leonardo da Vinci's fondness for painting madonnas resulted from displaced love for his mother. Young children have few objects that can satisfy their needs, but by displacing their needs to a variety of objects, they gradually develop a rich diversity of attachments and interests.

Freud believed that the first 6 years of life are crucial in the development of personality. During the first 6 years the id, ego, and superego become differentiated, the first and most important identifications occur, and through displacement children free themselves from the original object choices of their instincts. In addition, children pass through a series of stages that have profound effects on their personalities. Freud was so convincing in his arguments that the early years are decisive that many people today believe that personality is completely formed by age 6, without realizing that this belief comes straight from Freud's theory. Modern psychologists agree that early experiences are relatively more important than later ones, but most do *not* believe that personality development stops at age 6 years.

Each of Freud's stages is named for a *primary erogenous zone* (the part of the body that provides most physical pleasure). Freud theorized that the primary erogenous zones change with age and influence the behavior of children in predictable ways. He viewed

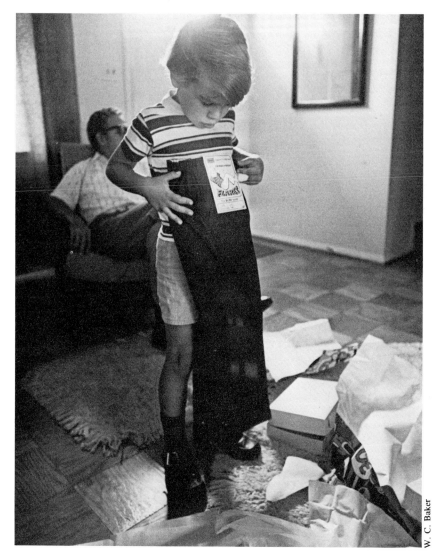

Fig. 11-1. Imitating the clothing style of adults is one form of identification.

W. C. Baker

the progress of an individual through the stages as a gradual process of growth, preset and timed by biologic forces. Each stage has characteristic conflicts. If these conflicts are not successfully resolved, an individual may become *fixated* ("stuck") at a particular stage, and traits associated with the stage will persist into adulthood. Fixation can occur when a need is frequently frustrated (not satisfied) *or* when a need is overindulged (too well satisfied), to the point that the child has no chance to learn to find satisfactions independently. Thus, repeated frustrations or overindulgences at age 4 can result in the persistence of some 4-year-old characteristics in a 40-year-old adult.

The first year of life is called the *oral stage,* because the mouth and lips are the primary erogenous zone at this period. Infants are almost entirely dependent on adults (or mother, in Freud's time), and the central problem for an infant is to become less dependent. An infant may fail to achieve the necessary independence because of too little attention and support (frustration) or because of too much *"smothering"* (overindulgence). Adults who were fixated at the oral stage are likely to be overly dependent or overly motherly (trying to induce others to depend on them) or overly involved in mouth pleasures, such as talking, chewing gum, eating, drinking, smoking, or chewing fingernails. Freud's sense of humor can be seen in his descriptions of some other oral traits: the oral personality may be sarcastic and verbally aggressive (makes biting comments) or may be gullible (swallows almost anything he is told).

From ages 1 to 3 years the child passes through the *anal stage.* The most pleasurable part of the body is the anus, and much attention is directed to this area during toilet training. The main problem for the child to overcome at this stage is control of elimination processes. The conflicts involved in toilet training can become a metaphor for the problem of controlling one's own behavior versus being controlled by parents and society. If adults are very strict and demanding about training a child, the child may react by refusing to eliminate and by being concerned and ashamed about being "dirty." Such a child is likely to develop into an adult who is stingy, stubborn, excessively neat and clean, a compulsive collector, or a saver of trivial items. On the other hand, a child may react to strict toilet training by relieving himself everywhere *except* on the toilet. This child is likely to become an uncontrolled personality who is hostile, messy, destructive, ill-tempered, and fond of "relieving" himself with exclamations related to toilet functions. A third type of personality may be fostered by parents who pay excessive attention to the production of feces and praise each "creation." Children of such parents may be unusually creative and productive, with their life's work as an adult playing the role that feces played in childhood. (Freud himself was said to be stubborn and meticulously neat; he had a remarkable collection of ancient art, and he had a notably creative, productive career.)

Personality development becomes more complicated in the *phallic stage* (ages 3 to 6). The genitals are the primary erogenous zone, and masturbation becomes common after the child discovers that rubbing the genitals releases sexual energy and tension. The problems of the phallic stage are somewhat different for boys and for girls because of differences in genital structure.

240
Even before the phallic stage, a boy has developed love for his mother. When the

boy discovers his genitals, he also experiences sexual desire for his mother. Freud called the boy's desire to have sexual relations with his mother the *Oedipus complex* (named for the Greek king who inadvertantly married his mother). The child's incestuous feelings cause him some concern because his mother is already sexually involved with his father, who is much bigger and more powerful than the boy is. Specifically, the boy fears that his father may discover his feelings, become jealous, and cut off the boy's penis to prevent him from having sex with his mother. Freud called this fear *castration anxiety.* Castration anxiety causes the boy to repress his sexual feelings for his mother and to identify with his father. Identification with his father and assuming some of his father's characteristics makes the boy feel safer (how could father castrate a little replica of himself?) and allows him some vicarious satisfaction of his desire to sleep with his mother. In the process of dealing with the Oedipus complex, the boy develops a strong superego, which controls, among other things, his later sexual activity. Failure to resolve the conflicts of the phallic stage may cause a boy to remain excessively fond of his mother or to become homosexual,* impotent, or perverted.

Little girls, according to Freud, experience a different problem during the phallic stage. Girls make the "momentous" discovery that they have no penis. "They notice the penis of a brother or playmate, strikingly visible and of large proportion, at once recognize it as the superior counterpart of their own small and inconspicuous organ, and from that time forward fall a victim to envy for the penis" (Freud, 1925). Freud theorized that *penis envy,* or the wish for a penis, causes girls to feel inferior to boys and "to share the contempt felt by men for a sex that is the lesser in so important a respect" (Freud, 1925). Soon after she experiences inferiority feelings, the girl becomes angry at her mother "who sent her into the world so insufficiently equipped." The girl then falls in love with her father, both because she is angry at her mother and because her father has the exalted organ that she lacks. To replace the penis she cannot have, the girl wishes for a baby, to be provided by her father. One final consequence of penis envy, according to Freud, is that the girl develops an aversion to masturbation, because any activity involving her genitals merely reminds her "that after all this is a point on which she cannot compete with boys and that it would therefore be best for her to give up the idea of doing so" (Freud, 1925). Unlike a boy, who represses his love for his mother because of castration anxiety, a girl has no strong need to overcome her love for her father. Eventually she concludes that she has no realistic chance of luring her father away from her mother (though Freud never explains exactly how), but she does not require a strong superego to reach this conclusion. As a result, Freud believed, girls do not develop as strong a superego as boys, and throughout life women tend to be less moral than men. In a mature woman, signs of unresolved penis envy and Oedipal feelings include excessive fondness for her father, problems relating to men, jealousy, frigidity,

---

*Freud thought members of both sexes were constitutionally bisexual. Desire for the same sex would become repressed during resolution of the Oedipus complex, but normal people would still have latent (hidden) homosexual feelings. Overt homosexual behavior, according to Freud, was a sign that the normal repression of love for the same sex never occurred.

failure to experience "vaginal orgasm,"* envying the social position of men, and engaging in masculine behavior, such as wearing men's style clothes or doing "men's work."†

A period of *latency* follows the phallic stage. From 6 years of age until adolescence, some of the child's sexual energy is repressed and some is redirected toward developing mental and social skills. At adolescence the child enter the *genital stage* and develops mature sexuality. Self-centered sex gives way to sexual activities with other young adults. If the child has not experienced significant fixations before this age, a normally socialized adult will emerge.

Children's dreams

Dream analysis was one of Freud's favorite methods of probing the unconscious. His dream analyses, however, were almost entirely restricted to dreams of adults. Freud's own children sometimes told him about their dreams, which he interpreted as examples of *wish fulfillment* (mental attempts to satisfy the id). If a child dreamed of a Christmas tree, for example, Freud might conclude that the child wished Christmas would soon arrive. On occasion, Freud did analyze children's dream in detail, but these dreams were related to him by adults who knew the young dreamers or by adult patients who recalled dreams from their childhood.

One patient whose childhood dream Freud interpreted has come to be known as the Wolf Man. Just before his fourth birthday, the patient dreamed he was lying in bed when "the window opened of its own accord" and he saw six or seven white wolves sitting in a tree outside the window. The wolves had "big tails like foxes," and their ears were "pricked like dogs when they pay attention to something." The boy screamed in terror and awoke because the dream had "such a clear and lifelike" quality that it thoroughly frightened him (Freud, 1918).

Freud analyzed this dream in terms of experiences and thoughts the patient described in therapy. As a child the patient had been told a story about a wolf whose tail was pulled off because of some mischief; he also owned books with drawings of wolves, and in each book the wolf's body was mutilated in some way. Since the patient's associations with wolves all related to loss of a body part, Freud interpreted the wolves as a symbol for castration anxiety. The patient also recalled that, when about 1½ years old, he had awakened from an afternoon nap and witnessed his parents having sexual relations. Freud related the dream at age 4 to this earlier experience, now complicated by the 4-year-old's Oedipal feelings. In the dream, as in the actual experience, the boy was lying in bed. The boy opened his eyes, as act represented by the window that opens

---

*Freud believed that normal women achieved sexual satisfaction through stimulation of the vagina only. Enjoying stimulation of the clitoris, in his view, was a sign of penis envy. Research on female sexual response disproves this notion of Freud's. Masters and Johnson (1966) found that female orgasm *requires* stimulation of the clitoris, either directly or indirectly.

†To the female reader who may be wearing slacks and dreaming of a career in astrophysics, allow for the fact that Freud grew up in a society with narrow, rigid sex roles. His sexist beliefs can be discounted without rejecting his entire theory.

"of its own accord." He watched his parents intently, which is translated into attentive wolves. The big tails of the wolves can be both a symbol for the father's enlarged penis and a reminder of castration anxiety. The boy's parents were wearing white under-clothes, which accounts for the unusual color of the wolves. Even though the wolves in the dream were not about to harm the boy, the dream was terrifying because it dealt with anxiety-provoking feelings of desire for his mother and competition with his father.

This dream interpretation emphasizes several common Freudian themes: the sexual conflicts of the Oedipal complex, the role of the superego in producing guilt and anxiety, and the need to release sexual energy. It also demonstrates the importance of *dream symbols*. Freud proposed that unconscious thoughts cannot be expressed directly in dreams; instead, the dreamer unknowingly censors these frightening thoughts, distorts them, and represents them symbolically. Freud believed that many dream symbols are universal but others are peculiar to the dreamer. In the Wolf Man's dream, a wolf rep-resenting castration is an individual symbol, based on stories the boy had heard. A uni-versal symbol for castration would be the breaking or discarding of a symbol for a penis (guns, knives, pencils, trees, umbrellas, or other elongated objects). Any dream in-corporates both actual experiences of the child (images of wolves like in a picture book) and symbols that tend to obscure the dream's meaning. Are all children's dreams sexually oriented? Certainly not. A child's dream can be symbolic, complex, and difficult to un-ravel, but ordinarily it will be "short, clear, coherent, easy to understand, and free from ambiguity," and a simple expression of the child's wishes (Freud, 1924).

Children's fears

Freud viewed most children's fears as normal products of our evolutionary heritage. Based on Darwin's theory of evolution, he suggested that fears are biologic hand-me-downs, leftovers from ages when our ancestors survived only by avoiding dangerous situations. Children typically fear realistic threats to their well-being, such as animals, high places, fire, and thunderstorms. "Psychological" fears common among children are also adaptive. Fear of the dark, fear of being left alone, and fear of strangers all reduce to fear of loss of a loved person, according to Freud, and help protect a child from wan-dering into danger. These simple fears, normal results of our biologic makeup, appear early in childhood.

After the age of 3 years, fear of loss of a loved one is transformed into castration anxiety, which is also a fear of loss. Eventually, fear of castration develops into a dread of the conscience, and by the end of childhood, tracing fears back to their original roots becomes difficult. Freud believed that after the phallic stage, children normally out-grow most fears. In neurotic individuals, though, childhood fears grow more intense and persist into later life (Freud, 1936).

Freud's only thorough study of a child was an analysis of *phobia* (intense, irrational fear) in a 5-year-old boy, Little Hans. Freud's information on the case was supplied by the boy's father, a physician and close friend of Freud. Little Hans had a strong fear of going out into the street; the fear then became attached specifically to horses. (Horses were the main means of transportation at that time; this phobia would be comparable to a fear of cars today.) Many of the elements of Little Hans' case are similar to those seen in the case of the Wolf Man.

Little Hans' father told Freud about the phobias and asked for help in dealing with them. He reported that at the age of 3 the boy had discovered his penis (which he called his "widdler"). Hans' mother observed him masturbating and threatened him with castration if he continued. She told Hans "If you do that, I shall send for Dr. A. to cut off your widdler. And then what will you widdle with?" (Such a threat was a common response to masturbation in Freud's time.) Hans then developed intense curiosity about the penises of other people and animals, and he particularly wanted to see his mother's widdler.

When Hans was about 3½, his sister Hanna was born. Hans was told to stay in another part of the house, but he sneaked into his parents' room for a moment just after the birth of the baby. He saw Dr. A., his mother's white legs spread apart, lots of blood, and no widdler; one can imagine what conclusion Hans drew. Some months later, Hans dreamed of sleeping with his mother and having sexual relations with her. The phobias of the street and horses appeared soon afterwards.

Freud gave Hans' father some suggestions for handling the phobias. Meanwhile Hans had a fantasy of two giraffes, one of which he made to go away (separating his parents), and a fantasy of squeezing himself into a forbidden space (having sexual relations with his mother). Soon afterward, the boy dreamed of a white horse that fell down in the street with its legs in the air. The horse was cut open, bled profusely, and died. Hans also told his father he had been frightened the year before when his sister was warned "Don't put your finger to the horse; if you do, it'll bite you" (a reminder of his mother's castration threat). Hans then developed fears of big things, heavy things, things that fall down, and feces.

From this information Freud concluded that Little Hans' phobias resulted from unresolved Oedipal feelings exaggerated by the birth of his sister. Hans assumed that his mother had been castrated, as a punishment for masturbation, when baby Hanna was born. The fear of horses originated with the warning to his sister, which was similar to the castration threat. The horse phobia was intensified by the dream of a white horse falling down and bleeding, which reminded the boy of the birth scene. His fears then spread to objects symbolically related to birth: things that are big and heavy (pregnant women), things that fall down (the horse in the dream), bathwater (considered by Freud a universal symbol for birth), and feces (Hans shared the common belief of children that babies are born by defecation). Freud recommended that Hans' father encourage the boy to talk about his feelings about his parents. Later Hans told his father of two more fantasies. In one, the plumber gave Hans a bigger and better widdler. In the other, Hans married his mother, had many children with her, and promoted his father to marry his grandmother. With these fantasies, according to Freud, the boy's Oedipal feelings were successfully resolved and the phobias disappeared.

Though Freud considered most childhood fears normal, the case of Little Hans demonstrated that some fears of children can develop from hidden psychic conflicts. How can normal fears be distinguished from neurotic ones? Neurotic fears are more intense, less rational, less likely to decrease over time, and displaced from the originally feared object (as Hans' fear of horses was a displaced castration fear). Note that Freud's conclusions about both types of fears were based on theory and secondhand observations. Freud's methods clearly distinguish him from psychologists who study fears by observing children directly.

Evaluation of Freud's theory

Freud's theory has been roundly criticized and accused of many shortcomings. Some of the criticism is irrelevant to the developmental portions of the theory, but five points are worth noting.

1. The importance of the first 6 years is overexaggerated. Most child psychologists agree that early experiences are relatively more important than later ones, because early experiences form a foundation on which a child's later experiences are based. Six months of separation from one's family, for example, is likely to have a more serious effect on a 2-year-old than on a college student. The third year is relatively less important than the first, the tenth year is relatively less important than the eighth, and so on, but personality development continues throughout life. Some psychologists propose a life-long series of stages, each with its typical trials and rewards. Nothing magical happens at age 6 that halts the development of personality.

2. Too much emphasis is placed on instinct and too little on experience. Though biology definitely plays a significant role in development, experience plays a larger role than Freud acknowledged. Many readers of Freud find the sexual instincts expecially objectionable. In the words of Hall and Lindzey (1957), to many critics "Freud's chief offenses consisted of ascribing lustful and destructive wishes to the baby, attributing incestuous and homosexual urges to all human beings, and explaining man's behavior in terms of sexual motivation. 'Decent' people were infuriated by Freud's view of man and called him a libertine and a pervert."

3. Though much of his theory is based on childhood events, Freud did not study children directly. His ideas about children came from recollections of disturbed adults. Freud's patients were not a normal sample, and their memories were almost certainly distorted. Freud's notes were not made while the patients talked, but hours later, which introduces another possible source of bias. As evidence for a scientific theory, Freud's raw material was not ideal.

4. Many of Freud's general concepts, such as the id, ego, and superego, cannot be scientifically tested. Specific concepts that have been tested have been, in many cases, contradicted by facts. For example, Freud assumed that 4- and 5-year-old children have a rather sophisticated understanding of sexual activity. Unfortunately for this aspect of the theory, children do not discover the relationship between genitals and sexual identity, nor do they realize that their sex assignment is permanent, until they are about 5 years old. The discovery that babies result from sexual activity usually occurs years later (Bee, 1975). Another example is penis envy. Despite stories of girls trying to urinate standing up or asking mother to buy them a penis like baby brother's, there is no evidence that wanting a penis has any more lasting effect on a girl than wanting blond hair

or wanting a lacy pink dress. One noted psychoanalyst reported that in 50 years of practice he never encountered a clear-cut case of castration anxiety or penis envy. The psychoanalyst suggested that these concepts probably evolved from Freud's own sexual experiences as a youngster. A third example is that masturbation is equally common among boys and girls, in spite of Freud's belief that girls find this activity repulsive. (Girls, though, may be quicker to discover that masturbation is not acceptable in public.) A fourth example is morality. Freud theorized that boys are more moral than girls because boys develop a stronger superego while resolving the Oedipal conflict. In research studies of moral behavior, boys do not outshine girls; when sex differences are found, boys are usually less moral than girls.

5. Freud's theory violates the scientific principle of *parsimony* (accepting the simplest theory that fits the facts). A boy's imitation of his father, for example, can be explained more simply by principles of observational learning than by Freud's complicated notion of identification to defend against castration. Likewise, excessive talking, eating, and smoking can be explained more easily by reinforcement than by fixation at the oral stage.

If Freud's theory had all these weaknesses and no strengths, it would not have survived for 75 years. Four of the strengths are particularly relevant to the developmental aspects of the theory.

1. Though Freud overemphasized the first 6 years, one cannot deny that early experiences are important. Freud expressed the idea in his famous statement "The child is father to the man." The early years do not completely determine the direction of a child's life, but they do have a major impact on social attachments, temperament, perception, language, learning abilities, and other aspects of development.

2. Freud may have given too much credit to instincts and maturational stages, but the role of biologically based timetables in development cannot be ignored. Piaget, for example, argues for maturational stages in development of intelligence. Though few psychologists accept the psychosexual stages exactly as Freud described them, maturation undoubtedly plays a role in personality development.

3. Many of Freud's descriptions of child behavior have been confirmed. For example, children often imitate their same-sex parent and develop a special fondness for their opposite-sex parent. Children are interested in sexual activity (though this interest does not disappear during latency, as Freud proposed). Sexual identity is established within the first 6 years and is stubbornly resistant to change later. Relatively little change in personality occurs during latency (ages 6 to puberty). Children do experience moral conflicts (as if the superego were pitted against the id and ego). Failure to develop conscience in the early years is virtually impossible to correct later. The explanation of these facts may be argued, but they have been supported by research studies.

4. Freud proposed an original concept of mankind. He demonstrated the importance of motives we are unaware of, feelings we do not understand, and experiences we no longer remember. Freud shocked his contemporaries by challenging their belief that humans are rational creatures with free will to behave as they choose. Freud claimed that human behavior is irrational and predetermined by instincts and childhood events over

which we have no control. In the words of Hall and Lindzey (1957), Freud conceived of an "individual living partly in a world of reality and partly in a world of make-believe, beset by conflicts and inner contradictions, . . . moved by forces of which he has little knowledge and by aspirations which are beyond his reach, by turn confused and clear-headed, frustrated and satisfied, hopeful and dispairing, selfish and altruistic." We may quibble about the details of his theory, but Freud's essential view of the human condition is difficult to deny.

BEHAVIORAL APPROACH: RESEARCH STUDIES OF FEAR

Freud's treatment of fear was speculative, theoretical, and generalized. In contrast, the behavioral approach is characterized by observations of concrete reactions of children to specific fear-provoking situations. Each study is designed to answer one narrowly defined question. General questions, such as Freud discussed, cannot be answered by a single research study.

The first widely discussed experimental study of fear was John Watson's attempt to condition fear in Little Albert, published in 1920 (see Chapter 6). Watson successfully conditioned the 11-month-old boy to fear a tame rat. The experiment was designed to contradict Freud's claim that fears had sexual origins.

Relatively few studies of fear have been published since 1920. Although fear is a common experience for children, it is a difficult concept to define and control. These difficulties and ethical concerns about scaring little children probably account for the small number of studies. Most fear research can be divided into four categories: studies of development of fear over time; observations of children's reactions to naturally occurring, frightening situations; questioning children or their parents about fear; and experimental attempts to provoke or to reduce fear.

Development of fear

John Watson claimed that fear was evident in infants from birth. Bridges (1932), on the other hand, proposed that newborns experience only one emotion, "generalized excitement." The unpleasant emotion of distress appears at about 1 month of age and becomes differentiated into anger, disgust, and fear by about 6 months. By 6 months of age infants can be frightened more easily than when they are first born. Explaining this increase in fear with age seems more important than determining the absolute earliest age at which an infant can be frightened.

Development of fear is related to development of social attachments. In birds, fear is first apparent a few hours after hatching; shortly afterward, the baby birds begin to follow a moving object and become attached to it *(imprinted)*. Konrad Lorenz observed this pattern of attachment and, by removing the natural mother and parading around in front of baby birds, induced the gullible birds to become attached to him. The birds remained attached to Lorenz through adulthood. In the mating season they would even bring him desirable gifts, such as juicy worms. Because the birds were socially attached to Lorenz, they showed no interest in mating with other birds. In monkeys, as in birds, social attachments are formed immediately after fear develops. **247**

In humans, fear of strangers appears at about 7 to 9 months; shortly afterwards human babies become attached to mother and show signs of distress when she leaves *(separation anxiety)*. Thus, whether the infants are birds, monkeys, or humans, development of a strong fear response sets the stage for development of a strong attachment.

Bronson (1968) described three stages in the development of fear. Generalized distress reactions are typical of the first stage, which lasts up to about 7 months in humans. When distressed, the babies can be comforted only by direct contact with the mother or another person. In the second stage, fear of visual novelty appears. The first sign is fear of strangers, followed by fear of seeing other unfamiliar objects. Children in this stage often try to escape the frightening object. Merely seeing mother might calm the young child, but some children continue to seek direct physical contact (holding or rocking). The third stage, appearing in middle childhood, is characterized by fear of new situations. By this age the child often can master the new situation and reduce the fear without appealing directly to mother. Bronson observed that these three stages are remarkably similar, although the time frame differs, for humans, chimpanzees, monkeys, and dogs. He suggested that this pattern of development of fear is a species characteristic, part of our biologic heritage. He also noted that humans, chimps, or monkeys that were deprived of normal mothering remained more fearful than normal throughout their lives.

Children's reactions to frightening situations

Approaching the problem of fear from a different perspective, Bronson (1970) observed reactions of infants and toddlers to a strange person in an unfamiliar setting while their mothers were present. Crying was his measure of fear. At 1 to 2 months, babies rarely cried in the unfamiliar surroundings. At 4 to 6 months, 20% of the babies cried. At 7 to 9 months and still at 10 to 15 months, nearly half of the children cried. By 24 months, though, crying in the strange situation had virtually disappeared. One way to make sense of the increase *and* decrease in fear with age is to consider what else the children are doing. By 7 to 9 months the child can crawl around fairly well; fear of unfamiliar people and places could be quite healthy. By 24 months, the child can talk and follow directions, although these skills are still limited. Ability to communicate makes the fear less necessary. Fear of new situations that persists beyond age 2 will interfere with the child's curiosity and eagerness to learn. Fear apparently plays a role in developing social relations, protecting a vulnerable child, and (by decreasing after 2 years) encouraging exploration.

A natural place for observing fear in older children is the dentist's office. Children aged 5 to 10 were rated by their dentists (who were not told the purpose of the study) on degree of fearfulness and three other characteristics. Fear was not related to sex or (surprisingly) age, but it was related to birth order. Children who were the first or only child in a family were more fearful than later-born children (DeFee & Himelstein, 1969). The greater fearfulness of first and only children is consistent with results of other studies (even with adults!) and might be explained by the tendency of inexperienced parents to be overly cautious and protective.

Fig. 11-2. A distressed infant will seek a familiar person for comfort.

Asking children about fear

Parents can be asked about their children's fears, but the answers of the parents and the children will not necessarily be the same. A mother reported that her 4-year-old boy was afraid of loud noises (thunder, fireworks, and a hippopotamus that snorts) but nothing else. When the boy was questioned, he replied seriously ''pricker things on the ceiling.'' He would not elaborate on that answer, but when questioned further he said monsters and turtles. Most parents would probably be surprised to hear what their children regard as scary.

Children may be questioned about fears formally (with a questionnaire) or informally (in an interview). The most well-known questionnaire designed to measure children's fearfulness is the Children's Manifest Anxiety Scale (CMAS), adapted from an anxiety scale for adults. It successfully distinguishes between highly anxious and less anxious children, but a number of other factors may also be involved (intelligence and social awareness, for example). Unfortunately, it is most suitable for children older than 8 years.

For younger children, a structured interview is more appropriate because the questions can be more general and easier to understand. Maurer (1964) used this technique with children ages 5 to 14, in the study described in the reading at the end of this chapter. **249**

She found that the most common fear at ages 5 and 6 is fear of animals; this fear decreases gradually with age. It is surprising that most of the feared animals (such as lions, tigers, and bears) are not realistic dangers in our society. The second most common category at this age is "spooks" (monsters, ghosts, witches, and the like). Realistic dangers (fire, car accidents, kidnappers, and so on) are less frequently mentioned by 5- and 6-year-olds, but older children are likely to name them. The predominance of unrealistic fears among the youngest children would be difficult to explain with learning theories, but it coincides well with Freud's suggestion that childhood fears are evolutionary leftovers from more dangerous times and also with Piaget's idea that preoperational children cannot separate fantasy from reality.

Inducing fear

Psychologists rarely frighten children deliberately; when they do, they try to frighten the children only mildly. One way to scare toddlers is to separate them from their mothers in an unfamiliar place; another way is to make a loud noise. Maccoby and Jacklin (1973) used both of these methods to study how boys and girls react differently to fear. The toddlers, just over a year old, were placed in an unfamiliar room with their mothers either nearby (18 inches) or farther away (8 feet, but still in the room). After the child settled down to play, a loud male voice came over a loudspeaker hidden among the toys. The fearful noise made many children run to mother and cling to her, but it did not increase mere looking at mother or crying. Most fear was shown when the voice was loudest and when the children were farthest from mother. Contrary to the psychologists' prediction, girls and boys reacted in the same way; girls did not show more fear.

Reducing fear

Psychologists are reluctant to frighten children, but they are eager to find ways to reduce children's fears. One method is to arrange for a frightened child to watch someone deal calmly with the feared object. Fears of mothers and of their preschool children are highly correlated, which suggests that children can learn fears by observation (Hagman, 1932). Bandura, Grusec, and Menlove (1967) tested the proposition that a child can also overcome fears by observation. Preschool children who feared dogs attended "birthday parties" twice a day for 4 days and observed one of three events: a 4-year-old child playing happily with a friendly dog; a friendly dog, but no child playing with her; or no dog and no child model. A fourth group saw the model play with the dog, but the birthday party atmosphere was absent. The children's fear of the dog decreased at least slightly in all conditions, but the most remarkable improvement occurred in the groups that observed the child playing happily with the dog (with or without the birthday parties). A month later, the children's fears had not reappeared, even when the children were tested with an unfamiliar dog. One effective way to reduce a child's fear, therefore, is to arrange for the child to watch another child play calmly with the feared object.

Another method is to reward a child for interacting calmly with the feared object. Jones (1924) used this technique to reduce fear of fuzzy objects in a 3-year-old boy,

Peter (no relation to Little Albert, except psychologically). Jones fed Peter food he especially liked, while bringing a caged rabbit gradually closer. Eventually Peter could touch the rabbit without crying, and his fears of other fuzzy objects also decreased. Lazarus (1960) used a similar approach to cure a boy's fear of cars. At first the child was given chocolate merely for making pleasant comments about cars. Then he was given toy autos and fed chocolate when he played with them. Eventually, the boy was given chocolate for actually sitting and riding in a car.

Sometimes more than one learning technique is needed to help a child conquer fears. A variety of principles was used by Patterson and Brodsky (1966) to modify a "multitude of deviant behaviors" in 5-year-old Karl. When separated from his mother, Karl became intensely aggressive; he kicked, bit, screamed, cried, threw toys, and had temper tantrums. On one occasion he clung to his mother's dress with his teeth when she tried to leave him at school. Karl's kindergarten teacher was covered with bruises obtained while trying to calm the boy. The psychologists guessed that Karl's extreme aggression arose from fear of being separated from his parents, especially his mother. They planned a program to reduce his separation anxiety and reinforce sociable behavior.

W. C. Baker

Fig. 11-3. A child's fear of dogs can be reduced by watching another child play comfortably with a dog.

(The parents, teacher, and classmates were all involved in the reinforcement strategy.) When Karl was left alone with a psychologist, he had a tantrum. The psychologist explained that Karl could rejoin his mother when he stopped crying. On the first day, Karl screamed and fought for 30 minutes before he calmed down and rejoined his mother; on day 2, the tantrum lasted only 30 seconds; on day 3, Karl did not have a tantrum. In addition, the psychologist enacted (with dolls) scenes of separation and reinforced Karl for saying the boy doll was not afraid to leave the mother doll. The third part of the plan was a "Karl box" at school, which would ring a bell and deliver candy (for the whole class) whenever a classmate talked to Karl. Karl was soon playing peacefully with the other children. The final element of the plan was to teach Karl's parents to reward Karl's good behavior and *not* to reward his misbehavior by accident. Within 9 days Karl's aggressive behavior was markedly decreased and he showed no more signs of fear.

One final method of reducing fear is to help the child feel in control of the feared situation, to prevent the child from feeling helpless. This technique was used successfully to help children overcome their fear of the dark (Kanfer, Karoly, & Newman, 1975). The children were told to sit in a dark room for as long as they could without turning on the light. All the children were shown how to turn on the light and how to use an intercom to call for help, if needed. On the average, the 5- and 6-year-old children could tolerate the dark for less than 30 seconds. The children were then trained with special words to say in the dark. One group learned to say "I'm a brave girl (boy). I can take care of myself in the dark." A second group learned "The dark is a fun place to be. There are many good things in the dark." The control group learned to recite a nursery rhyme. When the test of tolerating the dark was repeated, the nursery rhyme group still averaged less than 30 seconds. The other groups, after only a few minutes of training with the special words, could tolerate the dark for as long as 90 seconds. A practical application of this study is that parents should *not* call a child a baby for fearing the dark. Children are much more likely to learn to control their fears when parents train them to say brave words when they confront a fear-provoking situation.

SUMMARY

Fears are normal for children in the sense that all children experience them. In young children, some fears are even desirable because they help protect the child from dangerous situations. Fears occur in varying degrees and are not necessarily consistent over time and in different situations. A 5-year-old friend of ours who is considered a daredevil at home, willing to rush in where even his father fears to tread, is considered apprehensive at kindergarten. Adults are inclined to consider children's fears silly or to ignore them. Methods are available for reducing fear, though. Observation of a fearless playmate, rewards delivered for fearless behavior, and training to confront a feared object with brave words are three effective techniques. Most children eventually outgrow most fears, but by understanding the origins and dynamics of fears, we can help children conquer this unwelcome feeling more easily.

Personality development can be explored with specific research studies, as in the case of fears, or with more general theories, as in the case of Freud's theory. The grand theories have been valuable for providing insights into personality. The topical research approach is more popular among psychologists today because it provides more reliable answers to psychological questions. The following chapters emphasize the research approach, but theories are not entirely neglected.

REFERENCES

Bandura, A., Grusec, J. E., & Menlove, F. L. Vicarious extinction of avoidance behavior. *Journal of Personality and Social Psychology,* 1967, **5,** 16-23.

Bee, H. *The developing child.* New York: Harper & Row, Publishers, 1975.

Bridges, K. M. B. Emotional development in early infancy. *Child Development,* 1932, **3,** 324-341.

Bronson, G. W. The development of fear in man and other animals. *Child Development,* 1968, **39,** 409-431.

Bronson, G. W. Fear of visual novelty: developmental patterns in males and females. *Developmental Psychology,* 1970, **2,** 33-40.

DeFee, J. F., & Himelstein, P. Children's fear in a dental situation as a function of birth order. *Journal of Genetic Psychology,* 1969, **115,** 253-255.

Freud, S. The dream and the primal scene. (1918) Reprinted in G. Lindzey & C. S. Hall, *Theories of personality: primary sources and research.* New York: John Wiley & Sons, Inc., 1966.

Freud, S. *A general introduction to psychoanalysis.* New York: Washington Square Press, 1924.

Freud, S. Some psychical consequences of the anatomical distinction between the sexes. (1925) Reprinted in G. Lindzey & C. S. Hall, *Theories of personality: primary sources and research.* New York: John Wiley & Sons, Inc., 1966.

Freud, S. *The problem of anxiety.* New York: W. W. Norton & Co., Inc., 1936.

Hagman, R. R. A study of fears of children of preschool age. *Journal of Experimental Education,* 1932, **1,** 110-130.

Hall, C. S., and Lindzey, G. *Theories of personality.* New York: John Wiley & Sons, Inc., 1957.

Harari, H., and McDavid, J. W. Teachers' expectations and name stereotypes. *Journal of Educational Psychology,* 1973, **65,** 222-225.

Jones, M. C. A laboratory study of fear: the case of Peter. *Pedagogical Seminary and Journal of Genetic Psychology,* 1924, **31,** 308-315.

Kanfer, F. H., Karoly, P., & Newman, A. Reduction of children's fear of the dark by competence-related and situational threat-related verbal cues. *Journal of Consulting and Clinical Psychology,* 1975, **43,** 251-258.

Lazarus, A. A. The elimination of children's phobias by deconditioning. In H. J. Eysenck (Ed.), *Behavior therapy and the neuroses.* New York: Macmillan, Inc., 1960.

Maccoby, E. E., & Jacklin, C. N. Stress, activity, and proximity seeking: sex differences in the year-old child. *Child Development,* 1973, **44,** 34-42.

Masters, W. H., & Johnson, V. E. *Human sexual response.* Boston: Little, Brown and Company, 1966.

Maurer, A. What children fear. *Journal of Genetic Psychology,* 1964, **106,** 265-277.

McDavid, J. W., & Harari, H. Stereotyping of names and popularity in grade school children. *Child Development,* 1966, **37,** 453-459.

Nichols, R. C. Heredity and environment: major findings on ability and personality. Paper presented at American Psychological Association Convention, 1976.

Niem, T. C., & Collard, R. R. Parental discipline of aggressive behaviors in 4-year-old Chinese and American children. *Proceedings of the 80th Annual Convention of the American Psychological Association,* 1972, **7,** 95-96.

Patterson, G. R., & Brodsky, G. A behavior modification programme for a child with multiple problem behaviours. *Journal of Child Psychology and Psychiatry,* 1966, **7,** 277-295.

What children fear

Adah Maurer

A. INTRODUCTION

Children do not fear the atomic bomb (Escalona, 1963; Schwebel, 1963). They do not even fear the things they have been taught to be careful about: street traffic and germs. The strange truth is that they fear an unrealistic source of danger in our urban civilization: wild animals. Almost all 5- and 6-year-olds and more than one half of 7-to-12-year-olds claim that the things to be afraid of are mammals and reptiles (most frequently): snakes, lions, and tigers. Not until age 12 or more do most children recognize actual sources of danger and, when they do, these dangers are almost always highly personal rather than politically or socially determined (A. Freud & Burlingame, 1943).

One 12-year-old boy said that the things to be afraid of are "wild animals, fierce dogs and cats, and snakes." Another of the same age answered, "Not being able to get a job." Both boys had earned intelligence scores within the normal range (low 90s) on the Wechsler Intelligence Scale for Children; both had mild learning problems, but there the similarity ended. After an assessment that included achievement tests, the school history, parent interviews, and a study of the family dynamics, a marked difference became apparent. The first boy had been overprotected and lacked opportunity to care for himself and to make decisions. He was the youngest of a large family and had been babied and restricted in experiences. The second boy had been overwhelmed with excessive demands from his parents. His irresponsible father had drifted from one menial job to another and was unemployed at the time of the study. The boy, the eldest of his siblings, had borne the brunt of his father's disgust at the latter's incompetence and had been belittled and criticized to an excessive degree. Compared to that of the first boy, the conversation of the second boy seemed mature.

Did the answers these boys gave to the question about fears reflect in some measure the underlying problem? In the second case, it would seem that it did, yet without knowing the kinds of answers one might expect from normal children, it would be easy to jump to unwarranted conclusions. Was the first boy's fear of animals due to some traumatic experience? Had he lived in a primitive area where wild animals actually were a threat to his safety? Or had his father been a pioneer and entertained the boy with tales of the dangers of the woods? And if any of these suppositions had been true (which they were not) did they relate in any way to his learning problem? To answer questions such as these and to determine the etiology of fear in children became the purpose of a year-long study of normal children.

A 5-year-old boy, referred because of excessive aggressiveness, answered the question thus: "Dogs!" He was encouraged to go on. "And what else?" He grimaced and said, "Dog, dog, two dogs!" In the silence that followed he screamed, "DOGS!" Again he was asked, "Anything else?" More quietly, but still firmly he said, "Ten dogs." He proved to be a very fearful child, uncertain of the stability of his home and of his place in it. His belligerence in school seemed to stem from a psychological need to defend himself.

Children's fears have been explained by several diverse theories. The first, a folklore, denies that children fear by calling the emotion "stubbornness." The parents of the boy who feared dogs, dogs, ten dogs said, "We've told him that dogs won't hurt him but he won't listen!" The attempted cure had been repeated spankings for this and much else, and spankings again for passing the punishment on to his contemporaries.

The Freudian considers fear as a displacement of the son's fear of the father who, so the child believes, will retaliate for the son's incestuous desire for his mother by castrating the son. The Freudian postulates that, during the oral stage characterized by sucking, the child fears being eaten because he feels guilt about his desire to eat (or bite) his mother's breast (S. Freud, 1925). Psychoanalytic therapy has consisted of an effort to resolve an oedipal triangle, thus permitting the child to enter the genital phase of his development. The American Academy of Child Psychiatry has reevaluated this formulation, as have many of the neo-Freudians; but the emphasis remains firmly rooted in the dynamics of the child's emotional involvement with his parents (Josselyn, 1962; Maurer, 1964).

The behaviorist finds that fears are conditioned responses based upon associational ties with one or another of the fears present at birth. John B. Watson, the earliest behaviorist to apply the theory to child rearing, was certain that the fear of dogs proceeded from a traumatic experience in which the loud barking of a dog had triggered the original fear of loud sounds. His recommended cure consisted of unconditioning the fear by the introduction of a dog or a toy dog at some pleasant time, such as during a meal, and gradually bringing it closer until it could be tolerated on the tray (Watson, 1959). This theory, too, has undergone considerable modification; but the emphasis remains upon the learning, unlearning, and modification of fear through environmental experiences.

A follower of Jung's early theories (1962) would explain a fear of animals as an expression of the collective unconscious. In more primitive times, the boy's ancestors feared the rampaging wolf, the stealthy poisonous snake, and other natural enemies. Although the boy lives in the midst of the trappings of civilization, and the descendants of the wolf have been tamed to family pets; yet deeply submerged is the tribal fear, built in perhaps to the neutral network present but dormant at birth. Thus the child goes through a stage that he outgrows as he matures into succeeding phases of the ontogenetic recapitulation of the history of his race. This theory has been muddied by mysticism and has been neglected in the ongoing debate between the psychoanalysts and the experimentalists. Animal ecologists (Masserman, 1962), however, have demonstrated the specificity of fears in animals, notably in the giraffe, which animal, though born in captivity and raised on a bottle, nevertheless startles and shies away from the mock-up of a lion, the traditional enemy of his species; but approaches and sniffs at the mock-up of a giraffe. Humans, however, generally are considered to have lost their instincts and to have become dependent upon learning.

Gesell (1941) and the maturation theorists have demonstrated the primacy of growth in physical and mental functions, yet for the most part they have omitted similar studies of the maturation of the emotions, especially of fear. It may be that they have thought of fear as an abnormal manifestation or a malfunctioning rather than as an aspect of normal growth.

The eclectic finds it difficult to choose among the theories for they have little in common. Psychoanalysts have been concerned chiefly with the abnormal, and their preemption of the subject of fear has colored general thinking along these lines. The behaviorists have dealt with fear largely as a means to eliminate unwanted responses. Their use of punishment is empirical, with no discussion of fear it arouses since fear is a subjective phenomenon. Yet it should be obvious that a judicious, rational fearfulness is life preservative and therefore an inescapable aspect of the normal child (Maurer, 1961). Excessive, irrational fears are widely known to be intimately connected with learning difficulties, delinquency, and withdrawal. Preventive methodology requires more knowledge of the normal fears of normal children, thus defining, highlighting, and permitting evaluation of the unique and the aberrant.

Based upon the results of this study, each of the major theories appears to contain some part of the truth. It also becomes clear that the amount, depth, and kind of fear as well as its objects is ascertainable and definitely of diagnostic value.

B.   METHOD

Over a period of a year, each child who was given the Wechsler Intelligence Scale for Children was asked an additional question. At the conclusion of the comprehension subtest, in

PART
FOUR
═══

the same neutral tone used for other questions, the examiner said, "What are the things to be afraid of?" Each answer was recorded as nearly verbatim as possible, as were all answers for all subtests. Silent approval and recognition that the fears were legitimate was given by a sympathetic nod. When the child stopped speaking he was encouraged to go on. "And what else?" and then, "Anything else?" Four children replied, "Nothing." One answered, "You shouldn't be afraid of anything." In these cases, to provide the ease of replying by projection, the question was re-phrased. "Some children are afraid of some things some of the time, aren't they?" All nodded or said, "Yes." The examiner continued: "What are these children sometimes afraid of?" In all cases this brought a satisfactory reply.

The direct question "What are you afraid of?" was not used because children might interpret this as critical and tend to reply defensively. Since the question necessarily came after four fail-ures (except for the brightest who scored very high in comprehension) most of the children seemed relieved by an "easy" one and, with some exceptions, the answers flowed smoothly and without shock. For severely disturbed children, the question was omitted.

C. SUBJECTS

The subjects of the study consisted of 130 children of whom 91 were boys and 39 were girls. In age they ranged from 5 years and 5 months to 14 years and 6 months. All of them were in regular attendance at elementary schools in middle- or lower-middle-class suburbs. Eighteen of them proved to be mentally retarded (nine boys, nine girls), two of them severely (one boy, one girl). Since the study was for the purpose of tabulating the fears of normal children, these eighteen were eliminated from all calculations except one. In this one calculation, the attempt was made to determine whether replies conformed to a chronological or mental-age pattern and the retarded were included in the group of their mental-age mates. In all other tabulations and discussions, the subjects are the 112 students whose IQs fell between 80 and 144 (see Tables 1 and 2).

Each of the children had been referred to the school psychologist and to that extent was perhaps atypical. The reasons for referral covered a wide range. For some, testing was requested to help determine the advisability of retention or double promotion. Some had speech defects or verbal infantilisms. Some had reading problems. A few merely needed glasses. Some were noisy, defiant, failed to do their homework, or to conform in some way to the demands of teachers. A few were shy and apparently friendless, while others were the center of playground disputes. Some were the entirely normal siblings of disturbed or retarded children. None was so severely disturbed that referral for psychiatric care was deemed mandatory, thus all could be considered within the normal range. If the somewhat unexpected results were a function of atypicality, the study nevertheless is of value because *(a)* the technique proved to be an important diagnostic clue and *(b)* the need for additional studies along this line is clearly indicated.

The number of responses ranged from a single answer followed by "That's all!" to a spon-taneous eighteen responses, which number was unique in that the next largest number was nine. Boys averaged slightly higher than girls (4.23 *vs.* 4.00), but the difference is not significant. There was very little difference between the age groups perhaps because of the technique used, and there was no observable tendency for the younger or older children to give more or fewer replies. The more fluent children tended to elaborate or modify their answers or go on to relate personal experiences. The shy children and those with speech difficulties tended to be slower and more patience was required in drawing them out, but they averaged as many responses as the others.

D. RESULTS

Of the 467 responses, 233 or 50 percent, consisted of a single category: animals. Seventy-two of the 112 children, or 64 percent, replied solely or partly by naming animals in general or

256

Table 1. Subjects in the study by age and sex

Age	Boys	Girls	Total
5 and 6	13	7	20
7 and 8	20	9	29
9 and 10	21	10	31
11 and 12	18	1	19
13 and 14	10	3	13
Total	82	30	112

Table 2. Subjects in the study by IQ scores*

	Intelligence quotient		
Age	Slow 80-89	Average 90-110	Bright 111-144
5 and 6	2	14	4
7 and 8	8	12	9
9 and 10	7	18	6
11 and 12	4	12	3
13 and 14	8	5	0
Total	29	61	22

*The distribution approaches the normal probability of 22, 68, 22 percent in the three divisions, respectively, closely enough to consider this a fair sample of schoolchildren.

one or more specific animals including: alligator, ape, bat, bear, bee, bird, black widow, bobcat, buffalo, bull, cat, centipede, cow, crocodile, deer, dinosaur, dog, eel, elephant, fox, gorilla, hawk, hippopotamus, horse, insect, leopard, lion, lizard, mosquito, mountain lion, parakeet, pinchbug, rat, reptile, rhinoceros, scorpion, shark, snake, spider, spit-monkey, tarantula, tiger, turtle, wildcat, whale and wolf.

The most unpopular animal is the snake. Thirty-three of the subjects, twenty-three boys and ten girls (28 percent and 33 percent respectively) mentioned them. Next in order came lions, mentioned twenty-eight times; tigers, fourteen times; and bears, nine times.

The most striking fact that emerged from the study, besides the near universality of fear of animals, is that fear of animals decreases sharply with age (from 80 percent of the 5- and 6-year-olds to 23 percent of those 13 and 14 years old). The older children also tended to qualify their responses. Rather than simply "Lion, tiger," they said, "Wild animals if you are in a jungle without arms," "Dogs with rabies," "A cow that might kick you," or, "A parakeet that's infected."

Fear of the dark seems to disappear after age 7, with only two stragglers who admitted to it after that age, both of them qualifying their responses: "Little kids are afraid of the dark," and "Highways at night." Similarly, fears of nonexistent entities, such as monsters, the boogie man, ghosts, witches, and animated skeletons, are left behind after age 10. Thus the questions about the effect of television drama highlighting horror become a matter of age. Fright films would seem to be traumatic before the child thoroughly understands that they are only imaginary; after that age, the possibility of their being therapeutic may enter. Age 9 to 10 appears to be the dividing line.

Unique and individual responses rise from zero at 5 and 6 years to 46 percent as children reach early adolescence. The subject matter becomes more realistic and more closely tied to learned or experienced objects and situations (see Table 3).

Table 3. Subject matter of fears

Age	Percent*						
	Animals	People	Dark	Spooks	Natural hazards	Machinery	Miscellaneous
5 and 6	80	20	20	33	0	20	0
7 and 8	73	17	3	17	34	34	14
9 and 10	61	42	3	10	35	35	16
11 and 12	68	42	0	0	26	42	26
13 and 14	23	39	0	0	31	46	46

*In each age group, the percent of subjects who replied that things to be afraid of were such as to be classi-fiable under the categories. "People" includes "bad men," "kidnappers," "people who . . . ," "if some-body . . . ," as well as members of the family and playmates mentioned by name. "Spooks" includes "monsters," "ghosts," "witches," "man made of iron," "Frankenstein," etc. "Natural hazards" includes storms, fire, water, waves, flood, volcano, etc. Machinery includes all man-made gadgets and inventions, such as weapons, cars, electricity, trains, etc.

Table 4. Responses tabulated by mental age

Mental age	Percent*						
	Animals	People	Dark	Spooks	Natural hazards	Machinery	Miscellaneous
4 to 6	75	21	11	39	11	7	3
7 and 8	59	25	7	12	19	12	12
9 and 10	57	30	0	5	27	35	15
11 and 12	54	37	0	0	42	54	17
13 to 15	11	44	0	0	22	11	55

*The figures refer to the percent of the responses (not to percent of the children) of 130 children, including 112 normals and 18 mentally retarded children. The sharp drop in fear of the dark and of spooks after age 8 and of animals after age 12 is even more marked when mental age rather than chronological age is considered.

The question arises: Is this maturational trend a function of chronological age or does intel-ligence play a part? Two severely retarded children, whose replies were not tabulated with the above, gave immature replies. The boy (age 14:7, IQ 44, MA 6:8) said, "Cow, horse, goat, snake." The girl (age 15:6, IQ 46, MA 7:5) said, "Bears, lions, train if you go in front of it, and alligators." On the other hand, an exceptionally bright boy (age 9:6, IQ 134, MA 14:2) answered the same question, "Things you can't overcome." Asked to explain, he added, "Well, if you are afraid of water, for example, you probably will never overcome it." His home life showed an excessive responsibility for his mother who lived under the constant tension of having her husband away from home for long stretches on cruise as a Lieutenant Commander in the Navy.

To determine if these children typified dull and bright intelligences, the replies of all of the children in the study, plus those of the 18 mentally retarded children, were evaluated on the basis of mental age (see Table 4). On this basis, the sharp dropping away of fear of the dark and of spooks is even more marked. The fear of animals maintained a high level through age 12, but only one child with a mental age of 13 or more admitted to it. There were only nine cases in this most mature group, and thus it is difficult to determine whether this is a universal phenomenon. Each of the nine gave a unique answer. One boy (age 13:5, IQ 110) said, "Getting killed, parents getting a divorce, falling off a bike. The world is full of fears." Another (age 13:0, IQ 96) shrugged and said, "Trouble, the principal, spankings, going home if you lose money."

But it was also true that the younger children often gave personal clues in their replies. A boy (6:6, IQ 104) said, "Spiders, pinchbugs, a big boy beating you up." Thus, IQ alone does not tell the whole story. A precocious sense of danger in the specifics of living may be found in nonacademic children. A girl (8:9, IQ 84) gasped and rattled off a long story that was caught only in part as "Falling down and getting hurt. You might go to a hospital. . . . If you get stitches in your eye, you might have an operation and you might die." She was a member of a large, dependent family, whose troubles constantly recurred. At the time of the test, her mother was in the hospital but for what purpose could not be determined.

Nor does a high IQ necessarily move a 6-year-old to considerations of a realistic assessment of the world of dangers he lives in, perhaps because his home and environment were particularly safe, congenial, and supportive. Such a boy (age 6:5, IQ 144, MA 9:2) said without concern, "Lion, tiger, rat, buffalo and bull." He read words on the fifth-grade reading list without hesitation; in class he was so bright and well adjusted that his teacher had recommended double promotion. He was tall for his age, handsome, and in excellent health. Nothing about him suggested "immaturity" as that word is used by educators to characterize the egocentric crybaby.

Educators long have been dissatisfied with the IQ as the sole index of expected achievement. Motivational and emotional factors, it is generally agreed, play a strong part in determining progress, but attempted measurement of these has fallen short of usefulness. Personality type and preferences have proved less than predictive. It is strongly suggested by this study that the kind and level of fearfulness may act as a brake on usable intelligence, and that its measurement by a highly polished tool may prove as enlightening as the studies on creativity, which have uncovered another additional dimension.

Fear of fire is the traditional example used to prove that children learn by experience. "A burnt child fears the fire" seems to imply that the unburnt child does not or that only by experience does the child learn to fear or learn what to fear. The folk saying is older than central heating and seems to have little specific pertinence in today's world. Among our twenty children of 5 and 6 years (who gave a total of 91 replies), fifty-four replies were of animals, only one was fire. Four percent of the 7- and 8-year-olds, 5 percent of the 9- and 10-year-olds, 16 percent of the 11- and 12- year-olds and 9 percent of the oldest group included fire (forest fire, burning house, etc.) among the things to be feared. In no case, however, could it be ascertained that this response sprang from a personal experience. The one child known to have suffered extensive burns, a girl (age 11:6, IQ 60, MA 6:9) replied with a standard "Lion, tiger, dog, cat, snakes, rattlers, spiders." Her scars, which extended from neck to buttocks on her back, had been covered with grafts from her thighs. They had come to be her one claim upon her contemporaries for awed attention and upon adults for sympathy. Accordingly, she valued them and was quick to lift her skirts for strangers, a habit that tended to be misinterpreted. Asked directly if she feared fire, she looked puzzled and then smiled happily, "I guess so."

Other natural hazards mentioned by this group of children included storms, deep water, waves, earthquake, volcano, hurricane, tornado, quicksand, sharp rocks, cliffs, a tunnel cave-in, avalanche ("snow falling down from the hill"), poison oak, and the desert. No one of them was mentioned often enough to have any general significance. Individually, some seemed merely to represent the most recent subject of adventure stories read or viewed; others proved to have deep personal significance in the light of subsequent parent interviews. As a group, natural hazards (including fires) supplied one of the responses of the 5- and 6-year-olds, but from one fourth to one third of the responses of the 7- to 12-year-olds. The age of adventure thus begins at 7.

Machinery is perhaps an inadequate title for a category that includes cars, trucks, trains, construction, buildings, airplanes, guns, knives, electricity, a trapdoor, explosions, a submarine, helicopter, firecrackers, rusty nails, bicycles, a tractor, a crane, a hatchet, electric chair, gas, falling bricks, trolley car and a stairwell. What was intended was a grouping of those hazards that are man made and that are elements of an industrial civilization. Here it is obvious that learning has taken place. There is no possibility that a collective unconscious could have suggested to a boy that tractors are dangerous because "you might move the wrong lever and it would start up." The amazing discovery lies in the fact that teaching has had so little effect.

Surely every kindergartner and first-grader listens to lengthy lessons about the dangers inherent in highways, traffic, cars, and trucks. Yet when asked what are the things to be afraid of, not one gave evidence of having learned his lesson. Among older children—7 to 14—only 15 percent of the replies referred in any way to the Number 1 threat to life in America today. Automobile accidents account for more deaths and disabilities among school age children than any disease and far more than all the dangers that children fear put together. Perhaps this is just as well. We would not want our children to be terrified of crossing a street in the same unreasoning sense that some of them are terrified of dogs. Establishing the habit of stop, look, and listen before you cross is apparently enough; to add warnings of peril is ineffective because, for whatever reason, it is not learned.

Trains, usually qualified, were mentioned eleven times; weapons only seven times. All the others were unique replies. Many of them were qualified or explained. Some children went on to tell of personal experiences that gave important clues to their life style. The boy who replied, "Walking down the highway at night you might be hit by a car" had indeed been doing just that. His wanderings in search (it would seem) of a lost father helped to explain his listlessness in school. Another who listed, "Big cranes, big trucks, when you're tearing down a house" was describing his father's occupation and admitting inadvertently both his fear of his father and his fear that his father would leave.

The category "people" was also revealing of underlying difficulties. Forty-five replies involved "people who . . . (come with guns, hit you, try to give you trouble," etc.) or specific persons. Alas for learning, only five mentioned, "Somebody who tells you to get in his car." All children should have been warned against child enticers; perhaps most had been, but spooks, monsters, and ghosts remained frightening to more children than kidnappers. One boy blurted out, "My brother! He comes up behind me in the dark and says, 'Boo!'" Another, a girl, replied, "People who might try to make you nervous or give you a heart attack." She was describing not her own, but her mother's palpitations. Five children said, "If your parents get a divorce." This should perhaps be a separate category since it indicated not a fear of people but a resurgence of the separation anxiety of infancy. In these cases there was little need to hunt further for the cause of poor schoolwork. A family breakup, almost without exception, causes at least a temporary emotional upheaval in the children that is often reflected in an inability to concentrate.

Miscellaneous responses included: war, five; the atom bomb, two; punishment, four; disease, four; separation ("if you're all alone," "if you get lost," etc.), four; breaking the moral code, two; death, six; unemployment, one; and Hell, one. Some of these seemed to be thoughtful assessments of dangers in the abstract. Others were obviously specific to the particular life situation of the child. A few were so strange as to be baffling. One boy replied, "My little brother sleeps with me," possibly implying that otherwise he would be afraid of the dark or that there was danger in this arrangement for either the brother or himself. It could not be determined, and was not necessary. The parents, with very little persuasion, agreed to provide bunkbeds. Another changed the subject: "We planted some flowers in our garden," and would say no more. There is a far-fetched possibility that the "flowers" might have been marijuana and that the girl sensed her parents' concern about being caught or that a body was buried in the garden and camouflaged, but such speculations were considered out of bounds and the matter was not pursued.

E. CONCLUSIONS

The question, "What are the things to be afraid of?" asked routinely in the course of the Wechsler test proved to be an important clue to the emotional dynamics of the child being tested.

Eighty percent of children of 5 and 6 reply to the question by naming one or more wild animals, with snake, lion, tiger, and bear predominating. Sixty percent or more of children between the ages of 7 and 12 answer similarly, but after mental age 12 it is rare.

One third of children under 7 admit to fear of imaginary beings (monsters mainly), and a fifth of them fear the dark. Both of these replies drop off sharply after age 7.

The things that children are taught to fear (traffic, germs, and kidnappers) are rarely mentioned. Punishment, war, and the atom bomb are also scarce replies at any age although it is likely that children would answer "Yes" if they were asked directly, "Do you fear . . . any of these?"

As children mature, the kinds of things they regard as frightening become diverse, unique, and are often tied directly or indirectly to their central concern.

Refusals to answer, replies of "Nothing," long pauses, changes of volume or pitch of the voice, and facial expressions (while not common) provide clues to the intensity of the fear.

An "immature" reply may characterize the well-protected child and in some cases the mentally retarded. The child who has been burdened with excessive responsibility or hardship is more likely than others to give a unique, "mature" reply, as is also the bright child with a mental age of 12 or more.

Much caution is needed in interpretation, for recent events and the child's mood during the examination may be the fleeting cause of any particular answer.

All four of the major theories of childhood (psychoanalysis, behaviorism, the collective unconscious, and maturation) contribute, albeit incompletely, to an understanding of childhood fears.

A strong maturational factor, partly influenced by intelligence and partly influenced by the amount of responsibility thrust upon the child, seems to be at work upon an archaic instinctual base. The child is born with the capacity to fear, apparently more than is necessary to preserve his life. Although he feels fear, the child does not know with the same certainty as the smaller-brained mammals just what objects or situations are to be feared. Much infant questioning (Piaget, 1955), especially that relating to life and death, is prompted by a curiosity about the missing information and by a desire to locate accurately the causative objects of the amorphous sense of possible danger. If archaic instincts to avoid specific hazards are lacking, it may be that the fear of being eaten by wild animals or poisoned by snakes retains a certain ease of arousal. Among the uneducated, the folk habit of enforcing obedience by suppling incorrect information to children for the purpose of controlling them ("The wizard man will eat you if you stray!") is enormously effective, but also, by rousing archaic fears, it may be a limiting factor to the full use of mental powers.

As the child matures, the emotion of fear fastens upon more and more realistic objects depending upon experience learning rather than upon instruction.

The intensity of the child's fear depends for the most part upon the family relationships.

REFERENCES

1. Escalona, S. Children's responses to nuclear threat. *Children,* 1963, **10,** 137-142.
2. Freud, A., & Burlingame, D. *War and children.* New York: Willard, 1943.
3. Freud, S. Analysis of a phobia in a five-year-old boy. In *Collected papers. Vol. III.* London: Hogarth Press and the Institute of Psycho-Analysis, 1925, pp. 149-288.
4. Gesell, A., & Amatruda, C. *Developmental diagnosis.* New York: Harper, 1941.
5. Josselyn, I. Concepts related to child development: The oral stage. *J. Child Psychiat.,* 1962, **1,** 209-224.
6. Jung, C. G. The Archtypes and the collective unconscious. *Collected works—Bollinger series.* New York: Pantheon Books, 1962.
7. Masserman, J. Ethology, comparative biodynamics and psychoanalytic research. In Scher, M. D. (Ed.), *Theories of the mind.* New York: Free Press, 1962, pp. 15-64.
8. Maurer, A. The child's knowledge of nonexistence. *J. Exist. Psychiat.,* 1961, **2,** 193-212.
9. Maurer, A. Did little Hans really want to marry his mother? *J. Hum. Psychol.,* 1964, **4,** 139-148.
10. Piaget, J. *Language and thought of the child.* New York: Meridian, 1955, pp. 171-240.
11. Schwebel, M. Nuclear cold war: student opinions. Unpublished manuscript read at the convention of the American Orthopsychiatric Association, March, 1963.
12. Watson, J. B. *Behaviorism.* Chicago: Univ. Chicago Press, 1959.

Chapter 12

Social development

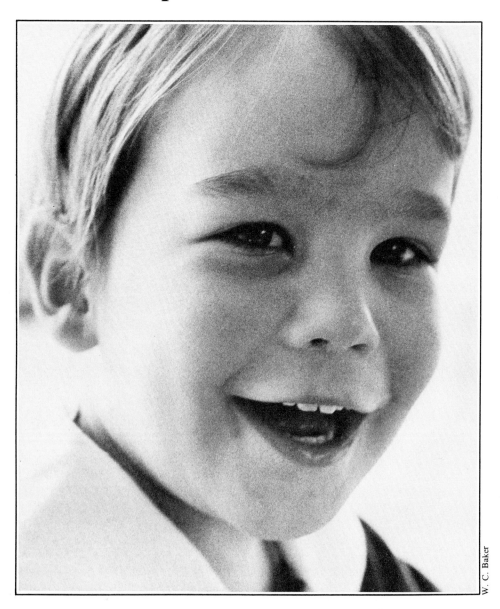

W. C. Baker

Several psychological theories emphasize the idea that infants are born with no particular inclination to either love or dislike others. These writers emphasize that the child's experiences with others determine whether that child will grow into a sociable, responsive other-directed person or will have difficulty relating to others. With this thought in mind, consider the general responsiveness most people exhibit toward infants. Infants elicit social behaviors even from total strangers. People peer at our infants, poke them, chuck their chins, coo at them, and cuddle them if given the opportunity. Most infants are generally tolerant of this behavior and in some instances even responsive. It would appear that infants should in most cases grow to trust and relate to others.

Yet the development of social behaviors in children is much more complex than this would suggest. First, it is generally believed that the infant's socialization depends on the formation of a close intense relationship with the mother, called attachment. Once this bond is formed, the child is able to expand his or her social relationships to include other members of the family. As the child's abilities to process information increase and the child becomes more mobile, he or she begins to interact with peers and to develop more and more social contacts.

Again the picture of social development is oversimplified, as the actual process involves periods of both social expansion and withdrawal. For example, most people who have spent any time with children are aware of two behavioral phenomena, called stranger anxiety and separation anxiety, which occur during the course of social development. In both cases the child begins to react negatively to experiences that have occurred previously with no disturbance. In stranger anxiety the child who has been tolerant of advances from strangers begins to fuss when a well-meaning stranger attempts to hold him or her. In separation anxiety the child becomes disturbed when left by the mother, although such separations may have occurred frequently before with no ill effect.

Psychologists have examined these phenomena in detail in an attempt to understand the child's development of attachment to the mother. These processes are considered later in this chapter. At this point they should illustrate the complexity of social development in children.

In this chapter we will first consider infant sociability and formation of an attachment bond to the mother. Then we will examine the child's relationship to family and the possible effects birth order in that family may have on development. Finally we will discuss general socialization and the child's increasing interactions with peers.

ATTACHMENT AND INFANT SOCIABILITY

How a child comes to love its mother has been the object of study by many psychological theorists and even more researchers. Psychologists call this process the attachment process in an attempt to be more specific and allow for more objectivity in research.

Maccoby and Masters (1970) describe attachment behavior as an attempt to be near certain people and to resist separation from these same people. As already mentioned, most researchers consider the attachment bond to be a strong, specific relationship directed to the mother or the primary caretaker. Its presence is assumed when the child seeks closeness to the mother and engages in behaviors designed to maintain that closeness. Although most researchers agree on descriptions of attachment behaviors, there are several differing viewpoints as to how attachment develops.

Theories of attachment

Freudian psychoanalytic theory considers the attachment bond between the mother and child to be the result of biological predispositions both to relate to other people and to satisfy body needs. If the child has a tendency to relate to people as well as a tendency to satisfy needs, a mother who cares for her child physically satisfies two conditions and becomes a powerful object choice for the child.

Not too different from the psychoanalytic position is that of social learning theory. This position also holds that the child becomes attached to the mother because she nurtures him or her, or in other words satisfies his or her needs. The major difference between these viewpoints is that social learning theory explains the attachment process further by stating that as the mother reduces discomfort in the child, for example by feeding him or her, the pleasant feelings as a result of having hunger reduced become associated with the mother. Therefore, the mother becomes a reinforcing event in the child's life. The child has learned to love her.

This viewpoint had much support until Harlow's work with infant rhesus monkeys began to complicate matters. Harlow raised several infant monkeys in isolation with surrogate (substitute) mothers. In his initial explorations Harlow raised his infant monkeys with two surrogate mothers. One mother constructed of wire fed the infant through a bottle and nipple inserted in her wire framework. The other mother had a covering of terry cloth over her wire frame, but she did not feed the infant. Among several findings, Harlow noted that the infants spent more time clinging to the soft mother and that in her presence they were more likely to explore (Harlow, 1973). Harlow theorized that contact comfort was important in the infant's attachment development. He saw the cuddling and close proximity necessary in nursing as being vitally important in the child's development. It should be emphasized that Harlow was not disputing the idea that the mother gains reinforcement value by being associated with feeding. He was simply pointing out that other factors may also be important in the process.

Since Harlow proposed the concept of contact comfort with rhesus monkeys, researchers have been interested in exploring this phenomenon in human infants. However, it is much more difficult to study contact comfort with human infants, as they cannot be given surrogate mothers.

Schaffer and Emerson (1964) interviewed the mothers of 37 infants on behaviors related to close physical contact, such as the infant's behavior during periods of contact and whether the infant actively sought close contact with the mother. On the basis of the interviews, they classified some of the children as cuddlers—babies who relished close physical contact—and noncuddlers—infants who resisted attempts at cuddling. Once the infants had been classified in this manner, Schaffer and Emerson tried to determine if there were any other differences between the two groups of infants and whether the noncuddlers were less attached to their mothers. They found that the noncuddlers apparently were just as attached to their mothers as the cuddlers in that they did not seek comfort from other people, objects such as blankets, or themselves through autoerotic behaviors, such as rocking or body rubbing. Noncuddlers sought the nearness of the mother when disturbed, just as the cuddlers did. Recall that attachment behavior generally is considered to involve seeking to be near the mother, particularly under stressful conditions. There were differences between the two groups, however, in that the noncuddlers were more likely to hide behind the mother and cling to her clothing, while the cuddlers signaled to be picked up.

Investigating the differences between these two groups further, Schaffer and Emerson explored the notion that the noncuddlers did not mind close physical contact as such, but objected to the restraint of movement that goes along with being held and cuddled. They determined that noncuddlers did not object to handling, particularly if the handling came in the context of roughhousing. Further, they also were more resistant during dressing than cuddlers were. Although Schaffer and Emerson did not find any difference in attachment between cuddlers and noncuddlers, this should not be interpreted as evidence disproving Harlow's belief in the importance of contact comfort. It should be apparent that studying contact comfort in infant humans will not produce straightforward results, as in the isolation work with monkeys.

So far we have considered briefly two theories of atachment, the psychoanalytic and the social learning theory. A third major theory on the development of attachment is an ethologic theory proposed by John Bowlby. Bowlby sees the development of attachment as being a process common to mammals in general and perpetuated through evolution as a behavior rich in survival value.

Bowlby sees both the infant's behaviors and characteristics and the mother's behaviors and characteristics as important and necessary to formation of the attachment bond. For instance, the infant has a repertoire of signaling responses, such as crying, babbling, and smiling, that serve the function of eliciting, or calling out, caretaking responses in the mother. In turn, the mother has certain characteristics, such as her face and voice, that elicit responsiveness on the part of the infant. You might recall from Chapter 4 on perception that infants are attracted to objects with sharp contrast and movement. The mother's eyes have these characteristics, as does her mouth. These factors should cause the infant to stare at the mother. The mother in turn might possibly respond by cooing to the child, and the child might then vocalize back. Each event in this sequence in effect elicits the next and sets up a circular reaction of positive interaction between the mother and child. In the same manner, a distressed infant cries and the mother responds, easing the infant's distress, another positive, rather circular set of interactive behaviors. Bowlby feels that the behavior of the mother can elicit responsiveness in the infant and that the infant's behavior has the same effect on the mother.

Beyond the formation of attachment, Bowlby theorized that the infant's attachment determines how far the infant is likely to roam from the mother. The survival value of this behavior is obvious. However, Bowlby felt that this system gets weaker as the child develops and that other characteristics, such as curiosity, get stronger. These formulations would account for the child's gradual growing away from the mother and his expanded interest in peers and the environment.

In regard to the eliciting characteristics of the infant's behavior, a consideration of Wolff's (1970) detailed description of the infant's tendency to smile should illustrate this process. Some theorists and many parents feel that the infant does not smile in a social sense for quite a time after birth. Early smiles are considered grimaces in reaction to internal distress. Wolff apparently does not agree with this belief, and has traced the development of smiling in eight infants from birth to 1 to 3 months of age.

Wolff observed that smilelike expressions can be obtained from infants 1 week old during sleep. He found that these infants smiled in response to a variety of sounds, including tape-recorded stimuli of mothers talking to babies. This behavior seems to be much more socially relevant than an infant grimacing in discomfort.

During the second week of life voices become much more effective than other auditory stimuli in eliciting smiles from infants. By the third week, Wolff is willing to classify infant response with smiles to high-pitched voices as social smiling. At this time the infant smiles while awake and attentive.

During the fourth week the mother's voice, as opposed to even the father's, elicits more smiling from the infant. Also by this time the infant smiles at slightly discrepant or surprising visual events. There is a change in smile eliciting by the fifth week. At this point a nodding head elicits smiling. If, as Wolff suggests, the very young infant is capable of social smiling in response to human voices and faces, Bowlby's suggestion of

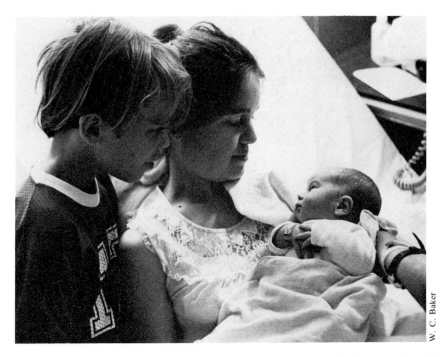

W. C. Baker

Fig. 12-1. Several theories attempt to explain how an infant becomes attached to its mother. Most psychologists believe that the infant must first form a close bond with the mother before other social relationships are possible.

circular releasers of infant-mother responses is quite possible. The mother speaks, the infant smiles, and the mother cuddles the child in pleasure.

One final theory of attachment is proposed by Schaffer and Emerson (1964). Their theory is a cognitive theory of attachment, and they add an element to the attachment process that other researchers ignore. They feel that the child's mental capabilities must develop to a point where the child can recognize the mother among other people and that the child must believe that the mother continues to exist even when she is not present. In other words, before the child can form an attachment to the mother, he or she must be able to discriminate and must have developed the concept of object constancy as outlined by Piaget. This means the child must develop the belief in the independent existence of objects (and people) apart from immediate experience of them. If the child has not established a cognitive belief in the permanence of the mother, he or she cannot become deeply attached to her.

While all these theories differ in what they consider to be important in the development of the attachment bond, they are not incompatible. All agree that certain behaviors and characteristics are necessary for the development of attachment. With any complex human behavior, it is not unusual for there to be variances of opinions as to causative factors. It is quite possible that all these factors are involved in the formation of the attachment bond. As we consider the experimental work on attachment behaviors, including stranger anxiety and separation anxiety, we should see data or information relevant to all of these theories of attachment.

Studying attachment

Since most theorists agree that the infant's attachment to the mother affects the child's relationships with others, researchers have been interested in defining the attachment behaviors of infants more precisely. This definition has taken the form of both experimental exploration of attachment and more precise descriptions of attachment, such as the following explanation by Ainsworth (1973).

Ainsworth defines attachment by listing at least 16 behaviors that she feels indicate that the infant is attached to the mother. These include differential smiling, crying and vocalization toward the mother as opposed to others around the child, and orientation toward the mother. Orientation toward the mother may be simply looking at the mother or approaching her for physical contact. Other indicators of attachment are crying when the mother leaves and signs of glee when she returns. It is also believed that fleeing to the mother and clinging to her under stressful conditions are strong indications of the existence of an attachment bond.

Experimental exploration of attachment has had as one of its major focal points specifying the developmental course of attachment. That is, much research has been aimed at determining when attachment behavior develops and whether there are changes in its intensity or form as the child matures.

Two major research projects have explored the developmental course of attachment using very different groups of children as subjects. Ainsworth (1973) studied this question using children from Uganda, and Schaffer and Emerson (1964) studied Scottish children. Ainsworth found that before 14 to 26 weeks, it was not possible to describe the Ganda infants as attached specifically to their mothers. She indicates that prior to this period the infants were differentially responsive to their mothers, but that it was not until after 14 weeks that strong indications of attachment developed, such as crying when left by the mother and attempts to follow her. Ainsworth also noted distinct changes in attachment behavior after this period. Between 27 and 39 weeks, the infants were active in seeking to maintain contact with their mothers and showed more signs of wariness of strangers. As the infants developed further beyond 41 weeks, a new characteristic of their attachment behavior occurred. Now under certain situations, such as the stress of strangers present, the infants would cling physically to their mothers. The developments of these later periods may not be simply indications of the existence of a stronger bond of attachment but may also reflect the increased physical capabilities on the part of the child.

Schaffer and Emerson found the same general patterns of behaviors in their population of Scottish infants. Not until approximately 28 weeks of age did these infants show signs of specific attachment to their mothers. At this age the infants protested when separated from their mothers, whereas before they simply protested at being put down, no matter who was holding them. Shortly after indications of specific attachments appeared in these infants, they began to show wariness of strangers. This observation coincides with Ainsworth's. Both researchers found increased wariness of strangers occurring at around 8 or 9 months of age.

Schaffer and Emerson also described the effectiveness in eliciting protests that different degrees of separation from the mother had on the infants. Initially the infants protested when simply put down in their cribs after being held. Then, in order, they began to protest at being left alone in a room, being left with another person, and being left alone outside.

Each of these situations seems to indicate an increased awareness on the part of the infant of the discrepancy of the situation from normal conditions. Although we have been discussing attachment in terms of the development of an emotion—love—it is important to recognize the part the child's developing perceptual, motor, and cognitive skills play in the formation of the attachment bond.

Most discussions of attachment indicate at first general responsiveness on the part of the infant, followed by increased attention focused on the mother. After indications of differential responsiveness to the mother appear, definite signs of attachment to her appear, generally in the form of protest when separated from her. At some point after the development of obvious attachment to the mother, the infant generally begins to fuss or indicate a reluctance to being held by unfamiliar persons. A second development that frequently occurs a few months later is a general disinclination on the part of the child to be left in the care of others, even familiar others. While these developments point to decreasing sociability on the part of the infant, this is not entirely the case. Although the child does center attention on the mother during this first year and a half, before the second year is far along the child becomes increasingly interested in exploring larger and larger areas of the world and consequently comes into social contact with many more persons.

One further change should be included in the sequence of attachment development at this point, that is, the attachment to others as well as the mother. Schaffer and Emerson indicate that after the indications of attachment to the mother appear, the child is also likely to give indications of attachment to other familiar people. In the context of the intact family, the possibility exists for attachment to any other person who regularly cares for the child or interacts with the child frequently. The most obvious question is whether infants become attached to their fathers in the same fashion that they become attached to their mothers.

In a study involving the stress of being left alone for a period of time with a stranger, Williamsen et al. (1974) found no difference in behavior of 1-year-olds towards their mothers or fathers. Separation from either parent caused fretting, and reunion with the parent relieved the distress.

In another study involving fathers as well as mothers, Bon and Lewis (1975) explored attachment in a nonstressful experimental setting. They found that 1-year-olds spent more time close to their mothers and actually touched their mothers more than their fathers. However, they noted that boys looked more frequently at their fathers than they did at their mothers.

That these studies have contradictory results should not be surprising, since one study involved a stressful situation and the other did not. What is important is the need to explore the child's relationship with the father much more specifically. Insofar as attachment is concerned, very little is known about the child's relationship to the father. We will return to this topic in Chapter 13 when we discuss the development of sex roles. At this point it is only safe to conclude that these studies do not contradict the belief that the primary attachment bond is to the mother.

The developmental course of attachment behavior presented here is only a descriptive overview of a very complex process. To even begin to understand the important implications of this process, it is necessary to look more specifically at the details of this process. Two important features of the attachment process are the infant's wariness of strangers (stranger anxiety) and the infant's protests at separation from the mother (separation anxiety).

Stranger anxiety

Stranger anxiety, if viewed in isolation, is a rather puzzling child behavior. An infant for the first several months of life is responsive to being held and cared for by anyone who performs these activities in an acceptable fashion. At around 8 or 9 months the child may become fussy if approached by a stranger. Consider the impact of this phenomenon in the following hypothetical situation.

Grandma's first grandchild is born in a city 900 miles away. Even though it is expensive, Grandma flies to see the baby and help out. She spend 2 weeks with her grandchild, then returns home to tell one and all about the baby. Having run out of details 8 months later and having saved enough money for a second trip, Grandma returns to visit her grandchild, with the happy expectation of hugs and kisses. On arrival, Grandma rushes over and scoops the baby up in her arms. She is welcomed with a terrified stare and sobbing. Is there anything anyone can say to ease the tenseness of the situation? Perhaps.

Researchers on infant attachment processes have been particularly interested in stranger anxiety because it is believed that for a child to show fear of strangers, he or she must recognize the strangers as different from normal caretakers. It has been proposed that children will not show stranger anxiety unless they have formed a close relationship with a significant person, generally the mother. If no one person is more important than any other, there is no reason for generally receptive infants to become wary of strangers unless they have had a bad experience with a stranger. However, stranger anxiety does develop in a good number of children who have previously been tolerant of handling by strangers and who have no experiential reason for the wariness.

With this theoretical base, research has been conducted to determine the developmental course of stranger anxiety, typical infant reactions to strangers, characteristics of strangers that may elicit wariness, and situational factors that affect infant responsiveness to strangers.

Although it has been indicated that stranger anxiety occurs at about 8 or 9 months of age, there is disagreement on this point. In reviewing research on stranger anxiety, Morgan and Ricciuti (1973) cite reports of stranger anxiety occurring anywhere from 7 to 15 months. Their own research indicates that infants under 12 months of age do not evidence stranger anxiety. At the other extreme Bronson (1973) found evidence of wariness as early as 3 months of age. Most likely this discrepancy is the result of major differences in the conduct of these two experiments. In the first study, where stranger anxiety occurs at 12 months, the children were tested with their mothers present and the stranger approached the infants only briefly. In the second study, the stranger approached the infants and remained close to them for a longer time than is usual in this type of study. These differences highlight the importance of situational variables in stranger anxiety. It should not be surprising that having the mother nearby might be related to more tolerance of strangers. Although we may find various reports of the time when stranger anxiety develops, the important point is that it is not going to occur until the infant is able to discriminate familiar from unfamiliar persons.

The discrimination of the familiar from the unfamiliar is a key concept in attempts to understand stranger anxiety and when it is likely to occur. Schaffer (1973) describes this relationship by explaining that a child cannot fear strangers until some pattern of the familiar person (the mother) is formed so that comparisons can be made. The more time the child has spent with the mother, the more likely the child is to have formed this pattern. Further, the fewer experiences with others, the more likely the child is to see others as discrepant and thus fear producing.

Others have suggested that the child who has spent little time with the mother and more time with a variety of people is less likely to show stranger anxiety.

Schaffer reports data that tend to support both of these points of view. He found earlier indications of stranger anxiety in first-born children as opposed to infants with siblings present during their first year of life. The implication is that first-born children spend more time with the mother and there are fewer people in their environments; therefore, these infants formulate a pattern of the mother earlier and react to those who differ from this pattern. On the other hand, children who have experience with many people are not as likely to view discrepant people as cause for concern.

Another major concern is to determine the characteristics of strangers most likely to elicit stranger anxiety. If these characteristics can be determined, not only will we know more about stranger anxiety but also more about the infant and what is important in identifying the mother. Informal observations can give us some hints as to what the infant sees as important or discrepant. For example, many infants have responded negatively to a mother's new glasses or haircut. Harlow and Suomi (1973) changed the head on one infant monkey's surrogate mother for purposes other than investigation and found that the infant became very disturbed by the change. In fact, the infant removed the head and discarded it rather than accept the change in its mother.

Identifying the characteristics of strangers that elicit fear is not easy. It is believed that people who closely resemble the mother are less likely to disturb the child, while people who are very different are likely to be more disturbing. Yet it is also possible that the child will be curious about the differences and not necessarily fearful. The question is complex. For instance, strange men appear to be more disturbing that strange women, but what is the source of the difference? It might be size.

One study attempted to assess the effect of size as well as other factors on stranger anxiety. Brooks and Lewis (1976) used three strangers in their study, a child, a woman of normal size, and a midget woman. They found that infants are not as disturbed by being approached by children as they are by adults, but size alone is not the crucial variable. The approach by the midget elicited fewer positive responses than did the approach by children and more staring than the approach by the normal sized woman. It is extremely difficult to pinpoint precisely the characteristics of strangers that elicit stranger anxiety.

Returning to the hypothetical example of stranger anxiety involving grandma, it might ease the tension of the situation if grandma knew that her grandchild's negative response to her was a positive developmental step. The infant was giving indications that she is attached to her mother and further is able to recognize unfamiliar people who approach her.

Separation anxiety

As puzzling as stranger anxiety may be when it appears in a previously social infant, separation anxiety may be frustrating. Separation anxiety is protest by infants at being separated from the mother. The form separation anxiety takes is largely determined by the child's capabilities at any point in development. During the infant's early months, separation anxiety may be seen as crying when the child is put down after being held. As the child becomes able to move around alone, separation anxiety may be seen as crawling after the mother as she moves from room to room. Separation anxiety may also involve vigorous protests at the prospect that the mother is about to leave the house. The early forms of separation anxiety may be the result of actual separation and an indication on the part of the infant that separation is unpleasant. The later forms of separation anxiety that develop after the child's first year involve to some extent the expectation that separation, which is viewed as unpleasant, is about to occur. For example, the parents make preparations to leave the house and leave the child in the care of a sitter. As soon as the child sees these preparations, he or she protests vigorously by crying and clinging. The parents may feel guilty or frustrated and may begin to worry about the care the sitter gives their child. In most instances their worries are unjustified. This unpleasant experience may occur even if the child knows the sitter and enjoys his or her company. What these protests may indicate is that the child realizes the parents are to leave and this sets up negative anticipation on the part of the child. Bowlby (1960) feels that the child senses on some level that certain needs will not be met during the mother's absence and that this prompts the development of anxiety and even fright on a general level in the child; consequently, the child reacts negatively. This anticipation is an indication that the child has developed cognitively to the point of awareness of the possibilities in future situations.

The child's protests should not be surprising, as the child lacks a more constructive means of handling the situation. The child can not explain his or her discomfort to the parents or ask them not to leave. Further, the child is not able to end the separation by following the parents, as when mother moves from room to room in the house. Also, if the child cries vigorously enough, the parents may not go out after all!

This frustrating experience can be tolerated perhaps more readily if parents realize that this behavior is a positive step on the part of the child. The child is only able to protest because of the awareness of the possibilities in the situation and also perhaps as a result of the frustration at lacking other adaptive responses. A child who has not developed cognitively to this point will not respond in such a fashion. Further, this behavior is an indication of the child's attachment to the mother. If the child is not attached to the mother, one caretaker (the sitter) should be as good as the other (the mother).

How parents respond to this situation is likely to determine the characteristics of this behavior. Parents who decide to remain home or severely curtail their activity outside of the home may only prolong this behavior by reinforcing it. Parents who wish to avoid the stress of separation may also resort to sneaking out while the child is not watching. This type of behavior may also intensify separation anxiety, as the child begins to learn that parents literally "disappear." This stress may increase the child's tendency to follow the mother and cling to her to prevent further disappearances. Perhaps the better way to handle this situation is for parents to reassure the child that when they leave they will return shortly. A child who has several experiences of being left for short periods by the parents should learn easily that separations can be tolerated.

THE CHILD IN THE FAMILY

Although we have been discussing the infant's social behavior only in relation to the mother, the child's family as a whole is important in the development of the child as a person and as a social being. Both the size and the atmosphere of the child's family contribute to the child's relationships with others. Even the child's particular position in the family (such as first-born, last born, only born) may be an important factor in the child's tendencies to relate to others.

Fig. 12-2. From studying social relationships of nursery school children, it has been determined that socially active preschoolers are likely to have a large number of both positive and negative interactions with other children.

For example, Baldwin (1948) studied more than sixty 4-year-old nursery school children and assessed their general sociability and activity level, then compared these behaviors with each child's home atmosphere. Baldwin rated each home as being either democratic or authoritarianly controlled. He also judged the general activity level that took place in each home. He found a relationship between the type of control exercised by the parents and the amount of activity in the home with the child's general behavior in nursery school. Baldwin concluded that children raised in democratic, permissive home atmospheres are likely to be leaders in nursery school. These children are aggressive and daring, while children reared in strictly controlled homes are more likely to be quiet and well-behaved. Further, Baldwin felt that democratic rearing held the danger of producing children who do not necessarily conform to social expectations, while children reared in controlled homes are more likely to be socially conforming. In other words, democratic rearing might encourage a child to be relatively individualistic at the expense of others. The second factor, activity level of the home, is a clarifying factor in Baldwin's position. Baldwin feels that a high activity level in the home is likely to lead to a high level of activity in nursery school, increasing the chances of both positive and negative behaviors in the children. If the activity in the home involves much warm interaction between the child and the parents, the child is stimulated to highly interact with others in other situations as well. A further implication is that if the child experiences a high rate of warm interchanges with the parents, the child is

273

more likely to experience this type of exchange with others. Part of the reason Baldwin feels that the nursery school children reared in democratic homes also experience many negative interactions with others is that they have not yet developed the ability to control hostility. Their democratically based homes lead them to feel they can be expressive, yet they have not yet learned the more socialized expressions of negative feelings.

While work such as Baldwin's emphasizes the parent-child relationship exclusively, other researchers have been concerned with the effect siblings and a child's birth order in the family have on the child's socialization. Hartup (1970), in discussing peer relationships, reviews the theory and findings of Schachter, who has investigated many birth-order effects on socialization in children. Schachter expresses a belief that birth order is related to popularity in college students. He found that later born students are more popular than firstborn children and that firstborn children express fewer friendship choices than do later-born children on tests designed to assess friendship patterns. Schachter feels these differences are related to the differing child-rearing experiences that first- and later born children receive. Specifically, Schachter speculates that firstborn children receive more inconsistent care than do later born children, due to the inexperience of new parents. Schachter believes this inconsistency can create anxiety in the firstborn child. Second, he feels firstborn children are more likely to be overprotected than are later born children and thus are more dependent and conforming than their younger brothers and sisters.

Many researchers have been interested in Schachter's hypothesis concerning differential care for first- and later born children. In a recent longitudinal study Jacobs and Moss (1976) studied the behavior of mothers with their first- and second-born children. Each mother was studied with both children when each child was 3 months old. Specifically, each of the 32 mothers in the study was observed caring for her first child when that child was 3 months old. When the second child was 3 months old the mother was again observed. In this manner the researchers were able to directly assess the hypothesis that mother-child interactions improve in consistency from the first child to subsequent children. Jacobs and Moss found that mothers spend less time interacting with their second child than they did with their first. This decrement was evident in caretaking activities and social interaction with the child. It is tempting to speculate that the experience gained with the first child leads to less time spent in caretaking activity with the second child and that the demands of two children decreases the time spent in social activity with the second child. However, Jacobs and Moss also found an interesting sex-related factor in this study. The decrement in time spent with the second child was greater for second-born girls than second-born boys. This decrement was greatest if the second-born girl had an older sister. The smallest decrements were found when second-born boys had older sisters. The effect of siblings on the mother-child interaction is a complex factor.

Other researchers have speculated on the greater sociability of later born children in a different fashion than did Schachter. Bigner (1974) assumes that second-born children have an advantage over firstborn children in socialization in that from the beginning they have the opportunity for more social interactions due to the presence of the older child in the home. Specifically, Bigner feels that second-born children are better able to assess age and sex roles than their older sibling and hence are better able to predict the behavior of others using role concepts. The implication is that better predictions of other people's behavior leads to smoother interpersonal relationships. Indeed, Bigner found that second-born children when assigning characteristics to hypothetical persons made more culturally standard assignments than their older siblings did. This seems to indicate that some facility in grasping age and sex role is associated with having older siblings.

The effect of older siblings shows up in many other ways as well. For example, Longstreth and Longstreth (1975) found that both boys and girls tend to be more active if they have an older brother, especially if the older brother is no more than 4 years older. The possibilities for imitation, direct learning, and reaction to the other child are probably unlimited. It should not be surprising that the presence of siblings is a major factor in the development of social relationships in any child. On the other hand, the absence of siblings in the case of only children must also exert some influence in the development of these children. Some psychologists have speculated that the only child should be similar to the firstborn child in many respects. First, the inconsistency in care from new parents should occur in the case of both firstborn and only children. Second, only children should also be likely candidates for overprotection, just as firstborn children are. Therefore, it should be expected that only children share the same anxiety and dependency of firstborn children, if one accepts Schachter's theory. However Hartup (1970) reports a study by Sells and Doff that found that only children are more accepted by their peers than are firstborn children with siblings, just as youngest children are. Yando, Zigler, and Letzinger (1975) found a difference between firstborn and only children in response to social reinforcement in an experimental situation. They speculated that only children were likely to have either more intense relationships with their parents or were relatively deprived in social reinforcement. For instance, if onliness is associated with disharmony in the home between the parents or negative attitudes toward children, it is possible that the only child will suffer deprivation in social contacts. However, if onliness is not associated with disharmony or ambivalence, it is quite likely the only child will enjoy warm social interaction with the parents and consequently with others.

The position of the child in the family is an important key to understanding any child. Although we have only considered the relationship of ordinal position and sociability, many other factors have been researched as well, such as the child's measured intelligence, adjustment problems, and achievements, all of which are interesting topics on their own.

THE CHILD BEYOND THE FAMILY

We have considered the child's social interaction with the family. No discussion of social development is complete without a consideration of peer relationships. Several topics are of importance in peer relationships, such as the types of characteristics and experiences that are likely to lead a child into satisfactory friendships with contemporaries. Another relevant question concerns the development of peer influences. Precisely at what age is a child capable of or interested in the company of others of the same age? Further, what is the relationship of the attachment to the mother and dependency on her to the child's other social relationships?

It has generally been believed that peer interaction and influence before the age of 2 years is minimal. In a 1975 study of peer relationships with very young children Eckerman, Whatley, and Kutz summarize the early belief of Maudry and Nekula that before 8 months of age children treat each other just as they do inanimate objects. By the end of the first year, peers are considered obstacles to enjoying toys. It is not until 2 years that other children are seen as possible playmates. Eckerman and co-workers investigated this position using children from 10 months of age to 2 years and found increasing sociability with age; however, even the youngest children interacted in a social fashion with each other to some extent. Earliest interactions involved watching the other child and vocalization as well as smiling. Contact with toys and interaction involving toys increased with age, as should be expected, but Eckerman and co-workers found more positive interactions than negative interactions at all ages, which conflicts with earlier beliefs that other children are obstacles to enjoying toys. Another related study was conducted by Rubenstein and Howes (1976), who studied eight 18-month-old children who had had extended opportunities to be together over a long time. These children interacted in a social fashion with each other at least 50% of the time they were together. These researchers also report very little conflict between playmates and the interesting observation that these children paid more attention to each other than they did to their mothers who were present during the play session.

These two studies indicate that very young children are able to interact socially with each other. These studies differ from early theories as a result of differing study techniques. Frequently in the early studies young infants were taken to an unfamiliar experimental laboratory and placed in a playpen with another unfamiliar infant and a few toys. In these two recent studies the children were observed under much more natural settings, and in the second study the children were observed with an actual playmate. It seems reasonable to assume that children are capable of interest in other children before age 2 years.

One contributing factor in the success of these early peer relationships is comparable levels of development. Another factor that seems relevant is the child's ability to relate to another's point of view, or declining egocentricism.

With the growing popularity of nursery schools and day-care centers, the question of peer interaction among preschoolers has become more and more important. Hartup (1970) summarizes many studies concerning preschool peer relationships. His review presents a comprehensive picture of the preschool child's social activity.

As would be expected, most researchers have found that both the frequency and the quality of social interactions increase with age for the preschooler. With the youngest children, size is generally equated with dominance, with the larger children being the dominant members of a play group. Preschoolers have been found to form definite subgroups within nursery schools, with cleavages as to sex and race, although these divisions

Fig. 12-3. By preschool age, most children are capable of relating to other children as persons. Some researchers believe that children as young as 18 months are capable of social interaction.

do not appear to be based on overt rejection. Hartup also described nursery school social interactions as on the whole more positive than negative. Children who are friendly and outgoing are generally well accepted by their peers. Although social interactions are basically positive with this age group, more complex positive responses, such as helping behavior and sympathy, are not particularly frequent.

Negative behavior in social relationships declines in frequency and its form changes with age. With the youngest children there is more direct physical aggression. With older preschoolers aggression is more verbal. There are also sex differences in aggression; boys are more aggressive than girls. It is not surprising that both cooperative behavior and competitiveness increase with age, because these characteristics require that the child be able to consider the roles of others. This is more difficult for younger pre-schoolers.

Since it is apparent that preschoolers are capable of positive social interaction, two additional questions remain to be explored. The first involves characteristics that might predispose a child to sociability; the second explores the stability of this characteristic.

It is believed that the child who is actively outgoing enters into more social interactions. Further it is believed that children who direct a majority of dependency responses towards adults are less likely to be popular preschoolers. Other researchers (Staub, 1975) speculate that children who have experienced warm nurturing from their parents are more likely to exhibit prosocial behavior for several reasons. First, the security of a warm relationship with the parents should serve to reduce the child's self-concern, a feature necessary before the child can show concern for others. Second, the positive parental relationship leads the child to expect positive relationships with others. Third, a warm environment makes learning easier and possibly the child learns social skills more readily.

Whatever the source of sociability in young children, there are indications that this tendency is relatively stable. Waldrop and Halverson (1975), in a longitudinal study, found that children who were socially oriented at 2½ years were also socially competent children at 7½. Their descriptions of the socially positive preschooler and elementary school child present apt summaries of peer-oriented children. The popular preschooler is active, aggressive, daring, and expressive. These same children at 7 tend to be leaders who spend a good deal of time in the company of their peers.

SUMMARY

Although we have not considered all areas or facets of social development, it is possible to conclude that the conception of children's sociability is increasingly positive. There are indications that children are capable of expressing social responses at very young ages and that, by and large, children's social interactions are more positive than negative. As more and more investigations of social development are conducted, the importance of an increasing number of contributing factors is established and our understanding of social relationships becomes more clear. The child's relationships with the mother, the father, siblings, and playmates is continually reemphasized in studies of social development, yet there is also an increasing awareness and belief in the importance of the child's cognitive development and the development of motor skills as contributing factors to the child's ability and skill in interacting with others.

REFERENCES

Ainsworth, M. D. S. The development of attachment in Ganda infants. In L. J. Stone, H. T. Smith, & L. B. Murphy (Eds.), *The competent infant, research and commentary.* New York: Basic Books, Inc., Publishers, 1973, pp. 1115-1120.

Baldwin, A. L. Socialization and the parent-child relationship. *Child Development,* 1948, **19**(3), 127-136.

Bigner, J. J. Second-borns' discrimination of sibling role concepts. *Developmental Psychology,* 1974, **10**(4), 564-573.

Bon, P. & Lewis, M. Mothers and fathers, girls and boys: attachment behavior in the one year old. *Merrill-Palmer Quarterly,* 1975, 195-205.

Bowlby, J. Separation anxiety. *International Journal of Psychoanalysis,* 1960, **41,** 89-113.

Bronson, G. W. Infants' reactions to an unfamiliar person. In L. J. Stone, H. T. Smith, & L. B. Murphy (Eds.), *The competent infant, research and commentary.* New York: Basic Books, Inc., Publishers, 1973, pp. 1139-1142.

Brooks, J., & Lewis, M. Infants' responses to strangers: midget, adult, and child. *Child Development,* 1976, **47,** 323-332.

Eckerman, C. O., Whatley, J. L., and Kutz, S. L. Growth of social play with peers during the second year of life. *Developmental Psychology,* 1975, **11,** 42-49.

Harlow, H. F., & Suomi, S. J. Nature of love—simplified. In L. J. Stone, H. T. Smith, & L. B. Murphy (Eds.), *The competent infant, research and commentary.* New York: Basic Books, Inc., Publishers, 1973, pp. 1040-1053.

Harlow, H. F., & Harlow, M. Learning to love. In L. J. Stone, H. T. Smith, & L. B. Murphy (Eds.), *The competent infant, research and commentary.* New York: Basic Books, Inc., Publishers, 1973, pp. 1054-1057.

Hartup, W. W. Peer interaction and social organization. In P. H. Mussen (Ed.), Carmichael's manual of child psychology (Vol. 2) (3rd ed.). New York: John Wiley & Sons, Inc., 1970, pp. 361-456.

Jacobs, B. S., & Moss, H. A. Birth order and sex of sibling as determinants of mother-infant interaction. *Child Development,* 1976, **47,** 315-322.

Longstreth, L. E., Longstreth, G. V., Ramilly, C., & Fernandez, G. The ubiquity of big brother. *Child Development,* 1975, **46,** 769-772.

Maccoby, E. E., & Masters, J. C. Attachment and dependency. In P. H. Mussen (Ed.), Carmichael's manual of child psychology (Vol. 2) (3rd ed.) New York: John Wiley & Sons, Inc., 1970, pp. 73-157.

Morgan, G. A., & Ricciuti, H. N. Infants' responses to strangers during the first year. In L. J. Stone, H. T. Smith, & L. B. Murphy (Eds.), *The competent infant, research and commentary.* New York: Basic Books, Inc., Publishers, 1973, pp. 1128-1138.

Rubenstein, J. & Howes, C. The effects of peers on toddler interaction with mother and toys. *Child Development,* 1976, **47,** 597-605.

Schaffer, H. R. The onset of fear of strangers and the incongruity hypothesis. In L. J. Stone, H. T. Smith, & L. B. Murphy (Eds.), *The competent infant, research and commentary.* New York: Basic Books, Inc., Publishers, 1973, pp. 95-106.

Schaffer, H. R., & Emerson, P. E. Patterns of response to physical contact in early human development. *Journal of Child Psychology and Psychiatry,* 1964, **5,** 1-13.

Staub, E. The development of prosocial behavior in children. *University Programs Modular Studies.* Morristown, N.J.: Silver Burdett, Co., 1975, pp. 1-20.

Waldrop, M. F., & Halverson, C. F., Jr. Intensive peer behavior: longitudinal and cross sectional analysis. *Child Development,* 1975, **46,** 19-26.

Williamsen, E., Fleherty, D., Heaton, C., & Ritchy, G. Attachment behavior of one-year olds as a function of mother vs father, sex of child, session, and toys. *Genetic Psychology Monographs,* 1974, **90,** 305-324.

Wolff, P. H. Observations on the early development of smiling. In L. J. Stone, H. T. Smith, & L. B. Murphy (Eds.), *The competent infant, research and commentary.* New York: Basic Books, Inc., Publishers, 1973, pp. 1070-1081.

Yando, R., Zigler, E., and Letzinger, S. A further investigation of the effects of birth order and number of siblings in determining children's responsiveness to social reinforcement. *Journal of Psychology,* 1975, **89,** 95-111.

Children's personal space as a function of age and sex

Jacob Lomranz
Ariela Shapira
Netta Choresh
Yitzchak Gilat

Tel-Aviv University, Tel-Aviv, Israel

Measures of personal space were gathered from 74 children (ages 3, 5, and 7) when they approached boys or girls of their own age. A significant difference was found between the 3-year-old subjects (who kept less distance from their age peers) and the 5- or 7-year-old group. No other differences attributable to age were found. For all subjects, the sex of the interacting child was relevant, in that less distance was kept from girls than from boys. The results are discussed in the light of learning and developmental processes.

The notion of personal space used in this research was derived primarily from the ideas of the anthropologist E. T. Hall (1959, 1966) and the psychological investigations of Little (1965), Guardo (1969), Meisels and Guardo (1969), and Guardo and Meisels (1971). Hall (1966) conceived of personal space as a series of spatial spheres with the individual person in the center. Little (1965) defined personal space as ''the area immediately surrounding the individual in which the majority of his interactions with others takes place'' (p. 237). Personal space is understood to be determined by a combination of specific factors such as the nature of the interaction (Dosey & Meisels, 1969), the degree of acquaintance and friendship between the interacting parties (Little, 1965), the subjects' personality (Horowitz, Duff, & Stratton, 1964; Frede, Gautrey, & Baxter, 1968), and cultural background (Little, 1968; Watson & Graves, 1966). Guardo (1969) and Guardo and Meisels (1971) emphasized developmental factors. However, the developmental factors of age and sex have not received sufficient attention, and the present status of the empirical findings related to personal space raises several questions.

A major question concerns the age at which personal space can be documented as a characteristic behavioral pattern, and the extent to which it is a learned mechanism. According to Klapfer and Hailman (1967) and Sommer (1969), the individual spacing mechanisms in animals are learned at a relatively early age. Sommer (1969) stated that when deprivation of contact between members of the same species has occurred, animals do not learn to space themselves appropriately. Fisher (1967) found that children who perceived their mothers as hostile generally had larger personal space. She assumed that a principle of learning operates as the mother models interpersonal interaction based on the distancing and hostility. Again the question arises: At what time in the child's life does such modeling occur? Which age would be critical for the child's learning of proxemic behavior?

In a study by Moreno (1953) it was found that as early as age 40 weeks, closeness or distance are obvious factors in social relations between infants. However, in the research carried out with older children the results are contradictory. Tolor (1968) found that children between the ages of 11 and 12 years seem to have a larger personal space than children of 10. In contrast, Meisels and Guardo (1969), who studied children between the third and the tenth grades, stated that older age children generally use less space in most of their interpersonal situations. Fry and Willies (1971) assert that the age at which spacing behavior develops in children has not yet been determined. It appears that a pronounced lack of clarity exists with regard to the developmental aspect of age and its relationship to personal space.

Little research, especially research using behavioral measures, has been carried out on preschool and early grade children to determine developmental differences in personal space in a social context. One study (Bass & Weinstein, 1971) found that kindergarten (age 5) and first-grade children keep less distance from a same-sex peer than do second and third graders. On the assumption that at this age an interval of 2 years is significant in the development of personal space, the present investigators focused on subjects in the age range between 3 and 7 years.

In addition to studying age changes in personal space, sex differences in personal space were investigated in this study. A number of studies (Meisels & Guardo, 1969; Bass & Weinstein, 1971) have shown that young boys and girls do not differ in the space they keep from same-sex figures. On the other hand the sex of the person being approached seems to be an important variable in determining personal space. Guardo and Meisels (1971) found that between the ages of 11 and 13 personal space towards the opposite sex decreases. Their study further indicated the interaction contribution of cultural norms insofar as they required children to introduce changes in their patterns of spacing toward the opposite sex. Tolor and Orange (1969) found that girls between the ages of 5 and 14 tended to have greater personal space than do boys at that age. The finding, however, is subject to question since it is based on a group of subjects with a large age range.

Regarding the interaction of age and sex factors, Mussen, Conger, and Kagan (1969) noted that the earliest friendships come about at the ages of 2 to 5 and that most of them take place between individuals of the same sex. However, pronounced change becomes apparent at the age of 5 to 6, when one finds mixed-sex play groups. This observation is supported by that of Moreno (1953), who found heterosexual attraction and sociometric choices across sex beginning at the age of 6. It should be emphasized, however, that Mussen et al. (1969) also found that at the age of 7 children return to organize themselves in same-sex groups. Hence, one may expect more same-sex interaction at the early age of 3, increased across-sex interaction around the age of 5, and again more same-sex interaction at the age of 7.

In this study the developmental process of personal space in several early age groups (3, 5, and 7 years) was investigated. An attempt was made to study differences between boys and girls across and within the various age groups and to determine whether these differences depend on the sex of the interacting subjects.

METHOD
Subjects

Seventy-four preschool and elementary school students in a central District School of Tel-Aviv served as subjects. All subjects were Israeli-born middle-socioeconomic-class children. Table 1 shows the sample distribution by age range and sex.

Materials

Subjects were tested in their usual classrooms. To maintain a natural atmosphere, no changes were introduced in furniture or arrangements in the classrooms. A carton with crayons and paper sheets (30 × 20 cm) was placed on the center of a table (200 × 80 cm). In front of the table was a bench (200 cm long), and a tiny centimeter measuring guide, identical in color with that of the bench and almost unrecognizable, was pasted along the back of the bench.

Procedure

The first subject was asked to sit on the bench, 40 cm from its edge. He was given a sheet of paper and was asked to draw. This child served as an approach object for the next subject, who was given the following directions upon entering the room: "Please sit on the bench next to the boy who is drawing." Five seconds after he was seated, two observers each recorded the distance in centimeters between the two children. The experimenter later gave the subject a sheet of paper and asked him to draw something. One minute after the second child began drawing, the first child was asked to continue his drawing in another adjacent room. The second child was asked to move to a point 40 cm from the edge of the bench and to continue his drawing. He now served as an object of approach for the third child, etc. This procedure was repeated for all subjects, with every child approaching the one before him and then serving as an object of approach for the one coming after him, except for the first child, who served only as an approach object, and the last child, who approached only. The order of approach was designed to assure that all four possible sex combinations would be realized; that is, boy to boy, boy to girl, girl to boy, and girl to girl.

RESULTS

Table 2 shows the mean distances of approach by boys and girls, respectively, to other boys and girls for each of three age levels.

A $3 \times 2 \times 2$ analysis of variance (Age $\times$ Sex of Approaching Child $\times$ Sex of Approached Child) was performed. The results show a significant effect due to age. The young 3-year-olds sat closer ($M = 17.7$ cm) to their peers than did the older 5- (23.8 cm) or 7-year-olds (22.6 cm), $F(2,60) = 5.57, p < .01$. No differences were found between the two older age groups. No differences were found between boys and girls in the distances they kept from other children. Their mean distances were 22.15 cm and 20.49 cm, respectively, $F(1,60) = 1.55$, ns. The sex of the child being approached was found to be a significant factor. Less distance was kept from girls (19.65 cm) than from boys (22.9 cm), $F(1,60) = 6.10, p < .05$. The Age $\times$ "Sex Approached" interaction yielded significant results, $F(2,60) = 4.34, p < .05$.

As can be seen in Table 2, the tendency to stay closer to girls than to boys is found mainly at the ages of 3 and 7. At age 5, no differences due to the "sex approached" were found.

A further analysis of the data did not find a tendency to keep different distances within sex and between sex. The mean distance kept from children of the same sex was 22.65 cm and from

Table 1. Sample distribution by age range and sex

Sex	Age (yr)			Total
	3.0-3.6	5.0-5.6	7.0-7.6	
Boys	10	11	13	34
Girls	10	15	15	40
Total	20	26	28	74

Table 2. Mean approach distance in centimeters for boys and girls at three age levels

Sex of approach object	Age (yr)					
	3		5		7	
	Boy	Girl	Boy	Girl	Boy	Girl
Boy	26.50	15.16	23.40	23.33	25.50	19.00
Girl	13.25	16.16	22.22	25.66	27.12	18.57

other sex 20.0 cm. (Only at age 3 did the subjects keep greater distances from children of their own sex [21.4 cm] than from children of the other sex [14.3 cm]).

It should be emphasized that many children, mainly at the age of 3, actually touched the other child body to body. These were recorded as zero distances and may have contributed to the relatively low interaction distances shown in Table 2.

DISCUSSION

Our findings reveal that there are significant differences in personal space between children of different ages. The significant effect due to age results from the fact that the youngest subjects—the 3-year-olds—have smaller personal space than do their 5- and 7-year-old counterparts in the two other groups. While 5- and 7-year-olds tend to have larger personal space, no significant differences were found between the two older ages.

These results support Bass and Weinstein's (1971) main finding that younger children maintain less distance than older children, and extends their findings to a younger age group (3 to 7 years old). It is interesting to note the congruence in the findings of the two studies, since the present study employed behavioral measures of personal space while Bass and Weinstein used quasi-projective measures.

The results of our investigation seem to support the possibility that personal space is a learned pattern of behavior (Fisher, 1967; Fry & Willies, 1971). It may well be that children at the age of 3 have not yet received sufficient exposure to positive or negative reinforcement for refined control of spatial behavior in shaping their personal distance, and to use distancing as an interpersonal, expressive tool of communication and reaction. Furthermore, if we conceive of personal space as a personality trait, then we may assume that in common with many other personality traits at the age of 3, it has not yet matured.

It may be that at this age children concentrate more on themselves, on sensorimotor experiences, and on self-exploration and that therefore their peers do not take a great part in their interests. It seems that at the age of 3 children do not respond to an invasion of their personal space. On the other hand, as they grow older, self-exploration is replaced by an interest in the interpersonal sphere. They spend more time in social interpersonal interactions and contact with others increases. At this time they might react to invasion of personal space and begin to use space as a communicative, nonverbal pattern of communication.

The investigation of the second variable, sex, yielded interesting results. Although no significant difference in approach behavior to other children was found, the sex of the object *being* approached was, however, highly significant. For all children, personal space was shorter when they approached girls than when they approached boys. This held mainly for children reaching age 7. These results with children coincide with those of Horowitz et al. (1964), who found adults of both sexes kept larger personal space when approaching men than women. It might well be that the effect of the sex being approached is not contingent on age, or that it is molded at a rather early age and remains constant during life. The general tendency to come closer to girls may also reflect the fact that mothers in our culture are the central figures with whom the child comes in contact, while the fathers are usually less available. Sears (1958) has suggested that in the preschool age the preferred parent by children of both sexes is the mother. In addition, females may be less threatening than males. Bandura, Ross, and Ross (1961) stated that girls are expected to be more reserved and less aggressive socially, especially with strangers and with people of the opposite sex. These may be additional factors explaining the fact that young girls do not resist closeness and are more comfortable with intimate proxemic behavior. Although the attraction to the mother figure may be a possible speculation, another may have to do with sex typing. This seems to be especially appropriate when considering the 7-year-olds. The boys at that age in our culture are supposed to be assertive, strong, and aggressive, while the girls are expected to be sociable, attractive, and avoid physical and verbal aggression (Bandura et al., 1961). Hence, **283**

**PART
FOUR**
═════

it may well be that boys nonverbally communicated greater resistance to invasion of their personal space, while girls may have sent cues encouraging, or at least not resisting, approach behavior towards them.

REFERENCES

Bandura, A., Ross, D., & Ross, S. A. Transmission of aggression through imitation of aggressive models. *Journal of Abnormal and Social Psychology,* 1961, **63,** 575.

Bass, H. M., & Weinstein, M. S. Early development of interpersonal distance in children. *Canadian Journal of Behavioral Science,* 1971, **3,** 368-376.

Dosey, M., & Meisels, M. Personal space and self protection. *Journal of Personality and Social Psychology,* 1969, **11,** 96-97.

Fisher, R. L. The social scheme of normal and disturbed school children. *Journal of Educational Psychology,* 1967, **58,** 88-92.

Frede, M. C., Gautrey, D. B., & Baxter, J. C. Relationships between body image boundary and interaction patterns on the map test. *Journal of Consulting and Clinical Psychology,* 1968, **32,** 575-578.

Fry, A. M., & Willis, F. N. Invasion of personal space as a function of the age of the invader. *The Psychological Record,* 1971, **21,** 385-389.

Guardo, C. Personal space in children. *Child Development,* 1969, **40,** 143-151.

Guardo, C. J., & Meisels, M. Factor structure of children's personal space schemata. *Child Development,* 1971, **42,** 1307-1312.

Hall, E. T. *The silent language.* Garden City, N.Y.: Doubleday, 1959.

Hall, E. T. *The hidden dimension.* New York: Doubleday, 1966.

Horowitz, M. J., Duff, D. F., & Stratton, S. O. Body buffer zone. *Archives of General Psychiatry,* 1964, **11,** 651-656.

Klapfer, P. H., & Hailman, J. P. *An introduction to animal behavior.* Englewood Cliffs, N.J.: Prentice-Hall, 1967.

Little, K. Personal space. *Journal of Experimental Social Psychology,* 1965, **1,** 237-247.

Little, K. Cultural variation in social schemata. *Journal of Personality and Social Psychology,* 1968, **10,** 1-7.

Meisels, M., & Guardo, C. J. Development of personal space schemata. *Child Development,* 1969, **40,** 1167-1178.

Moreno, J. L. *Who shall survive.* New York: Beacon, 1953.

Mussen, P. H., Conger, J. J., & Kagan, J. *Child development and personality,* New York: Harper International, 1969.

Sears, R. Personality development in the family. In T. N. Feidman (Ed.), *The child.* New York: Reinhart, 1958.

Sommer, R. *Personal space.* New York: Prentice-Hall, 1969.

Tolor, A. Psychological distance in disturbed and normal children. *Psychological Reports,* 1968, **23,** 695-701.

Tolor, A., & Orange, S. An attempt to measure psychological distance in advantaged and disadvantaged children, *Child Development,* 1969, **40,** 407-420.

Watson, O. M., & Graves, T. P. Quantitative research in proxemics. *American Anthropological,* 1966, **68,** 971-985.

Chapter 13

Sex-role development

Elaine M. Ward

285

A year ago some friends built their children a playhouse on stilts, which became a favorite place to play for many of the neighborhood's young children. Recently they commented on how differently boys and girls played in the playhouse. They had observed the boys climbing up and down the ladder, running in and out of the house, and shooting at each other from the windows. While the little boys were quite visible in their play, the little girls played more consistently in the house. When they did make appearances on the balcony around the house, they were airing the rug and rearranging the playhouse furniture. Are boys and girls really this different?

Until recently, the belief that boys and girls are basically different (possess different temperaments, interests, and behavior patterns) was relatively strong and unquestioned. Today in our society, where unisex hairstyling establishments are crowding out yesterday's beauty shops and barber shops, and everyone "wears the pants in the family," it is necessary to try to determine if sex or gender is an important determinant of behavior.

SEX-ROLE STEREOTYPES

Most of us have probably heard some child described as "all boy" and not needed any more information to conclude that this child was active, outgoing, and probably a little difficult to control. Such common beliefs or stereotypes are carried by most of us, and many of our stereotypes rest on the notion that men and women and boys and girls are different. The effect of such ideas may be varied.

Stereotypes serve a function in that they give us some idea of how to act toward an unknown person and what to expect in return from this same person. To the extent that the stereotypical beliefs are true, they become useful ways of organizing our information and behavior. Yet stereotypes also influence what we are likely to observe and remember. If we believe that little girls have a tendency to "nest," when we observe behavior that coincides with this belief we note it in an "Aha! I thought so" fashion. On the other hand, if we observe some little girls wildly racing around the playhouse shooting at each other, we might think it odd and dismiss the information.

A research study conducted by Condry and Condry (1976) examined the effect our beliefs have on our observations. College students were asked to judge the emotional response of a 9-month-old infant they viewed on videotape. To half the subjects the infant was identified on the data sheet with a common feminine name and to the other subjects the infant was identified by a masculine name. The effect of the name manipulation and consequently the belief that the child was either a boy or a girl was pronounced. When the child exhibited a negative emotional response on being presented with a loud buzzer, the emotion was labeled anger by the subjects who thought the baby was a boy and fear by the subjects who thought the infant was a girl. Our beliefs concerning male and female differences may indeed effect our interpretations of our perceptions.

The Condrys make a further point that goes beyond pointing out how our stereotyped beliefs can strengthen themselves. They suggest that if we believe one infant is angry and the other fearful, our behavior toward these infants will likely be different. For example, we are likely to comfort and protect the frightened girl.

It should be clear that our beliefs that boys and girls are different cause us to behave differently toward boys and girls. This difference in behavior is likely very pervasive and can be realized in many ways. One recent study tackled this question indirectly but broadly in an attempt to see if there were basic differences in parents' treatment of boys and girls. Rheingold and Cook (1975) examined the contents of boys' and girls' rooms to see if parents provide different settings and play material for their sons and daughters. They systematically indexed the furnishings and contents of the rooms of 96 children between the ages of 1 and 6 years. They found a distinct difference between boys' and girls' rooms. Boys' rooms were frequently decorated with animals, while girls' rooms were more likely to have floral decorations as well as ruffles and lace trim. The toys provided the two sexes were different as well and not quite what one might have expected. Boys

Elaine M. Ward

Fig. 13-1. Recent research investigating the toys that parents provide for their children found that girls still are generally given dolls and equipment for caring for dolls as major playthings.

had more toys and a greater variety of toys than girls did. This is surprising in that many people feel that the female sex role actually is broader than the male role and allows for more freedom. For example, girls may wear pants, but boys cannot wear dresses; a girl may be an executive, but a male secretary is likely to meet with sex-role prejudice. Therefore, we might expect to find boys possessing only masculine-type toys, while girls might have both masculine and feminine playthings. This was not the case. Boys had the predictable boy-type toys, such as cars, trucks, and trains, but also stuffed animals and dolls. The dolls generally were action figures and superheroes, yet dolls they were. The girls generally were supplied with dolls and equipment for caring for dolls. Interesting enough, girls did not have more books or musical toys than boys did. For the most part, it appeared to Rheingold and Cook that parents provide different experiences for sons and daughters and these differences reflect the common sex-role stereotypes.

Not only do sex-role stereotypes exist in the minds of adults, but even children share these beliefs. Many researchers have measured children's concepts of what behaviors are appropriate and likely for boys and girls and have found that children as young as 2 years of age are aware of the sex typing of some articles of clothing and some common household items. By 2½ years this knowledge is stronger, and by 3 years children can consistently identify objects as to their sex appropriateness (Thompson, 1975). Measuring this same ability with other children, Williams, Bennett, and Best (1975) found kindergarten children had a sound knowledge of sex-role stereotypes and that second-graders were even more knowledgeable.

This knowledge in the minds of children leads them to respond differently to situations and play materials. Montemayor (1974) had children 6 to 8 years old play a game of skill with a toy identified as appropriate either for boys or girls. The children who played with the toy when it was described as appropriate for their sex played more skillfully with the toy and rated it as more attractive than did the children who played with the toy when it was described as sex inappropriate. That is, if the toy was labeled for boys, boys played better with it than girls, and if the toy was labeled for girls, girls played better with it.

We have been considering the belief that males and females differ and have briefly pointed out what effect this belief might have on children's behavior. Now we should also consider that many people today strongly feel that the differences between males and females are artificial or exaggerated. They argue that if males and females are treated in the same manner and given the same opportunities, they will respond in the same ways. The results of this belief if carried into practice should help us answer the basic question of whether males and females are different behaviorally. However, it may be extremely difficult for people with a belief in the similarity of the sexes to escape influence from people who believe in differences. For example, several often-quoted studies have revealed that males and females are portrayed differently on television and in children's books. Sternglanz and Serbin (1974) surveyed popular children's television programs aired in 1971 and 1972 and found that male characters dominated the shows that children watched; four of the top ten children's shows had only male characters. In these shows a large majority of the characters performed in accordance with sex-role stereotypes. The males were aggressive, successful, and controlling, while the females were seen as neutral in their effect on the outcome of the plots. Many other surveys have also shown the same general trend in children's books.

With males and females portrayed differently in children's television and books, it is likely that children note these differences and in some ways are influenced by them. Jennings (1975) tested this possibility with 4 and 5 year olds by reading them stories with children acting either sex appropriately or sex inappropriately. She tested the children's recall of these stories and their preferences for the stories. She found that the children remembered better the stories where the behavior was sex inappropriate (possibly because it was novel to them), but that they preferred the stories that described sex-appropriate behaviors. The effects of sex-role stereotyping are indeed subtle and pervasive.

The belief that boys and girls are different can have several effects. First, it can cause us to note and remember events that support our belief. Second, our beliefs can influence how we interpret ambiguous or unclear events. Third, our interpretation of events and our beliefs can cause us to treat males and females differently. Fourth, our belief and our consequent differential treatment of boys and girls can cause them to respond differently, which reinforces our belief.

We have considered the effects of sex-role stereotypes without describing the content of these beliefs. Psychologists have conducted many research projects aimed at identifying areas of difference between the sexes. Some of these studies rely on naturalistic observations of children, some rely on ratings of behavior by parents and teachers, and some involve experimental manipulation, such as the emotion-judging study discussed earlier in this chapter. Before considering these areas of differences it should be noted that the evidence on this topic is far from consistent. With so many different behaviors to explore and so many techniques used to conduct the research, it is not surprising that very few solid, reliable generalizations can be made about the development of sex roles.

To illustrate how difficult it is to find real male and female differences consider the following personal experience. Almost from birth, people treat boy and girl infants differently. A few hours after my son was born, we received a large bouquet of flowers. Among the flowers were a small football and a basketball, both usable as toys and the appropriate size for an infant's grasp. The woman I shared the hospital room with had a new daughter. When the nurse brought her in to her mother, she had a pink bow taped to the top of her bald head. These observations indicate that even if we detect differences in boy and girl infants' behaviors, these differences may still reflect people's differential treatment of the infants.

WHAT ARE LITTLE BOYS MADE OF? WHAT ARE LITTLE GIRLS MADE OF?
Infancy

Several recent studies have found differences in the behavior and the characteristics of boy and girl infants. Some of the most reliable and physiologic differences, such as differences in average birthweight, size, and amount of body fat, are described in Chapter 5. Other initial differences include an indication that girl infants sleep more than boy infants

289

and that mothers hold boys for more minutes a day than they do girls (Moss, 1973), possibly because boys are awake longer.

Another common belief is that boys are more active than girls. Although this belief is widespread, Maccoby and Jacklin (1974) reviewed the literature on activity level and concluded that there were no reliable differences in activity level between boys and girls, at least in infancy. They reported, however, that by preschool age boys in groups tend to be more active. This observation is supported by others who find that nursery aged boys tend to play over a larger area and in a rougher manner than do girls (Lynn, 1974). Part of Maccoby and Jacklin's reluctance to consider boys and girls as different in overall activity level is their belief that activity level is not a very stable characteristic of a child's behavior.

Another major belief is that girls are more verbal than boys. Again the picture is unclear. Some studies report that girls acquire the skill more quickly than boys do; others, such as Koenigsknecht and Friedman (1976), note that girls do not show a distinct verbal advantage over boys until 4 years of age. Maccoby and Jacklin (1974) feel that the traditional female superiority in verbal areas does not occur until adolescence. Even though there is grave disagreement as to when female verbal superiority occurs, most researchers concur that females are more proficient at verbal skills. Another interesting finding relative to this point is the work of Cherry and Lewis (1976), who found that mothers of girls talk to their infants more than mothers of boys do and that their verbal stimulation to the two sexes is qualitatively different as well. They noted that mothers of girls use longer sentences, ask more questions, and use more repetition when talking with their daughters than with their sons. These are all techniques that should stimulate verbalization on the part of the child. It is difficult to determine whether the difference in the children's behavior precedes or follows the difference in the mother's behavior.

Aggression and dependency

As indicated earlier, somewhere between the ages of 2 and 4 years children are aware of their sex and behaviors that are considered appropriate to it. During this preschool period more distinct differences between the sexes can be detected. Two areas of interest have been researched very thoroughly and may serve to illustrate how difficult it is to study sex-role development. These areas are aggressive behavior and dependency. Beliefs about aggression and dependency are very strong. Most people readily agree that boys are more aggressive than girls and that girls exhibit more dependent behavior than boys. Research evidence tends to support the first belief, that boys are aggressive; however, the picture for dependency is not as clear.

Aggression. Of all the behavioral differences between males and females, aggression does seem to be highly sex typed as a masculine characteristic. Not only do many studies conclude that males are basically more aggressive than females (Mischel, 1970), but some researchers are inclined to point to a biologic base for differences in aggression. Lynn (1974) discusses what conditions are necessary for a behavior to be considered as biologically based:

> A trait that is more characteristic of one sex than the other is likely to have a biological component if it (1) occurs in that sex when the child is very young (has had less time to

learn), (2) is more characteristic of that sex in nearly all cultures, (3) is also more characteristic of that sex in other primates, and (4) is consistent with the findings on hormones.
(p. 143)

In his discussion of male and female behavior, Lynn, as well as Maccoby and Jacklin
(1974), present evidence from other cultures and primate studies that tend to indicate that
aggressive behavior is a characteristically male trait. Mischel (1970) in his review of the
literature of sex typing indicates that aggressive behavior appears more frequently in boys

W. C. Baker

Fig. 13-2. Although there are conflicting research data concerning differing play styles of boys and
girls, many feel that boys are more daring and aggressive in play.

as early as 3 years of age, and Maccoby and Jacklin (1974) in their literature review argue that aggression level does change in response to sex hormones.

Many researchers agree that males at all ages are more aggressive than females, and as indicated above, some believe that this difference may be biologically based. Others, however, have conducted studies designed to determine which environmental factors or situations may be related to the incidents of male aggression. One such study by Smith and Green (1975) investigated the response of adults to the aggressive behavior of nursery school children. They felt that the different rates of male and female aggression might be due to differential response by the nursery school teachers to acts of aggression by boys and girls. They found that most aggression in the nursery schools they studied could be classified as property fights. Further, they found that peer reinforcement for aggression was high in that if no adult entered the disputes the aggressive child was successful in obtaining the property at least 63% of the time. If an adult intervened, however, the aggressor's success rate dropped considerably. The major finding of this study is that adults respond in the same manner to aggression by boys and girls, an indication that the sex difference may not be the result of differential treatment.

Others, however, feel that girls may be less inclined to aggression, not because they are less aggressive but because they are much more likely to conform to an adult's suggestion that they "behave." This is the opinion of Maccoby and Jacklin (1974), based on their interpretation of the literature on aggression. They also indicate that not only do girls seem to instigate (start) fewer aggressive incidents, but they also appear to be the victims of such incidents less frequently than boys are. It is possible that this may be due to the self-segregation of boys and girls in play groups, even in preschools, and the more sedate manner of play observed in girls. Maccoby and Jacklin (1974) also reported that young boys tended to play in larger groups than did young girls and that when little boys played together, they tended to be wilder in their play.

Although there are many conflicting pieces of evidence dealing with aggressive behavior, it appears that from an early age males are more likely to behave aggressively and are quite frequently successful in gaining their goals. Some researchers believe that adults may be more tolerant of aggression in boys; however, some studies, such as the one by Smith and Green (1975), have found no such tolerance. Perhaps parents may be more tolerant of noninjurious aggression in boys, but in the structure of a preschool, apparently in the interests of maintaining order and providing for the safety of all the children, nursery school teachers are vigilant in their attempts to halt aggressive behavior. This possibility once again points to the difficulty in obtaining answers to complex behavioral questions. To study enough children to obtain reliable results for an experiment and to control for as many extraneous variables as possible, it is almost mandatory that child psychologists study children in groups, such as in day-care centers or nursery schools, because the great differences from one home situation to another make generalizations almost impossible.

Dependency. A second frequently researched topic dealing with sex differences is dependency. Many people believe that females are naturally more dependent than males. This belief seems quite compatible with the evidence that indicates that males are more aggressive. However, recent research dealing with the topic of dependency is not nearly as clear and conclusive as that dealing with aggression. Before discussing this topic further, it should be noted that perhaps the major source of conflict in data dealing with dependency is the lack of a uniform definition of dependency used from study to study. This problem also occurs in research dealing with social development (see Chapter 10).

Some studies of dependency consider dependent behavior as the tendency to cling to others and to seek to be near them. These others may be a central adult, such as a parent or teacher, or other children. Others consider dependency a tendency to ask for help in solving problems, such as asking a nursery teacher for aid in putting on boots or mittens. Still others define dependency as the opposite of or lack of independence. They consider that parents teach their children dependency by discouraging independent behaviors, such as crossing streets to play in a friend's yard, or aiding children in personal tasks, such as hair combing and face washing. In evaluating whether females or males are more dependent we need to keep in mind just what a particular researcher considers dependent behavior.

For example, in summarizing the early work on dependency Mischel (1970) observed that few distinct differences in dependency were found using subjects younger than school age. In their more recent survey Maccoby and Jacklin (1974) reached the same conclusion. There appears to be little difference in dependency behavior in young children. Yet there are some serious disagreements on this topic.

One of the most cited studies supporting the contention that girls are more dependent than boys is the 1969 study of Goldberg and Lewis. They studied dependency in an experimental laboratory with subjects 13 months of age. They found that in free play, girls were more hesitant to leave their mothers and returned more frequently to them during the session. They also found that girls have more physical contact with their mothers than boys do.

In observations conducted when these infants were 6 months old, they found that the mothers initiated more physical contact with the girls than with the boys. Goldberg and Lewis speculated that the child's tendency to seek contact with the mother at 13 months was related to the amount of contact experienced at 6 months. The observation that 6-month-old boys who received large amounts of contact also sought more contact at 13 months strengthens their belief that it is the differential treatment on the part of the parent that leads to the difference in the child's behavior.

Maccoby and Jacklin (1974) also observed that mothers tend to interact more with infant girls during feeding. However, just to point out the uncertainty of these kinds of observations we should recall that Mischel (1970) reports that boys are held longer than girls initially. He also reports that mothers tend to feed infant boys more on the first day of life, which would indicate more physical contact as well.

Not all experiments are in agreement with Goldberg and Lewis's. Corter and Bow (1976) set up a laboratory situation where infants 9½ to 11 months of age were left alone in an experimental room while the mothers watched them on a television screen. The mothers were told they could retrieve their infants at any time they wished. Mothers of boys returned to the experimental room and picked up their children sooner than did mothers of girls.

With such contradictory findings, it is no wonder that those who have surveyed most **293** of the work on dependency are reluctant to conclude that at a young age girls are more dependent than boys. But note that the studies reported here were conducted in laboratories; perhaps observational studies conducted in homes and schools would present a different picture. Maccoby and Jacklin (1974) indicate they could find no clear trend. They found instances of mothers letting girls roam as far from home as boys and mothers checking the whereabouts of unseen boys as frequently as that of girls. An interesting suggestion is proposed by Maccoby and Jacklin based on the longitudinal study conducted in England by Newson and Newson (in progress when Maccoby and Jacklin reported in 1974). They found no more restrictions placed on the movement of girls than on boys up to age 7 years. They did find girls being "chaperoned" more after age 7, in that parents were more likely to pick girls up at school or the bus stop than they were boys. This suggests that young children are treated in much the same manner. They are watched over carefully and protected equally. It is also assumed that they are given equal independence training, such as being encouraged to solve their own difficulties. Yet when school age is reached and both sexes move farther from home, it is felt that perhaps young girls need more protection. Indeed, this need may be unfortunately very real. It may be at this point that differences in dependency become pronounced, with girls being given more protection and this tendency generalizing to other areas such that girls perceive that they need defense and aid.

There are many areas of assumed difference between males and females, but because of the amount of conflicting evidence, we will not consider any other areas of difference in detail; rather, we will mention those areas and present the summary material provided by Maccoby and Jacklin (1974). Before doing so, it should be mentioned that Maccoby and Jacklin's conclusions must be regarded cautiously, as they themselves state. First, their conclusions are based on the reviews of many studies of different kinds. The aims, conditions, and conduction of these studies are not all compatible, and consequently, drawing conclusions in a summary fashion causes grave injustice to the original work and may be misleading even if not misinterpreted. However, due to the near impossibility of considering all possible sex differences, we shall rely on their conclusions. Maccoby and Jacklin conclude that many sex-role stereotypes rest on shaky ground at best or are distinctly incorrect at worst.

Maccoby and Jacklin (1974) summarized the following beliefs, among others, as apparently unfounded:

1. Girls are more socially oriented than boys.
2. Girls are more receptive to suggestion.
3. Young girls have lower self-esteem than young boys.
4. Boys and girls differ in learning ability.
5. Boys are naturally more analytic than girls.
6. Girls lack achievement motivation.

They concur that the following differences do seem to be real:

1. Girls are more proficient at verbal skills.
2. Boys seem more capable in making visual-spatial judgments.
3. Boys excel in mathematical areas.
4. Boys are basically more aggressive.

They list the following as open questions:
1. Are girls more sensitive tactilely?
2. Are girls naturally more anxious than boys?
3. Is there an overall difference in activity level between boys and girls?
4. Is one sex more competitive and dominant than the other?
5. Are girls more compliant and nurturant than boys?

It should also be indicated that some of the differences that Maccoby and Jacklin feel are reliable do not develop until middle childhood or adolescence, such as the male superiority in math and consequently logical reasoning. Ability in these areas is difficult to assess before these concepts are taught and encouraged to develop. However, predisposition to such ability may have roots in early childhood.

Lynn (1974) has proposed an interesting theory as to the possible impetus for male superiority in reasoning and analysis. It has been suggested in many places that one way in which boys and girls learn to behave in sex-appropriate fashions is to observe the same-sex parent. For little girls, Lynn points out that this is an easy task involving imitating the model present in the home, a female caretaker. It is likely that when a girl attempts to dust, stir the cookie dough, or curl her hair, she is supported. The task for a boy is much different and in a sense more difficult. The father is not readily available to be imitated, as he is frequently away from the home while the child is awake. Therefore, the little boy is going to have to guess or reason out appropriate male behaviors. For example, a little boy might decide to curl his hair using mommy's electric curlers. This behavior, considered male inappropriate, is likely to be halted with a "No; little boys don't curl their hair." Frequently there is no appropriate corresponding behavior (e.g., "Little boys don't curl their hair; they . . . instead."). So frequently the boy is left to *figure out* what little boys do. Consequently, Lynn reasons they become more likely to think in an analytic fashion because they are stimulated to do so early in life. It would be interesting to see whether in today's children, who have more available male models on television and more contact with fathers due to shorter work weeks, the boys continue to exhibit superiority in logical reasoning processes.

This discussion brings us to the final and perhaps more important question of how differences in the behavior of the sexes develop. There are several theories of sex-role development and much evidence dealing with differential treatment and pressures on children to conform with sex-role standards.

THEORIES OF SEX-ROLE DEVELOPMENT

As discussed in the beginning of the chapter, not only do most people expect boys and girls to behave differently, but children also expect these differences and frequently respond in the expected sex-role manner. It was also indicated that these expectations and differential responses appear to be relatively strong by the time the child is 3 years old. There are several theories and opinions as to how observed differences develop. Perhaps the best known theory of sex-role development, or the acquisition of sex-appropriate behavior, is the Freudian theory of identification.

It has been assumed by many that the child develops appropriate sex-role behavior by **295** identifying with the same-sex parent. Although the Freudian concept of identification is quite complex and proposes to account for a number of developments in the child, the important aspect of identification for sex-role development is fairly straightforward. First, it is believed that identification is the unconscious adoption of the traits and characteristics of another person. It is stressed that identification is not conscious imitation of another, but a tendency to become like another without actual conscious attempts at modeling. It is thought that the person chosen for identification is seen by the child as powerful and successful. One of the motivations behind identification is thought to be that if the child becomes like some powerful person, the child will share in that success. The theory further stresses that the child's most basic identification should be with the parent and that if all goes well that parent is the same-sex parent.

As the child becomes like that parent, the child acquires the appropriate behaviors for that sex. For several reasons, among them the reliance on unconscious factors and the difficulty of assessing the Freudian concepts directly by research, other theories relying on the modeling of the parent's behavior and characteristics have developed that deal with a child's conscious attempts to be like the parents.

One specific theory of this type is the social learning theory developed and researched by Sears and his associates, which adds to the concept of identification the notion of reinforcement. In addition to possessing power, if the same-sex parent is nurturing and reinforcing, behaving in the same manner as the parent can become reinforcing for the child, and these behaviors, which are like the parent's, can help the child at times when the parent is not present. This addition to the theory aids in explaining why a boy may become more like his father even when the father is not as available to copy. It is the copying of the father's behavior that helps the boy handle his father's necessary absences. Girls, however, as Lynn indicated, simply find attempts to be like a nurturing mother often directly reinforcing. Both of these theories make more or less use of the basic concept of identification.

Many others still feel that children learn to become like the same-sex parent through direct teaching and conscious reinforcement of behaviors that are considered appropriate. For example, a father may make a conscious effort to teach his son how to kick a football and praise him vigorously for any increase in his skill. It is easy to see how a child so treated would acquire the specific masculine activity taught. Along the same lines, many believe that when a child spontaneously exhibits a behavior that is sex appropriate it will be encouraged and an inappropriate behavior will be discouraged (e.g., "No, I won't teach you how to knit; girls knit.").

An addition to this belief that children learn to behave in a sex-appropriate way by direct teaching and conscious reinforcement is that through various previous reinforcements for such activity children begin to note behavior of people (or models) of the same sex and copy their behavior. For instance, Slaby and Frey (1975) found that as children become more sure of their own gender they are more likely to selectively attend to models of their own sex, especially boys. That boys would attend more selectively to male models over female models should not be surprising.

As was indicated earlier, there is seemingly more pressure on males to adhere strictly to the male role that there is on females to adhere to the female role. Lynn (1974), in his book dealing with the role of the father in child development, recounts evidence that fathers are concerned that their sons develop masculine traits. He states that this tendency is particularly strong among working class fathers. We all should be able to recognize this tendency from our own experience. Being a tomboy was never as bad or difficult for a girl as being a sissy was for a boy. It is also likely, if one examines the trend toward equality and similarity of the sexes, that we will find more masculine traits purposefully encouraged in females than we will find female traits added to the male role.

Fig. 13-3. Many fathers actively encourage activity considered masculine in their sons. This father is supporting his son's early attempts at daring to try a poolside slide.

Other writers have indicated that little boys frequently are aware very early of what are girl-type activities, and the purpose of this awareness seems to be so that they can avoid such activities, although both sexes are aware very early of sex-appropriate activities and objects. Fein et al. (1975) found that even 20-month-old children play more with sex-appropriate than inappropriate toys and that when given the opportunity to imitate play with these toys, both sexes do more imitating of sex-appropriate models.

The same tendency was found by Nadelman (1974) with children aged 5 to 8 years. Given memory tests and preference tests involving sex-typed objects, the children better recalled appropriately typed objects and indicated stronger preferences for appropriate objects. She reports that, as expected, boys are more rigid in their preferences than girls. Further, she noted that preferences of both sexes become more rigid with age.

An important point relevant to imitation and selection of appropriate behaviors is the child's awareness of his or her own gender and the fact that gender is stable over time and over situations. Kohlberg has formulated a theory of sex-role development that includes this point. Kohlberg feels that the development of gender awareness proceeds in stages, that first the child must be aware of his or her gender. Once gender is established, a boy must become aware that he will grow up to be a man, and a girl that she will become a woman. A third development is that the child must learn that gender is not only stable over time but consistent over situations (e.g., a boy who dresses up in the doll corner and plays he is the mommy is still a boy). Kohlberg's theory is consistent with data such as Slaby and Frey obtained showing stronger same-sex model preference with awareness of gender.

Another modification concerning sex-role development can be found in Kohlberg's theory and is discussed in Maccoby and Jacklin (1974). Kohlberg feels that children go beyond just imitating what they see and that they develop their own sense of what is appropriate and add their own interpretation to sex-role development based on what they have observed and been told. Kohlberg's formulation is very similar to the psycholinguistic explanation of language acquisition (see Chapter 7). Recall the McNeill explanation that a child listened to language, formulated rules or hypotheses, and then tested them. Kohlberg also indicates that the child develops rules of appropriate sex-role behavior that guide further behavior.

This type of formulization is in effect a self-socialization theory of sex-role development. Maccoby and Jacklin (1974) in their conclusion express the belief that some of the child's acquisition of sex roles involves an attempt to behave appropriately. They and Kohlberg emphasize the need for the child's own cognitive development to precede self-socialization (e.g., the child must be aware of his or her own gender and its stability before a consistent pattern of sex-appropriate behavior will emerge).

An interesting sidelight develops if one considers children as directing their own sex-role development; their interpretation of sex roles is childish and perhaps exaggerated (Maccoby and Jacklin, 1974). One cannot help but think of the preschool boy's overreaction to some activity with the typical "Yuck! That's for girls."

Although each of these viewpoints has its own distinct emphasis, it is likely that none is completely independent. What is proposed is that children are likely to acquire different patterns of sex-appropriate behavior by desiring to be like a parent, by being taught specifically to acquire or avoid certain behaviors, by selectively attending to previous reinforcement for such activity, and by becoming aware of their own gender and attempting to acquire the expected behaviors. Another possibility is that children acquire different patterns of behavior through some subtle and some not so subtle differential experiences.

DIFFERENTIAL TREATMENT OF THE SEXES

We have considered that people judge male and female behavior as different based on their expectations of differences, and we have noted that television programs and books present children with different pictures of males and females. Now we shall consider the further possibility that parents and teachers respond differently to girls and boys.

Throughout this chapter we have indicated different parental treatment of boys and girls that should be summarized. Parents decorate the rooms of boys and girls differently and provide them with different kinds of toys. It has been noted that mothers verbalize more to girls and that they stimulate verbal responsiveness more in girls. It has been found that boys are held more and fed more initially, but that by 6 months of age girls receive more physical contact. Although some researchers have found that infant girls cling more to their mothers in laboratory experiments, it has also been discovered that mothers of boys retrieve their sons earlier than mothers of girls retrieve their daughters to terminate a separation. Although there have been indications that young boys and girls receive the same kind of independence training, it has been found that older girls receive more parental protection.

Lynn (1974) discusses several areas of differential parental treatment of sons and daughters. He indicates that fathers roughhouse more with infant boys than girls and he also adds that these same men are likely to criticize their wives for handling the infant too roughly! Lynn cites several sources as indicating that fathers are more concerned about appropriate sex-role responses in their children than mothers are and that fathers exert more pressure on their sons to be masculine than they do on their daughters to be feminine. Lynn feels that the father's influence may be more direct than the mother's and that his influence is more direct with sons. Lynn feels that fathers may indirectly encourage femininity in their daughters by being very masculine themselves and treating their daughters in a protective, dominant fashion.

Fagot (1974) observed the behavior of mothers and fathers toward their children aged 18 to 24 months. She found that boys were more likely to be left alone to play but that parents were more likely to join a boy in his play than a girl in hers. It is interesting to speculate that boys are given more interesting playthings. Before we conclude that parents favor boys, Fagot also reports that girls received more praise than boys; however, they also received more criticism. One further difference observed was that, as anticipated, girls were allowed more freedom to participate in both male- and female-type activities. Fagot also reiterates the belief that fathers are more concerned about appropriate sex-role behavior than mothers are.

It is difficult to see any real trends or to draw any conclusions from the scattered evi-   **299** dence presented; unfortunately, this representation is fairly typical. It is difficult to see if or how parents are sex typing their children.

Another possibility is that teachers treat boys and girls differentially. A number of studies have been conducted to determine if this is so. We have already reported that nursery school teachers respond in the same fashion to aggressiveness by boys and girls. Cherry (1975) found that preschool teachers had more verbal interactions with boys and that their speech to boys was more directing. She also found that girls received more acknowledgement of their answers to a teacher's question. She further suggests that nursery school is a conflict experience for young boys. This would seem to indicate that the frequency of teacher verbalizations directed to boys is the result of a need to channel the boys' activity to a more desirable form. Note that the content of the teacher's speech was said to be directing.

Another study involving nursery schools (Etaugh, Collins, & Gerson, 1975) found that although boys and girls receive equal amounts of reinforcements from their teachers, a majority of reinforced behaviors are those traditionally considered feminine. This is compatible with the finding that teachers handle both male and female aggressiveness in the same fashion.

SUMMARY

After considering all the material presented, you may feel you know less than when you started considering the topic of sex-role development. This impression should not disturb you, as many researchers in this area feel the same way.

Maccoby and Jacklin (1974) present a plausible hypothesis. They suggest that most parents seriously attempt to foster positive traits in their children and that more and more traditionally held sex differences are being examined by thoughtful parents as to whether they are important. For example, it may be all right to let boys cry if they want. They suggest that parents may believe that the sexes are different but feel they can still foster the same traits in each by building up "perceived" weaknesses and changing "natural" tendencies through careful guidance and experiences. The major point is that parents learn to know their children as individuals and are therefore less likely to treat them in a stereotypical fashion. However, they feel that more differential treatment toward the sexes comes from people who do not know a child well. For example, your daughter may have the best curve ball or slider in the neighborhood, but the Little League coach may never give her the chance to prove it. What Maccoby and Jacklin suggest is that the subtle pressures that seem to create behavioral differences between boys and girls may be both difficult to pinpoint and even more difficult to control.

One final point is the consideration of the effect of the traditional belief in the superiority of the male sex and the subsequent superiority of the male role. What effect does it really have on a little girl to live in a culture that clearly advocates male superiority? For example, we pray to God the father, and our language is full of derogatory phrases and conceptions of women. Lynn (1974) points out that an aggressive female is castrating, a nagging person is a bitch, and a fussy person is old-maidish, never old-bachelorish!

REFERENCES

Cherry, L., and Lewis, M. The pre-school teacher-child dyad: sex differences in verbal interactions. *Child Development*, 1976, **46**, 532-535.

Condry, J., & Condry, S. Sex differences: a study of the eye of the beholder. *Child Development*, 1976, **47**, 812-819.

Corter, C., & Bow, J. The mother's response to separation as a function of her infant's sex and vocal distress. *Child Development*, 1976, **47**, 872-876.

Etaugh, C., Collins, G., & Gerson, A. Reinforcement of sex-typed behaviors of two-year-old children in a nursery school setting. *Developmental Psychology*, 1975, **11**(2), 255.

Fagot, B. Sex differences in toddler's behavior and parental reaction. *Developmental Psychology*, 1974, **10**(4), 554-558.

Fein, G., Johnson, D., Kosson, N., Stork, L., & Wasserman, L. Sex stereotypes and preferences in the toy choices of 20-month-old boys and girls. *Developmental Psychology*, 1975, **11**(4), 527-528.

Goldberg, S., & Lewis, M. Play behavior in the year-old infant: early sex differences. In L. J. Stone, H. T. Smith, & L. B. Murphy (Eds.), *The competent infant, research and commentary*. New York: Basic Books, Inc., Publishers, 1973, pp. 1244-1251.

Jennings, S. A. Effects of sex typing in children's stories on preference and recall. *Child Development*, 1975, **46**, 220-223.

Koenigsknecht, R. A., & Friedman, P. Syntax development in boys and girls. *Child Development*, 1976, **47**, 1109-1115.

Lynn, D. B. *The father: his role in child development*. Monterey, Calif.: Brooks/Cole Publishing Co., 1974.

Maccoby, E. E., & Jacklin, C. M. *The psychology of sex differences*. Stanford, Calif.: Stanford University-Press, 1974.

Mischel, W. Sex-typing and socialization. In P. H. Mussen (Ed.), *Carmichael's manual of child psychology* (Vol. 2) (3rd ed.). New York: John Wiley & Sons, Inc., 1970.

Montemayor, R. Children's performance in a game and their attraction to it as a function of sex-typed labels. *Child Development*, 1974, **45**, 152-156.

Moss, H. A. Sex, age, and state as determinants of mother-infant interaction. In L. J. Stone, H. T. Smith, & L. B. Murphy (Eds.), *The competent infant, research and commentary*. New York: Basic Books, Inc., Publishers, 1973, pp. 1237-1242.

Nadelman, L. Sex identity in American children: memory, knowledge and preference tests. *Developmental Psychology*, 1974, **10**(3), 413-417.

Rheingold, H. L., & Cook, K. V. The contents of boys' and girls' rooms as an index of parents' behavior. *Child Development*, 1975, **46**, 459-463.

Slaby, R. G., and Frey, K. S. Development of gender constancy and selective attention to same sex models. *Child Development*, 1975, **46**, 849-856.

Smith, P. K., & Green, M. Aggressive behavior in English nurseries and play groups: sex differences and response of adults. *Child Development*, 1975, **46**, 211-214.

Sternglanz, S. H., & Serbin, L. A. Sex role stereotyping in children's television programs. *Developmental Psychology*, 1974, **10**(5), 710-715.

Thompson, S. K. Gender labels and early sex role development. *Child Development*, 1975, **46**, 339-347.

Williams, J. E., Bennett, S. M., & Best, D. L. Awareness and expression of sex stereotypes in young children. *Developmental Psychology*, 1975, **11**(5), 635-642.

Effects of sex typing in children's stories on preference and recall

Sally A. Jennings

University of Missouri

Thirty-two preschool boys and girls heard 2 stories: 1 about a character of their sex and 1 about a character of the opposite sex. A significant number of subjects preferred the story where the character displayed accurate behavior for the sex. Higher mean scores for recall were recorded for the story where the character's sex role was atypical. The scores were significant for both male and female subjects.

Sex typing begins very early in the American culture. The child acquires the basic components of sex typing in his home through identification with, and imitation of, his parents. According to social learning theory, the consequences that occur when a child first attempts to perform sex-typed behaviors are critical determinants of the child's subsequent performance (Mischel 1966). Pressure to avoid inappropriate sex activities increases from a variety of sources, especially parents and teachers, about the time children are ready to enter elementary school (Hartup, Moore, & Sager 1963).

Books also provide children with role models of what they are supposed to be like when they grow up. Weitzman, Eifer, Hokada, and Ross (1971) examined several hundred picture books and found girls far less represented; when they did appear, they were depicted as dull and passive. The majority of attention they received was for their physical attractiveness, while boys were praised for their cleverness and achievements (Sutherland 1971).

Consequently, many girls have poorer self-concepts and lower levels of achievement. It has been found that girls wish to conform to adults' expectations of good academic performance but fear that such achievement may make them unpopular and appear to be unfeminine. As a result of these dual pressures, the brightest girls may do well in school but less than their best (Coleman 1961).

The aim of this study was to determine whether awareness of sex typing in literature exists in preschool children and whether they express sex-role character preferences. It was hypothesized that children would prefer a story where the character demonstrated behavior consistent with his own, or an appropriate, sex role. This hypothesis was based on research suggesting that a preschool child could determine which toy was appropriate for his or her sex and would choose that toy (Rabban 1950).

This project also attempted to study children's awareness and reaction to reversal of sex roles. Because novel items generally are remembered longer and more clearly (Wilcocks 1928), it was hypothesized that the children would have better recall of a story with reversed sex roles, probably because the reversed role was novel to them.

METHOD
Subjects

The subjects were 64 children, ages 4 and 5, enrolled in nursery school and day-care centers in Columbia, Missouri. The study included 32 girls and 32 boys.

From *Child Development*, 1975, **46**, 220-223. © 1975 by the Society for Research in Child Development, Inc.

Procedure

Each group of children ranged in size from five to eight children of the same sex. They were told two brief stories illustrated with a series of pictures placed on a flannel board one at a time. The children in the group were isolated from the other children in a separate room during the time the stories were being told and while being tested later.

In one story the main character demonstrated the usual sex-role behavior, while in the other story the main character behaved in a manner appropriate to the opposite sex. The main characters in the stories were always the same sex as the children in that particular group. The girls listened to one story about a girl who wanted to be a ballerina and one story about a girl who wanted to be a mail carrier. The main character in one story for the boys was a boy who wanted to be a male dancer, while the main character in the other story wanted to be a mail carrier. The order of presentation was reversed for half of the subjects.

Testing

Immediately after the stories, the children were tested individually for preference and recall. During these testing situations the child's responses were taped. All the pictures used in the stories were displayed on a table in proper sequence, and the child was encouraged to handle them. The child was first asked to indicate which story he liked best. To test recall, the child was asked to tell the story using the pictures. He was given nonspecific prompts when necessary. The prompts were kept very general so as not to disclose the entire theme. The most commonly used prompts were "What happened next?" and "Tell me what happened in this picture in the story." The child was then retested for recall 2 days later using the same methods.

Scoring

Each child's responses were transcribed and scored according to the number of correct themes the child reported. An additional scorer was used to determine reliability, and there was a .92 correlation between scores. Points were assigned for each theme as follows: 2 points—correct response without prompting; 1 point—correct response with prompting; 0 points—no response; − 1 point—incorrect response. The points for each child were added to yield a total recall score. The possible range of scores was from −6 to +12.

RESULTS

As hypothesized, a significant number of children of both sexes preferred the story with the usual sex-typed behavior ($\chi^2 = 9.24$; $df = 1$; $p < .005$). There was no significant difference between the day-care subjects and the nursery school subjects regarding percentage of preference (Table 1).

The mean scores for the recall data showed better recall for the story with the reversed sex roles

Table 1. Story preference as a function of sex-role behavior

	Prefer usual	Prefer reverse
Male:		
Nursery school	10	6
Day care	11	5
Total	21	11
Female:		
Nursery school	12	4
Day care	12	4
Total	24	8

Table 2. Mean story recall scores for day-care vs. nursery school children

	Usual sex roles		Reverse sex roles	
	Test 1	Test 2	Test 1	Test 2
Male:				
Nursery school	6.12	6.18	5.25	5.87
Day care	4.25	4.50	5.31	5.31
Total X	5.18	5.34	5.28	5.59
Female:				
Nursery school	4.43	5.00	6.18	6.25
Day care	4.81	4.62	5.81	6.18
Total X	4.62	4.81	6.00	6.21

for both male and female subjects. This was true for both testing sessions. An analysis of variance indicated this difference was statistically significant, F (1,62) = 16.55, $p < .01$. However, it was noted that when the male subjects were divided into the day-care group and the nursery school group, the day-care boys showed higher mean scores for recall of the story with the reversed sex roles. The male subjects from the nursery school actually showed slightly better recall for the story with the usual sex-role behavior displayed. Both groups of females had higher mean recall scores for the story with the reversed sex roles (Table 2). This disparity probably accounts for the significant sex × story interaction, F (1,62) = 10.07, $p < .01$.

The two different types of schools were not originally intended to be a variable, so the order of presentation was exactly reversed for the two groups. The stories were presented in the same order for all the subjects from a particular school. The day-care subjects heard the story with the usual sex roles first, while the subjects from the nursery schools heard the story with the reversed sex roles first.

Although the school variable was confounded with order, there did not appear to be any noticeable difference in the subjects' responses due to the order of presentation. An exploratory analysis of variance indicated that this school × sex interaction was not statistically significant, F (1,62) = 0.99, $p > .05$. None of the other main effects or interactions was significant, although the mean scores for test 2 were slightly higher than those for test 1.

Discussion

In general, the original hypotheses were supported. Both groups preferred the story with the sex role appropriate to their sex. The girls liked the ballerina better, and the boys preferred the mail carrier. Possibly it was easier for them to identify with these characters. The story they remembered longer and in more detail was the story with the reversed sex roles. The main character behaved in a manner appropriate to the opposite sex, which was the reverse of what the children were accustomed to seeing. Due to the novelty, their recall was improved for this story.

Although type of school was not intended to be a variable, the subjects from the different types of schools, especially the males, reacted differently to the stories. A large majority of the day-care boys coming from low-income, one-parent homes did not approve of the story about a male dancer. They labeled it "stupid" and even refused to listen. Research clearly suggests that boys show clear-cut preference patterns earlier than girls. Appropriate preference patterns for sex typing also appear earlier in low-income children (Rabban 1950). Hall and Keith (1964) tested children and found that low-income boys scored in the highest, most masculine areas of the preference scale. They felt this pattern indicated a greater rigidity of the definition of the male role.

On the other hand, the male subjects from the nursery schools apparently found the male dancer acceptable. They appeared interested in the story, and several said that they could dance like that. All of these boys were from middle- and upper-income homes.

Both of the groups of girls seemed to accept the woman mail carrier. None of them suggested that they might like to deliver the mail, but many had great aspirations to become ballerinas. In general, the girls found the male role much more acceptable than the boys found the female role; this finding is supported by research on sex-role preference (Sher & Lansky 1968).

It is not suggested here that sex roles in literature be reversed because, as demonstrated, children would prefer these stories. However, since books are a medium that can be changed, it is suggested that girls be depicted in more active and competent roles. Boys also need wider choices. Weitzman et al. (1971) concluded after studying literature that the narrow view of reality presented is confusing and misleading to children of both sexes. The sex roles were found to be unnecessarily rigid, and they especially discouraged and restricted a woman's potential.

REFERENCES

Coleman, J. *The adolescent society.* Glencoe, Ill.: Free Press, 1961.

Hall, M., & Keith, R. Sex-role preference among children of upper and lower social class. *Journal of Social Psychology,* 1964, **62,** 101-110.

Hartrup, W.; Moore, S.; & Sager, G. Avoidance of inappropriate sex typing by young children. *Journal of Consulting Psychology,* 1963, **27,** 467-473.

Mischel, W. A social learning view of sex differences in behavior. In E. Maccoby (Ed.), *The development of sex differences.* Stanford, Calif.: Stanford University Press, 1966.

Rabban, M. Sex-role identification in young children in two diverse social groups. *Genetic Psychology Monographs,* 1950, **42,** 81-158.

Sher, M., & Lansky, L. The IT scale for children: effects of variations in the sex specificity of the IT figure. *Merrill-Palmer Quarterly,* 1968, **14,** 323-330.

Sutherland, Z. Make no mystique about it. *Saturday Review* (March 20, 1971), 30-31.

Weitzman, L.; Eifer, D.; Hokada, E.; & Ross, C. Sex role socialization in picture books for preschool children. Paper presented at the meeting of the American Sociological Association, August 1971.

Wilcocks, R. The effect of an unexpected heterogeneity on attention. *Journal of Genetic Psychology,* 1928, **1,** 266-319.

Chapter 14

Play

W. C. Baker

306

In Chapter 1 it was indicated that the activities or behaviors of children are many, varied, and perhaps unpredictable. Some of the activities of children are explored in previous chapters, and we have seen that, if not precisely predictable, some of these behaviors are at least understandable, considering the particular characteristics of children at various ages. However, a major activity of children is still to be discussed, that is, play behavior. Studying play is a more difficult task than one might imagine because play activity is a broad category encompassing behaviors that are difficult to classify and define.

Most of us have pleasant memories of childhood hours spent at play. Yet if we were asked to define play or describe its essential characteristics, we might find ourselves at a loss. In answering the question "What is play?" we are likely to encounter some contradictions and complexities we had not before considered. Many of us would probably be satisfied with the answer that play is fun. So far so good. However, consider your present activities. Do you now engage in playing as you did as a child? You may participate in some type of recreation or sport and you may very well enjoy some games, such as card games or board games, but do you actively engage in "let's pretend" fantasies or enjoy dolls or small trucks and cars? Could you spend an afternoon constructing a jungle village in the dirt and grass? Probably not. Yet if play is fun, why does play behavior narrow in range and decrease in frequency with growth? The answer lies in the fact that play is more than having fun; play behavior serves many functions in the growth and development of the child, and as these functions are served or the child develops other behaviors to serve these functions, play behavior decreases.

It is through playing that the child exercises many skills and abilities, as when the infant puts one block on top of another, removes it, and places it on top of the other again and again. The child also develops social skills through playing. When two children pretend they are truck drivers talking on their CB radios, they are not only exercising their communication skills but are developing ideas about different roles in life and are also cooperating as they play. When a child stirs flour and water together in a small bowl and puts it out in the sun to bake, the child is exercising imitation skills and also acquiring information about adult activities. Playing also increases a child's cognitive capabilities, as a child pretending to be a lion in the circus draws on knowledge of lions and circuses and combines this knowledge into a game. Children not only explore reality in their play; they may also attempt to understand experiences more fully through play and sometimes gain some control over reality in their play, such as a child playing doctor with a doll after having a physical exam and telling the doll authoritatively that the shot it's about to receive is for its own good!

Just as play seems to serve various functions in development, there are various theories concerning play, each more or less stressing a particular function of play.

THEORIES OF PLAY

The study of play behaviors in development is one area where there are many extensive theories concerning the behavior and little research conducted in relationship to the theories. The reason may be that the major theories concerning play behaviors are parts of more general theories of development and as such are secondary to the general theories. **307**

Frequently the theoretical material concerning play is developed to support other concepts in the more general theory. For example, one of the major play theories is a psychoanalytic theory of play that stresses the usefulness of play in handling overwhelming emotional experiences. This theory explains play in terms of how it serves the development and protection of the child's ego. A second reason as to why there appears to be more theoretical speculation than research on play behavior is that the theories concerning play behavior are stated in rather general terms and do not lend themselves directly to explaining or testing specific child play activities (Singer, 1973). On the other hand, several researchers have conducted studies on specific play behaviors not related to any theoretical framework; consequently, many bits and pieces of information on play behaviors are available that do not relate to any theoretical orientation.

Older formulations

To illustrate the speculative nature of material concerning play, briefly consider two theories of play behavior that are no longer particularly viable or of interest to many of today's researchers in child development. The first of these is referred to as the surplus-energy theory of play. Its formulation is credited to the poet Schiller. The basic contention of this theory was that since children are not generally involved in work activity or fights for survival, they have excess energy in their systems that must be used. Children play to burn up this excess energy.

A second speculative formulation concerning the play of children is the instinct theory of play. This theory contends that play behaviors are the initial instances of skills necessary for survival that the child practices before their survival usefulness actually occurs (Singer, 1973). Any research based on this theory would be aimed at showing the relationship of specific play behaviors to actual survival skills of adults. This kind of research would be concerned only with children's play activities that could be related to adult skills. If this were the case, a large body of play activities would fall outside the boundaries of these studies.

More recent formulations

Several theories of play are more recent or at least more enduring than the two mentioned briefly above. The two major theories are the psychoanalytic theory of play and Piaget's theory of play. Although these theories are very different from each other, they both see play as serving a useful function in the child's life. In other words, play is more than simply having fun.

Psychoanalytic theory of play

The psychoanalytic theory of play emphasizes the relationship of the child's play and the child's emotional development. Specifically, this theory sees much of children's play as an attempt to satisfy drives, fulfill wishes, and control disturbing events that threaten the child's developing personality. The example of a child giving a painful shot to a doll illustrates the child's attempt to overcome a threatening experience. Through reliving a bad experience in play, the child is able to control the situation and make it less overwhelming. Other aspects of the psychoanalytic viewpoint concerning play are discussed by theorists working in the Freudian framework. Stamm (1976) discusses the psychoanalytic play theories of Walder, a follower of Freud's, and Erikson.

To the idea of the child controlling reality by repeating painful experiences, Walder added the complementary idea that the child may also repeat pleasurable experiences to relive them. For example, a child might for weeks play that he is visiting the post office after making the trip with the kindergarten class.

Erikson emphasizes the developmental changing nature of the child's play. Stamm (1976) discusses the major types of play Erikson proposes. This first type, autocosmic play, involves play that is related to the child's body. After the body has been examined, the child may use this resource to further examine the world. Erikson's second stage of play, microsphere play, is play expanded to include the young child's toys. Play with toys is thought to help the child develop mastery skills over objects. Erikson's last stage, macrosphere play, involves the preschool child's interaction with others in a social fashion. Here the emphasis is on the acquisition of sharing skills. This theoretical viewpoint is more extended and developmental than the other psychoanalytic theories; however, all share the idea that the child's well-being is involved in successful manipulation of emotions and skills in play.

Perhaps one of the best known aspects of the general psychoanalytic viewpont on play is the use of play in diagnosis and treatment of emotional problems in children. In play therapy, children are encouraged to work through their feelings in play and resolve their conflicts. For example, in playing with doll families intended to represent the patient's family, a child may be able to express feelings that he is not able to express directly in reality, such as aggression toward a parent or sibling. It is believed that this play experience can drain off some of the pent-up emotion that is troubling the child and thus reduce the hostility. Others argue that such behavior only increases the child's aggression. The argument is far from resolved.

An interesting sidelight of Erikson's work on play was his belief that boys and girls play differently. Erikson claimed that boys built things up out of play materials, while girls closed things in. The psychoanalytic symbolism here should be apparent; boys preoccupied with phallic symbols and girls in interior spaces are direct parallels with the physiology of sex.

We will see examples of psychoanalytic concepts of play in a later section when we examine categories of play activity in a more specific fashion.

Piagetian theory of play

Piaget's theory of play is an important part of his general theory of cognitive development. The play portion of this theory parallels the general developmental stages of the major theory. Piaget's general statement pertaining to play involves discussing three major types of play, each serving the child's cognitive development and stemming from the child's level of cognitive development. In terms of the major processes of development, assimilation and accommodation (see Chapter 9), play is an act of assimilation. In play the child may manipulate and distort experience and reality to serve particular needs.

309

The first type of play is mastery play, which occurs when a new skill is acquired (Miller, 1974). A new skill is exercised over and over again, apparently for the mastery of that skill and the pleasure gained from these repetitions. This type of play is more frequent during the sensorimotor period, when numerous new skills are acquired. In this stage of mastery play the child acquires some control over his or her body and familiar objects. This corresponds with Erikson's first two stages of play.

In this mastery stage of play, the child is also likely to begin imitative play during the sensorimotor period. Piaget felt that the child's ability to imitate involves the complex coordination of various perceptual schemas. Obviously, much systematic imitation is not likely to occur before the child's basic perceptual schemas are well established. Indeed, Piaget felt that children are not able to imitate actions they cannot see themselves perform, such as make faces, until they are 9 months of age. By 18 months, Piaget felt imitation in play can involve actions of models not present, such as "scolding little brother just like mommy would if she were here."

Apparently one of the major functions of imitative play is to acquire skills possessed by others. Piaget felt children's imitations are likely to be inaccurate and that when the child acquires the skill of accurate imitation at about 8 years, the activity is no longer play (Miller, 1974). Although Miller does not clarify this distinction, it implies that the accurate imitations of the 8-year-old no longer serve the process of assimilation but may be rather serious attempts to pattern behavior to a model's in order to learn (accommodation).

Although these two types of play continue for as long as new skills need mastering, they are not the major style of play between 2 and 7 years of age. During this period symbolic or make-believe play is important in the child's development.

Symbolic play seems to serve several functions for the developing child. Symbolic play parallels the preoperational period of development described in detail in Chapter 9. Recall that when the child acquires the use of symbols, he or she reorganizes the developments of the sensorimotor period into a system of symbolic thought and words. The relationship of the first two play periods is the same. In the first play period the child plays for mastery of new skills; in the second period, the symbolic play period, the child extends play activity to involve the manipulation of objects, emotions, and experiences in a symbolic fashion. The symbolic play period involves make-believe play.

In one sense, Piaget's conception of make-believe play is similar to the psychoanalytic view. Piaget includes the possibility that the child works on frightening experiences in play and through the process of assimilation rearranges the experience to better suit his or her level of cognitive functioning. Piaget also sees the child repeating pleasant experiences for the joy the repetition generates. For Piaget, as well as the psychoanalysts, make-believe play can be considered as involving emotional development. However, for Piaget there is a major cognitive component to make-believe play.

The actual talking and acting out that occurs in make-believe play can be seen as a transition from sensorimotor thinking to symbolic thinking. Again recall that Piaget felt that thinking develops from action and is only internalized as a covert thought process after the acquisition of the symbolic function. The acting out of real experiences is a transition step in the internalization of the thought processes. Further, Piaget explains the distortion of reality in children's make-believe as due to their egocentrism, or their being confined to understanding reality only from their own point of view. In make-believe the child may rearrange events, change reality, and translate reality into a form that is sympathetic and more understandable. Because of the egocentric quality of the preoperational child, make-believe or symbolic play is not generally a social type of play. Children may pretend together; however, each is involved in the play from his or her own particular point of view and cooperation is superficial.

Fig. 14-1. Many psychologists feel children imitate the activity of adults in their play in order to acquire new skills.

At the end of the preoperational period, generally around the age of 7 years, the child has acquired the ability to represent reality in a more straightforward fashion and is able to manipulate experience internally in a truly symbolic fashion. As this occurs, the need for make-believe play diminishes. While the child's egocentrism declines, the possibility for socialized communication and consequently true cooperation increases. The child is now cognitively capable of enjoying a new form of play, games with rules that exercise the new skills of social cooperation. We will not discuss this style of play in detail, as its major development occurs past the age of 8 years and consequently extends beyond the scope of this text.

In summary, Piaget's conception of play involves three major types of play: mastery play, symbolic play, and games with rules. Each serves the development of cognitive capabilities in the child and at the same time reflects the level of the child's cognitive capacities. As we discuss the particular characteristics of play patterns further, we will roughly follow Piaget's categorization of play activity and consider mastery types of play, symbolic play, and social play in children of various ages.

PLAY PATTERNS OF EARLY CHILDHOOD
Mastery play

Most theorists who discuss the play activities of children agree that a large portion of children's play seems to be directed toward exercising developing abilities. Miller (1974), in discussing Piaget's conception of mastery play, indicates that mastery play involves not only the exercise of a new skill through repetition but also manipulation of objects and exploration. This conceptualization parallels Erikson's first two styles of play, which involve exercising the body and then using the body to explore the environment and manipulate the child's toys.

This idea of play involving the exercise of new skills is not confined to theorists who discuss play directly. Recall from the discussion of motor development in Chapter 5 that Shirley, in her discussion of the development of locomotion skills, stated that children played at the level of their motor-skill development. As Shirley outlined the five orders of motor-skill development, she presented parallel orders of play involving the newly developed motor skills.

The function of this type of play should be obvious. As the child exercises a new skill, he or she increases the usefulness of that skill and gains further competence. The exercise of motor skills in particular should help speed the rate at which they become automatic sequences of movements so that the child is able to use these skills in the service of further environmental exploration and manipulation.

Developmentally, mastery play is the earliest form of play behavior and occurs most frequently during the earliest years of life, when there are more new skills to be acquired. However, mastery play can occur throughout the childhood period at any point when new skills are developing.

It is easy to see the mastery nature of play during infancy. Fenson and co-workers (1976) present a description of the development of manipulative play over the first 2 years of life, based on their observations of children at various points of development during this period. The first manipulative skill exercised is that of banging an object against something, such as the floor or a table surface. The next major event involves the relating of one object to another, such as putting one object on top of or into another. The next development is seen as distinctly more complex and involves the addition of symbolism in the child's manipulation of objects. For example, a child may place a toy cup on a toy saucer. This relationship is thought to be more cognitively meaningful than putting a toy car into the cup, which would actually be at the second level of relating objects. The final and more complex manipulative development of the first 2 years involves symbolic combining of objects and sequential ordering of the activity. The child might add a toy teapot to the objects being related, and once the cup is placed on the saucer, the child might "pour tea" into the cup. These investigators felt this ability to sequence play activities just begins occur during the first 2 years of life. Although these researchers emphasize the cognitive development related to manipulative skills, they should still serve to illustrate the practice nature of early mastery play.

Gesell and co-workers' discussions of play activity (1940) also provide examples of mastery play in infancy and early childhood. The play of the 15-month-old child is described as involving extensive exercise of the new ability to walk. At this age the child is described as interested in throwing objects to the floor and picking them up over and over again. A final type of mastery play described for this period involves putting objects into containers, taking them out, and putting them back in again. In fact, Gesell's description of the play of the 15-month-old involves nothing but practice of motor skills.

By 18 months of age the child's play involves both pulling toys around and carrying objects from place to place. These developments indicate some degree of mastery of the walking skills to the point that the child can now add other elements (pulling or carrying) to it. Another mastery skill at 18 months involves exploration. The child is now able to "get into everything." It should be noted at this point that Gesell and co-workers describe other play activities at 18 months that represent symbolic play.

By 2 years of age the Gesell play description involves fewer mastery of skills activities and more symbolic and social play activities. At 2 years, skill mastery play involves manipulation of toys, such as filling a wagon and pulling it and stringing beads.

Gesell and co-workers do not emphasize mastery play again until describing the 5-year-old's play. At 5 years the child's play includes an avid interest in cutting and pasting, which are new and relatively complex skills. These examples should illustrate the general decline of sheer mastery play with age in favor of more complex and meaningful play activities.

The stimulation of mastery play also changes with development. Initially, mastery play is relatively independent of the environment; the child simply exercises motor skills, such as movement of the body. As the child begins to develop further, however, simple objects to be manipulated are important for further skill development. Initially the child's toys may be quite simple, as the major developmental value comes from having objects to grasp, drop, pick up, and combine. As the child progresses, however, mastery play requires toys that can be manipulated in a more varied fashion, for example,   **313** form boards to fit various shapes into and objects with moving parts. More will be said about toys specifically in the last section of this chapter.

Insofar as sex differences in mastery play are concerned, very little is said directly, possibly because it is assumed that young boys and girls acquire and master new skills at the same rate.

Fantasy play

The make-believe play of children seems to be much more complex than pure mastery play. Not only does the activity seem more complex, the theories dealing with make-believe are more complex. Make believe play may deal with both emotional and cognitive elements. The major characteristics of play that may be designated as make-believe are complex also. In make-believe play the child is not confined by the reality of time, space, or the physical properties of the objects included in the play. Make-believe play can be very simple, such as a child cuddling a stick doll, or very complex, as when a child creates a make believe playmate and then engages in a detailed activity such as playing jungle explorer with the imaginary friend.

The functions one sees in make-believe play are influenced by one's theoretical viewpoint. If we have a psychoanalytic viewpoint, we see the function of make-believe as relating to emotional development. The specific functions of make-believe are to overcome threatening experiences or to fulfill wishes. If we endorse Piaget's view of make-believe, we see the function of make-believe play as developing the child's ability

Elaine M. Ward

Fig. 14-2. Make-believe play may involve the exercise of the child's imagination as well as social skills when other children take part in a child's fantasy play.

to use symbols. There are other possibilities to consider as well. Although Piaget stresses the egocentric characteristic of make-believe as opposed to the social functions or possibilities of make-believe, Singer (1973) stresses the social nature of make-believe in that it may involve other children or other characters that may or may not be present in reality. Singer sees the creation of pretend friends as serving a social function.

Singer also stresses that when the child creates a pretend environment or series of events, the child is both exercising cognitive capabilities and learning. This idea is echoed by Miller (1974), who in discussing the complexities of make-believe summarizes it as stimulating the abilities involved in receiving, validating, and storing information.

Still another function of make-believe is seen by Rosen (1974), who feels dramatic play or role taking may be useful in teaching disadvantaged children better problem-solving skills. The general idea is that through make-believe role playing we may decrease dependence on our own point of view (perhaps decrease egocentrism) and begin to see events from more perspectives, which should be a useful skill in problem solving.

Just as the functions of make-believe are varied, make-believe activity is varied. The variety of make-believe seems dependent both on the situations that stimulate it and the characteristics and developmental stage of the children who engage in make-believe. Most psychologists agree with Piaget that it is difficult to find much if any make-believe activity before 18 months or much after 7 years of age.

Returning once more to Gesell and co-workers (1940), the first play activity described that might be considered make-believe occurs at 18 months. This activity includes hugging dolls or stuffed animals. If we assume that this activity involves loving the doll or animals as an animate entity, it is pretending. However, if the hugging is simply to enjoy contact with a soft object, it is not considered make-believe but some type of stimulation seeking. Gesell and associates specifically cite imaginative play as a characteristic of the 3-year-old and add this characteristic to their descriptions of the 4- and 5-year-old as well.

Singer (1973) feels that, as the child develops, the range and richness of fantasy increases. The possibility that other children will become involved in sharing a make-believe session also increases with age as the children become more capable of entering each other's play situations. It is also likely that environmental stimuli that might prompt make-believe increase as well, as the child becomes more able to incorporate more objects and situations into play activity.

At around 7 years of age make-believe play begins to decrease. Piaget's formulation that the child no longer needs to think through activity offers a plausible reason for this change. Also, his belief that the child is no longer so egocentric is compatible with the decline in make-believe play. If the child can cognitively handle differing roles and interact socially, there should be less distortion of reality. There is also the possibility that if the child has been learning through make-believe experiences, at 7 there are many more direct avenues of learning to take advantage of. Singer also comments on the possibility that children today engage in less make-believe play than before, due to the availability of make-believe prepackaged on television.

Because Singer feels that make-believe play contributes in many positive ways to the child's development, he specifies in detail the conditions likely to stimulate a child to engage in make-believe play. One of the more important conditions for fantasy play is that the child has the opportunity to interact with an adult that the child views positively. The adult functions as a model, furnishing the child with many activities that may be imitated and incorporated into make-believe play. The adult's behaviors are likely to become part of the child's play when the child is alone. Singer implies that play involving the adult's activities or characteristics helps fill the lonely times for the child. Again note how Singer sees make-believe as serving a social function.

A second condition supportive of make-believe play is a variety of materials to use in play. By materials Singer means both physical props, such as dress-up clothes and miniature tools, but also cognitive material, such as stories, poems, and information the child may recall and act out in some fashion.

A third condition likely to foster make-believe play is privacy. The child is more likely to try out new roles and explore possibilities if given time alone away from other people and other types of stimulation. A child is not likely to play freely if others criticize or correct his or her characterizations of the world. It should also be obvious that children are not likely to play at anything if television entertains them constantly.

Singer in observing the make-believe play of young children has found support for some of the conditions described above. He has found that preschool children do not interject much fantasy into structured play situations in nursery school even when teachers design the activities to be creatively stimulating. Instead, Singer found that most make-believe play occurs during free play. Singer also found a sex difference in make-believe play. Of surprise, he found that in interviews girls report more fantasy play, but when he observed children playing in nursery school he found boys actually engaged in more fantasy play. He further judged the boys as engaging in more concentrated fantasy and seemingly enjoying this play more. Singer speculated that the particular range of toys available and the nursery school setting may encourage more fantasy play on the part of the boys. In another study involving nursery school children Ruben, Maioni, and Horung (1976) also observed more "dramatic" play by boys than girls.

As indicated, fantasy makes up a large portion of the preschool child's play; however, not all play activity may be considered either mastery play or fantasy play. A third major category of play is play involving other children directly as important elements in the play activity. We will call this third category of play social play.

Social play

Social play as a major category of play is not discussed in the theoretical section of this chapter because the major theorists considered do not discuss social play during early childhood in any detail. Recall that Piaget felt that the child would not be able to play in a truly social fashion until the end of the preoperational period of development. Psychoanalysts tend to see play as serving an individual's unique developmental needs and as such they give minimum consideration to play involving others.

Although these theorists are not concerned with the social aspects of play, anyone who has observed a nursery school group or watched preschoolers in a park should be aware that young children engage in social play with peers to some extent. As with any other major behavior, there are wide individual differences as to the amount of social play a child engages in and the success or satisfaction gained from that play.

As with the other categories of play, social play changes in nature as the child changes and develops. One of the most noticeable changes of social play that occurs as the child develops is the number of children likely to be found in a play group. Most psychologists feel that before 2 years of age children are not likely to play socially with other children. In Chapter 12 on social development we mentioned the belief that very young children treat each other as objects or obstacles to play. At the same time we also indicated a study that found that if children are familiar with each other, they are likely to at least react to each other as children and not as objects. The exact point at which we can say children are able to appreciate other children as potential playmates has not been determined; however, it is relatively safe to assume that the very young preschool child is not likely to engage in play with more than one other child in any organized or coherent fashion, as it may be difficult for the child to attend to multiple stimuli.

Miller (1974) indicates that, as might be expected, the size of a preschooler's play group increases as the child grows. She has found that 3-year-olds rarely play in groups of more than three children and that by 5 years of age the child's play group may be made up of four or five children. As the size of the group increases with age, so does the length of time the group is likely to be involved in a play session. The play of 3-year-olds is likely to be very sporadic with short, changing play periods.

Miller also indicates that many situational factors influence the likelihood that young children will play together. For very young children the familiarity of the playmate is an important factor in whether the children will interact in a playful fashion. Also, the availability of toys is an important stimulus for young children. As children enter elementary school, toys become less important in the play of a group of children. Older children are much more skilled in social interaction and are able to carry on more socially cooperative activities than are younger preschool children, who are more dependent on toys to ensure the involvement of another child. Another factor that is likely to increase the length and stability of a play period is whether the young participants have acquired the art of sharing and taking turns. Again Miller indicates that these skills develop with experience.

It is interesting to watch the success and failure of young children as they learn to interact with their peers. The sooner a child learns to share and take turns, the smoother play periods with others will be. Children develop their own techniques for handling each other. A 4-year-old playmate of my son has his own technique for controlling their play periods: ''If you don't play _____ with me, I'll go home!''

So far we have been discussing social play in a relatively nonspecific fashion, considering the presence of more than one child as a social play period. However, it is more meaningful to look at social play in a more specific fashion. The social skills of a child change as the child develops. The play of 6-year-olds differs from the play of 3-year-olds in more ways than the size of the play group and the length of the play period.

In 1932 Parten observed the play of nursery school children and described their social

317

play as developing through a specific sequence of changes. Parten's work has been often quoted and generally accepted by most researchers who have observed the social interactions of young children.

Parten's sequence of the social interactions in play begins with unoccupied behavior. Unoccupied behavior is considered the least social and least mature form of play behavior. In unoccupied behavior the child may simply stand around or sit alone, apparently doing nothing special and not observing other children's play.

The second level of play is solitary play. In solitary play the child is occupied in playing alone. This play might involve toys or other objects but not other children. The next development is onlooker behavior. In onlooker play the child is not actually engaged in an ongoing play activity, but stands on the fringes of an activity and watches its progress. While being a bystander a child may occasionally interject a comment into the play of others but will not join in. It is speculated that the child has the desire to join in the play but is not yet ready to do so socially.

The next play level, according to Parten, is parallel play. In parallel play children are engaged in individual play in close proximity to other children. For instance, two children

Barbara McClinton

Fig. 14-3. The third level of Parten's sequence in the development of play is onlooker behavior. In onlooker behavior a child stands on the fringes of a play group, observing other children at play.

may be working on puzzles in the corner of the room, but neither actually enters the play of the other. The children may occasionally exchange a comment or toy, but not for any extended period. You might see parallel play as similar to the collective monologues Piaget describes. The children seem to be enjoying the presence of another child but apparently do not have the skills to maintain a true social interaction.

The next step in the play sequence is associative play. In associative play children play together in the sense that they join in each other's activities, may exchange comments, interject ideas, and exchange play materials. This level of play involves interest in and enjoyment of other children's presence and their activities. Again, however, due to lack of extensive social skills, the children's ability to maintain the play is shaky and the play may disintegrate into more individualistic play.

The final level of social play is true social cooperation, or cooperative play. At this level children have enough social skill to truly cooperate and subordinate their individual wishes to the wishes of the group to maintain the group's activity. At this point children are capable of both creating a goal for a group and working to reach it. The goal may be simple, such as building a 5-foot tower of blocks, or quite complex, such as taking roles for dramatic play.

Parten's sequence is assumed to depend on the acquisition of social skills. At the lower levels children are thought not to interact with others because they do not have the skills necessary for interaction. As the child's skills increase, so does his or her ability to participate in the activities of others. The most mature form of social play requires the ability of the child to cooperate on more than a superficial level. In other words, for mature social play the child needs to learn more than simple sharing and taking turns or, we might add, the fine art of threatening to go home.

Parten's sequence is fairly well accepted, and it is generally felt that the majority of 2-year-olds function at the solitary play level, 3-year-olds at the level of parallel play, and 4-year-olds at the associative play level (Ruben et al., 1976).

Recently, researchers have become interested in verifying this information that was obtained so long ago, and some have questioned the ordering of the levels in the sequence. For instance, Moore, Evertson, and Brophy (1974) have argued that solitary play may not be a more immature activity than either onlooker behavior or parallel play. They argue that for years people have considered solitary play in nursery school as immature and possibly unhealthy. However, when they subdivided solitary play activities into different activity categories they found that a large percentage of the solitary play they observed was positive activity on the part of the child. A third of solitary play involved goal-directed activity and 10% involved some form of educational activity, such as looking at books. Obviously, it is wrong to assume that the child who actively pursues a personal play goal, such as setting up the school's racetrack or looking at a book, lacks the social skill to participate in associative or cooperative play. It may be wrong to consider solitary play as less mature than other forms of play.

A second recent reconsideration of Parten's sequence has been undertaken by Ruben and co-workers (1976), who were interested in, among other things, replicating Parten's work and comparing the play activity of middle- and lower-class children. They found that lower-class children spend more time playing in a parallel fashion, while middle-class children play more frequently on the associative and cooperative levels. They speculated that this difference might be due in part to a lack of familiarity with nursery school toys on the part of the lower-class children. These toys may be more novel to them, and consequently they spend more time exploring the toys than they do interacting with their peers. That this may be an important possibility is supported by the work of Scholtz and Ellis (1975), who found that as the novelty of new play equipment wears off, preschool children spend more time interacting with their peers than they did when the play items were new and unfamiliar.

Incidentally, Ruben and associates (1976) also argue that solitary play is not necessarily a more immature form of play than parallel play and onlooker activity. Apparently solitary play needs to be reexamined and perhaps subdivided into major activity categories to be better understood.

It should be readily apparent that preschool children engage in social play activities with other preschoolers and that the success and stability of these interactions depends to a large measure on the child's ability to interact in a positive fashion with the other child. Social play is an important area of experience and learning for the child, just as mastery play and make-believe play are.

TOYS

As we have seen, children at play are doing more than filling their days. They are actively acquiring skills, knowledge, and feelings that are important to healthy development. Once we are aware of the importance of play to a child's development, we should also be concerned with the type of play materials that we provide.

Toys and play objects may strongly influence the play of a child. Miller (1974) has expressed the belief that not only the type of toys available to the child influence the child's play, but also the number of toys available. This is particularly relevant with young children, who are much more likely to be distracted by several play possibilities present at once. Whether this should be considered a negative situation is debatable. Having several toys available may distract the 3-year-old so that play with any one toy is short, reducing the child's opportunity to fully explore the toy's possibilities. However, if the child is likely to be distracted anyway during play, having several toys available may offer more and varied opportunities for stimulation.

A more straightforward question about toys for children involves the amount of structure in the toy. For example, some toys, such as clay or Play-Doh, are unstructured completely in the sense that the child determines how the toy will become involved in play. The child might fashion objects from the clay, make designs in it, attempt to stick paper to the wall with it, or use it to support Tinkertoys in an upright position. Other toys are highly structured in that they are so detailed or realistic that their function is determined before play begins. A good example of a highly structured toy is the miniature stove that looks just like the one in the child's kitchen.

Many people have debated the benefits and shortcomings of highly structured toys. It is almost impossible not to notice how realistic dolls are today. Not only are some dolls, including boy dolls, anatomically complete, but they talk, crawl, wet, sleep, fuss, and so forth. Some people argue that the realism of these dolls stimulates the child to interact with the doll on a more realistic level, thereby exercising social skills and presumably child-care skills. Others argue that this realism in dolls reduces the likelihood that the child will exercise imagination during play. Even without considering the thoughts of psychological researchers on this topic, a sensible resolution of this debate might be to suggest that the child have access to both highly structured and minimally structured playthings, if possible.

Researchers themselves indicate a belief that both structured and unstructured playthings have their usefulness. Singer (1973) expresses the belief that unstructured toys may stimulate more make-believe play. Not only does the lack of structure almost require that the child create uses for the toy, it also makes the toy more appropriate for varied play situations. A large piece of cloth may be at times a tablecloth, a piece of clothing, a tent, a pillow, or a magic carpet, whereas a miniature helicopter is always a helicopter.

Singer (1973) also sees highly structured toys as particularly useful to the 2- to 2½-year-old child. Miniature versions of adult items may be very stimulating to children of this age. Small plastic tools, for example, give the young child an opportunity to imitate the behavior or activity of an adult and therefore the opportunity for role playing. Without the miniature tool, the child might not be stimulated to try the adult role in play.

Both Singer and Miller express a belief, however, that children may tire more quickly of highly structured toys because all their play possibilities may be exhausted in a few play sessions. The effect of this might be heightened in older children. On the other hand, the structured nature of some toys also makes them more complex, therefore affording the child more opportunity to manipulate the toy. This benefit appears to be particularly worthwhile to the child developing fine motor skills. Small children are very frequently intrigued by opening doors in little cars or buildings. One final word on structured toys seems relevant. As any mother can tell you, the more complex a toy is, the more likely it is to break.

Once a decision has been made as to the selection of highly structured or unstructured toys, another consideration becomes important. A toy must be suitable for the child's developmental stage. A toy that requires the child to exercise some skill or ability not yet developed can only be frustrating or uninteresting to the child. Not only should a toy buyer consider the skills a child might need to enjoy a particular toy, but should consider the size of the toy and its parts relative to the size and age of the child. Infants should never be given toys with removable parts small enough to be swallowed. On the other hand, toys given to infants should not be so large as to be overwhelming. Try to imagine what a beach ball rolling toward you would be like if you were 6 months old.

Gesell and Ilg (1943) suggest toys appropriate for children of various ages, which may be a useful guide. They suggest rattles and squeaking toys (without removable squeakers) for infants under 3 months. For slightly older infants teething toys and cradle gyms are considered appropriate. For infants nearing a year they suggest nested measuring cups that may be placed inside each other as well as serving as containers to be filled and emptied. Other items appropriate for the year-old child include blocks, balls, bowls, and water toys. As the child becomes increasingly mobile, toys that may be ridden, pushed, or pulled are appropriate.

For the preschooler, toy choices are nearly endless. Some of the suggestions made by Gesell and Ilg include climbing apparatus, sandboxes, wagons, clay, crayons, easels and paints, musical toys, and furniture items.

One final word on toy selection. A child's toys may be very influential in the play patterns of the child, and they should be chosen with this in mind. Many toys have traditionally been deemed appropriate for only one sex (recall the discussion on toys and sex typing in Chapter 13). A thoughtful parent or teacher will consider the impact toys may have on the child's opportunity to develop one set of skills over another. For example, consider what a child given dolls and toy stoves learns, as opposed to the child given an erector set.

Optimally, toys given to a child should be appropriate for the child's skill levels, allowing the child to exercise these skills for mastery and possibly stimulating the child's development further. Toys should also be fun; it is not necessary to choose only educational toys for a child.

SUMMARY

It should be clear that although there is no agreement among theorists concerning the play of children, children's play is important to their healthy development. Through play, children learn and grow in many ways. They exercise newly emerging physical, cognitive, and social skills. They also give expression to strong emotions and learn to cope with troubling experiences in play. Play may be fun for the child, but it is also a very serious process in the child's development.

REFERENCES

Fenson, L., Kagan, J., Kearsly, R. B., & Zelage, P. R. The developmental progression of manipulative play in the first two years. *Child Development,* 1976, **47,** 232-236.

Gesell, A., Halverson, H. M., Thompson, H., Ilg, F. R., Castner, B. M., & Ames, L. B. *The first five years of life: a guide to the study of the preschool child.* New York: Harper & Row, Publishers, 1940.

Gesell, A., & Ilg, F. R. *Infant and child in the culture of today: the guidance of development in home and nursery school.* New York: Harper & Row, Publishers, 1943.

Miller, S. *The psychology of play.* New York: Jason Aronson, Inc., 1974.

Moore, N. V., Evertson, C. M., & Brophy, J. E. Solitary play: some functional reconsiderations. *Developmental Psychology,* 1974, **10**(6), 830-834.

Rosen, C. E. The effects of sociodramatic play on problem-solving behavior among culturally disadvantaged preschool children. *Child Development,* 1974, **45,** 920-927.

Rubin, K. H., Maioni, T. L., and Hornung, M. Free play behaviors in middle- and lower-class preschoolers: Parten and Piaget revisited. *Child Development,* 1976, **47,** 414-419.

Scholtz, G. J. L., & Ellis, M. J. Repeated exposure to objects and peers in a play setting. *Journal of Experimental Child Psychology,* 1975, **19,** 448-455.

Singer, J. L. *The child's world of make-believe experimental studies of imaginative play* (chapters by E. Biblow, J. T. Freyberg, S. Gottlieb, & M. A. Pulaski). New York: Academic Press, Inc., 1973.

Stamm, I. The multiple functions of play: a review and examination of the Piagetian and psychoanalytic points of view. In J. Travers (Ed.), *New children: the first 6 years.* Stamford, Conn.: Greylock Publishers, 1976, pp. 79-96.

The contents of boys' and girls' rooms as an index of parents' behavior

Harriet L. Rheingold
Kaye V. Cook

University of North Carolina at Chapel Hill

The furnishings and toys of boys' and girls' rooms were canvassed on the assumption that differences, if found, would indicate parental ideas about appropriateness by sex. The children were 48 boys and 48 girls under 6 years of age, each having his own room. The results showed that the boys were provided more vehicles, educational-art materials, sports equipment, toy animals, depots, machines, fauna, and military toys. Girls were provided more dolls, doll houses, and domestic toys. The rooms of boys were more often decorated with animal motifs; those of girls, with floral motifs and lace, fringe, and ruffles. The differences do indeed show differences in parental behavior.

Differences in the behavior of boys and girls are attributed in part to differences in how parents behave toward them (see Mischel 1970 for a review). Differences in parental behaviors have been obtained from questionnaires, interviews, and observations in the home and laboratory. The present study offers another measure of such differences: the furnishings and contents of the rooms of young boys and girls. We propose that how parents furnish the rooms of their sons and daughters, including the toys they supply, provides an index to their ideas about appropriateness by sex and thus indirectly may indicate differences in their behavior toward their sons and daughters.

The proposal holds especially when, as here, the rooms of children under 6 years of age are studied. Children so young may indeed express their preferences and wishes, but it is the parents—now the mother, now the father—who decide which toy to buy or to place in the child's room (if a gift from others), as well as the kind of curtains, pictures, etc., that furnish the room. Thus, any differences found in the contents of boys' and girls' rooms are held to reflect differences in parental behavior.

The effect on children of the furnishings and objects in their rooms can only be surmised. Still, since they offer children different experiences, the contents may indeed instruct them in what is proper for their sex.

The primary purpose of this study was to look for sex differences, but since the children were selected by age, age differences are also reported.

METHOD
The sample

The contents of the rooms of 96 children between the ages of 1 and 71.6 months were recorded. Each child had his own room. The children included four boys and four girls at each half-year of life. Year 1 designates the children under 1 year of age; year 2, those in the second year of life, and so on.

From *Child Development*, 1975, **46**, 459-463. © 1975 by the Society for Research in Child Development, Inc. All rights reserved.

The subjects were obtained primarily from the census of births at the North Carolina Memorial Hospital in Chapel Hill but also from names volunteered by parents already visited. Homes in well-to-do residential areas were selected to insure the likelihood of a child's having his own room. The purpose of the study was explained to the parents by telephone, and only three refused permission.

All the children lived in privately owned homes except for five of the younger children, who lived in rented apartments. All but one were white. Order of birth was approximately similar by sex; for example, 27 boys and 29 girls were firstborn children. The occupational status of the majority of the fathers (40 of the boys' fathers and 34 of the girls') fell into the first of Hollingshead's seven categories—that of executives and proprietors of large concerns and major professionals (Hollingshead & Redlich 1958); 72% of the fathers held university-related positions.

Procedure

The survey was carried out between December 14, 1972 and February 28, 1973. On any one day the rooms which were visited as nearly as possible kept the age-sex categories equally filled.

The observer recorded on a checklist all the furnishings and toys in the room. In addition, color photographs were taken of each part of the room to supplement the checklist data. Toys elsewhere in the home were not canvassed, although a record was made of the number of children's rooms that did not contain the major part of their toys.

Classes of items

Classes of items were established from the furnishings and toys of the rooms; when the number of objects was too small to form a class by itself, related objects were combined. For the 13 resulting classes the data were the number of items present in a room. These classes, in alphabetical order, were defined as follows: *animal furnishings*—furnishings (including furniture, bedspreads, curtains, pillows, rugs, pictures, posters, and mobiles) bearing the figures of animals; *books*—children's books; *dolls*—small-scale figures of human beings, including toy soldiers, cowboys, and Indians; *educational-art materials*—a combined class of items including charts of numbers or letters, typewriters, materials for drawing and coloring, and clay; *floral furnishings*—furnishings (as above) bearing the figures of flowers and plants; *furniture*—beds, chests, toy boxes, etc.; *musical items*—musical instruments, radios, record players, etc.; *"ruffles"*—bedspreads, pillows, curtains, and rugs bearing ruffles, fringe, or lace; *spatial-temporal objects*—a combined class of items relating to the properties of space, matter, energy, and time, including shape-sorting toys, outer-space toys, magnets, clocks, etc.; *sports equipment*—toys such as balls, skates, and kites; *stuffed animals*—material marked or shaped like an animal, with a soft filling; *toy animals*—toy animals and their houses, such as barns and zoos; and *vehicles*—toys representing carriers of people or goods, such as cars, airplanes, and trains. A frequency of 10 was arbitrarily assigned to large collections of small cars and trucks.

Some very infrequent classes of items were tallied by the number of children's rooms containing them instead of by the number of items in a class. These classes, in alphabetical order, were defined as follows: *depots*—toys representing places for the storing or servicing of vehicles, such as garages, train stations, and airports; *"doll houses"*—houses, beds, carriages, etc., for dolls; *domestic objects*—toy stoves, refrigerators, set of dishes, etc.; *fauna*—live animals and animal cages; *flora*—live and artificial flowers and plants; *machines*—toys representing equipment for doing work, such as tractors, cranes, and bulldozers; and *military toys*—toys relating to soldiers, arms, or war, excluding dolls.

A number of other objects were identified but occurred too infrequently to analyze even by the number of rooms in which they were present. These objects included Bobo dolls and puppets; banks and cash registers; combs, brushes, and mirrors on the tops of dressers; and doctor and nurse kits; these are not reported.

Color of course was a characteristic of all objects but was in most instances too variegated to yield to tallying.

Statistical treatment

The 13 classes of items tallied by the number present in a room were analyzed by a multivariate analysis of variance, using the F approximation for Wilks's Λ criterion, for the main effects of sex and age and their interaction. Because of inequality of the cell variances, the analysis was carried out on a square-root transformation of the frequencies.

The other seven classes of items that were tallied by the number of rooms containing them were analyzed for sex differences by χ^2 test.

RESULTS

The findings are based on the contents of the 96 rooms, even though for 21 children the major part of their toys were stored elsewhere in the house. Inspection showed that these 21 subjects were approximately similar by age and sex to the other 75 subjects.

The multivariate analysis of variance of the 13 classes for which the numbers of items were counted yielded a statistically significant sex $\times$ age interaction, $F\ (65,344) = 1.42, p < .03$, a significant sex effect, $F\ (13,72) = 10.42, p < .001$, and a significant age effect, $F\ (65,344) = 2.74$, $p < .001$. The individual univariate F tests can therefore be reported.

The sex × age interaction: vehicles

The univariate p value for vehicles was $< .001$; the other 12 classes of items as a group yielded a nonsignificant multivariate interaction ($p > .10$). Therefore, only the class of vehicles was responsible for the reliable multivariate sex $\times$ age interaction. As the actual nontransformed frequencies in table 1 show, boys had more vehicular toys than girls at every age. In fact, the mean number for girls was always less than one. The analysis also showed a reliable age effect for males ($p < .001$), but not for females ($p > .10$). Furthermore, the analysis of sex effects within age showed that the difference was not reliable at year 1 ($p > .10$), but was at year 2 ($p < .05$) and also at years 3-6 ($p < .001$).

The number of vehicles summed over all ages was 375 for boys and 17 for girls. The difference must be still larger because a count of 10 was assigned to large collections of small cars and trucks. A more detailed analysis showed that no girl's room contained a wagon, bus, boat, kiddie car, motorcycle, snowmobile, or trailer, a subset of vehicles of which boys had 36.

Table 1. Mean number of vehicles by age and sex of child

Age (yr)	Male	Female	Mean
1	0.1	0.0	0.1
2	2.8	0.0	1.4
3	11.4	0.6	6.0
4	10.4	0.8	5.6
5	17.2	0.5	8.9
6	5.0	0.2	2.6
Mean	7.8	0.4	

Note: Mean number in the eight rooms of each sex at each age.

Sex differences

Table 2 shows the nontransformed mean numbers by sex of the remaining 12 classes of items, together with their levels of reliability by univariate tests. The rooms of boys contained more animal furnishings, more educational-art materials, more spatial-temporal toys, more sports equipment, and more toy animals. The rooms of girls contained more dolls, more floral furnishings, and more "ruffles."

Table 2. Sex differences in mean number of items

Class of items	Male	Female	p Value
Animal furnishings	6.8	5.0	<.05
Books	28.1	23.9	N.S.
Dolls	3.6	7.0	<.001
Ed-art materials	1.1	0.6	<.05
Floral furnishings	3.0	4.5	<.001
Furniture	6.2	6.3	N.S.
Musical objects	1.4	1.2	N.S.
"Ruffles"	0.9	2.0	<.01
Spatial-temporal	1.7	0.8	<.001
Sports equipment	1.0	0.4	<.05
Stuffed animals	4.1	4.4	N.S.
Toy animals	4.8	2.3	<.01

Note: Mean number in the 48 rooms of each sex.

No differences by sex appeared in the number of children's books, furniture, musical objects, and stuffed animals.

Types of dolls. Even though the rooms of girls contained more dolls—almost twice as many as those of boys—the boys' rooms also contained dolls. Inspection, however, suggested differences in the kinds of dolls found in these two sets of rooms.

To measure the difference, all dolls were first separated into three categories: male, female, and baby. Because many rooms of the boys contained none of some of these classes, the analysis was carried out by χ^2 test of the number of rooms in which each class was found. The results showed that only eight of the 48 boys' rooms contained a female doll; in contrast, 41 of the 48 girls' rooms did, $\chi^2 = 42.69, p < .001$. Similarly, only three of the boys' rooms contained a baby doll, while 26 of the girls' did, $\chi^2 = 23.91, p < .001$. Male dolls, however, were present in 36 of the boys' rooms and 28 of the girls' rooms, a difference that was not reliable. Thus, although girls as well as boys were provided male dolls, girls were provided female and baby dolls much more often.

To measure still another difference, all dolls were now divided into two classes: jointed or not. The results showed that jointed dolls were present in only eight of the boys' rooms but in 30 of the girls', $\chi^2 = 19.21, p < .001$.

Age differences

Only five of the 12 classes of items showed age differences by the univariate tests. The frequency of animal furnishings decreased from a peak of 8.9 at year 2 to 2.1 at year 6 ($p < .001$). The number of children's books increased markedly from a mean of 1.9 at year 1 to a mean of 60.2 at year 6 ($p < .001$). The number of dolls also showed an age difference, increasing from a mean of 1.6 at year 1 to a peak of 10.5 at year 5 ($p < .01$). The number of educational-art materials increased with age ($p < .001$), while floral furnishings decreased from a peak at year 2 ($p < .05$).

Sex differences of infrequent items

Objects that occurred too infrequently to be included in the multivariate analysis were tallied by the number of male and female rooms containing them. The results showed that males were provided more depots, $\chi^2 = 14.13, p < .001$, fauna, $\chi^2 = 5.55, p < .05$, machines, $\chi^2 = 5.69, p < .05$, and military toys, $\chi^2 = 5.69, p < .05$; females, more "doll houses," $\chi^2 = 16.44, p < .001$, and domestic items, $\chi^2 = 6.77, p < .01$. Although the girls' rooms contained more flora, the difference was not reliable.

No girl's room contained a depot of any kind, or a live animal or an animal cage. No girl had a crane, cement mixer, front-end loader, corn harvester, or lawnmower, toys that were found in seven of the boys' rooms. In the class of military toys, the boys had four cannons; the girls had none. In contrast, in the "doll houses" category, girls had 12 doll carriages, strollers, or swings; boys had none. Finally, in comparison with the 12 girls' rooms containing refrigerators, stoves, sinks, irons, pots and pans, and entire tea sets, in the rooms of two boys, both under 2 years of age, there was in one a coffeepot and in the other a set of spoons.

Quantity of toys

These children were well supplied with toys, as the data show. The recorder was often overwhelmed by the task of enumerating such quantities of objects. To document this fact, the number of all toys was subjected to an analysis of variance on the square-root transformation of the data. Although boys had more toys than girls at every age but year 4 (in fact, twice as many at year 3), the difference was not reliable ($p < .09$). The difference by age was reliable, $F (5,84) = 9.81$, $p < .001$, the mean frequency of the actual count increasing from 27.8 at year 1 to 90.6 at year 6. Since for a considerable number of the children the major part of their toys were stored elsewhere, these counts were surely an underestimate of all the toys they possessed.

DISCUSSION

The parents of these children did indeed provide different furnishings and toys for their sons and daughters. The rooms of boys contained more vehicles, more toys related to the physical properties of matter, more educational and art materials, more sports equipment, and more toy animals. More of their rooms contained toy depots, machines, and military toys. Animal motifs more often decorated the furnishings of their rooms. The dolls in boys' rooms were more often male dolls—cowboys, Indians and toy soldiers. The rooms of girls, in contrast, contained more dolls in all, especially more female and baby dolls, and more jointed, hence more realistic, dolls. Their rooms also contained more objects for the care of dolls and the home. The furnishings of their rooms were more often decorated with floral designs and more often embellished with lace, fringe, and ruffles.

These differences may come as no surprise. Still, they do contain a measure of surprise. The boys were provided more toys of more classes (depots, educational-art objects, machines, military toys, spatial-temporal objects, sports equipment, toy animals, and vehicles) than the girls (dolls, "doll houses," and domestic objects). Then, too, some differences were much larger than anticipated. Impressive was the much greater number of vehicles, the boys' most frequent class of toys, than the number of dolls, the girls' most frequent. As impressive was the complete absence of such toys as wagons, boats, buses, etc., in the girls' rooms, a class of objects frequently found in boys' rooms. Equally striking, on the other hand, was the almost total absence of baby dolls and toy domestic equipment in any boy's room. If, as is generally believed, our culture permits greater latitude for girls to behave like boys than for boys to behave like girls, one could account for the poorer showing of dolls among boys, but not for the very small showing of vehicles among girls. (In our laboratory 18-month-old girls spend as much time as boys playing with a large plastic truck.) Finally, counter to expectation, girls were not any better supplied than boys with books and musical objects.

The conclusions are based, of course, upon the choice of classes. Straightforward as the classes seem, the category of dolls especially presented difficulties. Although toy soldiers met the definition of "a small-scale figure of a human being used especially as a child's plaything," they could as well have been classified as military objects. But how then to classify cowboys and Indians? Nevertheless, had some or all of these figures been classified as military objects, the results would not have been much different; girls would have had still more dolls and boys still more military objects.

The conclusions reached here apply to a small sample of a population, special in many ways (high educational and socioeconomic level), that was studied at a certain time. The characteristics that make this sample special are those very ones that might lead one to expect fewer rather than more sex differences, the parents being informed on current efforts to provide more similar opportunities for boys and girls, more ready to challenge cultural stereotypes, and presumably more sensi-

327

tive to the effects of their behavior on their children. Yet in many ways the rooms of their sons and daughters closely resembled the rooms of boys and girls pictured in mail-order catalogs and home-decorating magazines. What would we expect in the larger culture? Even though having one's own room may not be modal, still the majority of the children in the United States have some commercially produced toys. It seems likely that among these other samples of children, the sex differences reported here would be at least as large.

The effect on children's behavior

The rooms of children constitute a not inconsiderable part of their environment. Here they go to bed and wake up; here they spend some part of every day. Their rooms determine the things they see and find for amusement and instruction. That their rooms have an effect on their present and subsequent behavior can be assumed; a standard is set that may in part account for some differences in the behavior of girls and boys. Clear in the findings of this study was the extent to which the boys were provided objects that encouraged activities directed away from home—toward sports, cars, animals, and the military—and the girls, objects that encouraged activities directed toward the home—keeping house and caring for children.

The sex differences aside, the objective bystander may well ponder the effect of the sheer quantity of toys found in these rooms on children's distractibility today and their attitude toward the exploitation of the environment tomorrow. Children—or rather the parents—are heavy consumers of toys.

An index of parental behavior

By their youth we have ruled out children as the providers of their toys or the furnishings of their rooms and have assigned the responsibility to the parents. Yet one might counter this conclusion by arguing that the parents were guided by what they found their children enjoyed playing with and, despite their young age, might assign a measure of responsibility to them. But that argument by itself would not account for the large number of toys of any one class and certainly not for the complete absence of any object of a class; the children's interest could have little influence if they were given no opportunity to exercise an interest. In the last analysis, the parents need not be influenced by their children's interests, or even requests or demands, if they are guided by some more compelling set of principles.

The many sex differences found in the contents of the rooms, therefore, do indeed qualify as evidence of differences in parental behavior. It is not parsimonious to assume that one set of principles guides their behavior in providing their children one setting rather than another, one toy rather than another, and that different sets of principles guide other behaviors. It may therefore be concluded that the differences in how parents furnish the rooms of their boys and girls may well document differences in other classes of their behavior toward their sons and daughters.

REFERENCES

Hollingshead, A. B., & Redlich, F. C. *Social class and mental illness: a community study.* New York: Wiley, 1958.
Mischel, W. Sex-typing and socialization. In P. H. Mussen (Ed.), *Carmichael's manual of child psychology.* (3d ed.) Vol. 2. New York: Wiley, 1970.

PART FIVE

FOSTERING
DEVELOPMENT

Chapter 15

Applying psychology to children

Elaine M. Ward

Throughout this book applications of specific research findings and theories have been suggested. Parents and teachers, though, often seek more general advice about handling children. This chapter is intended to provide general advice for dealing with common problems encountered with normal children.

"EXPERT" ADVICE FOR REARING CHILDREN

Plenty of people are willing to give advice to others about how to be good parents. Some of the would-be advisors have special training and experience with children, which qualifies them as "experts." Experts cannot provide a solution for every problem, but their suggestions are often useful. One clue to help separate valid from invalid advice is to look for themes that are repeated in several sources. Helpful techniques for rearing children are likely to be discovered by more than one expert.

Benjamin Spock

If you are not yet 30 years old, chances are that Dr. Spock had a hand (at least indirectly) in your upbringing. Spock's encyclopedic *Baby and Child Care* is loaded with practical advice on every conceivable question parents might ask (even sizes and styles of babies' undershirts!).

One of Spock's central themes is that children are flexible. Parents need not worry about ruining their children, because children can adapt to a variety of situations. Spock suggests that parents trust their own feelings and not rely too heavily on the advice of others and that even his own advice should not be taken too literally! Parents should enjoy their children. A child cannot be spoiled by too much affectionate fun.

Spock has been accused of being permissive because he advocated a relaxed, loving approach to childrearing at a time when most experts recommended a strict approach (feed on a 4-hour schedule, avoid picking up a crying baby, and so on). Spock's views on childrearing have not changed in this respect since the first edition of *Baby and Child Care* was published in 1945. Now that most everyone else has become more tolerant, Spock seems almost old-fashioned in his advice regarding discipline. Spock states that parents must sometimes be strict in order to guide a child toward acceptable behavior.

> Good hearted parents who aren't afraid to be firm when it is necessary can get good
> results with either moderate strictness or moderate permissiveness. On the other hand,
> a strictness that comes from harsh feelings or a permissiveness that is timid or vacillating
> can lead to poor results. The real issue is what spirit the parent puts into managing the
> child and what attitude is engendered in the child as a result.*

Permissiveness will not result in unruly, uncontrolled monsters. Studies of delinquents demonstrate that "most of them had suffered more from lack of love in childhood than from lack of punishment." Punishment is not needed as often as some parents use it; children can develop responsibility and respect without ever being punished. If parents do use punishment, though, it will not necessarily warp a child.

Baby and child care. Copyright © 1945, 1946, 1957, 1968 by Benjamin Spock, M.D. Reprinted by permission of Pocket Books, a Simon & Schuster division of Gulf & Western Corporation.

What causes parents the most trouble, according to Spock, is "today's child-centered viewpoint."

> Many conscientious parents [tend] to keep their eyes exclusively focused on their child, thinking about what he needs from them and from the community, instead of thinking about what the world, the neighborhood, and the family will be needing from the child and then making sure that he will grow up to meet such obligations. (p. xvi)

The child-centered viewpoint often is expressed in "needless self-sacrifice." Some parents give time, attention, and material things to their children and then feel guilty for sneaking out for an evening alone. Parents who act like martyrs harm both their children and themselves. This behavior causes parents to resent their child, and it makes the parents no fun to be around.

Spock advises parents to recognize their own feelings and to encourage children to do the same. Parents have needs of their own. They get frustrated and cross. If parents cannot accept these antisocial feelings, their child will develop a dread of his or her own feelings. A child (or parent) who habitually denies natural feelings eventually becomes an emotional cripple.

Parents should recognize three other common, though unpleasant, feelings.

1. New parents may not love their infant. They must realize that affection for any new person develops gradually. Considering how unattractive newborn babies are, it is no surprise that parents do not automatically feel love.

2. Parents may like one child more than another. They may be disappointed that one child is not as charming or attractive or intelligent or physically coordinated as they had hoped. Different feelings for different people are completely natural. Instead of trying to love them all the same, the parent should recognize the differences and love each child for what he or she is.

3. Children are sometimes angry and resentful. This is especially hard to accept for parents who resented their own parents and resolved to rear their children differently. Anger and resentment can never be entirely eliminated. Parents who try to avoid any expression of negative feelings prevent a child from learning how to deal with these feelings.

Four of Spock's emphases, then, are that children are adaptable, that the spirit of discipline is more important than being strict or being permissive, that parents should attend to their own needs as well as the needs of their children, and that parents must accept negative feelings in themselves and in their children.

Toward the end of his book, in a discussion of working mothers, Spock recommends that women not work outside the home if they have children younger than 3 years.

> Useful, well-adjusted citizens are the most valuable possessions a country has, and good mother care during early childhood is the surest way to produce them. It doesn't make sense to let mothers go to work making dresses in a factory or tapping typewriters in an office, and have them pay other people to do a poorer job of bringing up their children. . . . The important thing for a mother to realize is that the younger the child, the more necessary it is for him to have a steady, loving person taking care of him. In most cases, the mother is the best one to give him this feeling of "belonging." (p. 563)

Many psychologists (including your authors) disagree with this recommendation. The scientific evidence bearing on the proposition that an infant needs *a* steady, loving caretaker is not sufficient to justify any definite conclusions, for or against. Would two steady, loving persons who alternated caring for the child be just as beneficial? We simply do not know. If we eventually confirm that a single constant caretaker is best, why must this person be the mother? Many fathers are undoubtedly more suited than mothers for caring for children. Advice regarding working mothers is merely opinion based on personal observations. Spock has one opinion, shared by a number of prominent experts on children; the opposite opinion is also held by many respected authorities

Fig. 15-1. Can grandparents be effective substitutes for parents who work?

333

on children. The only opinion on this subject that most psychologists share is that unhappy mothers are likely to have unhappy children. It seems reasonable, then, for mothers to pursue the career they prefer, whether it is working outside the home or full-time childrearing.

Haim Ginott

Haim Ginott first burst on the advice-to-parents scene in 1965 and has become almost as famous as Benjamin Spock. In *Between Parent and Child,* Ginott expressed in slightly different words some of the same suggestions Spock made 20 years before.

Ginott's message is that parents would get along better with children if they (the parents) spoke to the children in a different manner. Criticism, writes Ginott, should be directed at a *behavior,* not at a child's *personality.* If a child loses a sweater at school, for example, the parent may be tempted to call the child stupid or forgetful. Ginott suggests that the parent should comment on the loss of the sweater and perhaps point out the consequences of the loss, but not engage in name calling. A possible comment is "You lost another sweater. I guess you'll be wearing your gray one for the rest of the school year." Assaults on the child's character lower self-esteem, but they will not teach the child acceptable behavior. In the same vein, praise should be directed at a behavior; if the child's personality is praised, he or she may feel pressured to be "good" all the time. "The table looks pretty; you did a good job of setting it" is more appropriate than "You are such a helpful child," because children know they are not always helpful.

In addition to criticism and praise, Ginott also suggests a method for phrasing rules. Rather than "Stop hitting your sister," a parent should state the general rule "People are not for hurting." This particular device can grow tiresome. A mother who continually told her boys "Beds are not for jumping," "The bath is not for swimming," "Food is not for throwing," and so forth, was finally told by a friend "Ginott is not for copying!"

On the subject of responsibility, Ginott warns parents not to expect that giving a child chores will automatically foster responsible behavior. A child has a *choice* on some matters, such as whether to have beans or peas for dinner or whether to buy the blue coat or the green one (if the parent approves of both coats). On other matters, the child merely has a *voice.* Matters such as whether to go to school are ultimately the parents' responsibility. The child's views should be considered, but the final decision is the parents'. Responsibility is developed by allowing the child to accept the consequences of choices. Children can only learn from their mistakes if they are allowed to make them.

Ginott also warns against self-defeating behavior, such as threats, bribes, sarcasm, rudeness, and sermons, which in the long run cause more harm than good. Note, however, that when Ginott discusses threats and bribes, he does not distinguish between practical uses of incentives (see Chapter 6) and irrational threats and bribes. If used improperly, incentives are counterproductive, but the same can be said of any device. Ginott does not address himself to productive uses of threats and bribes.

Ginott offers two items of advice with which we cannot agree. Both indicate a Freudian bent to Ginott's thinking, which is not appropriate in this day and age.

1. Ginott adopts a restrictive attitude toward normal curiosity about the human body. He claims, for example, that seeing a parent's nude body will stimulate incestuous desires; that masturbation is inherently offensive, and parents should state clearly that this activity is unacceptable; that certain words should be expressly forbidden; and that children should satisfy their curiosity about other children's bodies only by asking questions of their parents, not by looking. Such restrictive attitudes usually encourage intense interest and silliness about sexual matters. Children are more likely to develop a casual, matter-of-fact attitude toward their bodies if their parents are casual and matter-of-fact.

2. Ginott encourages sexist methods of childrearing. He advises, for example, that mothers avoid working outside the home and fathers avoid mothering activities, such as feeding a baby, lest the child's sex roles become confused; that the father defend the mother from an abusive child (as if she cannot defend herself); and that parents deliberately foster behavior conforming to traditional sex stereotypes.

> Boys should be allowed to be more boisterous [than girls] both because of their greater energy and because society requires them to be more assertive. . . . They should not be expected to be as neat and as compliant as girls, or to have ladylike manners. The dictum that "boys will be boys" is a valid one. . . . It is appropriate for a Father to compliment his daughter on her looks, dress, and feminine pursuits. It is inappropriate for him to engage her in [energetic play]. (Ginott, 1965, pp. 203-205)

Ginott goes on to say that feminine behavior in boys is sufficient reason to seek psychotherapy. Most psychologists strongly oppose these restrictive and sexist standards. Ginott's views on sex and sex roles place him in a small (some would say miniscule) minority of psychologists.

Thomas Gordon

Like Haim Ginott, Thomas Gordon proposes new ways of talking with children to encourage responsible behavior and harmonious family relationships. In *P.E.T. Parent Effectiveness Training,* Gordon states that parents want to attain these goals but must be trained to react differently to their children. P.E.T. is based on the assumption that children can become responsible, self-controlled individuals with *no* punishment or methods based on fear. Parents can teach responsibility by helping children find their own solutions to their problems. The parent does not *solve* the child's problem; the parent simply sets the stage for the child to develop his or her own solution. The parent accomplishes this by *active listening,* which includes reflecting the child's feelings (but not parroting words). When a son says "The other boys won't play with me; they all hate me," a reply demonstrating active listening is "It must make you feel crummy when they all ignore you." (An example of parroting is "You feel like the boys all hate you because they won't play with you.") By reflecting the child's feelings, the parent acts like a mirror, which helps the child perceive his own feelings more clearly. Both the words and the nonverbal messages (e.g., gestures, tone) of the parent should indicate *acceptance* of the child's feelings. The parent need not believe that the feelings are justified by the facts; the parent must only accept that the child's feelings are real, no

335

matter the events that gave rise to those feelings. Through active listening and acceptance, the parent can learn to resolve family conflicts so that all parties "win"; no one "loses." Parents trained to use Gordon's method have been quite successful in settling normal family arguments. A word of caution: parents must guard against using only the form, not the substance, of the method. Application of the form alone can lead to mechanical language, as sometimes occurs with Ginott's suggested style of talking with children.

Lee Salk

Emotional disturbance is the most serious health problem in the United States today. Lee Salk urges parents to help prevent this problem by attending to the emotional development of their children. Parents want their children to be happy and well adjusted, but often they do not know how to encourage healthy emotional development. To help parents learn ways to foster healthy adjustment, Salk has written *What Every Child Would Like His Parents to Know*.

Salk's book provides specific advice on a variety of issues. Five themes can be abstracted from his suggestions.

1. An interesting environment is necessary to stimulate a child's perceptual, motor, and mental development.
2. Parents should meet a child's needs, which are often expressed by crying. Children in distress should be comforted. Parents need not worry about spoiling children by taking care of them.
3. Patience is required for tasks such as weaning and toilet training. Children will let their parents know when they are ready for these accomplishments. Trying to force a child to learn independence at an early age will produce frustration and failure.
4. Children need discipline. Learning about acceptable behavior and developing a sense of right and wrong should begin when the child first begins to crawl around and get into things. Discipline is not the same as punishment. Punishment may be a necessary evil at times, but ordinarily a sense of self-control can be established most easily by rewarding acceptable behavior.
5. Trust is a sign of healthy emotional development. In the first year of life, trust is established by taking good care of the child. With an older child, trust is established by honesty. When children ask about going to the doctor or sex or strained relationships with relatives, a straightforward, truthful answer is best.

Salk believes that the best person to care for a child is the parent. Like Spock, he recommends that mothers not work outside the home, at least until an infant is 9 or 10 months old. Mothers of older children who prefer to work should try to arrange a schedule that allows them to be home half of the day. Salk recommends that fathers definitely play a role in caring for a child, but "for obvious reasons, fathers are generally not able to spend as much time with their children as mothers are." (One might wonder how working mothers can rearrange their careers so easily if working fathers find it so difficult.)

Burton White

The four experts discussed have emphasized social and emotional development. Burton White, in contrast, offers advice about stimulating a young child's intellectual growth. The greatest impact on a child's mental development is the informal education provided by a family in the first 3 years, according to the views of White expressed in *The First Three Years of Life*.

The first 8 months, writes White, are "probably the easiest of all times for parents. If they provide the baby with a normal amount of love, attention, and physical care, nature will pretty much take care of the rest." (White, 1975, p. 9) Parents of an infant should make the infant feel loved and cared for, help the child develop specific skills (such as sitting or reaching), and encourage curiosity by providing interesting surroundings. Natural play with an infant is a fun way to accomplish these three goals. The end of this period of child development is marked by the child's ability to move around and to understand a few words.

After 8 months, the task of guiding mental growth becomes more difficult, and most parents do not know the best ways to stimulate mental growth between 8 months and 3 years. "Relatively few families, perhaps no more than ten percent, manage to get their children through the eight- to thirty-six-month age period as well educated and developed as they can and should be." (p. 103) White and his associates located families doing an outstanding job of fostering mental development and observed what these families did. Based on these observations, White makes the following recommendations to parents.

1. Recognize what motivates the child. By 8 months, a normal child is motivated by physical needs, such as hunger and freedom from pain. The child also has three major interests: attention from the primary caretaker, exploration of the surroundings, and mastery of motor skills.

2. Stimulate language development. By 8 months, children understand a few words. By 3 years, they understand most of the language they will use the rest of their lives in ordinary conversation. The child does not *use* language in an adult way, but understands almost everything adults say.

3. Encourage curiosity. Young children, like young kittens, are immensely curious. "Nothing is more fundamental to solid educational development than pure uncontaminated curiosity." (p. 112)

4. Facilitate social development. By the end of the third year, a child learns about parents' expectations, moods, and soft spots. "He may have . . . developed into a delightful human being who is a pleasure to live with, . . . or he may have developed into an overindulged child who constantly badgers his mother, . . . [or he may have] learned to be an isolate, one who has never had the pleasure of a free and easy rewarding relationship with other human beings." (p. 112)

5. Nurture the roots of intelligence. Between 8 months and 3 years, a child learns about simple cause-and-effect relationships. This understanding is the structure on which later intelligence is based. Allow active exploration.

6. Design a physical environment in which exploration is safe for the child and not too nerve-wracking for adults. Instead of confining the child to a playpen, White

advises putting away everything breakable and letting the child "have at it."

7. Be available for "consultation" when the child asks for information or help. Effective parents also know when *not* to assist, when to let the child proceed alone.

8. Set limits. Realistic limits, consistently enforced, help a child become more agreeable *and* more intelligent, because they help the child learn about causes and effects. White found that effective parents rarely told a child to behave more than twice. If the child continued the forbidden activity after an order and one reminder, effective parents responded by removing the child from the situation, delivering a light pat to the child's bottom, or distracting the child's attention. Ineffective parents, on the other hand, tend to repeat an order several times and fail to follow up when the child continues misbehaving.

Like Salk and Spock, White advises mothers of young children not to work outside the home. He admits, however, that a child of a working mother can develop quite well if the mother devotes considerable time to the child every day, especially if the father is also an active participant in the child's affairs.

A more serious problem than working mothers is siblings of nearly the same age. With two (or more) children less than 3 years old, parents simply do not have time to provide each child with needed attention. The parents are exhausted, and the children are short-changed. White urges parents to space children at least 3 years apart.

Contrary to what one might expect, White does *not* recommend enrolling a child in an "educationally powerful" nursery school. He favors nursery schools, both for the sake of the child and the sake of the mother, but he views them primarily as social, not intellectual, experiences. Nor does White recommend expensive educational toys. He believes that most toys of this sort are useless. Simple toys that appeal to the child's interests are more suitable.

What happens after the third birthday? White proposes that children become less flexible. Major changes in the child's mental development can be accomplished easily before 3 years, but only with difficulty after this age. Despite fictional stories about older children (and adolescents and adults) who undergo a sudden personality transformation, the likelihood of such an event is remote.

Despite differences in language and emphasis, these experts agree on some points:

1. Young children need lots of consistent, loving attention.
2. Young children are flexible. There is not one right way to raise children; several approaches produce good results.
3. Interesting environments stimulate intellectual growth.
4. Young children need discipline (which can be established with little, if any, punishment).
5. Children should be treated with respect. They should not be insulted or ridiculed.
6. Children's feelings should be taken seriously.
7. Children may have trouble expressing unpleasant feelings constructively, especially if their parents deny their own feelings.
8. Nursery school is recommended, especially for children who have little contact with other children.

EDUCATING YOUNG CHILDREN

The process of education begins at birth. Burton White argues that the most important aspects of education occur in the home during the first 3 years of life. The attention of parents and teachers, on the other hand, is usually directed toward educational programs outside the home. What are schools for young children like, and how do they affect a child's development?

Virtually all children attend school after they are 6 years old; most attend kindergarten when they are 5. Preschool for 3- and 4-year-olds and day care for even younger children are still somewhat controversial areas. Of our panel of experts, the three who address these issues (Spock, Salk, and White) recommend preschool, primarily for social experiences. They disapprove of day care, though they do admit that if parents have no alternative, some day-care arrangements "may not cause much harm."

Preschools

In 1906 Dr. Maria Montessori established the Casa dei Bambini (Children's House) in Rome to educate poverty-stricken children. Montessori's philosophy was that busy children are happy children. Her highly structured system of sensory, motor, and language activities was designed to develop mental abilities. At about the same time, Margaret and Rachel McMillan founded a nursery school in London to care for neglected children of poor families. The McMillan sisters emphasized health, nutrition, and cleanliness, but their school was not educational in the same sense as modern preschools are.

In the United States, public nursery schools were first established in 1919. The nursery school concept grew slowly through the 1920s and 1930s. During World War II, nursery schools quickly became popular among mothers who for the first time were working outside their homes. Another growth spurt occurred in the middle 1960s when the federal government invested heavily in preschool for disadvantaged children. By 1971, over one million 3- and 4-year-old children were enrolled in formal educational programs.

Preschools today vary widely in educational goals, method of instruction, content of instruction, typical activities, and social atmosphere.

Montessori method. Maria Montessori has had a tremendous influence on many aspects of preschool we now take for granted. She designed the first child-size furniture, for example; in a more philosophic vein, she emphasized respect for the child. Montessori advised against treating children like miniature adults. She firmly believed children had a separate life and a different viewpoint from adults.

Montessori favored *autoeducation,* a natural process of soaking up experiences into an absorbent mind. Children cannot be educated by adults, she said; they must teach themselves. Another of her concepts was *sensitive periods,* times at which children are most susceptible to learning certain skills. All children pass through sensitive periods for the same skills (such as language), but the timing of these periods varies from child to child. The adult's role is to watch for sensitive periods and capitalize on them when they appear by arranging the environment to encourage learning. The teaching method

Fig. 15-2. Motor activities such as washing objects are stressed in a Montessori preschool.

used almost exclusively by teachers trained in the Montessori method is *demonstration.* Montessori believed that children learn more by watching than by listening.

Five skill areas are of special interest in a Montessori school:

1. *Motor activities,* including exercises in walking on a line, offering someone a chair, lacing, tying, zipping, housekeeping chores, washing objects, and washing hands
2. *Sensory skills,* such as coordinating vision and touch, observing details, and isolating distinguishing characteristics of an object
3. *Language skills,* such as naming objects, expressing relationships, and understanding adult speech
4. *Academic knowledge,* including simple reading, writing, and arithmetic
5. *Concentration*

There is a "right" way to do each Montessori task; children practice till they learn this right way.

Montessori schools stress active rather than passive learning. Age groups are mixed so that older children have opportunities to help younger ones and younger children benefit from the wisdom of their elders. Though lessons are presented in a predetermined order, a child's progress through the lessons is self-paced. The Montessori system seems formal and overly structured to some educators, especially because of the lack of spontaneous play. Fantasy play in particular was discouraged by Montessori. Ironically, although the original Casa dei Bambini served poor children, Montessori schools typically are quite expensive compared with other preschools.

Fig. 15-3. Social interaction is encouraged in a Piagetian preschool.

Schools inspired by Piaget. Many schools claim a Piaget-based curriculum. Since Piaget did not endorse specific educational practices (see Chapter 9), these schools vary considerably. In some schools, skills studied by Piaget, such as classification, measurement, and matching, are taught. In other schools these skills are benignly neglected on the assumption that children eventually learn them on their own.

Most Piagetian schools focus on:

1. Mental traits important for learning, such as independence, curiosity, and confidence
2. Interaction among children and opportunities for children to resolve their own conflicts
3. Cooperative and equalitarian attitudes
4. Coordination of physical actions
5. Respect for a child's ideas, even if they are "wrong"
6. Mild challenges to egocentric thought
7. Play as a method of learning
8. Learning by doing rather than by seeing or hearing

Teachers who adhere to Piaget's theory recognize that children of the same age may be functioning at different levels of development and plan activities appropriate for the child's mental level. Activities are intended to encourage systematic, logical thought, not to teach specific concepts. Experiences with concrete objects as emphasized. Relatively little attention is given to abstract concepts, such as words, numbers, and symbols.

Open schools. Open schools are characterized by a maximum of choices for the children and a minimum of instruction (''snoopervision'') by the teachers. The children are allowed to choose when and how to learn. Freedom in an open school is not absolute. Children are free from arbitrary rules (such as lining up before going to lunch), but rules are enforced regarding safety, property, and respect for other people. Children must also spend some time on academic activities. When a rule is enforced, the reason for the rule is explained.

British Infant Schools are successful examples of the open school concept. Children from 4 to 7 years old are combined in ''family groupings'' (also called vertical groupings). Peer tutoring, with more able children helping less skilled ones, is an important element of the system. There are no set times for lessons. Several activities are underway at any one time, and the teacher goes from one child to another to lend assistance where necessary.

Noise, motion, and apparent chaos are typical of open schools. In one observation, different children in one class were simultaneously engaged in: the ''grocery store'' (exchanging merchandise for play money), art activities (painting, drawing, clay, and sand table), the reading corner (a secluded, quieter area with comfortable chairs and lots of books), carpentry, feeding pets, watching birds outside, inspecting plants, arranging large and small blocks in designs, writing, counting and drawing charts, and the ''Wendy House'' (dress-up and fantasy play in a child-sized dollhouse).

Open schools are intended to be joyful places where learning progresses naturally. No artificial incentives are used. This self-motivated approach to learning can be seen in reading. American schools teach children to read in the hope they will later find an interesting use for reading. British Infant Schools whet the child's appetite for reading; then learning to read is motivated by the child's own interest. Teachers in open schools have little concern for the child's educational future. ''If a child does not learn to read this year, don't worry; he will learn to read next year.'' Children are treated as if they ''can be trusted to do their own learning.''

There is an important difference between open schools British style and open-space schools American style. *Open-space* schools are an architectural concept, with huge rooms occupied by numerous learning centers. The educational philosophy of an open-space school can be free, but it can be authoritarian and restrictive and still be open space. *Open* schools are a philosophic concept. The physical arrangement of the class is irrelevant; the essential element is freedom of choice for the children.

''Academic'' preschools. So-called academic preschools offer a highly structured, coordinated system of activities designed to teach basic skills involved in language, reading, and arithmetic. These systems ordinarily extend into the primary grades. A well-known program of this type is Distar, developed by Bereiter and Englemann.

Distar consists of specific objectives taught in a standardized, almost scriptlike fashion. Objectives include such items as polar opposites (tall/short, light/heavy), use of prepositions (in, on, around, under), affirmative and negative statements (''The paper is orange. It is not green.''), conjunctions (and, or, because), and simple if-then deductions. Lessons occur in small groups and last about 30 minutes. The lessons are preplanned exchanges between the teacher and the group of children. For example:

Teacher: (holding up a blue round block) Is this block blue?
Children: Yes!
T: Is this block round?
C: Yes!
T: Is this block blue and round?
C: Yes!
T: Say the whole thing!
C: This block is blue and round!

Such exchanges are conducted at a brisk pace and sometimes assume the quality of cheers at a football game.

Three academic lessons are presented in each half-day session. Relaxation activities, such as music, art, or listening to stories, occupy the time between lessons. Distar and other academic preschool programs ordinarily place little emphasis on sensory experiences or play.

Traditional preschools. Many preschools emphasize social and emotional development rather than a specific educational theory. These preschools are called traditional or mainstream because in the United States they have been the most popular schools for the longest time.

Traditional preschool programs are characterized by freedom of movement for children, flexible planning by teachers, general language experiences (not particularly structured), variety of activities, and lots of play. Activities ordinarily include story

Fig. 15-4. Learning about the work of adults is one way to gain social knowledge in a traditional preschool.

343

time, acting out of stories, listening to music, moving to music, art experiences, walks in the neighborhood of the school, informal discussions, growing of plants, television, science experiments, snacks, naps, and free play (especially outdoors).

Major emphasis is placed on social relationships. Children are encouraged to play peacefully with others, to cooperate, to share, and to help out. One teacher is present for every eight or ten children, and teacher aides may also be employed. A main goal of the teachers is to establish trusting, friendly relationships with the children. If a preschool does not advertise any particular educational philosophy, it is most likely traditional.

Which type of preschool is best?

There is no simple answer to the question of which type of preschool is best. Research studies suggest that Montessori schools improve a child's attention, Piagetian schools help a child acquire certain concepts, open schools encourage independence and self-motivation, academic schools boost scores on reading-readiness tests, and traditional schools foster sociability. Most research on effects of specific preschool programs is inconclusive because the children are assigned to particular preschools by their parents rather than by random chance. Parents who choose an open school, for example, may also encourage independence and self-motivation at home.

One thorough experiment comparing four types of preschool programs is reported by Miller and Dyer (1975). Disadvantaged 4-year-old children were assigned at random to one of 14 preschool classes: two Montessori, four enriched traditional, four academic (Distar), and four emphasizing both academic skills and positive attitudes toward learning (DARCEE). Several classes of each type were included to minimize effects of particular teachers and neighborhoods. Other children from similar families who lived in the same areas but attended *no* preschool were included as a comparison group.

More than a dozen tests (IQ, motivation, perception, creativity, and so on) were administered to each child before entering the program and again after preschool, kindergarten, first grade, and second grade. No method clearly emerged as the "winner." Immediately after preschool, some differences among children were found. Each type of program was successful in fostering the behavior it emphasized. The structured academic programs produced the greatest improvements in IQ, the motivation-oriented programs produced the greatest gains in ambition, and so on. By the end of second grade, there were no longer significant differences in IQ or achievement among the four programs (or between the preschool and control groups!). Some changes in motivation and attitudes did persist through second grade. It appears from this study that parents can confidently choose any of these programs or choose not to send their child to preschool at all. (Remember, though, that the children were already 4 years old when the study began.)

Other studies indicate that carefully planned preschool experiences can produce lasting benefits in intelligence and motivation, especially if the children's families are poor and the children enter preschool at a younger age (see Bee, 1975, for a review of these studies).

Choosing a preschool

If the theoretical orientation of a preschool program makes little difference in the long run, how should parents choose a preschool for their child? Educators of young children recommend that parents visit several preschools and look for the following qualities.*

General orientation
1. Concern about health and safety, including nutritious food, clean toilet facilities, space for exercising, and time to rest
2. Stimulation of intellectual capacities, including interesting toys, opportunities for music and art, language, and activities appropriate for the ages of the children
3. Opportunities for social development in activities with adults and with other children
4. Interest in emotional growth, especially encouraging independence, accepting children's feelings, and making the children feel wanted

Specific characteristics
5. Variety of activities; some choices left to the children
6. Flexible scheduling of time
7. Balanced mixture of quiet and boisterous play
8. Time for music, books, and conversation
9. Experiences with nature and basic sciences
10. Get-acquainted games
11. Opportunities for the children to dress themselves, hang up their own coats, help set tables, serve food, put away toys, and so on
12. Health routines that encourage good habits
13. Encouragement of sharing, being courteous, and respecting feelings of other people
14. Chances for children to express their own feelings in acceptable ways

Do the teachers . . . ?
15. Have warm, friendly personalities
16. Really listen to what the children say
17. Set a good example for the children
18. Have special training in child development and child care
19. Encourage parent-teacher interviews
20. Allow parents to visit the school often
21. Show respect for the children and their parents
22. Show obvious pleasure in learning and in helping children learn

Thoughtful parents let their child visit prospective preschools. Many children are shy about joining in right away, but parents who wait till the child relaxes and wanders around a bit can get an idea of their child's evaluation of the preschool.

What about day care?

Day care is a controversial issue, just as preschool was 30 or 40 years ago. Many psychologists and educators (especially those associated with preschools) are skeptical of day care. Other authorities believe that first-rate day care is an entirely acceptable substitute for home care.

---

*From Langford and Rand. *Guidance of the young child* (2nd ed.). New York: John Wiley & Sons, Inc., 1975, pp. 17-18, (with modification). Copyright © 1975. Reprinted by permission of John Wiley & Sons, Inc.

Day-care programs typically last all day, accept children at a very young age, and have relatively little intellectual content. Many large day-care facilities are publicly supported and intended to attract low-income families. Small privately run family-day-care operations are also available. For parents who work outside the home, have children younger than 3 years, and have no housekeeper or relative to care for their children, day care may be the only alternative. Is day care as harmful as some experts would lead us to believe? Probably not. Even Burton White, who advocates full-time home care of children younger than 3, admits that day care can be helpful if it allows a mother to pursue her own interests. White warns that day-care facilities vary tremendously in quality. He regards with suspicion day-care centers that claim to be inspired by Piaget, Erikson, or any other well-known authority. For parents who choose day care, White recommends small, home-based centers run by women who like children and who have successfully reared children of their own. The potential benefits of a top-notch day-care center are clearly demonstrated in the reading following this chapter. Because day care is the only alternative for some families, it seems that the crucial issue is not whether there should be day care but how to provide day care of the highest quality.

SUMMARY

There is no shortage of "expert" advice on rearing children. The most widely read child-care authorities agree on several points, notably a child's needs for loving attention, interesting surroundings, respect, discipline, and freedom of emotional expression. Education of young children, both at home and in preschools, is recommended by most psychologists. Many types of preschools are available, including those based on theories of Montessori and Piaget, open preschools, academic preschools, and traditional (social-emotional) preschools. No single method of preschool education has been proved to be best. Before selecting a preschool, parents should visit several and compare them. Day care is a controversial issue. Some experts are adamantly opposed to day care, but others recognize a need for quality day-care facilities and believe that first-rate day care can be beneficial.

REFERENCES

Bee, H. *The developing child.* New York: Harper & Row, Publishers, 1975.

Ginott, H. G. *Between parent and child.* New York: Avon Books, 1965.

Gordon, T. *P.E.T. Parent effectiveness training.* New York: Peter H. Wyden/Publisher, 1970.

Langford, L. M., & Rand, H. Y. *Guidance of the young child.* New York: John Wiley & Sons, Inc., 1975.

Miller, L. B., & Dyer, J. L. Four preschool programs: their dimensions and effects. *Monographs of the Society for Research in Child Development,* 1975, **40** (Whole No. 162).

Salk, L. *What every child would like his parents to know.* New York: David McKay Co., Inc., 1972.

Spock, B. *Baby and child care.* New York: Pocket Books, 1974.

White, B. L. *The first three years of life.* Englewood Cliffs, N.J.: Prentice-Hall, Inc., 1975.

Longitudinal development of very young children in a comprehensive day care program: the first two years

Halbert B. Robinson
Nancy M. Robinson
University of North Carolina

In September 1966 the Frank Porter Graham Child Development Center of the University of North Carolina at Chapel Hill opened a day care center offering comprehensive services to a small number of infants and very young children. This center was established as a pilot facility for a much larger multidisciplinary research project. The latter was to be devoted in part to a longitudinal intervention study of a sizable cohort of children ranging in age from birth to 13 years given education and comprehensive day care under conditions as optimal as could reasonably be devised (Robinson 1969). This study presents the assessment of the development of the 11 children admitted in 1966 and the 20 enrolled in 1967 and 1968. The data reflect the results of a complex experimental plan which combined several rather unusual characteristics:

1. Almost all Ss admitted as infants were selected before their birth, with the conditions only that the sample be roughly balanced for sex and race and that no gross anomalies be detected during the neonatal period. They entered day care when the mother returned to work, which ranged from 4 weeks to 6 months after the birth of the child.
2. The sample was broadly representative of the community's socioeconomic spectrum of Caucasian and Negro children of working mothers.
3. Comprehensive daytime care was given, including complete health care; children attended the center whether sick or well.
4. A carefully structured educational program, beginning in early infancy, constituted a strong focus of the center. Pilot curricula were developed in language, sensorimotor skills, perception and reading, scientific and numerical concepts, music, art, and French.
5. The basic organizational pattern consisted of two cottages of up to 16 children of all ages represented in the center for basic activities such as eating, sleeping, and free play. All center children in the same family were housed together. Grouping by developmental level for instruction and play occurred for approximately 3 hours each day, children ages 2½-4½ going from their cottage to an educational unit.
6. Child-focused work with parents occurred through daily conversations with staff, frequent contact with the pediatrician, and home visits by the public health nurse. There were also occasional newsletters, parent meetings, and parties.

SUBJECTS
Center sample

During this pilot phase of the study, infants and 2-year-olds were admitted in order to provide for some heterogeneity. Most infants were selected through routine interviewing of all employed women receiving prenatal care in the university hospital, the only hospital in Chapel Hill. A few in-

From *Child Development*, 1971, **42**, 1673-1683. Copyright © 1972 by the Society for Research in Child Development, Inc., By permission.

Table 1. Test results for Ss admitted as infants and controls

Group	Bayley Mental Scale					Bayley Motor Scale					Stanford-Binet	
	6 mo	9 mo	12 mo	15 mo	18 mo	6 mo	9 mo	12 mo	15 mo	18 mo	24 mo	30 mo
Center:												
N	17	18	19	10	11	17	18	18	8	7	4	4
$\bar{X}$	108.00	115.94	112.16	116.60	115.18	110.94	109.22	99.61	107.62	107.29	116.25	117.25
SD	8.95	14.71	9.91	9.19	8.95	14.06	11.90	14.45	9.29	16.71	8.67	4.76
Control:												
N	11	11	11	10	8	11	11	11	10	8	4	—
$\bar{X}$	105.90	113.27	110.91	110.70	99.75	103.82	105.00	101.09	103.60	94.00	99.75	—
SD	10.15	12.23	9.97	8.79	11.61	13.11	11.45	14.96	10.95	7.17	11.23	—

fants, and all older children, were admitted after applications by families not initially contacted prior to the birth of the child. Four infant siblings born to families already having a child in the center were automatically admitted. Efforts were made to keep each of the three annual waves (1966, 1967, 1968) as varied and balanced as possible in race, sex, and socioeconomic status.

During the fall of 1966 four children were admitted between the ages of 2.0 months and 5.5 months (mean age, 3.8 months) and seven others between 26 and 36 months (mean age, 28.7 months). In the fall of 1967, seven infants between 1.5 and 5.5 months old were admitted (mean age, 2.7 months), and five children who were 23-28 months of age (mean age, 25.6 months). In 1968, all eight new Ss were infants, 1.1-4.0 months (mean age, 2.1 months). Of the 31 children, 12 (7 Caucasian and 5 Negro) were admitted at age 2; 19 (8 Caucasian and 11 Negro) were admitted as young infants. One additional child, however, was a congenital athyreotic admitted before his condition was diagnosed at age 3 months. Borderline retarded, he is omitted from this report. One boy admitted at age 2 was withdrawn when his family moved 18 months later. He is included in the comparison with community controls, but not in the longitudinal analysis. By the end of the 2½-year period covered by this report, the 31 Ss ranged in age from a few weeks to 4½ years.

Twenty-four families were represented. Total incomes of the 12 Caucasian families (i.e., all adults with legal responsibility for child) ranged from $4,500 to above $40,000, the median family income for the 15 children being $10,976. Incomes of the 12 Negro families ranged from zero (unmarried student mothers) to $10,000, the median for the 16 children being $3,519. Median education for the Caucasian mothers was 14.5 years and for the Caucasian fathers, 16.5 years. Median education of the Negro mothers was 12.0 years, and of the Negro fathers, 11.0 years. One Caucasian child and four Negro children had no father in the home.

The dramatic differences between the Caucasian and Negro families in the sample are, in large part, a reflection of the disparities in this community. Its Caucasian wage earners are largely university staff and merchants, while its Negro population has traditionally performed supportive services. Community acceptance was also an issue, however. The early appeal of the center was to the poorer Negro parents, attracted by the low cost, and to the more affluent Caucasian parents, attracted by the potential benefits for their children. Eventually, however, the center's reputation began to attract blue-collar Caucasian parents and middle-class Negro parents. Included in the 1968 sample are, for example, the infant sons of a white policeman and of a Negro social worker.

Control groups

Two separate control groups were studied. One was followed from early infancy onward and is compared with center infants; the other was tested only once and was compared with center children who were at that time 2½-4½ years old.

From 1967, when pediatric services became available as part of the center's program, control groups of infants were selected by the same prenatal interviewing methods as center infants, an attempt being made to equate the annual waves as closely as possible on sex, race, number of siblings, education and occupation of parents, and number of rooms in the house. These groups were evaluated medically and psychologically on the same schedule as the center population, and additional health records were kept in conjunction with medical studies being carried out in the center. Complete medical supervision was given to the control children, in part to enlist the families' cooperation, but more important, to attempt to equalize medical care, the better to evaluate the effects of the enriched daily experience of the center children. Eleven control group infants were followed during the period of this report.

By 1968, the 16 oldest center Ss were 2½-4½. Four of these children had entered in 1966 as infants; 12 had entered in 1966 or 1967 at age 2. None had attended less than 1 year. As a rough comparison, a completely different group of noncenter children was matched with them individually on the basis of race, sex, parents' education and occupation, and the age at which the center child had last been given the Stanford-Binet and PPVT (see below). The controls were chosen from applicants to the center for whom there had not been space ($N = 5$), from friends of the family of the child for whom matching was sought ($N = 9$), and from another local day care center ($N = 2$). Mean CA of each group was 41 months, the mean within-pair age difference being 1.8 months. Exceedingly close matching on occupation and education of both parents was achieved, except that six control mothers were not currently employed.

BEHAVIORAL MEASURES

The data reported here represent only the results of standardized testing over the period being considered. Tests were scheduled every 3 months to age 18 months, the Bayley mental scale, the Bayley motor scale, and the Bayley behavior profile (Bayley 1961) being completed on each occasion. Table 2 lists most of the subsequent tests administered to age 4½. In addition, several language-assessment measures were administered in June 1968 to the 14 oldest children (ages 2-7 to 4-3) and three additional tests (WPSSI, Frostig, Caldwell preschool inventory) were given at age 4.

Testing through age 18 months was conducted by the staff of the University of North Carolina Laboratory of Infant Behavior to which the infants were transported by a caretaker from the center or by the mothers of the control infants. Testing of center children 2 and over was conducted at the center by a member of its staff. The control children for the special one-time comparison with the older Ss were seen in their own homes or regular day care settings by the same examiner who tested the older center children. The Stanford-Binet and Peabody Picture Vocabulary Test (PPVT) were administered. Effort was made to establish rapport through an initial period of play and the presence, when apparently desirable, of a trusted adult. For almost all of the Negro children, whose homes had no telephones, the testing visit constituted the second to the fourth contact with the examiner, who had played with the child during each previous visit. Nevertheless, these comparison data suffer the obvious drawbacks of the greater familiarity of the examiner with the center Ss and the unknown practice effects of their previous testing.

TEST RESULTS
Subjects admitted as infants

Test results for all children admitted as infants are shown in Table 1, together with those for the control infants. A 2×5 analysis of variance (Dixon 1965) nested on treatments (center-control) with repeated measures on comparisons over time and using a general linear hypothesis to handle

Table 2. Test scores of children admitted at age 2

Test	Admitted 1966 ($N = 6$)					Admitted 1967 ($N = 5$)	
	2-6	3-0	3-6	4-0	4-6	2-6	3-0
Stanford-Binet							
$\bar{X}$	112.3	124.5	132.7	—	127.2	118.4	123.8
SD	23.5	20.2	17.5	—	13.4	23.1	13.9
PPVT							
$\bar{X}$	93.8	100.8	114.0	111.5	108.5	111.4	107.2
SD	15.5	19.7	7.2	6.9	6.9	17.9	10.8
ITPA							
$\bar{X}$	104.3	124.5	122.2	—	—	—	115.0
SD	14.0	17.0	12.8	—	—	—	15.0
Leiter							
$\bar{X}$	—	128.0	128.3	—	126.8	106.6	130.0
SD	—	19.6	16.4	—	8.7	26.1	14.9
Draw-a-Man							
$\bar{X}$	—	—	96.8	—	98.5	—	—
SD	—	—	15.3	—	9.9	—	—

missing data values was applied to the infant test scores. Analysis of the Bayley mental scale scores yielded a between-groups F ratio of 7.99 (df 1/116, $p = .01$) for the treatments, an F ratio of 2.72 (df 4/116, $p = .05$) for the comparisons over time, and a nonsignificant interaction ($F = 1.45$, df 4/116). For the Bayley motor scale, the only significant F ratio (4.75, df 1/109, $p = .05$) occurred in the comparison of center and control groups. A t test of the mental scale scores at 18 months was significant at the .01 level, but a t test of motor scale scores at that age failed to reach significance at the .05 level. A t test of the small samples tested on the Stanford-Binet at 24 months also failed to reach significance.

In other words, scores for center and control Ss were significantly different on both tests, but a significant trend over time was found only on the mental scale, consisting of an initial rise for both groups, and a drop for the control group at the 18-month level. The suddenness of that drop probably accounts for the lack of significance in the interaction. The scores on the Bayley motor scale favored the center group but were less consistently different over time.

Subjects admitted at age 2

The test results for children admitted to the center at age 2 are described in Table 2. Additional tests administered to the 1966 group at age 4-0 yielded the following mean scores and standard deviations: Wechsler primary and Preschool Inventory full scale IQ 124.6 (SD 12.4), verbal IQ 126.0 (8.8), performance IQ 117.7 (14.5); Frostig test of visual perception IQ 100.0 (20.9) and Caldwell preschool inventory, median percentile 90 (middle-class norms).

Scores on most primarily verbal measures were high, as shown by the Stanford-Binet (Terman and Merrill 1960), the verbal scale of the WPPSI (Wechsler 1967), the Caldwell preschool inventory (Caldwell 1967), and, as an exception, the nonverbal Arthur Adaptation of the Leiter scale (Arthur 1952). Peabody Picture Vocabulary Test (Dunn 1959) scores were consistently lower than the other measures.

On the nonverbal measures, most of the children's scores fell below their verbal scores. On the Frostig test of visual perception (Frostig, Lefever, and Whittlesey 1964), the draw-a-man test (Harris 1963), and portions of the Illinois Test of Psycholinguistic Abilities (McCarthy and Kirk 1961), this lower performance was evident. Sensorimotor items (motor encoding, visual-motor sequential) were consistently the lowest of the mean ITPA scores, with the exception of the visual-motor association test, which is "motor" only to the extent that a pointing response is required. Similarly, on the WPPSI, the mean subscale scores for the seven children tested at age 4 ranged from a high of 16.43 on arithmetic to a low of 12.29 on geometric designs, the single exception being a mean score of 9.71 on the highly motoric mazes. The WPPSI performance IQ was approximately ½ SD below the mean verbal IQ.

The language assessment in June 1968 likewise revealed advanced verbal behavior. Of the 12 children given the Templin-Darley scale (Templin and Darley 1960), the score of each S was at or above CA level, the mean speech age exceeding the mean CA (42 months) by approximately 22 months. On the action-agent test (Gesell 1940), 10 of the 12 scored at age level or better, three Ss exceeding the CA by at least 6 months. On the Michigan Picture Language Inventory (Lerea 1958; Walski 1962) given to the seven oldest children, mean standard score of expression was +.96, while the mean comprehension standard score was +.65.

Test results for the 16 older center children and 16 matched controls are shown in Figures 1 and 2. The most striking findings on both tests are the differences, on the order of two standard deviations, between the center Negro children and their controls. Mean Stanford-Binet IQs were 119.7 for these seven center children and 86.1 for their controls; both groups showed a marked clustering of scores (SDs 8.16 and 6.59, respectively). On the PPVT, center Negro children attained a mean IQ of 107.4 (SD 10.03) while that of the control Negro children was only 77.6 (SD 13.75). There was no overlap of scores between these groups on either test.

Differences between the nine Caucasian center children and their controls appeared on the Stanford-Binet but not on the PPVT. Mean IQs on the Stanford-Binet were 129.7 (SD 17.00) and 116.9

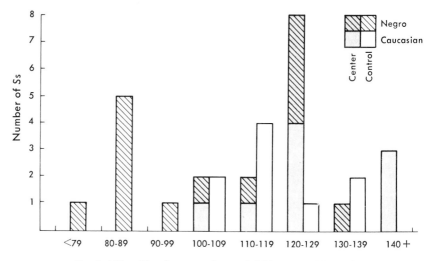

Stanford-Binet IQs of center and control children, ages 2¼ to 4¼.

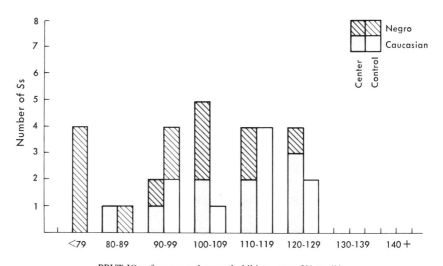

PPVT IQs of center and control·children, ages 2½ to 4½.

(SD 11.71), respectively. On the PPVT, mean IQ of the center Caucasian group was actually lower (108.1, SD 12.42) than that of the controls (110.2, SD 12.81).

According to an analysis of variance (Dixon 1965) of Stanford-Binet scores, F ratios were highly significant for the comparisons of racial groups (F = 22.27, df 1/28, p < .001) and center control groups (F = 28.89, df 1/28, p < .001), the significant interaction (F = 5.81, df 1/28,

$p = .05$) highlighting the much greater magnitude of the difference between the Negro groups. In the analysis of scores on the PPVT, there were also significant effects of race ($F = 14.29, df \ 1/28, p = .001$) and of the center/control variance ($F = 9.90, df \ 1/28, p = .01$). The interaction term ($F = 13.14, df \ 1/28, p < .01$) demonstrated that the significant differences were limited to the Negro groups. Center Ss who were 3-6 and older attained somewhat higher scores on both tests than did center Ss 3-0 and younger (mean Stanford-Binet IQs 129.1 and 121.5, respectively; mean PPVT IQs 113.5 and 102.1), but a t test of these Stanford-Binet differences was not significant, and the PPVT difference ($t = 2.346, df \ 14$) was significant at only the .05 level. The control group showed no such age trends. Practice effects cannot be ruled out. Sex differences were not significant.

DISCUSSION

Within the serious limitations which characterize the data, a number of tentative suggestions emerge:

1. Enriched group care of the young infant, when carefully designed and fully staffed, may enhance cognitive development, especially during the time when verbal abilities are beginning to emerge. The differences between experimental and control groups which were apparent at the 18-month level suggest that the period before this may be a crucial one. Earlier concern about the possibility of detrimental cognitive effects of ''institutionalization'' (i.e., any form of group care) is apparently unjustified. On the contrary, a decline in scores was found for the control group, while the center's group maintained its status on cognitive measures at about 1 SD above the mean of the national normative sample.

2. High quality group care combined with educational efforts during ages 2-4 years may have its major impact upon culturally disadvantaged children. Although the center Caucasian (more advantaged) children in the study obtained higher scores on the Stanford-Binet than the control Caucasian children, the really dramatic differences occurred between the center Negro (less advantaged) children and their controls. Indeed, the center Negro children attained a mean Stanford-Binet of approximately 120, as opposed to the control Negro mean IQ of approximately 86. The crucial variables of the day care, educational, and health programs cannot be identified in this pilot study, but that the ''package'' made a difference in the lives of the children is unmistakable.

3. The major impact of the program was in verbal rather than motoric areas. The nonverbal scores of the center children were ''normal'' but not particularly advanced.

The lack of well-standardized instruments to assess social-emotional functioning of young children is a major handicap to a study of this nature. A series of attempts to devise a problem-behavior checklist or interview with the mothers was unsuccessful because of the inability of some poorly educated mothers, even with considerable prompting, to think in differentiated terms about their children's behavior. Overall evaluation by a team of psychoanalytically-oriented clinicians yielded interesting individual assessments which were based on limited observations of center children and did not yield useful research data. Similarly, detailed behavioral ratings by the staff, useful in many ways for longitudinal research, are not reported here because they yielded only within-group comparisons. There was unanimous agreement among all the staff, who were of diverse cultural and educational backgrounds, that as a group the children were extremely amicable, stable, and outgoing, and that none exhibited behavior deviant from the normal range of childhood behavior patterns.

A study such as the present one raises many more questions than it can answer. What are the long-range residuals of a program such as that provided by the center? In the long run, will the development of children who enter as infants differ significantly from that of children admitted at age 2, later, or not at all? What elements within the program are most effective? Can these elements be packaged and delivered more economically than through comprehensive full-day programs? What positive impact may the availability of reliable day care have on the stability of families, and on the mother's employment and personal adjustment? What are the immediate and delayed effects on the children's relationships with their parents? Major longitudinal research efforts will be required to answer these compelling questions.

353

REFERENCES

Arthur, G. A. *The Arthur adaptation of the Leiter international performance scale.* Washington, D.C.: Psychological Service Center Press, 1952.

Bayley, N. Manual of directions for infant scales of development (temporary standardization). (Mimeographed.) Bethesda, Md.: National Institute of Neurological Diseases and Blindness, Colloborative Research Project, 1961.

Caldwell, B. M. *The preschool inventory.* Princeton, N.J.: Educational Testing Service, 1967.

Dixon, W. J. (Ed.) General linear hypothesis (BMDO5V). Biomedical Computer Program. Los Angeles, UCLA Health Sciences Computing Facility, 1965.

Dunn, L. M. *Peabody Picture Vocabulary Test* manual. Minneapolis: American Guidance Service, 1959.

Frostig, M.; Lefever, D. W.; and Whittlesey, J. R. B. A development test of visual perception for evaluating normal and neurologically handicapped children. *Perceptual and Motor Skills,* 1964, **12,** 383-394.

Gesell, A. *The first five years of life.* New York: Harper & Row, 1940.

Harris, D. B. *Measuring the psychological maturity of children: a revision and extension of the Goodenough draw-a-man test.* New York: Harcourt, Brace & World, 1963.

Lerea, L. Assessing language development. *Journal of Speech and Hearing Research,* 1958, **1,** 75-85.

McCarthy, J. J., and Kirk, S. A. *Illinois test of psycholinguistic abilities.* (Exp. ed.) Urbana: University of Illinois, Institute of Research on Exceptional Children, 1961.

Robinson, H. B. From infancy through school. *Children,* 1969, **16,** 61-62.

Templin, M. C., and Darley, F. L. *The Templin-Darley tests of articulation.* Iowa City: University of Iowa Bureau of Education Research and Service, 1960.

Terman, L. M., and Merrill, M. A. *Stanford-Binet intelligence scale.* Boston: Houghton Mifflin, 1960.

Walski, W. Language development of normal children, four, five, and six years of age as measured by the Michigan Picture Language Inventory. Unpublished doctoral dissertation, University of Michigan, 1962.

Wechsler, D. A. *A manual for the Wechsler preschool and primary scale of intelligence.* New York: Psychological Corp., 1967.

Index

A

Abandonment, 5
Abortion, spontaneous, 78, 80
Absolute response to transposition problem, 157, 165
Abstract of research report, 37, 38, 48
Academic preschools, 342-343, 344
Accommodation, 181-182, 199, 203, 309, 310
Accommodation, visual, 57, 65
Acquisition, in memory, 162
Action schemes, 93-95
Activity level, 290
Adaptation, 181, 202
Age and IQ, 214-215
Age changes
  in aggression, 111
  in attention, 167-170
  in classical conditioning, 100-101
  in cross-modal transfer, 159-160
  in dimension preferences, 159-160
  in dominant sensory mode, 158-159
  in effective reinforcement, 163
  in fear, 248
  in hypothesis testing, 158
  in imitation, 107
  in inhibition, 166-167
  in intelligence test skills, 161
  in learning, 100-101, 105, 107, 155-158
  in memory, 162-163
  in operant conditioning, 105
  in perception, 158-160
  in spatial orientation, 160-161
  in thought, 155-171, 180-198
  in transposition, 156-157, 164-165, 167-169
  in use of words, 161-162, 163-166
  in verbal mediation, 163-166
  in word associations, 161-162

Age comparisons, 23, 26, 31-32
  Cross-sectional, 31
  Longitudinal, 31
  Time lag, 32
Aggression, 107-111, 277, 290-292
  age changes in, 111
  and arousal, 109, 110
  classical conditioning of, 100
  definition, 107
  and frustration, 111
  imitation of, 109-110
  operant conditioning of, 110
  origin of, 108-109
  and pain, 116
  punishment of, 116
  sex differences in, 109, 111
  stimuli for, 111
  and television, 110, 121-125
Ainsworth, M. D. S., 89, 93, 104, 267, 268, 278
Albert, Little, 97-99, 247, 251
Aleksandrowitz, M. K., 81, 93
Anal stage, 240
Anger, 7, 13, 17, 18, 286
Animal behavior, 7, 8, 18, 19, 21, 127, 264
Animism, 191
Anoxia, 80
Anxiety; *see also* Fear
  castration, 241-244, 246
  separation, 248, 251-252, 263, 268, 269, 271-272
  stranger, 263, 268, 269-271
Applefield, J. M., 110, 121-125
Aronson, E., 68, 71, 107
Artificialism, 191
Assertiveness, 107

Assimilation, 181-182, 199, 202, 309, 310
  functional, 183, 200
  generalizing, 183
  recognitory, 183, 184
Associative level of thought, 166
Associative play, 319, 320
Attachment, 263-270
  theories of, 264-267
Attention, 167-170, 337-338
  age changes in, 167-170
  as a reinforcer, 101-103, 104
  to same-sex models, 296
  visual, 55
Attention span, 167
Attention theory, 167-170
Audition, 17, 56, 67-69
Auditory acuity, 68
Authoritarian home, 273
Autoclitic behavior, 137
Autocosmic play, 309
Autoeducation, 339
Axline, V., 24, 32

B

Babbling, 128-129
Babinski response, 82
Baby biography, 6-8, 15
Baker, C. T., 214
Baldwin, A. L., 273, 274, 278
Ball, W., 58, 71
Bandura, A., 106, 109, 146, 250, 283
Baron, R. A., 110
Bass, H. M., 281, 283
Baxter, J. C., 280
Bayley, N., 31, 161, 209, 216
Bayley Scales of Infant Development, 212
Becker, W. C., 115
Bee, H., 245, 344
Bell, S. B., 104
Belmont, J. M., 162
Benek, J., 67, 71
Bennett, S. M., 288, 301
Bereiter, C., 342
Berkeley Growth Study, 31
Berko, J., 161
Best, D. L., 288, 301
Bigner, J. J., 274, 278
Bilingualism, 133
Binet, A., 10, 11, 180, 209, 210, 223
Biologic predispositions, 235, 237
Birth, 80-81

Birth order, 263, 270, 272, 274, 275
Birth-traumatized infants, 71
Blank, M., 148
Blasdale, R., 144, 145
Blatchley, M. E., 73-75
Blinking, 82
Blood types, 78
Bloom, L., 132, 140, 145
Bobo doll, 109, 110
Bon, P., 269, 279
Books and stories, children's, 288-289, 302-305
Bow, J., 293, 301
Bower, T. G. R., 57, 67, 71
Bowlby, J., 265, 266, 272, 279
Brain damage, 80, 127
Brain development, 81, 84, 85, 132, 133
Bridger, W., 71
Bridges, K. M. B., 247
Brodsky, G., 251
Broen, P., 146, 149, 150
Bronson, G. W., 248, 270, 279
Brooks, J., 271, 279
Brophy, J. E., 319, 322
Brown, J. V., 55, 72
Brown, R., 138, 145, 146, 148, 149, 151, 161
Burt, Sir Cyril, 220-221
Butterfield, E. C., 162
Bzoch, K. R., 147

C

Cardiac monitoring, 55, 56, 63
Caron, A. J., 167
Casa dei Bambini, 339, 340
Case study, 24
Castration anxiety, 241-244, 246
Cause-and-effect relationship, 27, 28, 45
Cazden, C., 139, 141, 145, 146
Centered perception, 61, 62
Centered thought, 192-193, 195
Cephalocaudal development, 17, 71, 84
Cerebral cortex, 81, 133
Cherry, L., 290, 300, 301
Child laborer, 5, 16
Child rearing, 331-338
Children's books and stories, 288-289, 302, 305
Children's rooms, 323-328
Chomsky, N., 137, 138
Choresh, N., 280-284
Church, 5
Circulatory system, 78, 81
Circumcision, 70

Classical conditioning, 97-101, 103, 105, 155
  age changes in, 100-101
  compared with operant conditioning, 103
Classification of objects, 184, 197
Cline, V. B., 110
Cochran, W., 149
Cognitive level of thought, 166
Cognitive processes, 4, 73, 75, 132, 267, 298,
    307, 309, 310, 313, 314; see also Thought
    processes
Coleman, J., 302, 304
Collard, R. R., 235
Collective monologue, 190
Collins, G., 300, 301
Color perception, 57, 58
Communication, 12, 20, 21, 104, 127, 129,
    130, 132, 307, 312
Complex motor skills, 90-92
Compos, J. H., 63, 72
Conception, 77, 78
Concrete operational period, 196-197, 201, 203
Conditioned response, 99, 106
Conditioned stimulus, 98-100, 105
Condry, J., 286, 301
Condry, S., 286, 301
Conger, J. J., 71, 72, 281
Conscience, 237
Conservation problems, 194-196, 197
Contact comfort, 264, 265
Cooing, 128, 135
Cook, K. V., 287, 301, 323-328
Cooperation, 307, 311, 312, 317
Cooperative play, 319, 320
Coordination of sight and sound, 68, 69
Correlates of IQ, 211, 212, 213-215, 223
Correlation, 26-28, 43-45, 157, 166
  negative, 44-45
  positive, 44
Correlation coefficient, 43-45
Corter, C., 293, 301
Courrier, S., 110
CR; see Conditioned response
Crawling, 86, 87
  "regressive," 101-103
Cretinism, 215
Critical period, 91, 132
Criticism, 334
Croft, R. G., 110
Cross-modal transfer, 160
Cross-sectional age comparisons, 31
Crying, 104, 128, 135

CS; see Conditioned stimulus
Cuddling, 264, 265
Cultural-familial retardation, 219, 224-227
Culture, 25, 235
Curiosity, 19, 265, 337

D

DARCEE, 344
Darwin, C., 6-8, 15, 16-21, 24, 210, 243
Davies, P. A., 94
Davis, B. B., 141, 142, 145, 146, 149
Davis, D. R., 214
Davitz, J. R., 110
Day care, 345-346, 347-353
Deep structure in language, 138-143
De Fee, J. F., 248
Definitions, operational, 39-40
Delivery anesthetic, 54, 69, 81
De Loache, J. S., 61, 72
Democratic home, 273, 274
Denenberg, V. H., 73-75
Denes, P. B., 136, 145
Dennis, M., 9, 16
Dennis, W., 216
Dependency, 240, 292-294
Depth perception, 62-63
Developmental norms, 12
Developmental problems, 11, 12, 77, 80, 82,
    83
Developmental psychology, 3, 13
Diabetes, 78
Differential treatment by sex, 289, 299-300,
    323-328
Dimension preferences, 159-160
Discipline, 331-332, 335, 336, 338
Discrepant visual stimuli, 64, 65, 266
Discussion of research report, 37, 46-47
Disease in pregnancy, 80
Displacement, 238, 245
Distar, 342-343, 344
Doctors, 3, 5, 53
Dolls, 9, 288, 315, 320-321, 326
Dominant sensory mode, 158-159
Dorman, L., 214
Dosey, M., 280
Down's syndrome, 215
Dramatic play, 315, 316
Draw-a-Man test, 213
Dreams, 242-243
Drugs in pregnancy, 79-80
Dudgeon, J. A., 80, 93

Duff, D. F., 280, 283
duPreez, P., 144, 145
Dyer, J. L., 344

E

Ear structure, 67, 68
Early experience, 9, 14, 89-91, 245-246
Early prediction of behaviors, 83
Eckerman, L. B., 276
Education, preschool, 339-345
Educational toys, 338
Ego, 237-238, 245
Ego-ideal, 237
Egocentrism, 183, 189-192, 197
  in language, 190-191
  in moral judgment, 192
  in play, 311, 312, 315
  in reasoning, 191-192
Eichorn, D. H., 80, 93
Eifer, D., 302, 305
Eimas, P. D., 68, 72, 158
Eisenberg, R., 67, 72
Elkind, D., 62, 72, 220
Ellis, M. J., 320, 322
Embryo, 78
Emerson, P. E., 264, 265, 267-270, 279
Emotions, 13, 14, 17-19, 77, 101, 286, 309,
    310, 314
Endsley, R., 109
Engen, T., 71, 72
Englemann, S., 115, 342
Environment and IQ, 213-220
Equilibrium, 182
Erikson, E., 309, 310, 312, 346
Ervin-Tripp, S., 139, 142, 145
Etaugh, C., 300, 301
Ethics, 23, 98
Etzel, B. C., 104
Evertson, C. M., 319, 322
Evolution, 6, 265
Expansion of language, 139, 140-142, 146-150
Extinction, 112
Extroversion, 77
Eye structure, 57

F

F ratio, 43
Faces, perception of, 64, 65
Fagot, B., 299, 301
Family, 272-275
Family size and IQ, 214

Fantz, R. L., 55, 58-60, 63, 72, 74
Fathers, 269, 297, 299, 333, 335, 336
Fear, 7, 13, 16, 18, 63, 64, 236, 243-245, 247-
    252, 254-261, 286, 310; see also Anxiety
  common, of children, 249-250, 254-261
  conditioned, 97-99
  development of, 247-248
  of dogs, 106-107
  of furry objects, 99
  of rats, 97-99
  reduction of, 250-252
Feelings, 332, 335, 336, 338; see also Emotions
Fein, G., 298, 301
Feldman, C., 141, 145, 146
Fenson, L., 312, 322
Fetal movement, 79
Fetal period, 78-80
Fetal responsiveness to sound, 69
Figure-ground reversals, 62
First words, 21, 128, 129, 138
Fishbein, H. D., 84, 88, 89, 93
Fisher Exact Probability Test, 43, 45
Fisher, R. L., 280, 283
Fixation, 240-242, 246
Flavell, J., 192, 198
Fleherty, 269, 279
Fontanelles, 81
Forgetting, rate of, 162
Form perception, 62-65
Formal operational period, 197-198, 201,
    203
Fovea, 57
Frede, M. C., 280
Fredrickson, W. T., 55, 72
Freedman, J. L., 116
Freud, S., 8, 13-15, 236-247, 250, 253, 295,
    296, 309, 334
Freud's theory of personality, 236-247
  analysis of children's dreams, 242-243
  evaluation of, 245-246
  interpretation of fears, 243-245
  stages of personality development, 238-
    242
  structure of personality, 237-238
  view of mankind, 246-247
Frey, K. S., 296, 298, 301
Friederich, L., K., 110
Friedlander, B. Z., 141, 142, 145, 146, 149
Friedman, P., 290, 301
Frustration, 111
Fry, A. M., 281, 283

G

Galton, Sir Francis, 209-210
Games with rules, 312
Garber, H., 219, 224
Gardner, J., 107
Gardner, H., 107
Gautrey, D. B., 280
Gender awareness, 298
Generalization, 99
Genetic influences, 77-78, 109, 235
Genital organs, 79, 240-242
Genital stage, 242
German measles, 80, 215
Germinal stage, 78
Gerson, A., 300, 301
Gesell, A., 10-13, 16, 79, 88, 93, 313, 315, 321, 322
Gesell Developmental Schedules, 228-230
Gewirtz, J. L., 104, 135, 145
Gibson, E. J., 62, 63, 72
Gilat, Y., 280-284
Ginott, H. G., 334-335
Ginsburg, H., 107, 192
Glietman, L. R., 140, 143, 145
Goldberg, S., 37, 293, 301
Golden, M., 213
Gordon, H., 216
Gordon, T., 335-336
Green, M., 110, 292, 301
Greene, D., 114
Greenman, G. W., 58, 72
Groves, T. P., 280
Growth rate, 85
Grusec, J. E., 106, 250
Guardo, C., 280, 281
Gustation, 71

H

Habituation, 55, 60, 61
Hagman, R. R., 250
Hailman, J. P., 280
Haith, M. M., 57, 69-72
Hall, C. S., 245, 247
Hall, E. T., 280
Hall, G. S., 8-10
Hall, M., 304
Halverson, C. F., 278, 279
Hand-eye coordination, 17
Handedness, 17, 77, 79
Hanratty, M. A., 110
Hans, Little, 243-245

Harari, H., 235
Harlow, H., 264, 265, 271
Harris, A., 146
Harris, F. R., 101
Hartup, W. W., 111, 274-277, 279, 302
Haynes, H., 57, 72
Head Start, 219, 221
Heart development, 78, 79, 80
Heaton, C., 269, 279
Hebb, D. C., 53, 72, 73
Heber, R., 219-220, 222, 224
Height, 77, 85, 86
Held, R., 57, 72
Hepatitis, 215
Heredity, 23, 25, 45
Heredity and intelligence, 220-222
Hess, R. D., 165
Hicks, D. J., 109
Himelstein, P., 248
Historical concept of childhood, 3
Hokoda, E., 302, 305
Hollingshead, A. B., 324
Holophrastic speech, 129, 143
Home economists, 3
Hood, L., 132, 145
Hormones, 108
Hornung, M., 316, 319, 320, 322
Horowitz, M. J., 280, 283
House, B. J., 169
Howes, C., 276
Hypothesis testing, age changes in, 158

I

Id, 237-238, 242, 245
Identification, 238, 241, 295, 296
Imitation, 19-21, 106-107, 139, 146, 150, 295, 307, 310, 316, 321; *see also,* Observational learning
    of aggression, 109-110, 121-125
    deferred, 107
Imprinting, 247
Impulsive style of thought, 167
Incentives, 117-118
Infant focal distance, 57, 58, 64, 65
Infant sensory systems, 56
Inflections, 138
Inhibition of associative thought, 166-167, 169, 170
Instinct, 108, 237, 245-246
Institutionalized infants, 73

Intelligence; *see also* Intelligence tests; IQ
  definitions of, 209
  and early stimulation, 224-232
  and environment, 215-220
  fostering development of, 337
  and heredity, 220-222
  measurement of, 209-223
  Piaget's theory of, 177-207
  role of attention in, 169
Intelligence quotient; *see* IQ
Intelligence tests, 10, 209-223
  Bayley Scales of Infant Development, 212
  Draw-a-Man Test, 213
  history of, 209-210
  misuse of, 222, 223
  Peabody Picture Vocabulary, 213
  Piaget-based method, 199-200
  skills measured by, 161, 210-213
  Stanford-Binet, 210-213
Interference, in memory, 162-163
Internalization of speech, 161
Interviews, 15
Intonation, 21, 128, 129, 135, 144
Introduction of research report, 37, 38
Introspection, 8
Introversion, 77
IQ, 31, 39, 155, 161, 199-200, 210-232, 347-
  353; *see also* Intelligence; Intelligence tests
  and age, 214-215
  calculation of, 210
  and contagious diseases, 215
  correlates of, 211-215, 223
  and deprived environments, 215-217
  and early experience, 215-217, 219-220,
    223, 224-232, 347-353
  and enriched environments, 220
  and family size, 214
  and general learning ability, 214-215
  and genetic disorders, 215
  and heredity, 220-222, 223
  and home environment, 214
  and nutrition, 215
  and parents' education, 213
  and parents' IQ, 214
  and personal characteristics, 214
  and place of residence, 213-214, 221
  and racial or ethnic background, 213
  and school performance, 211, 213
  and sex, 214
  and socioeconomic status, 213, 215-216
  and teachers' expectations, 217-219
  and type of preschool attended, 344

Irregular verbs, 139
Irreversible thought, 192, 193-194, 195

J

Jacklin, C. N., 250, 290-295, 298, 300, 301
Jacobs, A. C., 141, 142, 145, 146, 149
Jacobs, B. S., 274
Jacobson, L., 217
Jealousy, 18
Jennings, S., 289, 301, 302-305
Jensen, A. R., 221-222
Jensen, P., 144, 145
Johnson, D., 298, 301
Johnson, V. E., 242
Johnston, M. K., 101
Jones, M. C., 250-251

K

Kagan, J., 71, 72, 167, 169, 281, 312, 322
Kanfer, F. H., 252
Karoly, P., 252
Kaye, H., 99, 100
Kearsley, R., 312, 322
Keith, R., 304
Kelley, C. S., 101
Kendler, H. H., 164-165
Kendler, T. S., 164-165
Kennedy, B. A., 172
Kent, N., 214
Kessen, W., 3-5, 9, 13, 16
Klopfer, P. H., 280
Koenigsknecht, R. A., 290, 301
Kogan, N., 167, 169
Kohlberg, L., 298
Kopp, C. B., 93-95
Koppenaal, R. J., 163
Korson, N., 298, 301
Krowitz, A., 63, 72
Kuenne, M. R., 157, 164
Kutz, S. L., 276

L

Laboratory research, 13, 14, 25
Langer, A., 63-72
Langford, L. M., 345
Language, 127-151
  acquisition of, 126-151
  collective monologue, 190
  complexities of, 127
  deep structure of, 138-143
  monologue, 190
  in preoperational thought, 188, 190-191, 201

Language—cont'd
  stimulating development of, 165-166, 337
  surface structure of, 138, 140, 141, 143
  theories of, 133-140
  and thought, 161-162, 163-166
  transformations, 138, 140, 143
Lansky, L., 305
Lanugo, 79
Latency, 242
Lateralization, 133
Lazarus, A. A., 251
Leach, E., 150
League, R., 147
Learning, 5, 13, 19, 56, 97-119, 127, 132-136,
    145, 296
  age changes in, 100-101, 105, 107, 155-158
  classical conditioning, 97-101
  observational, 106-107
  operant conditioning, 101-106
  theories of, 97-107, 118
  using principles of, to influence behavior,
    111-118
Learning theory of language acquisition, 134-
    137
Lenneberg, E., 132, 133, 145
Lepper, M. R., 114
Letzinger, S., 275, 279
Levy, E. A., 162
Levy, N., 71, 72
Lewis, M., 37, 269, 271, 279, 290, 293, 301
Liebert, R. M., 110
Light deprivation, 53
Lindzey, G., 245, 247
Lipsitt, L. P., 71, 72, 97, 99, 213
Little Albert, 97-99, 247, 251
Little Hans, 243-245
Little, K., 280
Locke, J., 5, 6, 13
Lomranz, J., 280-284
Longhurst, T. M., 146-151
Longitudinal age comparisons, 31
Longstreth, G. V., 275, 279
Longstreth, L. E., 275, 279
Lorenz, K., 247
Lourey, G. R., 78, 81, 84, 85, 93
Love, 13, 18, 263, 264, 268, 332
Luria, A. R., 161
Lynn, D., 290, 295-297, 299-301

M

Maccoby, E. E., 250, 263, 290-295, 298, 300,
    301

Macrosphere play, 309
Maioni, T. L., 316, 319, 320, 322
Make-believe, 310-312, 314-316
Malnutrition, 215-216
Mann-Whitney U, 43, 45, 46
Martin, R. M., 61, 72
Masters, J. C., 263
Masters, W. H., 242
Mastery play, 310, 312-314
Masturbation, 240, 241, 244, 246
Maturation, 5, 6, 12, 75, 78, 89, 132, 133,
    137, 202, 235, 237
Maurer, A., 249, 254-261
McClinton, B. S., 160
McDavid, J. W., 235
McDonald, F. J., 146
McGraw, M. B., 90-93
McNeill, D., 130, 137-141, 145, 146, 298, 302
Mean, 41, 42, 45, 46, 124
Measles, 215
Median, 41, 42
Mediation, verbal, 163-166, 167, 169, 170
Mediation deficiency, 165
Medinnus, G. R., 203
Meier, B., 144, 145
Meisels, M., 280, 281
Memory, 20, 23, 61, 162-163, 172-175, 289,
    298, 303, 304
Mendelson, M. J., 69, 72
Menlove, F. L., 106, 250
Mental age, 163, 210; *see also* IQ
Mental disorders, 77, 127
Meredith, H. V., 78, 79, 93
Method of research report, 37, 39-41, 48
Methods of child rearing, 112-118, 331-338
Methods of equalizing groups, 29-30
Methods, research, 6-16, 23-32
  correlational, 26-28
  cross-cultural, 25
  experimental, 28-31
  group study, 24
  in language, 130, 141
  in motor skills, 89, 90
  observation, 23, 25
  in perception, 54-56, 60
  in sex roles, 289
Microsphere play, 309
Miller, D. J., 172
Miller, L. B., 344
Miller, S., 310, 312, 315, 317, 320-322
Milwaukee Project, 219-220, 224-232
Miner, L. E., 148

Mischel, W., 290-291, 293, 301, 323
Mobiles, 65
Model, 106, 110, 116, 118
Moerk, E., 142, 144, 145
Monologue, 190
Montemayer, R., 288, 301
Montessori, M., 339-340
Moore, N. V., 319, 322
Moral behavior, sex differences in, 241, 246
Moral development, 20
Moral judgment, 178, 192, 203-207
Moreno, J. L., 280, 281
Morgan, G. A., 270
Moss, H. A., 274, 290, 301
Mothers working outside the home, 332-333, 336, 338
Mother's speech, 141-143, 146, 148, 149, 266, 290
Motivation, 113-114
Motor-skill development, 77, 86-92
Motor-skill training, 77, 89-92
Muma, J., 146, 148
Murphy's Law, 23
Mussen, H. P., 71, 72, 281

N

Names and personality, 235
Negative correlation, 44-45
Neonatal development, 81-83
    alertness, 54, 75, 81
    auditory perception, 69
    light sensitivity, 57-58
    visual capacity, 57
Nervous system, 12, 70, 71, 78, 81-83
Neurosis, 238, 243, 244-245
Neutral stimulus, 97-100
Newman, A., 252
Nichols, R. C., 235
Niem, T. C., 235
Nodelman, L., 298, 301
NS; see Neutral stimulus
Nutrition in pregnancy, 79

O

Obesity, 92
Object concept, 186-188, 200-201
Object constancy, 267
Objective responsibility, 203-207
Observation, 15, 16, 23-25, 54-56
    casual, 23
    laboratory, 25

Observation—cont'd
    naturalistic, 25
    systematic, 23
Observational learning, 106-107, 109-110, 118, 121-125, 155
    to overcome fear, 250
Oedipus complex, 241-244, 246
O'Neal, E., 110
Onlooker play, 318, 320
Open schools, 341-342, 344
Open-space schools, 342
Operant conditioning, 101-106, 155
    and age, 105
    of aggression, 110-111
    compared with classical conditioning, 103
    of "constructive" play, 110-111
    to overcome fear, 250-252
Operant response, 101, 106
Operational definitions, 39-40
Opinion as alternative to research, 23, 46
Opinions on child rearing, 331-338, 346
Opper, S., 107, 192
Optimal cognitive conflict, 199
Oral stage, 240
Orange, S., 280, 281
Organization, 181, 202
Orienting response, 54, 55, 67
Orphanage-reared children, 216-217
Osbourne, D., 109
Ossification, 78, 79
Ottinger, R., 73-75
Ovum, 77, 78

P

Pain sensitivity, 56, 69-71
Palmer grasp, 82, 83
Parallel play, 318-320
Parents, 3, 7-9, 12, 13, 53, 58, 62, 65, 67, 89, 112, 118, 129, 143, 144, 198, 213, 214, 216, 249, 251, 252, 272, 287, 299, 300, 323-328, 331-338
Parsimony, 246
Parten, M., 318, 319
Participation, 191
Patterson, G. R., 251
Peabody Picture Vocabulary Test, 213
Pearson's *r*, 43-45
Peck, M. B., 71, 72
Peeples, D., 57, 73
Peer influences on willingness to try difficult tasks, 33-35

Peers, 263, 265, 275-278
Penis envy, 241, 245, 246
Perception, 53-75
  age changes in, 158-160
  centered, 61, 62
  color, 57, 58
  of faces, 64, 65
  of pitch, 67, 68
  of speech, 67, 68, 136, 140-145
Perceptual schemas, 310
Performance, 106, 107
Permissiveness, 14, 331-332
Personal space, 280-284
Personality, 9, 14, 235-253
  behavioral approach to, 236, 247-253
  and biology, 235, 237
  and culture, 235
  genetic predispositions, 235
  and names, 235
  structural approach to, 236-247, 253
  theoretical approach to, 236-247, 253
  and unique experiences, 235
Phenylketonuria, 77, 215
Phenylthiocarbamide, 77
Phallic stage, 240, 243
Philosophers, 3, 5, 6, 53
Phobia, 243-244; *see also* Fear
Physical development, 76-95
Piaget, J. J., 6, 13, 14, 61, 62, 73, 93, 107,
    163, 170, 177-203, 209, 250, 267, 308-
    316
Piaget's theory of intelligence, 177-207
  accommodation, 181-182, 199, 203
  adaptation, 181, 202
  alternative interpretations, 202
  applications of, 198-201, 341, 344
  assimilation, 181-182, 183, 199, 200, 202
  basic concepts of, 180-182
  centered thought, 192-193, 195
  classification, 184, 197
  concrete operational period, 196-197, 201,
    203
  conservation, 194-196, 197
  egocentrism, 183, 189-192, 197
  equilibrium, 182
  evaluation of, 201-202
  formal operations, 197-198, 201, 203
  intelligence testing, 199-200
  irreversible thought, 192-195
  language, 188, 190-191, 201
  methods of research, 178-180, 201

Piaget's theory of intelligence—cont'd
  moral judgment, 178, 192, 203-207
  object concept, 186-188, 200-201
  optimal cognitive conflict, 199
  organization, 181, 202
  preoperational period, 188-196, 201, 203
  primary circular reaction, 184
  qualitative versus quantitative changes in
    thought, 180
  schema, 182, 184
  secondary circular reaction, 184
  sensorimotor period, 182-188, 200-201, 203
  static thought, 192, 193, 195
  symbols, 185, 188
  tertiary circular reaction, 185, 201
Pitch perception, 67, 68
Placenta, 78, 80
Placing response, 82
Play, 88, 307-328
  associative, 319, 320
  autocosmic, 309
  class differences in, 319-320
  cooperative, 319-320
  dramatic, 315, 316
  macrosphere, 309
  mastery, 310, 312-314
  microsphere, 309
  onlooker, 318, 320
  parallel, 318-320
  in preschools, 340-344
  sex differences in, 38-48
  size of group, 317
  social, 316-320
  solitary, 318, 320
  symbolic, 310, 311
  theories of, 307-312
  therapy, 309
  unoccupied, 318, 320
Positive correlation, 44
Postural control, 86-88
Poulos, R. W., 110
Praise, 334
Predictions, 27
Premature infants, 57, 80, 81, 93-95
Prenatal development, 78-80
Preoperational period, 188-196, 201, 203, 310-
    312
Preschool, 338-346
  academic, 342-344
  choosing a, 345
  compared with day care centers, 345-346

Preschool—cont'd
history of, 339
learning in, 344
Montessori, 339-340, 344
open schools, 341-342, 344
Piagetian, 341, 344
traditional, 343-344
Primary circular reaction, 184
Primary erogenous zone, 239
Privacy, 316
Probability level, 43
Production deficiency, 165
Protein deficiency, 215
Proximodistal development, 71, 84
Psychoanalysis, 8, 14, 264, 265, 308-310, 314, 316
Psycholinguistic theory of language acquisition, 134, 137-140
Punishment, 101, 103, 106, 115-117
contrasted with discipline, 331-332, 335, 336, 338
Pupillary response, 57

Q

Qualitative changes in thought, 180
Quantitative changes in thought, 180
Questionnaires, 8-10

R

Rand, H. Y., 345
Range, 41, 42
Rayner, R., 97, 99
Reading, 342
Recognition of pictures, 162
Redlick, F. C., 324
Reese, H. W., 97, 99, 213
References of research report, 37, 38, 48
Reflective style of thought, 167
Reflexes, 7, 13, 16, 82-84, 90, 97, 135, 183
Rehearsal, use of, as a memory strategy, 172-175
Reichle, J. E., 146-151
Reinforcement, 101, 103, 104, 107, 112-115, 163
of crawling, 101-103
of crying, 104
extrinsic, 113-114
intrinsic, 113-114
partial, 113
social, 103, 112-113
of thumb sucking, 115

Reinforcement—cont'd
token, 113
Relative response, to transposition problem, 157, 165
Reminders, 112, 115
Report, research, 37-48
abstract, 37, 38
discussion, 37, 46-48
introduction, 37, 38
method, 37, 39-41
references, 37, 48
results, 37, 41-46
Research methods; see Methods, research
Research reports, how to read, 37-48
Responsibility, 334
Results of research report, 37, 41-46
Retrieval in memory, 162
Reward, 101, 110-116
activity, 112
delayed, 112
to follow punishment, 116
material, 112
social, 112
Rheingold, H. L., 135, 145, 287, 301, 323-328
Ricciuti, H. N., 270
Risk taking, 33-35
Rist, R. C., 218
Ritchy, G., 269, 279
Robban, M., 302
Robinson, H. B., 347-354
Robinson, N. M., 347-354
Rocking, 73, 74
Rodgen, M., 141, 145, 146
Rooting response, 82
Rosen, C. E., 315, 322
Rosenbloom, S., 68, 71
Rosenthal, R., 217
Ross, C., 302, 305
Ross, D., 283
Ross, H., 135, 145
Ross, S. A., 283
Rousseau, J. J., 5, 6, 12
Ruben, K. H., 316, 319, 320, 322
Rubenstein, J., 276

S

Salapatek, P., 57, 73
Salk, L., 336, 339
Scarr, S., 221
Schaffer, H. R., 264, 265, 267-270, 279
Schema, 182, 184

Scholtz, G. J. L., 320, 322
School performance and IQ, 211, 213
Sears, R., 283, 296
Secondary circular reaction, 184
Selective attention to same-sex models, 296
Self-esteem, 334
Self-fulfilling prophecy, 217-219
Self-socialization, 298
Sensitive periods, 339
Sensitivity to locus of sound, 67-69
Sensorimotor period, 182-189, 200-201, 203, 310
Sentence building, 140, 141
Separation anxiety, 248, 251-252, 263, 268, 269, 271-272
Serbin, R. A., 288, 301
Sex and IQ, 214
Sex differences, 18, 71, 81, 85, 86, 95, 274, 277, 283, 286, 287, 289-295, 309, 316
   in moral behavior, 241, 246
   in play, 38-48
   in reactions to fearful situations, 250
Sex-role development, 285-305
Sex-role stereotypes, 286-289
Sex roles and child rearing, 335
Sexual identity, 246
Shaping, 136
Shapiro, A., 280-284
Sher, M., 305
Shipley, E. F., 140, 143, 145
Shipman, V. C., 165
Shirley, M. M., 83, 86, 87, 93, 312
Shyness, 7, 20
Siblings, 275
Significance, statistical, 43, 45, 100
Silver nitrate, 54
Simon, T., 210
Singer, J. L., 308, 315, 316, 321, 322
Single-gene traits, 77
Siqueland, E. R., 105, 120
Sitting, 77, 86, 89, 90, 132
Size of play group, 317
Skeels, H. M., 216-217, 222
Skeletomuscular system, 78, 81
Skinner, B. F., 134-136, 145
Smiling, 18, 19, 21, 64, 65, 128, 266
Smith, C. S., 140, 143, 145
Smith, P. K., 110
Smith, R., 110, 121, 292, 301
Smoking in pregnancy, 80
Snedecor, A., 149

Snow, C., 143, 145, 146
Social development, 262-284
   encouragement of, 337
Social-learning theory, 264, 265, 296, 302
Social play, 316-320
Social workers, 3
Socioeconomic status and IQ, 213, 215-216
Socioeconomic differences in play, 319-320
Solitary play, 318, 320
Solomon, F., 148
Sommer, R., 280
Sontag, L. W., 214
Spatial orientation, 160
Speech, 127, 128
   mothers', 141-143, 146, 148, 149, 266, 290
   production of, 68, 128, 129, 130, 133
   stress in, 144
   telegraphic, 130, 132, 134, 146
Speech corpus, 130-131
Speech perception, 67, 68, 136, 140-145
Sperm, 77, 78
Spielmeyer-Vogt disease, 215
Spock, B., 331-334, 339
Spontaneous abortion, 78, 80
Sprofkin, J. N., 110
Staats, A., 134-136, 145
Staats, C., 134-136, 145
Staby, R. G., 296, 298, 301
Stamm, I., 309, 322
Standard deviation, 41, 42
Standing, 77, 86, 87, 90
Stanford-Binet Intelligence Test, 210-213
States of infant alertness, 54
Static thought, 192, 193, 195
Statistics, 27, 30, 41-45, 48
   descriptive, 41, 43, 48
   inferential, 42-43, 48
Staub, E., 278, 279
Stechler, G., 54, 73
Stein, A. H., 110
Stepanich, L., 146-151
Steuer, F. B., 110, 121-125
Stevenson, H. W., 163, 215
Stewart, A. L., 94
Stimulating environments, 336-338
Stimulating visual development, 65, 66, 73-75
Stimulation, tactile, 73, 74
Stimulus-response learning theory, 164
Stork, L., 298, 301
Stranger anxiety, 263, 268-271
Strategies, in memory, 162

Stratton, S. O., 280, 283
Stress in speech, 144
Structuralism, 8
Structured toys, 320, 321
Subjects, 39, 40
Sucking, 99-100
Sulzer, J. L., 110
Superego, 237-238, 241, 245
Surface structure in language, 138, 140, 141, 143
Surplus energy play theory, 308
Survival skills theory of play, 308
Sutherland, Z., 302
Symbolic play, 310, 311
Sympathy, 18, 21

T

t test, 124
Tactile stimulation, 73, 74
Tanner, J. M., 78, 80, 81, 85, 93
Tantrums, 251-252
Taste receptors, 79
Tay-Sachs disease, 215
Teachers, 3, 9, 292, 300
Teachers' expectations and IQ, 217-219
Telegraphic speech, 130, 132, 134, 146
Television, 67, 288, 295, 315
  and aggression, 110, 121-125
  and arousal, 109, 110
  and helping, 110
Teller, D., 57, 73
Temperature regulation, 81
Terman, L. M., 10, 210
Tertiary circular reaction, 185, 201
Thalidomide, 80
Theories
  of age changes in thought, 163-171
  of attachment, 264-267
  of intelligence, Piaget's, 177-207
  of language acquisition, 133-140
  of learning, 97-107
  of play, 307-312
  of sex-role development, 295-299
  social-learning, 264, 265, 296, 302
Thomas, D. R., 115
Thompson, S. K., 288, 301
Thought, 155-171, 177-203
  age changes in, 155-171
  associative level of, 166
  cognitive level of, 166
  impulsive style of, 167

Thought—cont'd
  Piaget's theory of, 177-203
  processes, 14, 15
  qualitative and quantitative changes in, 180
  reflective style of, 167
  theories to explain age changes in, 163-171
Time-lag age comparisons, 32
Toilet training, 240, 336
Toine, M., 16, 19, 21
Tolor, A., 280, 281
Torrance, E. P., 33, 214
Toys, 288, 313, 317, 320-322, 324-328
Traditional preschools, 343-344
Transformations in language, 138, 140, 143
Transposition, 156-158, 164-165, 167-169
Tronick, E., 58, 71
Trust, 336

U

UCR; *see* Unconditioned response
UCS; *see* Unconditioned stimulus
Unconditioned response, 97, 98, 100, 105
Unconditioned stimulus, 97, 98, 100, 105
Unconscious, 237
Unoccupied play behavior, 318, 320
Unstructured toys, 320, 321

V

Variable, 31
Verbal fluency, 290
Verbal mediation, 163-167, 169, 170
Verbal skills, stimulation of, 165-166
Vision, 7, 17, 55-66
Visual accommodation, 57, 65
Visual acuity, 58, 59, 65
Visual attentiveness and position, 55
Visual cliff, 62, 63
Visual complexity in patterns, 60-62, 64-65
Visual development, stimulation of, 65, 66, 73-75
Visual novelty, 60, 61
Visual preference, 55, 58-61, 63-66
Visual response to movement, 58, 64

W

Wahler, R. G., 105
Waldrop, M. F., 278, 279
Walk, R. D., 62, 63, 72
Walking, 77, 83, 87, 132, 313
Wasserman, L., 298, 301
Watson, E. H., 78, 81, 84, 85, 93

Watson, J. B., 6, 13-15, 97, 99, 247
Watson, O. M., 280
Weight, 85
Weinberg, R. A., 221
Weinstein, M. S., 281, 283
Wertzman, L., 302, 305
Wertheimer, M., 67, 68, 73
Westone, H. S., 141, 143, 145, 146, 149
White, B., 57, 72, 337-339, 346
White, S. H., 155, 159, 160, 163, 166-167
Whotley, J. L., 276
Wilcox, R., 302
Williams, J. E., 288, 301
Williamsen, E., 269, 279
Willies, F. N., 281, 283
Wish fulfillment, 242
Witryol, S. L., 104

Wolf, M. M., 101
Wolf, R. M., 214
Wolf Man, 242, 244
Wolff, P. H., 54, 73, 266, 279
Word associations, 161-162
Words, use of, in thinking, 161-166
Working mothers, 332-333, 336, 338

Y

Yando, R., 275, 279

Z

Zajonc, R. B., 45, 214
Zeaman, D., 169
Zelaze, P. R., 312, 322
Zigler, E., 275, 279
Zygote, 78